GROWING UP LOCAL:
An Anthology of Poetry and Prose from Hawai'i

edited by
Eric Chock, James R. Harstad,
Darrell H. Y. Lum, & Bill Teter

Bamboo Ridge Press
1998

In association with

 and

ISBN 0-910043-53-1
ISBN 0-910043-55-8 (hardcover)
Copyright 1998 Bamboo Ridge Press.
Introduction copyright 1998 by Darrell H.Y. Lum

This is issue #72 of *Bamboo Ridge, A Hawai'i Writers' Journal* (ISSN 0733-0308)

Cover art: *Aloha Shirts* by Huy Van, Farrington High School
Title page art: *A Glimpse of the Past* by Rochelle Rivera,
        Farrington High School
Book design: Susanne Yuu
Typesetting: Wayne Kawamoto

Bamboo Ridge Press is a nonprofit, tax-exempt organization formed to foster the appreciation, understanding, and creation of literary, visual, audio-visual, and performing arts by and about Hawaii's people. Bamboo Ridge Press is a member of the Council of Literary Magazines and Presses (CLMP).

This project is supported in part by grants from the Hawaii Education Association, the National Endowment for the Arts (NEA) and the State Foundation on Culture and the Arts (SFCA) celebrating over thirty years of culture and the arts in Hawai'i. The SFCA is funded by appropriations from the Hawai'i State Legislature and by grants from the NEA.
Additional funding for this project and some of the educational activities associated with it was provided by the Hawai'i Community Foundation, the McInerny Foundation, and the Atherton Family Foundation.

Bamboo Ridge is published twice a year. For subscription information, direct mail orders, or a catalog please contact:

Bamboo Ridge Press
P. O. Box 61781
Honolulu, HI 96839-1781
(808) 626-1481
www.bambooridge.com

10 9 8 7 6 5 4   01   02   03

ACKNOWLEDGMENTS

We gratefully acknowledge the support of the following organizations and individuals:

University of Hawai'i Curriculum Research & Development Group
    Arthur R. King, Jr., Director
    Alice Santiago
    Gina Lujan

Hawai'i Education Association
    Hubert V. Everly, President
    Daniel W. Tuttle, Jr., Executive Director
    Grace Fujita, Chair, Educational Programs Committee
    Carol Yoneshige, Office Manager

Department of Education
    Tom Inhofe, Radford High School
    Fern Kashiwabara, 'Aiea High School
    Dyron Ota, Farrington High School
    Gail Teshima, Farrington High School
    Stanley Yamamoto

Beau Press, University of Hawai'i Board of Publications

Lyn Ackerman
Barbara Gearen
Joy Kobayashi-Cintrón

TABLE OF CONTENTS

INTRODUCTION

II

III

AUTHORS' NOTES

PERMISSIONS

INTRODUCTION

Shave Ice by Erin Morrison, 'Aiea High School

LOCAL GENEALOGY: WHAT SCHOOL YOU WENT?
Darrell H.Y. Lum

> . . . in the native Hawaiian way, personal introductions include these
> questions: What are you called (*i.e.*, your given name)? Who is your
> family (*i.e.*, your surname and genealogy)? Where are you from (*i.e.*,
> your neighborhood or district)? And who is your teacher (*i.e.*, your
> school or the way of thought to which you are loyal)? . . . without
> their knowing its Hawaiian origins, locals expect this genealogical
> exchange, this fine ritual of personal introductions, not for judging
> the superiority of one person over another, but for learning facts that
> relate somehow to inner values of the individual, on the one hand,
> and to already existing social and cultural connections on the other.
> This local ritual is expressively a way for two people to begin
> discovering their relationships with each other, however distant, in
> order to talk stories that sprout on common ground. It is a way to
> begin weaving their histories together—and this defines friendship,
> or an aspect of it, local style. (Stephen H. Sumida, *And the View from
> the Shore*, Seattle: University of Washington Press, 1991, p. xvii.)

The typical local party in Hawai'i might consist of a buffet table set
out in the carport with family and friends sitting on folding chairs or on
coolers of beer and soda, talking story. If you are a visitor, sometime soon
after the introductions you'll likely be asked, "What school you went?"
Locals know that the question refers to what high school you attended.
And that the next question might be, "You know my cousin? He grad in
'97." Invariably, after a few more questions, a connection is made to a rela-
tive who attended your school or a mutual acquaintance who lives in the
neighborhood or sometimes the discovery of a distant family relationship
("Eh, my cousin married to your sister-in-law!").

At the same party, the kids call all the older females "Aunty,"
whether they are related or not. Local kids have innumerable "aunties," not
all by blood, but all who act as family. In fact, a high school study hall
teacher once confessed that the most powerful warning she could use on
misbehaving students was, "I know your father," which made her like an
"aunty," a part of the family.

The "What school you went?" question has its roots in the native
Hawaiian way of identifying oneself by geography and genealogy much as

Kamakau described people in *Ruling Chiefs of Hawaii (Revised Edition)*:
"Liloa's wife was named Pinea. She was from 'Ewa and Ko'olaupoko and was
his mother's younger sister (p. 1)." In more contemporary times we simply
ask, "You related to the Heu's from Kahului?"

This impulse to establish how we are related is critical to understand-
ing local culture and local literature. The question "What school you
went?" rather than being a question that divides us, is fundamentally an
effort to discover how we are connected.

This sense of family and community characterizes local literature.
Like all families, the stories and poems in this collection may be marked by
conflict, disagreement, and discord yet retain a fundamental bond to the
islands and local culture. As diverse as these pieces are, each one has an
honesty of voice, a strong and sure sense of place, and a sense of genealogy
that invites us to share the experiences of being local.

Locals have always been well aware of class and ethnic differences
and their hierarchical relationship to the plantation bosses. From this per-
spective, local culture developed out of necessity: immigrant laborers and
native Hawaiians found themselves in a plantation system on the lowest
rung of the ladder and subject to deliberate efforts by the plantations to pit
ethnic groups against one another through pay differences and living in eth-
nically segregated camps.

Sharing a common enemy, local culture has often been characterized
as a culture of resistance against the dominant white culture and rooted in
the struggles of the working class of Hawaii's sugar plantations. The immi-
grant laborers shared more than a common enemy, however. They entered a
native Hawaiian culture that valued interpersonal relationships and love for
the land. Their own values of family loyalty, obligation, and reciprocity
coincided with those of the native Hawaiians: an orientation that valued
harmony between people, minimized personal gain or achievement, and
shared natural resources. This cultural accommodation on the part of native
Hawaiians and immigrant labor was born out of a tradition of hardship,
struggle, and conflict that counters the romantic notions of blended cul-
tures, the melting pot, or a multiethnic Hawai'i based on a democratic shar-
ing of cultures.

*   *   *

Like Home

But I can't talk the way he wants me to. I cannot make it
sound his way, unless I'm playing pretend-talk-haole. I can make my
words straight, that's pretty easy if I concentrate real hard. But the
sound, the sound from my mouth, if I let it rip right out the lips, my
words will always come out like home.

—*Lovey*

Lois-Ann Yamanaka, *Wild Meat and the Bully Burgers*,
New York: Farrar Straus Giroux, 1996, p. 13)

While ethnicity and class play important roles in defining local cul-
ture's resistance to the dominant Western society, the bonds that tie it
together are the common values, common history, and common language
(Pidgin, or more correctly Hawai'i Creole English).

The emotional underpinning of local culture and the affirmation of
community might well be the sense of "home" of which Lovey so eloquent-
ly speaks. And while an immigrant people may never know the deep con-
nection to the land that perhaps only native Hawaiians can fully appreci-
ate, all local people can surely know and speak of home.

The use of language and story (and the practice of "talk story") to
convey the sense of home is also reflected in Hawaii's literature. The persis-
tence of Pidgin in the islands despite widespread assimilation of American
culture and the concerted efforts of educators to stamp it out, suggests that
it is less a matter of Pidgin speakers being *unable* to speak standard English
but their *choosing* it as a symbol of local identity. Despite this, Pidgin has
long been blamed for the ills of the educational system for over a century
when it was labeled in the 1880s "a hideous mongrel jargon," a "barbarous
perversion of English," a "bastardized language," and a "savage dialect"
(*Hawai'i: a case study in development education 1778–1960*, diss. by R. K.
Stueber, 1964, p. 148–149).

Not only does the use of Pidgin promote a sense of community, it
challenges our assumptions about language and culture. Pidgin serves to
unify local culture and to critique the dominant one. When Lovey speaks of
letting Pidgin "rip right out the lips," she recognizes that her language is
that of her heart and her home.

It's clear that local culture and local literature did not simply appear,
nor are they likely to remain static and unchanging. And it is not difficult
to see how the forces, so delicately balanced to draw us together, could
become the very issues that separate us. "What school you went?" might
easily become a question used to perpetuate public/private school distinc-
tions, socio-economic differences, and divisive stereotypes.

These stories, poems and essays remind us of our shared history, our literary genealogy. We are richer and have a deeper understanding of each other because of them. And like our own families they will continue to comfort us and sustain us and encourage us to continue to ask one another "What school you went?" so that we can find the points where we can begin to weave our histories together.

*　　*　　*

Growing Up Local is the result of the combined vision of three organizations, all dedicated to the enhancement of education in Hawai'i: Bamboo Ridge Press, Curriculum Research and Development Group (CRDG) and Hawai'i Education Association (HEA). Curriculum Research and Development Group is legislatively mandated to develop programs that benefit all the schools of Hawaii. It enrolls a statistically representative sampling of Oahu's population at the University Laboratory School, its program testing site. CRDG's Performance English Program strongly supports local literature as an important component of language arts study in classrooms throughout Hawai'i. In 1981 CRDG published *Asian-Pacific Literature*, a three-volume high school literature and writing textbook. Volume One became a favorite in many classes because of its generous representation of local writing. In 1985 Bamboo Ridge Press and CRDG co-sponsored a writing contest for Hawaii's secondary students and published the winners in a book titled *The Ten Rules of Fishing*. Winners came from as far away as Ka'u to present their work at a public reading at UH-Mānoa.

The Hawai'i Education Association is a broad-based professional association dedicated to the educational future of Hawai'i. The Association has sponsored annual statewide writing contests for island students since the early 1980s and in the tradition of *The Ten Rules of Fishing* has published the winners in *Write On, HEA!* since 1989. Contest winners are among the selections in *Growing Up Local*.

The Best of Bamboo Ridge, published in 1986, gained wide acceptance in the classroom as a reader for local literature. While it was not designed to be a classroom text, it was enjoyed by thousands of students and pointed out the need for a volume devoted specifically to the secondary school audience.

It was 1993 when Lyn Ackerman selected work from *The Best of Bamboo Ridge* and created a show called "Growing Up Local" at the Lizard Loft, a performance space above Java Java Café. She directed another version of the show for Honolulu Theatre for Youth in 1995 when it played to over 6,600 intermediate and high school students. Some of the authors in the original show, Eric Chock, Marla Hamabata, Mavis Hara, Violet Harada, Hina Kahanu, Māhealani Kama'u, Darrell Lum, Jody Manabe, and

Lois-Ann Yamanaka also appear in this book. All are part of this book's genealogy.

We've included in this anthology student work, new work by emerging writers as well as work by more established writers, and reprints from books and journals published since *The Best of Bamboo Ridge*. Some of the work has been edited slightly to make it more suited for use in schools, but we've tried to retain the integrity of each author's voice and his or her use of language.

We've also asked each author to tell us "What school you went?" and to reflect on how their particular story or poem got written and to share their thoughts on growing up local. Take a look at their comments in the Authors' Notes. We think you'll find their comments about their work, about growing up in Hawai'i, and about themselves and their families thought-provoking and insightful. You might even find someone you're related to!

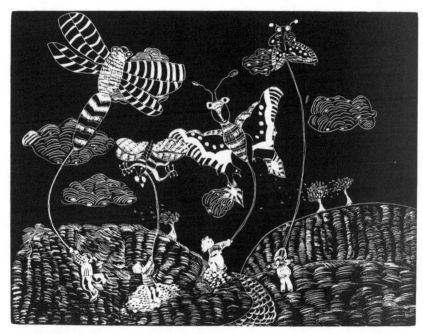

I

Kites by Czar Tagayama, Radford High School

ma ket stenlei
bradajo

ma ket stenlei
dablucross wensen om
wong kreesmess kaad ah
hinostey nau bot
histey free eswy

awen no damada bifo
eswenastey
veratenya shtrit ah
she neva lai kwaam clos
shistey wyl
eswy

bambai shikaam pragnet
deng kaam stenlei
endabradas
dey stey wyl tu ah

mawnin tym
awach om pley
onda da chree
delai cheys
da leevs ah

wonlym

damada

she weng get skwash
ontopda road

den stenlei endabrada
deykaam ontopma step ah

stey hong gray

eswy

den slo... slo...
hilan... me... ta chom
bol nol da brada
hisked

enso
me en stenlei
we wemek fran ah
embambai
hika meen sai

we wempley fyt fyt ah
goo fon dakyn
aget shorech vol

awembai om
won smawl kyn supabawl
en wen he wac om
he bounts
enekuzmpleys

wontym

amasmoov..ah

enstenlei

wadagondu..weed..heem

longtyma..teeng..kah

vambaia..feega

mobeda..lan om..go

ontopdamaunten

esmin..hees..free..ah

nomodameng

gombada..heem

so
apsood om eensai da box
ena lydom weeda shtreeng
ena jrujr ludamaun ten
asin om waan lym
efta det
hiluklyk wong ghos ah
hees hea
awl sten op
frana cold

hiloook me

hong tym..ah

jaluk

hilai talmis am lin

den

histego

ALLOWANCE
Eric Chock

It wasn't the amount, Daddy.
Five cents a week could've been enough
if I wanted to stretch the pennies
in your dresser ashtray back then,
when even lunch money was hard to find
if you were trying to buy a house
and raise a local family in Hawai'i
after the Big War.
But still I wanted more,
a little boy just barely tall enough
to tip toe my eyes
to the level of the dresser top
and curl my skinny arm over the edge
to pluck a silver dime
I hoped hadn't been noticed
among the brown pennies
filling the dish
like so many old monkey pod leaves
waiting to be burned.
More carefully than any game of fiddlesticks
I moved nothing from its place,
the quiet scrape of coins
grating in my heart,
the ashtray unmoved from its station
near the stack of unpaid bills,
your roll-up metal measuring tape,
the Elgin watch you hardly used,
and sometimes during a peaceful late afternoon
you'd lie on the bed
in the darkened room after work,
thin lines of sunlight glowing
on the Venetian blinds,
and I would pretend you didn't hear me
coming and going from your rest, as you would pretend too.

DA GLOVE

Eric Chock

Where he got um?
Was so old-fashioned,
on'y had five short fat fingers,
no moa even da webbing stuff between da tumb part—
jes one big fat glove dat even my hand
wen reach all da way to da end.
What kine glove dis? I tole my fada.
How come you neva get me one real glove?

Dis glove, you try bend um, no can.
Not like my friend's one, smood brown ledda
he used to rub wit some kinda oil
until was so easy fo fole in half could snap um
open and shut, open and shut
and pound yo fiss inside like was one line shot
from Mickey Mantle coming back at you
befo you had time fo follow true on your
full wind up karate kick stink eye fass ball.
Ho, wit my oven mitten potholder panty kine glove,
how you expeck me fo concentrate on my pitching?
Of course dey wen kick me off da mound.

Mo worse, I wen move to first.
Was soa you know, fo catch every ball
right in da middle of my hand!
After a while, I try fo catch em in between da tumb and finga,
but hard fo keep um in dat space when no moa webbing.
Every time somebody gotta trow one to me
I gotta whip my glove on da ground and hole my hand
and check if da bones inside wen broke yet.
Could see all da blood making designs on my palm
like pitchas I seen inside my astronomy book
of galaxies, 'cept dese was all red and pink
and da rest of my hand wen look white like one haole.

Wasn't wort it fo get da guy out!

One time, somebody wen hit one to tird base,
da big lava rock by da side of da bushes.
Earl wen whip da trow supa fass to me
so I wen stick my foot back
against da clothesline pole first base
and I wen stretch all da way reaching fo dat white moon—
but since my hand was in pain I wen try fo catch um
in between da tumb and finga, and da bugga went right true
and smash me in da nose.

Dat was my first glove.
He was so proud wen he brought um home
he even wen play catch wit me in da back yard,
him wit his bare hands, me complaining da whole time,
What kine glove dis, dis not one real baseball glove!
How come I no more one real glove?

Afta dat, no more he wen play catch wit me.

MY FIRST WALK WITH ASHLEY
Eric Chock

I can't understand any of your gurgling,
but when you raise your arm forward
and stare with raised eyebrows
beyond the opening and closing fingers
of your year-old hand,
I know I should follow that direction.
So with just one finger of mine in your grasp,
you lead me down the back stairs,
past the washing machine with its
audience of orchids and ferns,
and into the front yard.
You squat and smell some purple flowers,
giggling with complete pleasure.
Arm reaching again, we wobble out the driveway
toward the neighboring stream
where you know there are ducks,
one of the three or four words you know
besides mom and dad.
Your feet barely know which way is front,
so I've watched every step
just to make sure you don't fall.
Our path happens like a meditation.
Soon we are bending over the edge of the stone wall
trying to touch the water.
It's close enough.
We do it without having to get on our knees,
just by squatting again.
And the ducks are getting friendly.
You have already touched their wings as lightly
as if your fingers were feathers.
"Ducks," you say.
Now the white one that sits alone
is the one you want.
It runs away.

We pursue but can't get to it.
Once we got close.
It stopped and beat its wings as if
to lift off the ground
and you were in white feather awe,
your soft hands clasped together
as if in prayer,
your face in its light.
You're so young, but already
you know what you like.

FOURTH GRADE UKUS
Marie M. Hara

Until the right time came for me to meet my father, I would be patient. Mama made plans all the time. She had figured out what to do. Soon after we settled into a small rental house, we walked over to Lincoln School, a gracious stone building with many trees. None of the students there had to do any manual labor. They used the newest books. They were always featured in newspaper articles and photos that she pointed out to me. Mama had heard that the best Lincoln graduates were sometimes accepted into the private high schools, which was how they "got ahead." Once in the office I saw that all the teachers were *haole*, and it was a good thing I wore the socks and new shoes Mama had adjusted. I sat with each foot in her lap and great impatience to get accepted. Several teachers watched me watching the other kids playing on the immaculate playground equipment. This part was called The Observation. Once outdoors I took my time taking off my shoes and socks to keep them good for the next wearing. I kept munching softly on a strand of hair that hung comfortably near my mouth. Mama sat on a bench away from the other chatting mothers. She had one bare foot out of her slipper and rested it on top of the other foot still in its slipper. They, too, were new and hurt her. She looked tired. She was still waiting to hear about a better job than being a cook in a dormitory. I could see thoughts which made her cranky cross her face.

By the time we were back in the office for the part called The Interview, which was really a test to see if I could speak perfect Standard English, I knew something was funny. I could smell it.

The woman tester was young and Japanese and smiley. I relaxed, thought for sure I wouldn't have to act "put on" with her. But she kept after me to say the printed words on the picture cards that she, now unsmiling, held before my eyes.

"Da bolocano," I repeated politely at the cone-shaped mountain where a spiral of smoke signaled into the crayon-shaded air. She must have drawn it.

She shook her head. "Again."

"Da BO-LO-CA-NO," I repeated loudly. Maybe like O-Jiji with the stink ear on his left side, she couldn't hear: "We wen' go 'n see da bolocano," I explained confidentially to her. And what a big flat *puka* it was, I thought, ready to tell her the picture made a clear mistake.

"It's the vol-cano," she enunciated clearly, forcing me to watch her mouth move aggressively. She continued with downcast eyes. " 'We went to see the vol-cano.' You can go and wait outside, okay?"

Outside I wondered why—if she had seen it for real—she drew it all wrong.

Mama shrugged it off as we trudged home.

"Neva' mind. Get too many stuck shet ladies ova dea. People no need act, Lei. You wait. You gon' get one good education, not like me."

That was how I ended up at Ka'ahumanu School which was non-English Standard. Its front yard sported massive flower beds of glowing red and yellow canna lilies arranged in neat rows, which were weeded and watered daily by the students. Teachers at Ka'ahumanu were large in size, often Hawaiian or Portuguese with only an occasional wiry Chinese or Japanese lady in sight. There was a surprise *haole* teacher who came in to teach art and hug kids. Many teachers wore bright hibiscus blooms stuck into their pugs of upswept hair. They didn't hold back on any emotions as they swept through the main yard like part of a tide of orderliness, lining up their wriggly children into classes. They cuffed the bad and patted the heads of the obedient as they counted us. They were magnetic forces with commanding voices, backbones at full attention and bright flowers perched like flags on the tops of their heads. When we stood in formation, the first ritual of the morning, rumors of all kinds went through our lines. I learned right away that on special holidays the cafeteria might even serve *laulau* and *poi* which we would help to prepare. Now that was worth waiting for.

I had resolved that in Honolulu I would have friends "fo' real." To this goal I studied the children at play and kept a silent watch before venturing in. When I forgot this logic and opened my mouth, it almost cost me my appetite to get educated. Because I occupied a fantasy world of vividly drawn characters from books and people I had made up for the lonely times in Kohala, I could go "off on a toot" and momentarily forget the real ones in front of me. I had gotten used to amusing myself in that way even while other kids swirled in activity around me.

I was in a dreamy mood when I first ran into Mrs. Vincente, who was to be my teacher. As a human being she was an impressive creation, since her bulk was unsettling and her head quite small. As she waddle-walked toward me, I made a fatal error. I mistook her for an illustration in a library book I had grown fond of in Kohala. She was a dead ringer for the character I thought I was seeing right before my nose. And why not? The first day of school was supposed to be the beginning of new and exciting things in my life. Everything so far had been surprising.

Therefore, I squealed out loud in pleasure, "Oh, Mrs. Piggy-Winkle!" at the sight of the pink-fleshed mountain topped by a salad plate-sized orange hibiscus. Did I truly think she would be equally delighted to see me? Mrs. Vincente, as I learned later, would never forget me. At the moment of our meeting, she grabbed me by the back of my neck and shook me fiercely until I blubbered.

Teachers came running; students formed a mob around our frantic struggling, and the school principal, Mrs. Kealoha-Henry, saved me.

As I stood sobbing in shivers from the wild shaking, Mrs. Vincente lectured me and the others on good manners. I shook my head in no-no-no when she asked in an emotional voice, "Do you understand now?" It took all of Mrs. Kealoha-Henry's counsel to keep Mrs. Vincente away from me.

Grabbing the opportunity, I ran all the way back home where long after she came home from work, Mama found me hiding out in the laundry shed. I didn't return to school for several days after that. But my mother's continual nagging, bribery and my own plain boredom finally wore me down. I vowed not to talk at school, in the name of personal safety. And I would forget imagination.

When I returned, I learned another lesson, although this one, also, started out in confusion. Back at Ka'ahumanu School the white-columned building seemed enormous. Without Mama for support, I needed to report my string of absences to the office. Retreating into passive silence, I stood in the main hallway in front of the office with its impressive counter, convinced I was in trouble. The dark paneling and polished wood flooring came together into a tunnel of cool air where important things happened, and people spoke in official whispers.

Hanging high on the wall against the painted white wood, positioned to face the person entering up the broad steps through the columned entrance was a large portrait of Queen Ka'ahumanu, our school's namesake. Someone had placed an offering bouquet of many-colored flowers under the picture. I studied her fully fleshed face, the insignia of rank in the background and her guarded expression. In return her eyes reviewed me, a small girl who wasn't sure what to do next.

As I stalled and paced the corridor, the morning bell rang, and all the other children disappeared. Alone in my patch of indecision, with flashing eyes, I mapped out how and where I would run if I had to. I balanced on one bare foot and then the other, while I studied the ancient lady's clear-eyed regard.

When Mrs. Kealoha-Henry found me, she laughed in surprise.

"So you did come back. And now you have met the Queen. Do you know her story? No? Well, I didn't think so."

The principal, a plump woman who wore old-fashioned glasses which dangled from a neckpiece onto the front of her shirtwaist, told me then and there about Queen Ka'ahumanu, the *Kuhina Nui*. I learned that she was a favorite child and a favorite wife, that her hair was called *ehu*, meaning it was reddish unlike that of other Hawaiians of her time, and that she was *hapa*—of mixed blood, probably from Spanish ancestors. Mrs. Kealoha-Henry suspected the conquistadors, whose helmets the Hawaiian *ali'i* had copied in feathers, had been the first Europeans in Hawai'i. I heard the kindly stranger saying that I, too, must be *hapa*. To test me she tried out some Hawaiian, and when I answered correctly, "*Aloha kakahiaka*," she nodded favorably. She suggested a visit to the school library, where I would be welcome to read more about the Queen and what she did with the tremendous power she held at the end of her life.

Mrs. Kealoha-Henry put her hands on my shoulders and turned me in the direction of the polished *koa* wood steps that led to the second floor. She would take care of the absences.

Although I hoped that the principal had not confused me with someone else who was Hawaiian by blood, I was very pleased with the thrilling story. Her comments became the bond between the Queen and me. I felt lucky that I went to a school where a *hapa* was the boss—in fact, commanded tribute. After all, I did have the reddish hair, or some of it, and if I was *hapa* as she said, then that was the reason for my being different from the others. I felt lighter whenever I looked at Queen Ka'ahumanu's portrait from then on. Every day the Queen's round face gave me a signal that I was okay; a small thing, but necessary for someone so hungry for a sign.

Still, no matter how hard I squinted, the hair depicted in the painting showed no sign of being red. Never mind, I told myself, she was right there, up high, and she looked at me affectionately, if I kept up the squint. Whenever I needed to, I found my way back to the hallway to stand in the breeze and acknowledge the power of our kinship.

I had singled out Darleen Nishimura, a sixth grader, as my new model. I wanted to grow up to look just like her, even though she despised me.

Darleen looked so dainty and petite as she completed every action with grace. I tagged along behind her as she received smiles and praise, followed her as she delivered newspapers for her older brothers. But when she saw me, she looked annoyed and tried to shake me. She often escaped by cutting through a yard unknown to me. She made a clippety-clop sound

with her merry flopping slippers, a sound which left you with a carefree
rhythm. When she laughed, she covered her teeth delightfully with a hand
in the way some of the older Japanese women did. I practiced and got
nowhere. Never mind that Darleen wouldn't give me the time of day. Now I
could forget it. Queen Ka'ahumanu was somber and regal; she never giggled.

One day I spotted another girl, this one chubby and my own age,
standing in front of the painting. She quickly placed a white ginger blossom
on the *koa* table and disappeared with a smile at me. Later, I heard her
name was Monica. When we played in the school yard together, she
revealed the secret of her full name; Monica Mahealani Michiko
Macadangdang. Happily memorizing it on the spot, I learned that choosing
friends wasn't the only way you got them; some chose you, if you were
lucky.

Midway through the year I was happy enough to be going to school
there, skipping down the streets extra early, eager to help water the taro
patch and the red and gold lilies.

Three years later I was a bonafide Ka'ahumanu Kid, as accustomed as
any one of my classmates to the school routine. Our neighbor Mrs. Lee,
who lived on our block, must have seen my enthusiasm. She entrusted her
only son, who had been living in Makawao, Maui, to my care since we were
both in the fourth grade. Joseph and I walked to school together on his first
day.

I felt a nudge from one side and a soft pinch from the other.

Just before the first morning bell rang, the whispers traveled around.
We were aware that our teacher was moving down the line to study each
one of us. Our voices were high, and our faces as busy as the noisy birds in
the banyan outside. Always chattering, always in tune with our buddies,
always watching, we knew how to move together on our quiet bare feet,
without getting caught talking. We studied how to do it.

"Pssssssssst . . ."

"Joseph. Make quick. We gotta line up; no talk. Standupstraight.
Sing loud or she gon' make us guys sing one mo' time."

"She checking da guys' clothes first, if clean or what. Bumbye she
gon' look our finganail and den check our hair behind da eah, l'dat."

The clanging bell brought us to silent attention.

Joseph looked completely blank. Unconcerned, he, being new, had
no understanding of the importance of our morning classroom ritual. He
didn't even pretend to mouth the words of Mrs. Vicente's favorite greeting,
"Good Morning, Deah Tea-cha, Goooood Mor-ning to Youuu."

"W'at fo' she like check us in da eah?" Joseph's slow whisper tickled.

Before I could answer importantly, "'Cuz got *ukus*, some guys, you stupid doo-doo head," and think, "But not us guys," our teacher was standing right in front of us. Mrs. Vicente looked grim. Her gold-rimmed eyeglasses gave off glints in the pools of sunlight, evidence of real daylight outside, which invaded our dark, high-ceilinged and wood-paneled classroom.

She was the one who taught us to sing "Old Plantation Nani Ole" (Oooll . . . Plan-tay-shun . . . Na-ni . . . Ohlay) and "Ma-sa's (never her way, Massa's) in the Cold, Cold Ground," her favorite mournful melodies. She had turned to making us sing in order to drill us on our English skills, so lacking were we in motivation.

Frequently Mrs. Vicente spoke sharply to us about the inappropriate silences of our group. She complained that too often we spoke out of turn but "rarely contributed to the discussion." She must have believed that we didn't absorb anything that she lectured about repeatedly. She confided that she was "disappointed in" us or we had "disappointed Teacher" or she was "sorry to have to disappoint" us, "however," we had done something wrong again.

She was a puzzle.

The oriental kids—for that was our label—in the room knew better than to open their mouths just to lose face, and the part-Hawaiian and Portuguese kids knew they would get lickings one way or another if they talked, so we all firmly agreed that silence was golden.

Never would an adult female loom up as large to me as Mrs. Vicente did then. I could see her face only when I sat at a safe distance with a desk for protection. If she approached—in all her girth she was most graceful moving across her neatly waxed floor—her hands took my complete attention. When they were ready to direct us, I felt the way I did when Mama showed me what the red light at the crosswalk was for. When Teacher stood very near me, I couldn't see her tiny eyes, because the soft underpart of her delicate chin transfixed me so that I could not understand the words she mouthed. I got my mouth wrenched up to be ready for an alert answer, just in case she eyeballed me. Somehow whenever I had to respond to her I managed to get the subject and verb unmatched—"Yes, ma'am. We is ready fo' class"—even though she drilled us on the continual sin of the mixed singular and plural, because it was so fascinating to see her furious reaction to what she called Broken English, which none of us could fix.

Passing outside by Room 103, I overheard her passionate argument with another teacher who wanted to introduce the hula in our PE exercises. Mrs. V.'s reasoning escaped me, but I knew she was against it unconditionally. I stayed hidden in the *ti* leaves under her window just to hear the rush of her escaping emotions as she grew angrier and pronounced words more distinctly.

Mrs. Vicente's face was averted from the horrors she saw represented in the existence of our whole class. To her, we were not by any means brought up well, didn't know our p's and q's, often acted in an un-American fashion as evidenced by our smelly home lunches, dressed in an uncivilized manner, and refused moreover to speak properly or respectfully as soon as her back was turned. Her standards were in constant jeopardy.

Our concentrated looks centered on her totally. We followed her every move, a fact which unnerved her briefly each morning. To hide her discomfort, revealed by streams of perspiration, she swabbed her face delicately with a lace-trimmed hankie.

She shook her head at Francene Fuchigami, whose mother made her wear around her neck an amulet in a yellowed cotton pouch which also contained a foul incense and active herbs. The blessed *o-mamori* guaranteed the absence of both slippery vermin and casual friends.

Francene and I competed for Mrs. V.'s favor, no matter how much we accepted her obvious but peculiar interest in the boys only. She favored them shamelessly, but bullied them at every opportunity.

We brought Mrs. Vicente homegrown anthuriums, tangerines and sticky notes: "Dear Mrs. V., Your so nice. And your so pretty, too," with high hopes. *Maybe she will like me now*, ran the thread of wishful thinking. Winning her favor took all of my attention. I had to stay neat and clean and pretend to be a good girl, somebody who could "make nice-nice" and "talk high *makamak*." To win Mrs. Vicente over, I saw that I would have to be able to speak properly, a complicated undertaking demanding control of all my body parts, including my eyes and hands, which wandered away when my mouth opened up. Therefore, in a compromise with my desire to shine, I resolved to keep absolutely quiet, stand up with the stupid row and ignore the one I wanted to impress.

Mrs. Vicente was one of us, she claimed, because she herself had grown up in our "very neighborhood." Her school, too, she once let out, had been non-English Standard. We were surprised to hear her say that her family was related to the Kahanus who owned the corner grocery store. We knew them, the ones who used to have money. The brothers Eugene and Franklin Teves claimed they knew for sure she couldn't be kin to anyone they recognized, in answer to the other class who called her "The Portagee Teacha." She spoke, dressed and carried herself in a manner that was unlike any of the women I observed at home, but she fit right in with our other teachers who, like her, had gone to Normal School and shared her authoritative ways.

Difficult as she was, we could understand her preoccupation. Getting rid of ukus was a tedious job connected with beratings from your mother and lickings from your father. We always knew who carried ukus and were swift to leave that child alone. News traveled fast. All the same we could each remember what it felt like to be the "odd man out," which was the name of one of our favorite games.

To have ukus, to tell your close friends not to tell the others, and to have them keep the secret; that was the test of friendship. Like the garbage men who worked under the *uku pau* system, which meant that no gang or worker was finished until everybody on that truck helped the final guy unload his very last can, and everybody could quit, uku season wasn't over until every kid got rid of every last clinging egg.

At Christmastime, Mrs. Vincente wrapped up a useful comb for each and every one of us. At the end of the year we raced each other to be the first one lined up at her massive desk.

We would each shyly request her autograph with the suggested correct phrases, "Please, Mrs. Vincente," and, "Thank you, Teacha." So she must have been what we had grown to expect a teacher to be.

Because of Mrs. Vincente I wanted to become a teacher. I wanted to wield power and know how to get my way. I wanted to be the one who would point out a minute, luminous silver egg sack stuck on a coarse black hair, shake it vigorously with arm held out far away from body, and declare victoriously, "infestation . . . of . . . pediculosis!"

She would then turn to address the entire class. "This child must go directly to the nurse's office." She would speak firmly but in a softer tone to the kid. "Do not return to our room until you can bring me the white clearance certificate signed by both of your parents."

Completely silent during class, I practiced those words at home while I played school. I turned to the class. I gave the warning to the kid. Mrs. Vicente was not to be taken lightly.

The day Joseph learned about ukus, I figured out teachers.

Facing him, Mrs. Vicente demanded to know the new boy's name from his own mouth.

"Joseph Kaleialoha Lee."

"Say ma'am."

"Hah?"

"You must say 'Joseph Kaleialoha Lee, ma'am.' "

"Joseph-Kaleialoha-Lee-ma'am!"

"Hold out your hands, please."

Evidently he had not paid attention, the biggest error of our collective class, one which we heard about incessantly. He had not watched her routine, which included a search for our hidden fingernail dirt. He held his hands palms up. I shuddered.

Mrs. Vicente studied Joseph with what we called the "stink eye," but he still didn't catch on. She must have considered his behavior insubordinate, because he did not seem retarded or neglected as he was wearing his new long, khaki pants and a freshly starched aloha shirt.

She reached into the big pocket of her apron and took out a fat wooden ruler. Our silence was audible. She stepped up a little nearer to Joseph, almost blocking out all the air and light around us that her sharp features and steely voice cut through to reach our wobbly attention.

"What grade are you in now, young man?"

Joseph was silent as if in deep thought. Why wouldn't he say the answer? I nudged him quickly on his side with the hand nearest his body.

"Fot grade," he blurted in a small, panicky wheeze.

She turned on us all, enraged at our murmurs of anticipation. We knew for sure he would get it now.

Some girl giggled hysterically in a shrill whinny, "heengheengheeng . . ." Probably Japanese.

"Quiet."

Businesslike, she returned to Joseph with her full attention, peering into his ear. "Say th, th, th. Speak slowly." He heard the warning in her voice.

"Tha, tha, tha." Joseph rippled droplets of sweat.

"Th, th, th . . . everyone, say it all together: the tree!"

We practiced loudly with Joseph leading the chorus, relieved now to be part of the mass of voices.

"Say the tree, not da chree."

"The tree, not da chree."

"Fourth grade, not fot grade."

"Foth grade, not foth grade."

With a rapid searching movement which caught most of us off guard, Mrs. Vicente swung around to face Darcie Ah Sing, whose hand was still stuck in her curly brown hair when she was spotted scratching herself vigorously. Mrs. V. stared blackly into Darcie's tight curls with unshakeable attention. In a matter of seconds, with an upward swoop of her palm, Teacha found the louse at the nape of the exposed neck and pronounced her memorable conclusion, ending with "by both of your parents," indicting Darcie's whole family into the crime.

"March yourself into the office, young lady." Mrs. Vicente wrung a hankie between her pudgy hands with tight motions. Head hanging, Darcie moved out wordlessly to the school nurse's station for the next inspection.

We knew that she would be "shame" for a long time and stared at our dusty toes in hopeless sympathy.

When we were allowed to sit at our desks (after practicing the sks sound for desks: "sssk'sss, sssk'sss, dehss'kuss, dehss'kuss, dehss'kuss, not dessess, dessess, dessess"), we were hooked into finishing our tasks of busy-work and wearing our masks of obedience, totally subdued.

Then she read to us, as she explained that she was "wont to do when the occasion arose," while we sat quietly at our desks with our hands folded as she had trained us. She enunciated each word clearly for our benefit, reminding us that by the time we graduated we would be speaking "proper English" and forgot the *uku* check for the day. Her words stuck like little pearly grains into the folds of my brain. I pondered how to talk *haole* while she continued to lecture.

"The child . . . the school . . . the tree. . ." I could not hear the meaning of her words and scratched my head idly but in secret, my head dodging her line of vision. I yearned to master her knowledge, but dared not make myself the target of her next assault. I was not getting any smarter, but itchier by the minute, more eager than anyone to break free into the oasis of recess.

When the loud buzzer finally shattered the purring motor of her voice, we knew better than to whoop and scatter. We gathered our things formally and waited silently to be dismissed. If we made noise we would have to sit inside in agony, paying attention to the whole endless, meaningless story which sounded like all the ones before and wasted our precious time. Even Joseph caught on.

He said, "Whew, 'as waste time."

Once we were outside, surveying the situation, we saw two teams of the bigger boys who pulled at a heavy knotted rope from opposite ends. Joseph's bare feet dug into the ground right in back of Junior Boy, the tug-of-war captain. Clearly he wouldn't need any more of my guidance if Junior Boy had let him in. Beads of wetness sparkled off their bodies as the tight chain of grunting boys held fast under the bright sun.

Noisy clumps of kids skipped rope and kicked up the grass, twisting bodies and shining faces, all together in motion. Racing around the giant banyan, for no good reason, I scream-giggled, "Wheeeeha-ha-hah!" Like a wildcat I roared up the trunk of the chree . . . just to see if I could.

Joseph spotted me. "Too good, you!" he yelled.

While the girls played jacks, and the boys walked their board stilts, Joseph and I moved around groups trading milk bottle covers and playing marbles. We wondered aloud to each other. We spread the word.

"Ho, w'atchoo tink?"

"Must be da teacha wen' catch ukus befo'."

"Not . . . "

"Not not!"

"Cannot be . . ."

"Can can!"

"Yeah?"

"Ay, yeah. O' how else she can spock 'em dat fast?"

That made me laugh, the thought of Mrs. V. picking through her careful topknot. She would have to moosh away the hibiscus to get in a finger. I mimed her by scratching through the hair I let hang down in front of my face. When I swept it back professionally with the palm of my hand, I threw in a cross-eyed crazy look. Joseph pretended to "spock *uku*" in my hair as he took on Mrs. V's exaggerated ladylike manner to hold onto one of my ears like a handle and peer into the endless *puka*.

"Ho, man," he proclaimed, "get so planny inside."

The recess bell rang, ending our sweet freedom. We pranced back to the classroom in a noisy herd. Teacha gave us the Look. We grew cautious. We would spend the next hour silently tracking Mrs. Vicente's poised head, while Joseph and I smiled knowingly at each other.

Eyes gleaming, Mrs. Vicente never disappointed any of us, because she always stuck right on her lessons and never let up at all. She stayed mean as ever, right on top of the class. As for us, fourth grade *ukus* could appreciate the effort . . . so much not letting go.

RAINBOWS UNDER WATER
John Dominis Holt

Kawela Bay was a treeless, wind-blown place, with a matchless sand beach and excellent swimming. In the outer reaches of the bay, among coral reefs and stone outcroppings, reef fish of all kinds abounded. In season, schools of kala, akule, 'opelu, and 'o'io swarmed into the bay. Sometimes a lone shark found its way through the coral and rocks to the edge of the beach where we swam. We watched one once, swimming with her young safely hovering under her belly. As they approached shore, she seemed to regurgitate her brood to allow them to wiggle in the sand as the waves swept up and down the beach. A marvelous sight. Someone took pictures and we had them for years until we made a massive move from Makiki Roundtop Drive to a house in 'Aiea. All of our childhood pictures were lost at that time. It was a truly great loss and left me with a punishing gap in the period of years between my birth and mid-teens.

My grandmother, Emma Daniels Holt, owned some lots at Kawela Bay and left them to her children, who divided them among themselves, each taking two beach lots plus a taro patch—a typical kuleana arrangement. My father chose one beach lot at the western end of the bay's curve, where there was a lagoon fed by a tunnel from the sea. At high tide, fish would come in with the water—schools of mullet chased by ulua, the latter occasionally chased by sharks. My father's other lot sat dead center of the bay, where his three brothers Bill, Harry, and Mannie had also chosen lots. Their sister, my Aunt Ellen, preferred to be a little separated from her brothers and chose a beach lot several hundred feet away. She eventually sold a part of it to a childhood friend.

I first went to Kawela with my family during the summer when I was five or six years old, immediately following the end of the school year. I remember the continuous sounds of the sea at the shore and the groups of old people sitting around lanterns in the evenings, incessantly speaking Hawaiian. It was here at Kawela that I first became aware that Hawai'i is a place of mysteries, especially for old-fashioned Hawaiians—in the days and nights are woven magical happenings, seen in cloud formations, gusts of wind, and patterns of waves. In these elements, people were inspired to talk, letting the long hours pass as they spun tales and shared wondrous stories of the old days. At those times, I became partly separated from the twentieth century, a child, yes, but one caught in the golden web of imagination and fantasy, a product of the dream world who would never again be a devoted member of modern, scientific civilization with its cold separation of dream from fact.

There was plenitude all summer long and a very special sense of seclusion and privacy. In some places, mountains are separate from the ocean, like the great Rockies and the Urals and other continental masses; but in Hawai'i, mountains enclose the beaches, with steep slopes sometimes plunging to the very edge of the water. At Kawela, we sat before our own part of the huge Pacific Ocean sheltered by the mountains at our backs.

Low gray hills rose from the lowlands along the shore. The area had a serene beauty. Where now the fields are flattened and corn is grown for seed, there were numerous taro patches, some of which we owned. The parcels were called kuleana in the parlance of fee simple land title, usually meted out to maka'ainana as small awards during the Mahele. My uncles and aunt owned similar parcels. I suppose we were once the konohiki of Kawela Bay—owners of a chiefly land award.

Behind the hills, the mountains rose with their unusual combinations of greens—the cascades of distinctive yellowgreen kukui trees, woven into the dark green hillsides and the great groves of pale green koa covering the upper slopes. Wild tree ferns grew under 'ohi'a lehua trees with inimitable red puffs of blossoms—the familiar flower of Pele, ruling deity of volcanoes. Dark wild vines called 'ie'ie entwined the trunks of smaller trees. The native 'o'u bird, now in the darkness of near extinction, was then a beautiful dull green in the flourishing native Hawaiian biota. 'O'u were the source of green feathers used in the making of capes and cloaks during the golden age of Hawaiian civilization.

All of this natural beauty was in contrast to daily life in Honolulu where the routine involved going to school and studying, and there were street cars and the steady encroachment of the outside world which would eventually intrude on our romantic places beside the lagoon. Kawela had so much, it was all there, and so close. It was old Hawai'i, a true relic of the past. There were very happy times at Kawela—fishing night and day, swimming and romps on the sand, and horseback rides on mounts from nearby Kahuku Ranch, owned by the Rathburn family.

Directly in front of my father's lagoon lot sat an outcropping of rock and coral. This mass slanted downward into the ocean to a depth of about twenty feet. On its walls hordes of ula, or lobsters, gathered during certain times of the year, usually the summer months. All summer long, we were fed broiled lobster—partly cooked and mixed with wana, or sea urchin, when it was available. Directly across at the other point was a place known to be the home of myriads of he'e, or octopus. A part-Hawaiian family named

Andrews had a two-story house there. "Uncle Archie," as the father was called, was always being photographed holding up a massive octopus. My father was much taken with these photos, and when he showed one of them to anyone, he provided all the details of the catch—the time of day, the year, and the weight and length of the octopus.

Our near neighbors were the Heilbrons, Uncle Bert and Auntie Minnie, whose teen-aged son and daughter would at times bring hordes of Punahou classmates down for the weekend. The 'ukuleles were strummed continually, the popular songs of the time were sung, and, of course, there was much dancing to the tunes of the twenties; a marvelous air of frivolity prevailed. Aunt Minnie, an extremely kind and generous lady, with her small staff, provided exquisite picnic-type concoctions. At times, all the neighbors would share. One of the family lots left empty separated the Heilbrons from the Rosas, Uncle Mack and Aunt Helen—the beautiful Helen Robertson, a niece of Princess Ka'iulani. Aunt Helen had grown up next to my father's family, on School and Nu'uanu Streets. Her mother, Aunt Rosie Cleghorn Robertson, was also a famous beauty. She was married to James Robertson, the brother of Aunt Lizzie Shaefer and A.G.M. Robertson, the famous lawyer and judge who lived well into our times.

Aunt Helen and Uncle Mack's dinners were more regal than the dinners served by others of the community. Their diminutive cook, Fujii-san, prepared marvelous roasts of lamb and beef, great green salads, and wonderfully elaborate fruit salads. To be invited to dinner there was a joy and a privilege.

They drove a Pierce Arrow touring car with headlights on the fenders. Uncle Mack had had someone install in the engine a device that made sounds like bird calls, and when he and Auntie Helen drove down the little road to our houses, the bird calls announced their arrival.

Among the most treasured experiences were the evening picnics on the beach where all gathered to eat lobster, steak, and perhaps ulua filets—all broiled on kiawe wood fires. After the feasting, an enormous bonfire would be lit. Soon after the Punahou-ites would burst into song, and before long, someone would be dancing a hula.

At this point, we children would be gathered up by Julia, our Hawaiian nurse, and marched off to bed.

The enchantment of the evening's smells, sounds, and food would keep me awake for hours. From our beds, we could hear the laughter, chatter, and singing of the revelers. Sometimes it went on until dawn.

At dawn I could sometimes hear Kai'a, our caretaker, stirring in his little room at the back of the house. Soon he would make loud noises as he cleared his throat and mumbled things to himself in Hawaiian, as a way of telling me it was time to wake up. Kai'a was a great, renowned fisherman. He knew where the fish were and could always tell my father and the others where to go to catch what they wanted. He was somewhat heavy, with a tremendous long, white beard that flowed down over his stomach. He lived in the traditional way, always wearing an old-fashioned malo and speaking very little English—only when he had to. Although he had a little house of his own, he stayed with us. His nephews and his sister lived down the road. Kai'a was from an old family of that area, so he knew the land and sea extremely well, one of the last of the elder Hawaiians whose life was spent from birth to death on the north shore of O'ahu. He talked very little about all the history he had seen and lived, being a simple man of the sea and living in a complete, unaffected way.

He took a shine to me, and I became attached to him, accompanying him everywhere as he wandered along the seashore or examined the taro patches. Twice he took me into the hills above and south of Waiale'e—a long trek. Part of the time he carried me on his massive shoulders. He took me up to see the many burial caves located in the steep hills overlooking the sea, where 'ohana and kupuna lay in deep sleep. In some caves were pools of dark, cool, iridescent water, as clean as unpolluted rain.

"No ka wai ola," he would say—the waters of life. "Home o na 'aumākua"—home of the family gods.

We would view the remains—bones and artifacts. He knew the families and described them to me. He would show me where the date trees were planted as markers that identified the burial caves. Date trees were hardy and lived a very long time. I was not carried to heights of unfettered joy on these occasions—there was something spooky about examining those caves, as though I were intruding on some terribly private moment during a family gathering.

Often we walked along the shore together, a little hapa haole, sun-tanned boy with blond, almost platinum-white hair and the old pure Hawaiian, with his full white beard. He was always amazed at my blond hair, the only blond hair he had ever seen in his life. My hair bleached out even more over the summer, from the sun and sea, and grew longer and wilder as the weeks passed. We were quite a pair, walking along the reef in the early mornings, looking for fish and just observing what there was to see. It was dream-like. The fish were so beautiful, undisturbed in the clear waters. Hardly anyone was around in those days. We would go to the headlands, what was formerly a reef, and look down into the ocean where hundreds of fish passed beneath us, flashing in the sunlight.

The sight brought on waves of utmost delight. Decades later, when I read about the effects of taking hallucinogens like LSD, I realized that I had witnessed something similar, but the brilliant flashes of color were not illusions, but fish. One particular fish, the most unreal sight of all, had colored ribbons flowing from its sides. Seeing these beautiful fish erased momentarily my fear of the ocean. Kaiʻa would tell me which fish were safe to eat, which were poisonous, and which ones were to be appreciated just for their beauty.

After we were companions for some weeks, he told me about the sharks living under the ledge that sloped down into the water to the sand below the reef. As we stood on the coral, he pointed out the dark area, saying that in the deepest corner were the sharks, whole families of them.

One day he said quite confidently he would take me down and show them to me. I replied, quite sincerely, "No, no!" I was only five or six at the time. However, I trusted the old man so much and wanted to go wherever he went, so finally I agreed to dive with him. We walked out to where the water was deeper; then he crouched down and had me wrap myself around his body like a monkey. I rode on his back, with my arms around his neck and my legs around his chest. His arms were free to swim and dive. He paddled strongly across the surface of the lagoon, then with a sign to me, descended three or four feet and came up quickly. The first time I practically choked to death. He coached me to keep my mouth closed and not to drink the water and showed me how to hold my breath for the longest time possible. It was somewhat scary, but exciting, and it didn't take long to learn what to do.

Kaiʻa swam like a fish—his name implies the sea and fishing. When he dove deeper into the sea, my blood froze. As I gripped his body with my knees and his neck with my hands, all the glories of the Hawaiian reef were revealed. Schools of manini glided by, as happy as school children on an excursion. There were gorgeous hinalea, whose green blue-brown and pinkish streaks ran the length of their bodies. At times, a small school of pāpio swam by, searching for baby mullet, called pua, or other small fish. Kumu streaked in and out of coral formations. The sharp, nose-like head of a puhi, or moray eel, would pop out of a hole, its mouth ajar showing rows of teeth designed to rip flesh.

After we surfaced for air, Kaiʻa would say, "They are not showing themselves to us today."

"I saw a lot of fish."

"You saw nothing . . . but you all right, keiki." I would have nodded, and he would have kissed my cheek.

"This time we go see the niuhi, old John Jack mā." Off we went to the place in the reef where the sides slanted sharply to the bottom. Here we had to dive much deeper than before. Kaiʻa was old but extremely strong.

He had dived all of his life and knew how to get down to the bottom quickly, with little exertion. I clung tightly to my old friend and kahu, and we passed through layers of sunlight in the water. I saw brilliant fish scattering in all directions around us. I was transfixed by the beauty but held on firmly to Kai'a, feeling his muscles and bones moving as he pulled his way to the bottom, following the steep ledge. It was darker down there, with shafts of light slipping through the cracks in the coral above and illuminating the sand in a dim glow.

Then I saw these great living things lying on the bottom, rolling slowly from side to side in the lolling current. The sharks, apparently satiated by a previous feeding, were resting. We hovered about six feet above them for some time. They looked like tiger sharks and fish sharks with long tails. I was both exhilarated and terrified. My little legs jammed into Kai'a's sides and he understood. We shot to the surface, leaping out of the water like humpback whales. I remember being ready to burst just as we broke free. Once we were at the surface, I was relieved to see that no shark had followed us.

We would dive down again and again. Afterwards, when we rested on the warm coral surface at the water's edge, Kai'a told me of the ali'i makua—the old sharks that had been living in the bay for ages and ages. They all had names, odd names, personal names that he had given them. One in particular he called Haku-nui, Big Boss. He also told me of one that had been young when he was just a boy himself. As we dove down again and again, I would learn to recognize these sharks as he had. Whatever fears I had were lessened. I began to really enjoy these plunges and the creatures; they became very real to me.

Sometimes, with me on his back, Kai'a would go down and come up close to the older sharks and reach out slowly with a hand to pick off barnacles that had encrusted their eyes. Such a build up of barnacles could eventually blind the old animals. They somehow trusted him and allowed him to do the cleaning. The great yellow eyes stared at us, floating inches from us as Kai'a picked away at the hard material that was often covered with limu. It must have hurt the sharks at least a little. They moved around slowly like a herd of cattle in a corral. Kai'a jabbed at them and pushed them away in order to stay with the shark he was working on. It was quite unreal, hanging onto this white-bearded man shoving these large, dark creatures glaring at us. I would look up to the surface to see the brighter fish darting above, and the sky-blue of the surface and rolling waves. It was an ancient feeling, like something from Merlin's strange, enchanted world or the magical times of Pele and Hi'iaka.

Sometimes the sharks moved away and swam to the surface. It was a habit they developed because fishermen fed them 'awa to pacify them in order to prevent them from interfering with the fishing boats. When the sharks surfaced, they were of a different color in the brighter light. With growths of barnacles and limu on their backs, they looked like islands emerging from the sea. After the sharks left, we stayed out in the water for hours, rarely if ever, talking.

Once Kai'a told me that when he was fourteen or fifteen and had not slept with a woman, which meant he still had the mana of innocence, he was chosen as one of the youths to tie ropes of braided coconut fiber around the tail of a shark. The shark would be dragged out of the sea so that its skin could be used for making drums. I have never seen a reference to this particular practice of old Hawai'i, but Kai'a's mo'olelo was dependable.

Kai'a always carried a spear to hunt fish and we would swim above this astounding sea floor, over the puhi 'ula, red moray eels, darting in and out of their holes in the coral and sea urchins producing eggs. We would investigate small caves and holes where he knew fish would be. On other occasions, we visited the place on the steep sloping ledge jutting into the harbor where lobsters gathered in great numbers during the summer. My father joined us at these times. He and Kai'a kept the place a secret from the others. The two of them would dive down and pick lobsters off the bottom. I'd let myself down into the water with the help of a rope tied to the ledge and they would give me two lobsters, one for each hand. Then I'd kick back to the surface and put their catch into a box. When they had more lobsters, they would tug on the rope and I would descend again. We ate fresh lobster for days.

After a good day of fishing, Kai'a and I visited his ko'a where he prayed and offered up some part of the catch to the gods. I would stand stiff as a rock, thinking of my very Christian mother and what she would say if she knew I was there. My father knew and didn't care, allowing me the chance to have the experience. Eventually my mother learned only a part of it. Kai'a's rituals and prayers were all a great thrill to me. I loved dreaming and still do. I loved fantasy and building my own worlds. The old man fortified this instinct in me, this attraction to realms beyond what was apparently real. The experience certainly seemed unreal to me, like the sea and all its inhabitants.

Years later there would be events that would shatter the memory of the innocent pleasures of the bay and show me the modern world. My father and his friends carried out shark hunts in the outer reaches of the bay's deep water. There, the carcass of an old bull or mule or horse would be dragged out as bait, one of its feet lashed with cable, the other end of which

had been secured to rocks at the edge of the bay. Gruesome debacles result-
ed as the sharks eventually swarmed in to devour the bait. Using highpow-
ered rifles, my father and his friends slaughtered sharks by the dozens at
close range, shooting them directly in the eyes—eyes that I had watched
Kaiʻa delicately clean. When one shark was injured, the others in a feeding
frenzy would devour it.

Kaiʻa, hiding in the brush on shore, would be horrified, wailing over
the massacre of his ʻaumākua. He protected me for a long time from having
to watch these slaughters from the boat or sampan until my father insisted
—in the interest of developing my macho instincts—that I come aboard to
watch. I have been haunted ever since by the memory of the scene I
witnessed, the absolute enraged greed of the sharks and the strange joy that
showed in my father and his friends as they killed. At the time I witnessed
the slaughters, I was already familiar with Wagner and the stories of
Macbeth and Julius Caesar. I knew something about the beauty of the old
ways of Hawaiʻi and more about the impassioned heroics and the madness
of unloving love of the *Ring of the Niebelungen*. I came to realize that the
violence in the bloody acts of Macbeth was no different from the violence
in Pele's abrupt and arrogant decisions. There was something of the same
willful, cold-blooded intentions that incorporated love and hate into cruel
indifference.

My mother's experiences as a child on Maui concerning sharks as
ʻaumākua made her shiver with fright and confusion when these slaughters
took place. She came to hate Kawela Bay. At first, she was convinced by a
hapa haole Honolulu matron that a water goddess lived in the lagoon and
needed special feeding and prayers to remain happy and harmless. My
mother, rigidly Christian, was strongly affected by the story. She never rest-
ed until that lot was sold—to another prominent hapa haole matron who
eventually sold it to the first one, the mythologist who had planted the
seeds of dread in my mother. So went our favorite place to loiter as children,
watching mullet and awa swim in silvery, peaceful shoals until an ulua came
in from the ocean and scattered them, snapping up one or two to appease its
hunger.

CHINATOWN
Ashley M. Houk

Along the crowded streets I walk
staying close to my mother's side,
with the smell of fresh noodles cooking
drifting from bright red painted shops.
I pass a couple of people talking,
their clothes looking as dirty and old as the street does.
One is squeezed into a tight red top
and I cannot tell if it is a man or woman.
I turn away trying not to look.
We pass tiny markets,
my mother bending over baskets
filled with smells that are strange to me,
saying their names in a language I do not understand;
she is trying to teach me about her culture.
As we are leaving we pass a basket with blood on the sides
and things that look like an animal's heart;
I do not dare ask what it is.
We make our way through a long tunnel,
people hustling past me,
the noise of the street dying in the background.
We arrive at a noodle factory,
a man with a heavy accent takes our order
and wraps the look fun noodles in the familiar pink paper with a white
string around it.
After hurrying to our car on a deserted street that my mom didn't
want to park on,
we speed away to share our treasures with Grandma.

WHEN I WAS YOUNG ON AN ISLAND
Hina Kahanu

When I was young on an island
my brother caught gray baby sharks
on his bamboo fishing pole.
When he'd catch a shark,
he'd call the other kids and
we'd come running with clubs
of driftwood to beat the shark
to death.

When I was young on an island
my brother made moray eel traps
of silver pineapple juice cans
and a can opener, the kind that
makes triangle holes. When he'd
catch an eel, he'd give it to the
neighbor cat and we'd all watch
the tiger-striped cat
take the eel out of the can
and eat it.

When we were young on Paikō Drive
in Kuliʻouʻou and we played war,
my brother invented the battle charge.
He'd wait for a hard wind to pick
up the sand and just when the wind
was strongest, he'd yell, "Charge,"
and we'd run, head down, into a zillion
tiny bullets of stinging sand
hurled by the wind's hand.

When I was young on an island
my brother invented the jellyfish
test. He was an Apache Indian that day.
Tortured, he would not cry out.

We caught see-through jellyfish
in our hands and held them
while they stung us. Whoever
cried out first or dropped their
jellyfish, lost. I remember sinking
to my knees with pain and finally
lying down in the cool, shallow water.
Only my burning jellyfish hand
held out.

BECCAH
I record the lives of the dead:
Severino Santos Agopada, 65, retired plumber and member of the
Botanical Garden Society of Hawaii, died March 13, 1995.
Gladys Malia Leiatua-Smith, 81, died April 9, 1995. Formerly of
Western Samoa, she is survived by sons Jacob, Nathaniel, Luke, Matthew, and
Siu Junior; daughters Hope, Grace, Faith, and Nellie; 19 grandchildren and 5
great-grandchildren.
Lawrence Ching III of Honolulu, died April 15, 1995. Survived by wife,
Rose, and son Lawrence IV. Services Saturday, Aloha attire.

When I first started writing the obits for the *Honolulu Star-Bulletin*—
as a graduating journalism major in awe of my first adult lover, U of H leg-
end and the *Bulletin's* managing editor, Sanford Dingman—I read the cer-
tificates of death, faxed fresh from the mortuaries, with imagination: creat-
ing adventures for those born far from their place of death, picturing the
grief of parents having to bury a child, feeling satisfaction when someone
died old, surrounded by the two or three generations that came from his
body.

Now, however, after six years of death detail, treading water in both
my relationship and my job, I no longer see people, families, lives lived and
wasted. I no longer struggle over the script, thesaurus in one hand, hoping
to utilize obscure synonyms for "die" so that my obits would illuminate my
potential, attracting praise and admiration from the great Mr. Dingman.
Now I deal only in words and statistics that need to be typed into the sys-
tem. The first thing I do each day after I log on is to count how many inch-
es I have to fill, computing how many names and death dates need to be
processed.

I have recorded so many deaths that the formula is templated in my
brain: name, age, date of death, survivors, services. And yet, when it came
time for me to write my own mother's obituary, as I held a copy of her death
certificate in my hand, I found that I did not have the facts for even the
most basic, skeletal obituary. And I found I did not know how to start imag-
ining her life.

When I was a child, it did not occur to me that my mother had a life before me. Always, when I asked for stories about her past, they were about me, starting from my conception. "How did you and Daddy meet?" I would ask her. "When did you know you were in love? When did you decide to have me?"

In those days, I believed my mother's story that my parents met when she was a famous singer in Korea. "Once on a time, I sang on stage," my mother would boast, "and your father came to see me. He was in love."

I imagined hot spotlights blinding her eyes, a large stage empty except for my mother, dressed in stripes and glittering sequins. When I was in elementary school, and easily influenced by Auntie Reno's sense of fashion, that was my idea of glamour. The first outfit I chose for myself was a plaid and denim bell-bottom pantsuit, which I wore three times a week in the fourth grade. I wore it despite the hoots of the boys and the stinkeye and snubnose from Janice "Toots" Tutivena and her Entourage, until the crisscrossing stripes faded at the knees and the bell-bottoms flapped above my ankles.

I believed my mother's story, even though when I heard her singing to the spirits, I thought not of music but of crying, her songs long wails of complaints and demands and wishes for the dead.

I believed it because I wanted to believe that my voice would rescue me, transport me to a new world. I lived with the secret hope that I had inherited my mother's talent and that I would soon be discovered—perhaps singing "Rudolph the Red-Nosed Reindeer" in our school's Xmas Xtravaganza. When my class took its place in the cafetorium and began singing our carol, I knew my voice would float out above the voices of the other students. Slowly, one by one, the rest of the singers would fall silent. One by one, the parents and teachers in the audience would rise to their feet, drawn closer to the stage by my voice, as pure as a bell. Then, when the song came to a close, the audience would erupt into cheers and applause, and one man—preferably Toots's father (who in real life sold vacuum cleaners at Sears but in my perfect daydream was a movie agent)—would point to me and shout, "What a voice! What poise! What a smile! The new Marie Osmond!"

Whenever I was alone, I'd sing—usually something by the Carpenters or Elvis—in preparation for my discovery. I would sing so hard I'd get tears in my eyes. My singing moved me.

One afternoon I crawled into the bathtub, pulled the curtain to make a private cave for myself, lay down, and sang "Let It Be," over and over again. Somewhere between my third and seventh renditions, my mother came in to use the toilet.

"What's wrong?" she shouted.

"Nothing," I growled. "I'm singing."

My mother yanked open the shower curtain so hard the bar fell onto the floor.

"Hey!" I squealed as I sat up. My mother loomed over me, the curtain clutched in her hands and pooling into the tub. The bar, suspended by the curtain's rings, knocked against her thighs. I almost asked, "Are you crazy?" but stopped myself before the words escaped and became concrete, heavy enough to break into the real world.

"Are the spirits after you too?" she panted. "Do you hear them singing, always singing?"

"No!" I shouted at her.

"Sometimes they cry so loud, just like a cat cry, so full of wanting, that I worry you will begin to hear them, too." My mother closed her eyes and started rocking. "Waaaooo, waaaaoooo," she wailed. "Just like that." She stopped rocking and glared at me. "You have to fight it."

I put my hands over my ears. "I can't hear you, I can't hear you," I sang over and over again. "I can't hear you, I can't hear you," I chanted each time she opened her mouth to add something else.

Finally she shut her mouth and didn't open it again. Then she shook her head, just looking at me lying in the tub with my hands plugging my ears, singing tonelessly, "I can't hear you I can't hear you I can't hear you." When she turned and walked away, kicking the curtain out in front of her, I was still chanting, "I can't hear you," though the words had lost their meaning.

I was discovered not during Ala Wai E's Xmas Xtravaganza but during the tryouts for the May Day Pageant. And not by Toots's father but by Toots herself.

I was not naive enough to try out for May Day Queen or her court. I knew that I never had a chance, since I wasn't part Hawaiian and didn't have long hair. But I did want to be in the chorus that stood next to the stage and sang "Hawai'i Pono'i" as they ascended their thrones.

During the after-school tryouts, as I waited for my turn to sing next to the vice principal playing the piano, I watched the kids ahead of me turn shy and quiet, their squeaky voices breaking under the weight of the accompaniment. I vowed my voice would be strong enough to fill the entire cafetorium and rich enough to eat for dessert.

When my name was called, I marched down the aisle, a long gauntlet of chewed sunflower seeds spit at my feet by the Toots Entourage. My slippers kicked up the littered shells so that they flecked the backs of my calves. I kept my eyes on the stage, on the piano, and on Vice Principal

"Piano Man" Pili, who alternately smiled encouragement to each struggling singer and glared into the audience in an attempt to stifle whistles and hoots and shouts of "Gong." But as I walked past their seats, I heard Toots and Tim Sugimoto hiss, "Look dah fancy-pants! 'I stay blinded by dah light!'"

I tossed my hair and glided onto the stage. Clearing my throat, I nodded to Vice P Pili, smiled and waved to the crowd—right at Toots—and tapped my foot: one and a two and a three!

To this day, I am not sure what happened, or how it happened. I had practiced—in the bathtub, walking to school—until I knew I was good, until I made myself cry. But that day, some devil thing with the voice of a big, old-age frog took possession of my throat, and "Hawai'i Pono'i" lurched unreliably around the cafetorium: "Hawai'i Pono'iiiii, Nana i Kou mo'i . . . uh . . . la la la Lani e Kamehameha e . . . mmm hmm hmm . . . Hawai'iiiii Po-oh-no 'iiiii! Aaaah-meh-nehhhh!"

At least I was loud.

As I slunk off the stage, I heard Toots and her Entourage laughing and howling like dogs. "Guh-guh-guh-gong!" they barked.

They followed me out of the building and pinned me against the wall. "You suck," said Toots.

"Yeah," said Tiffi, a Toots wannabe. "You suck."

"You gotta be the worst singer in the school," Toots said. "We don't want you in our chorus."

"We don't even want you in our school, you weirdo," said another Toots follower.

"You're the weirdo," I snapped back. "Just so happens I got the talent of my mother, who was a famous singer in Korea." After I said this, I realized some things were better left unsaid.

"Yeah, right," said Toots.

"Yeah, that's right," I said, then added, compelled to defend myself, "They just have different singing over there."

"Hanyang anyang hasei-pasei-ooooh," Toots screeched. "Yobos must have bad ears!"

The girls laughed and stepped closer, the half-moon made by their bodies tightening around me. "You're nothing but a stink Yobo," said Toots. "Nothing but one big-fat liar. 'Oh, my mommy's a famous singer.' 'Oh, my daddy was rich, with a house on the Mainland, and I had one puppy.' 'Oh, next year my daddy going come get us and move us back.' Yeah, right."

Toots pushed my shoulder. "This is what's true: You so poor that every day you gotta wear the same lame clothes and the same out-of-fashion, stink-smelling shoes until they get holes and still you wear em. You so poor you save your school lunch for one afterschool snack—no lie, cause we seen you wrap em up in your napkin."

By this time Toots was so close I could smell a mixture of seeds and the kakimochi she always ate in class on her breath. I gave her stink-eye, but she kept pushing me.

"You talk like you better than everybody else, but you not. We all know you live in The Shacks, and you prob'ly sleep with dirty feet in the same bed as your crazy old lady."

"Not!" At the one thing I could call a lie—that I went to bed with dirty feet—I called Toots a liar and punched her in her soft, newly forming chest. When she fell back into her friends, I ran away and didn't look back, not even to see if they were chasing me. I don't think I ran home and asked my mother to verify her singing story right away. I probably went to my secret place, a spot under the Ala Wai Bridge, where runoff from the rains and the city drained into the canal. Underneath, I had flattened out a nest among the tall grass that stretched along the bank. Sheltered by the underbelly of that small pedestrian bridge, I would practice my singing. I liked to hear my voice bounce off the concrete that surrounded me.

I probably went there right after Toots and her Entourage told me I sucked. I know I would have wanted to hear the truth for myself.

Eventually, though it might not have been that night, I must have asked my mother to repeat the story of how she met my father. Because I have the distinct memory of another story.

We were at the kitchen table, sorting coins from the Wishing Bowl and packing them into paper sleeves, when, trying to sound casual, I asked her for the story of my parents' first meeting. "Mom," I told her, "tell me again that story, you know, that one about you and Dad meeting."

Without looking up from counting out a pile of dimes, she sighed. "Once was a hard time," she said, "but a happy time. I was helping to take care of all the orphans during the war—you know, so many children lost their mommies, lost their daddies at that time. Your father was one of the missionaries that gave us food and clothing. When he saw how good I was with the children, he fell in love with me, because he knew I would make a good mother."

She slipped the dimes into a roll, then began on the quarters. "When the war moved into my village, he helped us all, everyone, even the old mamasans, escape. We walked and walked, trying to escape from the communists. We hid in cemeteries and walked over the mountains of Korea until we were free to build a new home. In America."

My mother finished one stack of quarters, then looked up at me. She touched my cheek. "You remember anything about your father?" When I shook my head, she said, "Everything was nice and happy."

I don't recall if I challenged this new story or her old one. Sometimes I think I must have said, "Wait! That's not what you told me before! What's the truth?" because even then I must have recognized her story as an adaptation of *The Sound of Music*. Every year we'd watch that movie, after preparing a big bowl of boiled peanuts and a plate of dried squid as snacks. My mother liked the songs and would always cry at the ending.

Other times I think I must have said nothing, swallowing her new story without accusation or confrontation, even if I didn't believe her. When she spoke to me, calling me by name, I never wanted to do anything to spoil the moment. I feared my own words might break the spell of normalcy.

I grew cautious of my mother's stories, never knowing what to count on or what to discount. They sounded good—most of the stories she told me included the phrase: "It was a hard time but a happy time." In fact, I repeated several of her stories, telling teachers and other students versions of them that I supplemented with my own favorite movies: *West Side Story*, where Maria, my mother, was left pregnant with her love child, who was, of course, myself; *The Little Princess* and *The Poor Little Rich Girl* where I, the brave and suffering orphan, am reclaimed in the end by a rich and loving father, who was alive.

But I knew they were just stories told to people who didn't really matter, those who couldn't see into our Goodwill-furnished apartment in the row of dilapidated tri-story housing units nicknamed The Shacks. Those who couldn't see into the past when my father was alive and drunk and yelling about God. Those who couldn't see into my dreams of drowning and sinking and struggling for breath while unseen hands wrapped around my legs and pulled.

Not long after I started working for the *Bulletin*, I saw Tiffi Sugimoto. She wandered into the news building, looking for the marketing department, and even after all the years that had passed, I recognized her right away. With her spindly arms and her head that seemed overly large for her thin neck and scrawny body, she looked more like a ten-year-old as an adult than she had when she was really ten. When we were both ten, she seemed so big, her power as Toots's "right-hand man" larger than life.

I meant to look away when she walked near me, but I was caught staring. She smiled at me and sailed over to my cubicle. "Rebeccah!" she said as she bent over to hug me. She smacked the air near my ear. "You look exactly the same!"

I must have appeared dubious, because she leaned back and said, "Don't you remember me? Tiffany Sugimoto. Remember, me and Janice were always following you around, trying to be your friend?"

"Uh, yes, Tiffi," I mumbled.

Tiffi giggled, high-pitched and girlish, and as the men in the news-room—including Sanford, who back then always seemed to be nearby and ready with encouragement and advice—looked up, she batted her lashes. "What a wonderful place to work," she cooed. "How stimulating! How exciting to be the first to know the news!"

I grunted. "What I do is not glamorous," I said. Then, throwing a glance, a challenge, toward Sanford, I added, "At least not yet it's not."

"No, really, Rebeccah," Tiffi said, frowning her sincerity. "Wait till I tell Janice and the others what you are doing now. Now that Janice is back from California, learning how to be an EST instructor, I know she'd, like, love to see you! We always wondered what happened when you moved away—you went to the Mainland to live with your dad, right?"

She patted my head. "We really missed you. You always had such presence, an individualistic sense of style and color, and what a wit! Remember when Vice Principal Pili ordered you to sing "Hawai'i Pono'i" and you made up your own words? I thought he would, like, flip!"

Tiffi laughed and added how great it was to see me, that we should keep in touch, and maybe the "old Ala Wai gang" could get together for a mini-reunion. Hey—would I be willing to, like, put together a newsletter?

As I smiled and nodded whenever she took a breath, all I could think was: Is this the way she really remembers it? Her sincerity made me doubt my own version of events. Perhaps what I thought was true had been colored by the insecurities of a ten-year-old girl. At any rate, at that moment, looking at Tiffi chatting at me like we were the best of friends, I realized that not only could I not trust my mother's stories: I could not trust my own.

TONGUE

Juliet S. Kono

Dust flew into my eye.
My mother took my face
into her hands like a melon,
came at me with her tongue
and placed her lips around my eye.
It looked as if she were sucking
out my eyeball,
the way she sucks out fish eyes to eat.
She swirled her tongue
and cleansed my eye of its irritant.

Honeycomb of lungs
sticky with infection
held me to the sick bed for days.
She placed her mouth over my nose
and sucked the green muck
as if she were slurping noodles.
Her tongue helped clear
my blocked nasal passages,
and heaved my wheezing out like bath water.

After a walk in the canefields,
a bee in the ear
had me spinning like a top.
I banged into the wash buckets, gate, clothesline,
zigzagged like a drunk
or someone blind.
Mother grasped my hands
and secured me between her legs,
and came down on my ear with her tongue.
She slid the tip in and left it there.
Without a flinch,
she retracted her tongue
with the bee curled on its tip.

My lips on your lips,
my lips holding your tongue,
a learned truth.

FOURSCORE AND SEVEN YEARS AGO
Darrell H.Y. Lum

Six grade, we had to give da news every morning aftah da Pledge Allegence and My Country Tis of Dee. "Current events time," Mrs. Ching tell and she only call on maybe five kids fo get extra points, so first, you gotta raise your hand up and hope she call on you. You should always try be ready wit someting fo say cause sometimes nobody raise up their hands cause nobody went listen to da news on da radio or read da newspaypah last night so if you raise your hand, guarantee she call you. Bungy Lau was always waving his hand almost everyday fo give news. And if only get one chance left fo tell da news, Bungy give you da stink eye and raise his hand mo high and wave um and almost stand up awready fo make Mrs. Ching see him. Us guys and most times da girls too, dey jes put their hands down cause we no like Bungy get mad at us. Mrs. Ching try look around da room fo see if get anybody else she can call besides Bungy, but by den we all stay looking down at our desk so she gotta call Bungy cause he da only one left, yeah? And Bungy he stand up, he big you know, and he stay cracking his knuckles and he no mo one paper or anyting and we know dat he going give da wrestling results from da night before.

"Las night at da Civic Auditorium, fo da Nort American Heavyweight Belt, Nicky Bockwinkle pinned Curtis 'da Bull' Iaukea in two outa tree falls and retained da Nort American Belt. In tag team ackshen 'Mister Fooge' Fuji Fujiwara and da Masked Executionah was disqualified in a minute and thirty seconds of da first round fo using brass knuckles dat da Executionah went hide in his tights."

"Da cheatah!" Andrew go tell and everybody went laugh at him. Mrs. Ching shush da class.

"Da duo of Giant Baba and da Southern Gennelman Rippah Collins retained their tag team title."

Once I tawt dat I would try do dat too and I went listen to da radio, KGU Sports, da night before fo get da winners and I wrote um down because no fair if Bungy hog all da points just by giving da wrestling results. Dat wasn't news, was all fake. My fahdah said wrestling was like roller derby, all fake.

Anyway, da time I was going give da wrestling results, Bungy was looking at me cracking each knuckle in his fingers first one hand den da uddah and I went look down at my paypah wit da winnahs and da times and I tawt, maybe I better give da news about how da Russian astronaut Yuri Gagarin went around in space instead. After I was finished, Bungy raised his hand and said that da Indian guy Chief Billy White Wolf went fight Beauregarde, da guy dat always stay combing his hair, and he took Beauregarde in two minutes of da third round wit a half nelson. Exack what I had on my paypah! I saw Mrs. Ching marking down our points in her book.

One time, Mrs. Ching went ask me if I like get extra points. She said she would gimme extra points if I got all dress up like Abraham Lincoln and say da Gettysburg Address to da fit graders. I nevah like but she said I had to, cause I was da best at saying um las year. I still nevah like cause look stoopid when dey pin on da black construction paper bow tie and make you wear da tall construction paper hat, but she said it was one privilege fo say da speech and dat she would help me memarize um again. Das cause when I was in da fit grade, everybody had to learn da ting and had one contest in da whole fit grade and I went win cause everybody else did junk on purpose so dat dey nevah have to get up in front of da whole school, dressed up like Abraham Lincoln. Shoot, I nevah know. I nevah know dat da winner had to go back da next year and say um again to da fit graders either.

Everyting was diffrent. In da seven grade, you change classes la dat and had all dese rules and j'like da bell stay ringing all da time. Had da warning bell before school start, had da real bell, and had da tardy bell. And da bells between classes and da tardy-to-class bell and da first lunch bell and da second lunch bell. And you had to tuck in your shirt and wear shoes.

Bungy was Benjamen now. I know cause his muddah and my muddah went make us go Chinese school summer time and we had to be in da first grade class wit all da small kids even if we was in da six-grade-going-be-sevent. Anyway, whenevah da teacha call Bung Mun, he tell, "Benjamen!" So da teacha try call him dat only ting come out "Bung-a-mun" and Bungy gotta tell her again, "Benjamen!" Das how I knew he was Benjamen now. But most guys still yet called him "Bungy" even if he nevah answer.

And Wanda Chu had braces so she nevah smile anymore, not dat she used to smile at us anyways. Bungy, I mean Benjamen, would yell at her, "Hey, metal mout, you can staple my math papers wit your teet?" And all of a sudden, she get chichis. Six grade, nutting. Seven grade, braces and bra.

Benjamen would always wear slippahs even if he was supposed to wear shoes. He tell he get sore feet but his feet always stay bus up cause he like to go barefoot. His feet so ugly and dirty and stink, da nurse no like even look at dem, she jes give him da slippah pass. And if you had to go batroom during classtime you had to get one batroom pass. And had library pass and cafeteria pass and if you work cafeteria you had to wear da paper cap or if you get long hair, da ladies make you wear da girls hairnet and you had to wear covered shoes. Even had dis yellow line painted on da stairs and down da middle of da hallway all ovah da school and you had to go up only on da right side and go down on da uddah side. Dey could nab you and make you "stand hall" for doing stuff like going down da up side of da stairs. Crazy, yeah?

If you gotta stand hall, you gotta go da vice-principal's office before school, recess, lunch time, and after school fo so many minutes and stand in da main hallway of the school facing the wall. Das where everybody walk pass so dey can razz you any much dey like cause you no can talk when you standing hall. I tink Mr. Hansen went make up da rules. He was dis tall, skinny haole guy, mean-looking buggah. But he nevah do da dirty work. If you got reported to the office, you had to see da vice principal, Mr. Hirohata. He was one short, fat guy you had to go see if you was tardy or went fight and somebody said he da one who paddle you. Bungy said watch out if you gotta go his office and he close da door. Anyway, when Hirohata tell you you gotta stand hall, he take you to your spot and he take his pencil and he make one dot on da wall and he tell, "Dis is your spot. Don't take your eyes off it." You no can talk or look around cause every now and den he come out of his office and walk up and down da hallway real soft fo check if you still dere and you not fooling around.

So in da sevent grade, I wised up. Had me and Andrew and Bungy left in da classroom spelling bee. Da winner had to represent da class in da school spelling bee and no ways we was going make "A" in front da whole school.

"Tenement," Miss Hashimoto said.

"T-E-N-A-M-E-N-T," I went spell um.

"T-E-N-T-E-M-E-N-T," Bungy went spell um.

"T-A-N-E-M-E-N-T," Andrew said.

"This is easy, you guys," Hashimoto went tell.

"Nah, S-L-U-M!" Bungy went tell.

"Okay, nobody got um. Next word, syncopate."

"S-I-N-K-O-P-A-T-E," I went tell real fast. I was trying fo spell um as wrong as I could cause I nevah like spell um right by accident. Miss Hashimoto went sigh real loud.

"Definition, please," Bungy went jump right in. He chrow da ack, him.

"To shorten or produce by syncope."

"S-Y-N-C-O-P-A-T-E. . ."

"Yes!" Miss Hashimoto said. She sounded relieved.

"E!" Bungy went yell. He knew he went spell um correct. He went spell um again, "S-Y-N-C-O-P-A-T-E-E!"

Andrew was laughing and I was telling, "No fair! He had two chances. Da first one was good! Was correct." Hashimoto looked pissed, she caught on. "If you boys don't shape up and start being serious, I'm just going to dock your grade and send all three of you to the finals."

It ended up being me. I tink da uddah two guys was still yet missing on purpose but everytime came to me, Hashimoto went gimme da eye and made her mout kinda mean and I could feel my heart loud in my throat and she everytime had to say, "Louder, please. Repeat the spelling." And I would spell um diffrent jes in case I spelled um correct da first time and she would say, "Correct!" even when I tink I went spell um wrong. So I was da one.

When I was up on stage, da principal, Mr. Hansen was pronouncing da words and he went gimme "forefathers" in da first round. I went spell um "F-O-R-F-A-T-H-E-R-S" and I knew I had um wrong by da way Miss Hashimoto went look at me when I went look out at the seats and saw my homeroom class. I knew she was tinking I did um on purpose but actually I was figuring on staying in fo a coupla rounds fo make um look good before I went out. When I got back to my seat on stage, I went look at her and I tink she was crying. She had one Kleenex in her hand and she was wiping her eyes. I felt bad, man. Wasn't my fault. I was really trying dat time. I went aftah school fo tell her sorry I went get out on da first round and she started crying again. I wanted to cry too cause I nevah mean to make da teacha cry. I hate Hashimoto fo making me go up dere in da first place. Bungy and Andrew was smartah den me. My ears was hot, j'like dey was laughing at me.

Mostly da teachas was all dese old futs. But we heard dat had one cute new speech teacha, Mrs. Sherwin, and dat she was one hot-cha-cha. George Miyamoto said da eight graders said she was good-looking. He said dat how many times John Akimoto went catch da bone while he was giving one speech cause when you give one speech you gotta go to da front and she go to da back and sometimes when she cross her legs, can see her panties.

"Not," I couldn't believe dat. "Besides," I said, "she must be old if she married, she *Mrs.* Sherwin, yeah?"

Anyways we all wanted to see what she was going be like cause anyting was bettah den having chorus wit Miss Teruya who was one young old fut. And mean. She whack you wit her stick if she tink you not singing loud enough and if you nevah memarize da words, she make you stand next to da piano and sing solo. One time we went spend one whole class period practicing standing up and sitting down when she give da signal cause she no like when everybody stand up or go down crooked.

Da first day of da second semester we switched from chorus to speech and we went to Sherwin's room and everybody was quiet cause was j'like da first day of school again. Benjamen kept poking me in my back wit one book.

"She cute," he whispered to me, "I heard she cute!" even though we nevah even see her yet. Some of da girls went turn around and give him stink eye and tell him, "Shhhh!" He jes went stretch out his legs and tell loud, "You tink Wanda Chu wear falsies?" I donno if he knew she was walking in da door but everybody went laugh when Wanda came chru da door. Andrew guys was trying fo be quiet but dey was all trying fo grab da small paperback book dat Benjamen was reading behind his social studies book, *Lady Chatterley's Lover*. Andrew said dat was one hot book and only da guys in their club could read um. Andrew sat in front of me and Benjamen sat behind me, so I had to pass da book back and fort between dose two guys. Nevah look like one hot book. I went look inside and nevah see no hot parts.

"Das because you donno which page fo read," Andrew told me afterwards. "Benjamen get um all written down in his Pee Chee folder." Dey was passing da book back and fort reading da good parts all da way in social studies and now in speech. I wanted to read um too but if you stop and read um, Benjamen start kicking your chair until you pass um on. Dey was still yet passing um around when Mrs. Sherwin walked in the room and threw her cigarette case on the desk.

"Okay class, let's begin." She looked like one ninth grader or little older maybe and she was wearing one short dress and everytime her bra strap was falling out and she had to tuck um in.

"Whoa, she smoke," Bungy was telling Andrew, "she smoke!"

"See, I told you she cute," he said in my ear and put da hot book on my desk. I was supposed to pass um on to Andrew but even though I was poking Andrew wit da book, he nevah turn around and take um cause Sherwin went start class and he nevah like her see. I went put um undah my folder but I started fo get nervous about what if I get nabbed for having one hot book. Probably gotta stand hall for da rest of da year.

We went watch her reaching up to write her name high at da top of da board: "Mrs. Sherry Sherwin - Beginning Speech" in one loose, half-printing, half-scrip style. She was skinny and we was watching her ass and her arm and she even write sexy and all da boys started to adjust their pants in their seats. Even her name was sexy, Sherry Sher-wen. She turned around and we watched her lick her lips with the tip of her tongue. Da girls was looking at her and den turning around and looking at da boys. Dey probably was jes jealous.

Da rest of da time was regular. Pass out books, write your name on da card in da back of da book and hand um in, and she gave us work on da first day, man. Was boring da beginning part so I started to read da hot book. Dis time Benjamen wasn't kicking my chair and Andrew went forget about getting um, so I went read um. Mostly was about dis creepy gardener guy and he was trying fo get dis young girl. He was peeking in her window or someting or and was checking out her tits and he was reaching for his "member," das his dick, I tink. Somebody went kick my chair real hard and I went drop da book and quick Benjamen went kick um undah my chair.

"Stoopid!" he went hiss at me. Sherwin went look up at us.

Turn out, Sherwin was the sevent grade adviser and when came time fo the first canteen, she told the boys that we had to learn the etiquette of asking a young lady to dance. She made us practice.

"Make sure all the girls get to dance," she said. "If any of you notice wallflowers, I expect my boys to say what?" She looked around da room and went call on me, "Daniel?"

"May I have dis dance," I mumbled.

"And ladies, how should you reply? Wanda?" Sherwin said.

"Why I'd love to, Daniel," Wanda said, all sassy. All the guys laughed.

"Whoa, Dan-yo? She would love to dance wit you . . ." Dey made kissing noises.

"Maybe Wanda going ask you fo dance!"

Wanda straightened up and tucked her blouse in tightly into her skirt. She looked at me disgusted. I wonder if dey was falsies?

"Whas one wall-fla-wah?" Andrew asked.

"Stoopid," Benjamen said, "da ugly ones!"

Andrew raised his hand. "Geez," Benjamen said, "he going ask someting stoopid," and he put his head down.

"Yes, Andrew?"

"So what if we no like dance wit da wall-fla-wahs?"

"Then you have to dance with me," Mrs. Sherwin said. "Would you like to dance with me, Andrew?" she said doing a little Watusi.

"Oh, no! Ah, I mean, yes. Ah, I mean, it would be an honor ma'am."

"Don't gimme that bull," Mrs. Sherwin said laughing. "I just want to see everybody having fun. This is about the whole seventh grade participating. Okay?"

I wouldn't mind dancing wit her. I was looking at my shoes. If I had Beatle boots, maybe she would dance wit me. And afterwards we could go outside, have a smoke.

Benjamen said that if you had real shiny shoes you could look up the girls' dresses. No wondah he was always rubbing the top of his shoes on the back of his pants legs. He had Beatle boots with taps and anybody with new shoes he stomped on and scuffed um and said, "Baptize!" Like how he baptized everybody after they came back to school with a new haircut. Everytime he sweep his hand around my ears and tell, "Whitewalls!" Benjamen had sideburns and a sheik cut, a razor trimmed cut around his ears that made his head look like a black helmet, hard and glistening with pomade, swept into a ducktail in the back.

"And boys," Mrs. Sherwin was saying, "if I catch you combing your hair in the dance, I'm going to confiscate your comb. Get a nice haircut before the dance and comb your hair in the bathroom." Once, I got nabbed with my comb, da long skinny kine, sticking out of my pocket and Sherwin took um cause she no even like see one comb. She told me I had to come back after school if I wanted um back. So I went after school fo get um back and when she went open her drawer, had uku-billion combs, all hairy and greasy and probably had real ukus on top.

"Which one is yours?" she told me.

"Uh, das okay, I foget which one was mine," I said even though I could see mine, right dere, on top.

"You don't need to comb your hair anyway," she went rough up the top of my head and I could feel her hand go down the bristly back of my neck, almost like how Benjamen baptize you.

"Eh, no make," I said. Felt good though. Could smell her perfume. Spicy. I felt hot.

"And Daniel," she told me, "you don't have to be reading those kinds of books." She was smiling but I felt hot like the janitors caught staring at the young girls in school. Or the guys who come to mow the grass and hang out under the big monkeypod tree leaning up against their riding mowers, sucking on a toothpick. I felt like the gardener in the book. Caught. But excited about getting caught.

I wish I had one sheik cut. But I couldn't. Nutting was growing in front my ears. I no like when da barber jes buzz um off. I like get one sheik cut but I no mo nuff hair over dere to shave. Costs fifty cents more. Even my fahdah no get one sheik cut. He get the 85 cent special at Roosevelt Barbershop, one time around the ears wit da machine and scissors cut on top. Pau fast.

Everytime my fahdah go cut hair, I gotta go too. Even if I no like. Geez, I hope nobody see me cutting hair. Da barbah guy, Fortunato, still take out the booster seat, one old worn-out board that he put across the arms of the chair and I gotta sit on um cause da stuff fo crank up da seat stay broken.

Good ting da barbah shop was next to Roosevelt Theater, da one dat showed hot movies. Hard fo look at da pictures when you stay wit your fahdah but you can look side-eye at da Now Playing and Coming Attractions posters. "Alexandra the Great 48 in Buxom Babes!" and "Physical Education!" Couple times I went put da *National Enquirer* inside one of the old magazines, *Soldier of Fortune* or *Guns and Ammo* or *Field and Stream* and read the main story, "My Bosom Made Me a Nympho at Thirteen." I read um so many times I almost memorized um. Had this picture of one lady bending over wit big tits and you could see down her dress but da head was one young girl, but nevah match. Looked so fake. Wasn't even trick photography.

Sometimes when my fahdah stay in da chair and I stay waiting my turn, Fortunato stop cutting and quick I look up fo see if he went nab me but he only get his head tilted toward da radio listening to the announcer talking Filipino, fast, excited. He jes suck his teeth and make one "tssk" sound and cut again. And I would look at the picture again and try to imagine dat it was Mrs. Sherwin but I could only see Wanda's face in dat picture, bending ovah. Smiling at me, her braces shiny, glistening, "Why I'd love to, Dan-yo." Whoa, da spooky.

GIVING TANKS

Darrell H.Y. Lum

Da brown and orange crayons always run out at Tanksgiving time. You gotta use um for color da turkeys and da Indian feathers la dat. Yellow run out fast, too. My teacher, Mrs. Perry, used to tell us dat we suppose to use dose colors cause das da autumn colors. Suppose to be when all da leaves on da trees turn color, like da orange and brown crayons or da funny kine brown one in da big crayon box, burnt someting. I couldn't see how if da leaves turn color, was pretty. For us, dat jes means dat da tree going die, or maybe stay dead awready. Or maybe like our lychee tree in da back yard, when da leaves turn color, dey fall off and Daddy tell me I gotta go rake before I can go play.

Tanksgiving was when you gotta learn about da Pilgrims and all dat. Das when da Indians and da Pilgrims went get togedda, eat turkey or someting. Kinda hard to believe though, yeah? Me, I like da Indians mo bettah den da Pilgrims. Da Indians had, da kine, leather pants wit da fringes and da small kine beads and dey fight wit bow and arrow la dat. Da Pilgrims had to wear da black suits, even da small kids, and da funny kine hat. Dey even had da funny kine gun dat was fat at da end. My bruddah told me dat was one blundahbuss, dat da olden days guys wanted da bullets to spread all ovah so da gun was funny kine. He said da gun couldn't shoot straight, though. Das why da Indians mo bettah. I betchu arrows could shoot mo straight den dat.

Da teacha told me I had to do one report on da Pilgrims and draw one cornucopia. I nevah know what dat was. Even aftah I saw da picture, I still couldn't figure out what dat was.

"Das one horn of plenty," Louise went tell me. She smart, so she oughta know. "Stay like one basket fo put fruits inside, fo show you rich, dat you get food."

"Well, how come always stay falling down and all da fruits spilling out?" I went ask her. "Funny kine basket, eh?" I not so dumb. So when I went home, I went try draw one horn of plenty but I couldn't figure out what was fo. Look more like my bruddah's trombone den one basket. And you no can play music wit one horn of plenty. Ho, sometimes da teacher make us do crazy stuffs.

In school we always had to do da same old ting. You know, make one turkey out of one paper plate: da plate is da body and you paste on da head and da tail and da legs. Sometimes we make one napkin holder turkey: you staple half a paper plate to your turkey so get one place fo put da napkins. Den you paste da neck and da head and da feet and you gotta color dat too . . . brown and orange and yellow. Den you fold up da paper napkins and put um inside da plate and if you use kalakoa napkins, look like da turkey tail. Mama really went like dat one. She went hang um up on da wall and fill um up wit napkins and put away da regular napkin holder until came all had-it and da head went fall off.

Everybody like go to Auntie Jennie and Uncle Jim's house fo Tanksgiving dinner cause Mama said Auntie's turkey always come out moist. Me, I only like eat skin and gravy. Auntie Jennie make good gravy and I like da cranberry sauce da best. I no like da stuffing cause I tink dey hide all da ugly stuff from inside da turkey in dere.

Auntie Jennie's house was nice. Her kitchen table had real cloth kine tablecloth, not da plastic kine on top and she no put sheets on top her couch and had anykine knitted stuff, like dose hat things dat cover da extra toilet paper on top da toilet tank. And get anykine neat stuff all around her house . . . anykine souvenirs from all ovah da world, da places dey went go visit. J'like everyplace dey went, she went buy one salt and pepper shaker. Fo collect. Some look like animals and look like one house or one car or one famous building. Some you couldn't even figure out where da salt or da pepper come out!

Uncle Jim had dis teeny-tiny collection of knives dat was da best. Wasn't real, was imitation; each one was about one inch long or maybe two inches long. Was anykine knives, like bolo knife and swords from all ovah da world and put on one piece of wood, j'like one shield. Maybe he went collect knives from every place he went.

Uncle Jim was da fire chief so always had firemen at his house. And he park his car right in front his house, one big red station wagon. Da license plate says, "HFD 1," Honolulu Fire Department Numbah One. Dat means he da chief. Uncle Jim was tall and skinny and bolohead. Everybody call him "Chief" and I know he da fire chief but he remind me of one Indian chief, tall and old and plenny wrinkles on his face. I betchu he get one Indian knife someplace, wit one leather holder, too.

My grandma, Ah Po Lee, was always dere too, sitting down on da couch in her plain stay-at-home clothes talking Chinese to my Auntie. I think she get nice clothes, one time I seen one silk cheong sam, one fancy long dress, hanging up on her door wit da plastic from da dry clean man but I nevah seen her wear um. And she wear one wide cloth headband dat make her look like one old Indian lady: all small and bent ovah, plain blue khaki jacket and black Chinese pants and fancy cloth slippahs wit small beads making one dragon and anykine wrinkles and spots on her face. Look j'like warpaint.

So das what we did Tanksgiving time. Go Auntie Jennie's house and eat turkey and make paper plate turkeys and try fo figgah out what one cornucopia was. And in school, I kept tinking, when we going learn about one Indian holiday? Would be neat if we could, yeah? We could dance around . . . whoo, whoo, whoo, whoo! Anyways, all dat was jes one fairy tale. J'like wrestling at da Civic Auditorium, fake. Same like da uddah tings in da books and da National School Broadcast, all fairy tales. Ah Po told me one time, dat real Tanksgiving stay everyday. Das why every day she pray fo my grandfahdah. No miss. She burn incense and pour tea and whiskey fo him outside on da porch where get da bowl wit sand fo stick da red candles and da skinny kine incense. Sometimes I watch da ashes curl up, hanging on, hanging on. Da ting can go long time before it fall off.

I no can remembah my Ah Goong, my grandfahdah, except fo da big picture on da wall in da living room. But even my bruddah Russo said dat he nevah look like dat. He said he look mo old. Da picture stay one young guy. I guess das one fairy tale too. Ah Goong was old, Russo said. Tall and skinny and old. So Ah Po burn candles and incense and pour whiskey and tea fo dis tall, skinny, old guy and I watch da ashes curling and da smoke go up like smoke signals. Once, I went ask Ah Po how come she pray so much and she tell me she pray dat Ah Goong stay okay, she pray dat us guys, Russo and me, be good boys, she pray "tank you" she get rice to eat. She tell me she get lots to pray about.

Everytime get sale, she go buy one bag rice. Could tell she felt rich when she had one bag rice extra in da closet. And toilet paper. Lots of toilet paper. And Spam and Vienna sausages and Campbell's soup and can corned beef. Nevah mind she kept fixing and fixing her stay-home dress ovah and ovah, cause was stay-home anyways. Nevah mind dat she had one old washing machine you had to crank da clothes through da roller stuffs. Nevah mind sometimes she went eat hahm gnee, salt fish, and rice fo dinner fo tree days when me and Russo went sleep her house and we wanted to eat plain meat and not all mixed up wit vegetables kine.

And I seen her finish eating da little bit meat off da bone from my piece of meat and how hardly had any slop for da slop man and how she went look in her button bottle for two quarters fo wrap up in red paper fo give us lee-see fo buy ice cream from da ice cream man. Das how I knew dat my cornucopia wasn't one basket wit fruits and vegetables spilling out. Wasn't Indians and Pilgrims sitting down fo eat turkey. Was Russo and me sitting down at da table while Ah Po put her oily black frying pan on da stove and turn da fire up high until da oil smoke and she put noodles and carrots and little bit oyster sauce and tree, maybe four, pieces of green onion cut big, so dat we could see um and pick um out of our plates. She nevah used to have one big fat turkey fo Tanksgiving.

"Lucky," she used to say anyways. "Lucky da ice cream man come," even though he alway pass by about tree-thirty every Thursday. "Lucky you get lee-see to spend. Lucky. Lucky you come visit Ah Po," she would say. And we would tink about what if we nevah come and miss out on noodles and quarters and ice cream.

I guess we was lucky, yeah?

AN IMAGE OF THE GOOD TIMES

Wing Tek Lum

It would be at dinner
when I was just a kid
when my brothers were away in college
and there were just the three of us
around our small table in the kitchen
my mother sitting to my right
and my father to the right of her
—that is, sitting opposite me
with his back to our chopping block.
And we would be finishing our meal
our rice bowls empty
our chopsticks and spoons laid on our plates
the dishes on our lazy susan
waiting to be cleared.
And my father would turn to the bunsen burner
hooked up to a spigot by the counter.
In a stainless steel pot
he would bring water to a boil.
In turn the water would be poured
into a small clay pot
he had stuffed full of his favorite leaves.
While waiting for his tea to brew
he would raise his leg
resting its heel against the edge of his chair
his thigh tucked into his chest.
He would reach over
underarm supported by his knee
to pour the tea into his cup.
The cup, saucer and pot were a matching set
and we learned over the years
never to wash them
to add to the dark pungency.
He would finish off the tea
in large, measured gulps

smacking his lips at the end
with a loud sigh of satisfaction
as if it could echo
against the chaos of the world
that reigned outside our home
outside of that love that bound us together
through all our bad times and all the good.

THE ROOSTER

adapted from *Tales of a Hawaiian Boyhood, Vol. I (audiotape)*
Makia Malo

Aloha! Thank you. First, I'd like to share with you a little bit about Kalaupapa. It started in 1865 on the part of the Moloka'i peninsula called Kalawao, when the government started isolating those who had leprosy, now known as Hansen's Disease. The Belgian priest, Father Damien, made that whole experience world-known, and because of his efforts, we who had the disease in this century enjoyed the benefits of the humanitarian work he did in the late 1800s.

For most people, Kalaupapa represented an unknown world. We were sent there to die, so there was lots of fear and sadness and all that kind of stuff when you first arrived. But later, life within the community was as normal as a life can be under those circumstances. In fact, when people hear that the law took me away from my parents when I was twelve years old and that I had to live at Kalaupapa for 25 years, they tend to feel sorry for me. But the truth is that it really wasn't that bad, mainly for two reasons.

First, I had two brothers and a sister who had been sent there before I was, so when I arrived in 1947, it was like going from one part of my family to another part. My oldest brother Bill, who lives on Maui now, was the first to go, when he was 16. Then my kid brother Earl went in when he was seven years old. He was the baby of the family and closest to me in age. We always fought like hell, man, but we were best friends. I was nine when he had to leave home. We were apart for three years, and I missed him! My sister Pearl was eight years older than I was. She was a surrogate mother to me and Earl because mama worked, and that's how it was in big families: the older ones took care of the younger ones. She was about 22 years old when she had to go in. She had two babies Olga and Tweetie she had to leave behind with Mama and Daddy in Honolulu.

The second reason being sent to Kalaupapa wasn't sad for me was it meant I didn't have to work in our family's taro patch anymore. Our taro patch used to be where the main stage of the Polynesian Cultural Center is today. Every Saturday morning—early!—we had to drive from our home in Papakōlea to the taro patch in Lā'ie. And I mean every Saturday—birthdays, Christmas, it didn't matter. The taro patch, selling the poi, was how my parents helped feed our family, so you just did it from the time you could barely walk, carrying one taro at a time.

When I heard that I was being sent to Kalaupapa, honest, that was one of my first thoughts: Oh boy! I don't have to work in the bloody taro patch anymore! I couldn't believe my good luck.

Of course at Kalaupapa we all had Hansen's Disease and that brought suffering of another kind. But today I stand before you as a survivor of that illness and that place. I'd like to dedicate this program to my kid brother Earl who's buried up at Kalaupapa, and all my other friends who are buried there, people who never enjoyed the opportunities I have by being out here in the bigger community.

The first story I'd like to share with you, of course, is when I first went up to Kalaupapa. So, this story comes like around 1948. Now, the old airport up at Kalaupapa was much smaller than it is today. In fact, there were often times you'd find the cattle, the pipi, in the middle of the airfield because, somehow, the cow learned how to tiptoe across the cattle guard. And, on top of that, the grass is much greener inside the airfield because, you know, there's someone to care for the field.

Well, there was . . . there still are some beach homes close by to that place . . . but there was one in particular that we stayed there for the first summer I was there and was really fantastic! You know, as we were isolated in Honolulu, in Kalaupapa, we had the free run of that whole eleven square miles of land. And so, it was like, a small town. We were at this beach house, staying for the weekend, but one person had visitors from Honolulu, visitors coming to stay. They were non-patients but they came down to the beach house to be with us.

And so, I remember this guy Jimmy and I were outside, in front of the beach house, we had just come back from the beach. And then I heard the lady of the house call out, "Makia!"

"Hanh?"

"You know how fo' kill chicken?"

"Chicken?"

"Ah, nevah mind. You go kill da chicken, dat's for our dinner."

And me, I like ack macho, right? Twelve years old . . . tirteen . . . I wanna ack macho. I nevah know how fo' kill chicken, but I no can tell dem guys I nevah know how. So, I ack cool, eh? I walk inside da house, dis guy Jimmy was alongside of me. We passed tru the parlor, go tru da kitchen. As I was passing tru da kitchen, I see dis loooong bloody knife—you know, da kine da pakes use for chop-chop vegables? Long knife, you know! I look, whoa! I grab da knife, I tell da guy Jimmy, "Eh, Jimmy, you know how fo' kill chicken?"

He tell me, "No."

"Ah, nevah mind."

Go outside. When we came to da back porch, here was the oldest, the biggest old fut chicken you evah seen in your life. Was a damn biiiig roostah! And, you know da buggah, he walk around like *somebody*, you know, wid da hand in da pocket every time, eh? Going li' dat! And I look, dat buggah was so big! And I tought, Ohhhh . . . .

"Eh, Jimmy, Jimmy . . . you sure you don't know how fo' kill chicken?"

He tell me, "No."

Gee, I look at dat chicken. So I say, "Heah, heah, you hold da knife."

I walk up to da chicken. What dey did was dey tied one leg, the other end of the cord, dey pound 'em with a nail into da ground. So I grab da cord, I pull da cord, I lift up da chicken—was a biiiig roostah, man! I grabbed da two legs and I look around, we saw dis empty corn beef box. 'Cause no mo' table, I tell Jimmy, "Eh, eh, bring dat box ovah heah, turn um ovah!"

So. Slap da chicken on top. Da buggah was so big, you know, I trow him on top li' dat, da head hang ovah da odda side and da feets down around dis side! So, I had to twist da wings so da buggah no struggle, that much I can control. And den, I have to put my knee on top da wing, and I put my leg on da odda side, and I grab da neck and I tell Jimmy, "Okay, okay, cut, cut!" And I waaaiting! I look up at him . . . .

"No."

Ho! I tink, gee. I say, "Okay, okay, okay. Gimme, gimme!" And I push the knife li' dat, you know. And was so strange. What I recall, when you bend the neck of the chicken back, the feathers lift up like that, and it's all bare skin underneath. And so I see da knife pull the skin when go across. when the time wen come back, the skin separate, wen pop just like da kine ovah ripe tomato. And den I see da stuff shoot out. Oooh, my eye come big, man! And I had the knife kinda shaking in my hand and the darn chicken started to struggle and struggle and struggle! And I get so nervous, I drop the knife, I get off da chicken. The chicken starts kicking and futting and everyting! Ah!

Finally, he stood up, the wings unraveled, and he starts walking around li' dis . . . erp! . . . erp! And every time he did that, da blood shoot, you know! And you only can stare at this dumb chicken—he's supposed to be dead! And da buggah don't know yet, eh?

And, before we realized it, the chicken was heading straight for the house. But all we did, just stand ovah dere and waaatch dat chicken. By da time he's just going underneath the house, I said, "Jimmy, Jimmy, go get um!"

He tell me, "No!"

And da chicken wen undaneat da house, take his sweet time. So I run ovah dere, I watch da chicken, I said, "Jimmy, Jimmy, go da odda side, block um!" And we looked at the chicken.

Now, the ground that the house was resting on wasn't level. One end of the house was resting right on the ground, the other end was up about two and a half, three feet. And so we looking undaneat da house, looking way da hell . . . dat darn chicken go way the hell in da cornah, and lie down. I tell, "Jimmy, you go get um, I watch!" (He no like work, you know.)

I said, "Jimmy!" And I look dat chicken, I tink, God! Den I hear da lady from da house say, "Makia, whachu doing? Playing wid dat chicken?"

"No!"

And I watching dat chicken. And I figure I had to get um. But what going tru my mind was cockroach, scorpion, spidah, centapede . . . ho, and I look again. Well, I knew I had to go get it, so I really psyched myself up, you know. You know how when you squeeze your body real hard, eh, so da blood circulate mo' fast. And den I just wen down on da ground and I scramble undaneat and I go inside and I can feel all dat damn spidah web going on my head. But, you know, it's da kine you close da eye, right? Jes go and grab da damn chicken up! I pull um out, I backing out, I pull um, now stay outside. Ho! I shaking up, make sure everyting get off me, man!

By da time I look at dat chicken, da damn buggah was dead already. Ho, da buggah wasn't nice enough fo' die outside!

Well, anyway, as I said, Kalaupapa was a small town, and as you can see from this little story, basically, except for being sick and going to the hospital, our life was pretty much like life on the outside. Earl and I still fought and hung out together, we went to school, had chores, church, but we also had a lot more to do. Kalaupapa is gorgeous, you know. We had great fishing, hunting, horseback riding, swimming; we had baseball teams, a Boy Scout troop, a band, movie nights (free!), and we put on plays. There was one thing we didn't have. We didn't have a taro patch!

THE DREAM-FLYER
Elizabeth Manly

Denise flew. Spreading her arms even wider, she let the wind flap the baggy sleeves of her T-shirt and push against her face. To be free of the land was exhilarating.

Though the wind numbed her face, Denise didn't care. Instead, she viewed the land below, paying more attention as she neared her destination. Below were the banyan trees of Thomas Square, aerial roots reaching for earth.

Denise had been flying almost two months. Each night, she would seem to awaken, feeling as though she were dreaming. Walls and doors became mere illusions. With great ease, she walked into the yard, took off, and flew to the Honolulu Academy of Arts for her lesson from Pio.

Pio was an extraordinary teacher—a bird, an owl to be precise. His name, Pio, meant "prisoner" in Hawaiian; and since his left wing had been broken long ago, prisoner he certainly was, for he would never fly again.

Swooping towards the darkened building, Denise was warmed inside, thinking of her unlikely teacher. She landed, stumbling, then walked to the Academy's courtyard. Her footsteps silenced crickets chirping in the bushes. The pond surface rippled in the moonlight. All was peaceful. Seating herself on a tree root, Denise waited for Pio.

A sound like a muffled bark betrayed his presence. Looking up, Denise saw the owl perched nearby. His yellow eyes pierced the darkness. He ruffled his speckled feathers, making himself look bigger.

Denise smiled a greeting. Pio responded in kind, hopping to a lower branch, almost losing his footing. He stretched out his good wing to balance himself. "Ready for more?"

"Yes," Denise replied telepathically, as she had from their first meeting.

"Patterns." The word echoed in Denise's head. Though she didn't know what Pio meant, he had already taught her of patience. She waited for the explanation sure to come.

"Patterns . . . ." Pio gestured. "Patterns are everywhere."

"Where?" Denise interrupted, in total bewilderment.

"Everywhere. See the pond's ripples? A pattern." Pio indicated the leafy foliage above him. "Another pattern. All trees of the same kind have leaves of the same shape."

Denise considered this, then spoke. "I understand. But why is that important?"

Denise was sure she saw the great bird smile. "Ah, fledgling, let me teach you."

Smiling, Denise settled herself at the water's edge. She loved the great bird's explanations.

"Say you want to grow taro. You've always seen it thrive in water. But what if you were to plant it there, and the taro plant died? What if you were to experiment further and find that they did well in hot dry soil? How would you feel?"

Denise answered immediately, "I'd be surprised."

"That's all?"

Denise nodded.

"Not worried?"

"Why would I?" Denise didn't understand.

"Because," said Pio with a trace of irritation in his telepathic voice, "you wouldn't know if the next time you tried to grow taro it would thrive in water or sand, whether it would like moisture or sunlight, or both, or how much of each."

Finally comprehending, she smiled. "I see . . . . Patterns tell us what to expect. We then have that knowledge for future reference."

Pio blinked in surprise. "You are getting wiser, my owlet. I think my time is nearer than I expected."

Denise demanded an explanation. "Are you going to die?"

"Of course. All living creatures die." The owl's face softened. "But I have no intention of doing so anytime soon. I meant only that I can't stay long—just until you learn what I have to teach. After that . . . ."

"What?"

"I must go and teach another young one, as I am teaching you."

"To . . . ?" Denise urged Pio to continue.

"To also become a dream-teacher."

Denise was stunned. Never had she considered either that she would become as wise as Pio or that these lessons would come to an end. She stared into the dark water. How she would miss her friend.

Suddenly, Denise felt a jolt. She realized that it was time to wake up. But she still had one more question. Gazing up at Pio, Denise asked, "When will you have to . . . go?"

His words, though kind, helped little. "Soon. You'll know when the time has come."

Denise nodded as she turned away. She waved briefly to Pio as the world turned white . . . .

BUZZZZZZZZ!

Denise jolted as she woke up in her bed. It was morning and the whole day lay before her.

Six days later, she heard the words she dreaded. "Fledgling, it is time. You have learned all I have to teach you. This will be our last night together. I'll miss you, Denise."

Denise had a lump in her throat. She understood what was to happen and why, but she was sad. She knew that she would never see Pio again. Soon she would have the important job of being a dream-teacher; or so Pio had predicted.

Pio perched on Denise's forearm, his sharp talons gripping with great gentleness. She stroked the owl's magnificent head. How could she manage to teach alone?

As they stood, each felt the jerk of morning approaching. Pio reached down and plucked a flight feather from his useless wing. Handing it to her, he said, "It won't keep me from flying, you know; and with it you will soar." Gently she touched the unnatural stiffness of his injured wing a last time.

"I'll never forget you," bird and girl said together. "Good-bye."

BUZZZZZZZZ!

The alarm clock rang. It was 6:30. Wakening, Denise opened her clenched hand. It still held the feather. A tear splashed onto the treasure, though part of her didn't know why she cried. She had, after all, learned a lot from Pio.

Denise found a silk thread and looped it carefully around the quill, then hung the feather around her neck. Somewhere outside she heard a muffled bark. Denise strapped the prosthesis where her left leg had been. It was morning and the whole day lay before her.

GROWING UP BAREFOOT
L. Nishioka

(for M.U.)

Growing up barefoot,
feet free to roam
like roots of the banyan,
no need for shoes
until graduation from kindergarten.

My first pair:
red ballet slippers, suede,
buckled at the ankles
from back-to-front.
Me,
a twirling plumeria,
pirouetting on the tips
of the white rubber soles.

No Cinderella slippers
for these grown feet, though.
Broad at the front,
flat to the ground,
"luau" like the leaf.

Yet,
through these unshapely soles
I came to know you,
Father,
home from a full day's work,
coaching
as I stepped carefully along
your lumpy spine,
Olympic gymnast on balance beam,
tottering left, then right,
up and down each arm,
your knotted muscles letting go,
you sighing,

Ah, feels good!
my sunken footsteps
vanishing
behind
me.

THE POOR PAGAN CHILDREN
Susan Nunes

After old Mrs. Souza died, the corner house on Laimana Street stayed empty, the blinds drawn tight, the yard untended. Weeds took over the path to the front steps, and a passion plant began its curling pursuit of the clothesline. Wilhemine and Kate had been warned away when Mrs. Souza took sick; now they needed no reminding. It was a dead person's house, full of ghosts, and only a family could change that . . . preferably one with children their own age.

Then one day a For Sale sign appeared on the mailbox. The lawn got mowed and the vine cut back, and someone painted the front porch and repaired the broken window downstairs. Two weeks after school let out, the sign disappeared, and a moving van pulled up in front of the house, and Willie and Kate learned that their prayers had been answered in the form of the Chaffees, from Tennessee, with two children the right age.

"Judy's ten and I'm six and we're from Memphis," said Ernest. He pronounced Memphis "mimfis" and had slate blue eyes, thick glasses, and very red knees. "Don't you wear shoes?" he asked, staring at Willie and Kate's bare feet. Both the Chaffee children were wearing brown oxfords and white socks.

Kate shook her head and proceeded to wind a strand of hair around her right forefinger. Kate's hair was curly, some of it natural, some the result of her habitual winding.

"We're Baptists," said Judy.

In 1953, Memphis was a long way from Hilo. Willie had no idea what a Baptist was.

"Any relation to Saint John the Baptist?" she asked.

"It's a church, and we don't have saints," Judy sniffed. She scrutinized Kate's hair and Willie's wrinkled shorts. "Baptists don't allow saints."

Judy Chaffee had a turned up nose, freckles, and blond hair carefully pinned back with four pink barrettes. It occurred to Willie that Judy might be the kind of girl who wore dresses every day, even to play in. She hoped not.

Then Kate asked, "Do Baptists go to church on Sundays?"

"Of course, silly," said Judy.

Kate's face lit up. "So do we!"

Willie smiled indulgently at her little sister. She could always count on Kate to search for common ground, Kate with her cork screw curls and her turned-in feet and the limp their parents worried about.

Judy smiled, too, revealing a row of braces clamped to widely-spaced teeth. "Ernest and me, *we* go to Sunday school."

Sunday school? Kate shot Willie a questioning look, but Willie was still staring at Judy's braces.

Judy's mouth slammed shut. "It's rude to stare," she said.

"I'm not staring," said Willie. "I was wondering what you did at Sunday school."

There was a flash of silver and a narrowing of eyes. "Why? Are you heathens?"

"No," said Willie, "we're Catholics."

Now it was Judy's turn to stare. "Catholics?" she said in a tone that suggested that Catholics, like saints, weren't allowed either.

But Willie let it pass. She wanted her new friends to like her. And she was curious. She listened without interrupting as Judy explained that they sang songs, read Bible stories, and colored pictures in their Bible coloring books, like of Samson pushing down temples or Jesus converting the Jews, and then they had juice and cookies at break time.

Kate, a new communicant still struggling with the rigors of fasting, was shocked. "You get to *eat* at your church?"

"Of course," said Ernest. "Don't you?"

Kate told them the only thing they ate was the body and blood of Christ.

Which made Judy's mouth flash silver again, and Willie had to step in and explain that it wasn't like they ate a real *dead* body. Just a little round thing that tasted like bread. She wasn't sure *how* it got changed into a body, but the Catholic church was the only church where this happened. She said that Catholics went to church every Sunday, rain or shine, and if they didn't it was a sin.

"We go with my Dad," said Kate.

Judy's eyes narrowed again. "What about your mom?"

"She doesn't," said Kate, pulling at a strand of hair.

"Why?" Judy wanted to know.

"She's a Buddhist," said Willie.

"A Buddhist!"

"Buddhists don't have to go to mass," Kate explained.

"What's a mass?" Ernest asked, blue eyes wide and curious.

Now it was Willie's turn to explain. She told him that mass was what they did at church. It was like a long prayer, in Latin mostly, and it reminded them of Christ's sacrifice on Calvary. There were no refreshments.

"Well," sniffed Judy, "Buddhists are heathens."

Willie said she supposed they were, though she felt like a traitor saying it.

Then the Yamamoto Hauling Company truck was pulling away from the curb, and Ernest was asking whether they wanted to come to the Baptist Church some time, and Judy was saying how she'd ask her mother, and Willie saw Kate's face light up at the prospect of doing something special with their new friends. She didn't want to think about Buddhists and why being one seemed to bother people so.

The first time Wilhemine's father met Mrs. Chaffee, he called her a "real dynamo." Which was to say that Mrs. Chaffee's boundless energy and enthusiasm got on his nerves. She had ash blond hair that she wore in a tight little pageboy, like June Allyson, and she had a liking for full-skirted dresses with Peter Pan collars and lots of little buttons down the front. Mrs. Chaffee didn't get on Willie's nerves. Willie liked the smooth way of talking, especially the terms of endearment so rare in her own family.

One day in the Chaffee's big kitchen, Mrs. Chaffee was talking about the Bible and Willie asked whether they really had juice and cookies at Sunday school.

"Why, yes, Sugar," said Mrs. Chaffee. "Now, wouldn't you and Kate just *love* to come?" Mrs. Chaffee was frosting a cake, and what she did with the word *love* reminded Willie of what happened when a can of sweetened condensed milk got upturned.

"I'll ask my dad," she said.

Mrs. Chaffee smoothed the collar of Willie's shirt and patted her on the head.

"Why of course, you sweet thing."

When Willie asked her father, though, he said things like "Over my dead body," and "Who in the Sam Hill does she think she is?" The promise of refreshments didn't change his mind, either. He reminded Willie that they already belonged to the true church. He said Saint Peter had built the Catholic church on a special rock that lasted forever and that's why Catholics had the keys to heaven. He said faith was a gift, and one shouldn't take gifts lightly. *And*, he said, making a serious face, going to another church was a sin.

Willie looked up from the shrimp she'd just speared with her fork. "Mortal or venial?"

"Mortal," said her father.

Willie glanced at Kate and saw tears and disappointment.

Later, she felt called upon to explain the distinctions. They were lying in the dark bedroom, with the street lights slanting through the Venetian blinds and the tradewinds tossing the mango tree next door. Willie told Kate that if you were a Catholic and even *stepped* into another church, you got covered with mortal sin and everyone knew what happened then.

"What happens?" Kate asked.

Willie stared across the black stretch of floor between their beds and broke the news as gently as she could. "It makes you look like you have leprosy to God."

"Oh," whispered Kate. Then, "What's that?"

Willie told Kate what she'd learned about the disfiguring disease from Father Marius, who in catechism class related the story of Father Damien, the Belgian priest who'd ministered to the people of Kalaupapa until he himself died of the disease. The sinner's soul, said Father Marius, holding up a photograph of a man whose nose and lips had fallen off, was like this.

A metaphor works when one grasps the comparison. Willie had stared at the photograph, dog-eared and creased by many little hands, and known she didn't want to look like that to God or anyone else.

That was the idea she struggled to get across as she and her sister pursued the discussion late into the night. Finally, Kate seemed to understand. She also had nightmares for weeks.

Perhaps the story should have ended there. And had Mrs. Chaffee accepted graciously when Willie declined the invitation, perhaps it would have. But Mrs. Chaffee was an evangelist. The truest of true believers. Like all true believers she probably believed in salvation by faith. She rejected the efficacy of good works alone. What was the point of doing good if one's destiny was decided? No way out except to be reborn another believer.

And so one day she sat the two sisters down at the big, sun-splashed table in her kitchen and asked Willie, "Your mama's a Japanese, isn't she, Sugar?" She pronounced it *japanee*.

"Yes," said Willie, eyeing the plate of cookies placed before her.

Kate sat quietly, her little face barely clearing the table top.

"Go on, Sugar, have one," Mrs. Chaffee said to her. "They got pecans inside. You know what a *peekahn* is? It's a fine old nut. Tastier than your macadams, or whatever you call them here. Go on, help yourself." Mrs. Chaffee poured two glasses of milk.

Kate reached for a cookie.

Mrs. Chaffee took the opportunity to touch Kate's curly head. "She go to church with you, your mama?"

Kate shook her head and continued to solemnly chew.

"Now, why's that?" Mrs. Chaffee sat down next to Kate. She folded her hands in front of her the way Willie's mother did when she was waiting for an answer.

Willie didn't like the way the conversation was going. "She's a Buddhist," she said.

Mrs. Chaffee raised her eyebrows and looked at Willie.

Willie added, "An agnostic Buddhist."

Mrs. Chaffee's eyebrows disappeared into her blond bangs. "Goodness sakes! Where'd you learn words like that?" She leaned forward and cupped her chin in her hand.

Willie shrugged, trying to look casual. She didn't want to say that in fact she'd learned it from her mother, who'd used it to describe her own beliefs. But the words came out anyway. Willie couldn't blame Mrs. Chaffee for being shocked. Willie was shocked, too, the first time she heard it. She'd asked her mother, was being an agnostic as bad as being a heretic? Father Marius had said heretics were burned at the stake and deserved it. That was the law of the church.

Her mother had stared at her with profound astonishment. "What are they *teaching* you in that class?" she'd exclaimed.

Willie replied that it was a good thing she was with the True Church, that she wasn't a *pagan*.

Willie's mother's eyes looked like wet stones, which is how they looked when she felt something deeply. "Wilhemine," she'd said, "I'm sure you know that Grandpa and Grandma Shinoda are as good as any Catholic. Your Father Marius included."

Willie wanted to believe her mother. She loved her grandparents, loved them dearly. She didn't want them to end up in hell with the other pagans.

"But what's an agnostic?" she'd asked.

"An agnostic," said Willie's mother, "is someone who doesn't believe there's *proof* that God exists."

"Of course there's proof!" said Willie.

"Let me put it this way," said Willie's mother. "An agnostic isn't as convinced as you are."

Willie had thought hard about her mother's words. "Is that why you don't go to mass?" she finally asked.

Willie's mother seemed to find the question amusing. "I *choose* not to go, Wilhemine. And there's no God trying to force me, either."

Willie had tried to imagine a world where God wasn't watching. Her mother's words made her feel like two Willies in one, like the Trinity was three persons in one. Sometimes in the dark closet of her mind, one Willie questioned the existence of a God who banished babies to Limbo and their parents to Hell for what was essentially an accident of birth. But the other Willie worried. *What if this vindictive God really did exist and you found out only after you died?* Her thoughts were a maze of contradictions.

Only one thing seemed certain. Being an agnostic was risky business.

But Mrs. Chaffee was not easily put off with excuses. By the time she'd shown the children out the door, she'd convinced herself that the neighbors needed saving and that the way to accomplish this was to strike at the heart of the family. The assault began slowly. Invitations to church bazaars and suppers, which Willie's mother turned down. Then followed requests to accompany Mrs. Chaffee to Bible study classes and church meetings. Willie's mother retreated behind a fortress of polite excuses. ("Sorry, Betty. Maybe next time.") Mrs. Chaffee intensified her efforts. Not only did she proselytize, she baked and cooked. And she was a very good cook.

Willie's father was furious. "Why won't that woman let up?" he demanded.

"Shhh," said Willie's mother. "They'll hear you."

"I don't care!" said Willie's father.

"I do," said Willie's mother, which ended the conversation.

But not the religious wars, long simmering, which erupted in Willie's house.

With all the talk of Baptists and Buddhists and Catholics, it was perhaps no wonder that Willie would propose the passion play that would end all discussion.

It had not been easy convincing Judy Chaffee to act out the crucifixion of Jesus Christ. For one thing, Judy Chaffee wasn't interested in games that didn't include her dolls. For another, she wasn't sure what the word meant and wasn't about to ask.

It was Ernest who asked.

"What's a crucifixion?"

With Judy in listening distance, Willie told Ernest the stories behind the stations of the cross. She recounted the stripping of garments, the scourging at the pillar, the crowning with thorns. She drew out the long walk to the hill, the jeering crowds, the weight of the cross, and described in exquisite detail the nails driven into yielding flesh.

Oh Lord, why hast thou forsaken me?

Ernest was sold. Judy's face began to look like she'd stepped on something unpleasant. "That's disgusting," she pronounced when Willie told them about what the soldier did with his sword.

"It's not disgusting," said Willie, "it's the last passion."

"And what's *that* supposed to mean?" Judy asked.

Realizing that Judy and Ernest knew nothing of suffering, Willie embellished her account with her grandmother's stories of the epic wars between the Taira and Minamoto clans.

"They even beheaded the children!" she exclaimed.

Judy finally agreed to play, on condition that she could be Mary and carry a doll through the whole production. Willie said Ernest would be the Roman soldier and Kate, Saint Elizabeth or Mary Magdalene, whichever she preferred.

"Saints aren't allowed," said Judy.

"Okay, Mary Magdalene," said Kate.

"I'll be Jesus, of course," said Willie.

"How come you get to be Jesus?" Ernest wanted to know.

Willie had to explain that she was the only one tall enough to hang onto the cross. The cross was one of two T-shaped stands of metal pipe supporting the Chaffees' clothesline. To be Jesus, she explained, you had to climb up on the narrow concrete base and hang onto the horizontal bar of the T, while keeping your body in contact with the vertical pole. It was a delicate balancing act.

"You get to carry a spear," she assured Ernest.

And so they set to work. Using the illustrations from the children's version of *Lives of the Martyrs,* Willie created the right atmosphere. Soon Judy and Kate were draping their heads in blankets, and Willie was weaving a crown of thorns from an extension cord, and Ernest was cutting branches from the panax hedge, which they sharpened into spears with Willie's mother's sashimi knife. Judy even got a towel from her mother's laundry basket for Willie's loincloth.

In addition to her key role, Willie also served as director and stage manager. She honed the script, set the scene, and made sure everyone got their lines right. Soon they attracted the attention of other children in the neighborhood.

Linda and Bobby Desilva were Catholics and quickly fit in. But Melvin Nakashima had a hard time getting his lines right.

"What *are* you, anyway?" demanded Willie. "Don't you go to church?"

"Nah," said Melvin.

"What do you *do* on Sunday?"

"Go to the beach. Swim."

Willie threw up her hands.

Then Melvin said he also went to Bon dances, which set everything right, since *obon* was the Shinto harvest festival where the Japanese honored their dead, and Willie'd gone with her grandparents every year since she could remember.

Melvin turned out to be such a good Roman soldier that when it came time for the scourging at the pillar, Willie had to remind him not to hit so hard.

So there they were, Willie up on the pole, arms outstretched, hands grasping the ends of the T, Judy, Kate and Linda kneeling at the base with blankets over their heads and tragic expressions on their faces, and Ernest, Bobby and Melvin holding spears and looking mean. A perfect tableau.

That's when Mrs. Chaffee stepped onto her back porch.

"What are you *doing!*" she screamed from on high. She descended the stairs like something out of the apocalypse, shouting, "Savages! All of you!"

By then Willie was on the ground because Mrs. Chaffee's yelling had made her lose her balance.

"It's only a game," she protested, brushing dirt off her loincloth.

Mrs. Chaffee's eyes narrowed and her voice was not soft and smooth. "What *kind* of game?"

"The last passion of Christ," said Willie.

Mrs. Chaffee's mouth fell open.

Willie tried to explain, but Mrs. Chaffee was having none of it. She yanked the loin cloth off Willie's waist. "That's *ours!*" she shouted, beating the air above Willie's head. Then she shoved Judy toward the house, seized Ernest's left ear, and herded her children up the back steps.

"Heathens!" she shouted before slamming the door.

Then there was a lot of yelling from the house, and Willie knew Judy and Ernest were getting it.

Willie knew she was in deep trouble. Her father had barely gotten through the door when her mother started saying how upset Mrs. Chaffee had been. "She called me in tears!" she said, as if she were personally responsible for Mrs. Chaffee's pain. It seemed to Willie that her mother was less angry about the game than she was about Mrs. Chaffee's being upset.

"It was your daughter's idea," said Willie's mother, sending one of her looks in Willie's general direction.

It occurred to Willie that she was always her father's daughter when things went wrong. In fact, at that moment Willie didn't feel like her mother's daughter at all. She was not measuring up to her mother's standards of daughterhood. Why was it so easy for girls like Leona Hironaka, the daughter of her mother's best friend? Leona Hironaka was the perfect daughter. She never argued, she always helped her mother, and she sewed her own clothes. She even sewed her sister's clothes.

Willie hated Leona Hironaka.

She asked herself why she should be the perfect daughter. Her mother hadn't been perfect. She'd married Willie's father, after all.

Later, Willie felt bad about her thoughts. She asked her father what she'd done wrong.

He patted her shoulder. "Please, Willie. Find another game."

"Why?"

He sighed. "Because it upsets your mother."

Willie's hopes lifted. "You mean it's not a sin?"

Her father looked torn in two.

"Enough, Willie."

Her mother was quiet all through dinner. After dinner she banged the dishes around and complained that her feet hurt. She was pregnant, and her legs were swollen, and Willie felt like everything was her fault.

Willie said her prayers to herself in the darkness of the bedroom, the light from the street casting stripes across Kate's sleeping form. Kate had cried herself to sleep. Now the mango tree groaned in the night wind. Willie made an act of contrition in case she died before she woke and she asked the Virgin to pray for her and Kate and for the poor, pagan children.

Somewhere in the house, her mother was crying.

That made Willie think about her family and being born without what Father Marius called the gift of faith. Half the people she loved were pagans. She wondered what would happen when they died, whether they would go to hell like Father Marius said, or whether they'd qualify for Limbo, where God sent the unbaptized babies.

It didn't seem right, somehow. It wasn't their fault they were Buddhists.

The unfairness of it wasn't the least of it, either. On Sunday, Willie's mother went to the Baptist church.

Willie couldn't believe it. She felt confused and angry. None of her prayers had succeeded in getting her mother into the Catholic church and there she was, driving off with the Chaffees. Willie's father ranted and raved, but that didn't stop Willie's mother. Kate and Willie had to get ready for mass all by themselves, right down to sticking their hat pins.

Her mother didn't get home till late afternoon. Mrs. Chaffee saw her to the door. "See you next Sunday, dear," said Mrs. Chaffee.

Willie felt betrayed.

Then something unexpected happened.

As Mrs. Chaffee turned to leave, Willie's mother said, "Excuse me, Betty. But Sundays I save for my family." She said it in her most gracious and gentle way, but Willie recognized familiar steel.

Mrs. Chaffee must have felt it, too, for she blinked, hard, as if she'd been slapped. "The Lord's used to waiting," she said as she left.

He's going to wait a long time, thought Willie.

Later, she asked her mother what the Baptist church was like.

Willie's father rattled the newspaper he'd been reading all afternoon, and Willie's mother said it was fine, that she'd sat and listened and watched and the music was nice. "Dr. Tuttle gave a fine sermon," she added, sharing a secret smile with Willie when more newspaper rattling came from the front room.

"Then what happened?" Willie prodded.

Her mother had started cutting up a chicken. "People got extremely excited," she said.

"Excited?"

"Oh, yes. Some cried. Some began speaking in gibberish." She paused, frowning, and remarked that the knife seemed a little dull.

"They spoke of their pain," her mother continued, "their torment, their desires and wrongdoings."

"Right in public?" Willie asked.

Her mother took a chopper and whacked off the chicken's leg. "I didn't like that part." She glanced at Willie. "I don't like hanging out dirty laundry."

Willie tried to imagine her mother's serene, public face among the people in Mrs. Chaffee's church, people crying and hugging and singing. She tried to imagine her mother sitting there amongst all that commotion. She wondered if her mother had known what awaited her at the Baptist church. The thought wrenched her.

"So you're not going again?" she asked.

"No," said Willie's mother, whacking off the other leg, "just this once."

As Willie watched her mother go through the ritual of cooking, she realized that her mother had made what Father Marius called a sacrifice. A sacrifice was a giving up and a going through. For principle. And sometimes for love. Her mother hadn't gone to the Baptist church to save her *own* face. She'd gone there to save *Willie's*.

In the months after the religious wars cooled down, Willie would think on her mother's sacrifice on more than one occasion. That's what's called *making an impression*. The specific memory would fade in time, but sometimes it would rise to the surface of things to temper the pain of growing up and (much later) growing old.

Contradiction was at the heart of Willie's experience, and maybe it was a gift. Because somewhere along the way, Willie stopped worrying about her mother's soul, and once she did that it was only a short hop to not worrying too much about the souls of others. But first she had to confront Father Marius with many more questions, so that Father Marius took to regarding the ceiling whenever Willie raised her hand in catechism class. In time Willie saw that Father Marius had no final answers to the larger questions of life and faith, like wasn't love the most transcending commandment and shouldn't everyone just try to get along. So that when Willie's father reminded her to pray for the poor pagan children, she did it the way she prayed for Kate's legs. Whatever the legs decided to do, Kate was still Kate and she loved her just the same. Perhaps they were an abstraction, all those prayed-for pagans. What seemed more important than words was what she saw her father do every day—love her mother, the biggest pagan of them all.

THE GIFT
Gary Pak

It was the summer of 1962. It was the time around the Cuban missile crisis. I remember my parents watching that black/white/gray—a lot of gray—television and listening with a doomsday kind of attentiveness as President Kennedy went into the motions of that fateful blockade. I remember viewing on the television those secret maps taken by a U.S. spy plane of the Soviet bases in Cuba. It was a scary time, marked by the uncertainty that at any second the whole world would blow up. I remember that feeling very clearly. Everything seemed so gray, there was no good or evil, just that lousy feeling that something wasn't right and that the bottom of the world was about to fall out. A feeling of hopelessness. I was ten years old then, and I remember my parents watching the TV set in a glum silence, helpless, as if their lives were suddenly worthless and meaningless. It was a bad feeling that prevailed in our home.

A few days later, President Kennedy's gamble paid off, to everyone's relief. Nikita Khrushchev backed down and the whole world began breathing easily. But that helpless feeling did not leave my gut, I don't know exactly how to explain it, but it was like nothing seemed to matter anymore. The world around me—my home, family, the neighborhood, everything—seemed irrelevant. Nothing seemed to matter.

About a week after the Cuban crisis, when the whole country was resting but everyone was still nervous about the realness of nuclear war, we heard the rumor that our friend Chunky Kalama had died. Actually he wasn't really a friend of ours. (Our gang consisted of me, my cousin Davey who was a few months younger than me, and two other neighborhood kids, Willy and Georgie.) You see, Chunky Kalama was the neighborhood bully. He never used to fool around with me because we were the same height though he was heavier, but he used to push around most of the kids our age or younger because Chunky was super-strong for his age. Willy—whom Chunky also never used to bother because Willy was about Chunky's size, even though he was fat and couldn't scrap at all—told us a story once about Chunky beating up a kid two grades above. And Chunky used to hang around another neighborhood bully, Damien Mahoney, who was a year older than us.

Though he was much stronger than me, Chunky and I had kind of an "eye-balling" relationship; in other words, he kind of knew he could have taken me easily, but because I was just as tall as he was, he probably thought it wasn't necessary to physically lord it over me, he'd just give me the "third-degree" eye to keep me in my place. And anyway, I never made trouble with him to give him the excuse to beef with me because I was pretty afraid of him, though I tried not to show it.

It was my cousin who told me that Chunky had died. My cousin was just as skinny as me and shorter. And he used to get pushed around a lot by Chunky and Damien. It was night when I heard the news from my cousin. I was sleeping over his house that night, his house was just a few doors away from mine in a dead-end street, and he told me that he heard it from his mom that the night before Chunky had tried to get candy from the machine down at the service station after the station was closed, and when the machine jammed after he had dropped in his nickel, Chunky must have banged the machine and pulled on all of the knobs making the machine tilt forward, then fall on him, crushing him to death. I remember my cousin telling me this when we were in bed, with a thin blanket over us like a tent. He was holding one of those pencil flashlights, telling the story with his voice wavering and fearful. We couldn't sleep that night, or at least for a long time into the early morning hours because we weren't sure how to deal with this, a kid our age dying and he being the bully and not liking any of us, and we thinking that maybe his ghost might come back and search for us and haunt us in the dark of the night.

The next day we told the rest of our friends about what happened to Chunky and they, too, did not know what to make of it. We were sitting in the huge mango tree in the front of my cousin's house.

"You think Chunky going come back and make trouble wit' us or what?" Georgie asked, looking at me.

I shrugged my shoulders. "I dunno," I said. "He was mad at you?"

Georgie's eyes were wide and scared. "No," he said quickly. "I nevah do nothing to him. But he always picking on me." He looked up into the higher branches of the tree, then quickly corrected himself, thinking perhaps Chunky might be listening in and might not like what he had just heard. "Nah-nah, he nevah pick on me . . . dat much. Nah, he wasn't bad to me."

"What . . . you scared his ghost?" Willy said, then started laughing.

"Not. I not scared of ghost," Georgie protested.

"Not. You scared of his ghost," Willy said.

"Not! You scared his ghost!"

"Not! If I see his ghost, I whack him wit' my fist!"

But we all knew that Georgie was scared of Chunky's ghost. We were all afraid of his ghost, even big tough Willy.

Then a week later, a strange coincidence happened. Georgie's oldest sister died. He told us about her death when we were all in the mango tree again. He told us that his sister was sick for a long time, something inside of her that the doctors had said was "incurable," and that his parents and everyone else connected with his family had known that his oldest sister was going to die sometime soon. But he didn't know, he said, or wasn't supposed to know. He told us that his parents didn't want him to know about her condition, but that his sister had taken him to the side one day and told him there was something wrong with her. And we knew that Georgie liked his sister a lot, in fact, we all kind of liked her because she used to make these real ono-licious chocolate chip cookies for us once in a while and Georgie used to bring them up into the tree and we all used to eat up every crumb, they were so delicious. Georgie cried that day, up in the tree, and though we had often kidded Georgie of being a crybaby, we didn't that day because we knew Georgie was very sad and hurt. When he finished his silent crying on his branch of the tree, wiping his tears and hanabata on his t-shirt, we all told him how sorry we all were and then we started playing Superman and Batman and Georgie said he was going to be Flash Gordon and then I said that I was going to be the Blob from Outta Space.

We never liked Chunky and Damien, the big bullies of the neighborhood. And we should have been kind of glad that Chunky was not around. But something inside of us was telling us—I know that's how we all felt at the time, though we never told one another this feeling—that maybe it was all right when Chunky was around, even though he bullied us about, that it was okay for him to do so if that meant him not dying and still being alive. It was an awfully hard thing to think about: that someone we knew, someone our age, had died. We didn't quite understand what it meant to be dead. All we knew was that it was a horrible thing, that it meant that Chunky, or any other kid if that happened to him, would not be able to play in the park or climb the trees or hike up the side of the hill, or do anything for that matter anymore. Period. No presents to open. No birthdays. No friends to play with. No pets. No soda water to drink from the machine at the gas station. No fooling around with the pay phone at the station and getting two dimes to drop into the change return slot after tapping the dial tone five times, the two dimes we would buy two bottles of Diamond Head soda water with.

We were afraid of catching Chunky's misfortune, we didn't want to be the next kid to die, so we avoided the service station like we avoided Willy's house whenever his father was drunk and raving mad. Or especially how for a long time we avoided going near the empty lot near Georgie's house because that was where we saw that mad dog with saliva dripping from its mouth and Mr. Wong coming out of his house with a rifle and killing the crazy dog with two shots, and Mr. Wong telling us that we would catch something bad if we went near that spot where the dog had died. After a while, though, we cautiously went back to use the soda machine. That was the only place in our neighborhood where we could get sodas. But we never used the candy machine ever again.

It was a horrible summer for us. Watching the television watch the world was no fun. And two people we knew were dead. And we not able to understand any of this at all.

In the beginning of the summer, just before Chunky died, another family moved into our neighborhood. The Rezentes family. There was a father and a mother and three children, all girls. And Cynthia Rezentes was the youngest of the girls and very pretty.

I remember the day we first saw her. My cousin and Willy and I were walking down the street going to Georgie's house when we saw them moving in. That's when we caught a glimpse of Cynthia. She gave us a shy glance, then scurried inside the house. Willy was all jazzed up. He took out the short black comb he always carried in his back pocket, the comb he had swiped from his big brother, and began combing his hair, a big grin on his face.

We were ten years old then and entering the sixth grade in the fall; and yet, we all had that inkling for the opposite sex already, though we didn't know what we were supposed to do or why we felt that way. We just had that warm and tender feeling swelling inside of ourselves that felt embarrassing but good. We knew that when we got older we were supposed to be interested in girls; we'd watched Willy's older brother and Georgie's older brothers and my cousin's two older brothers go out with their girlfriends. Often we kidded each other about having a girlfriend, which each of us, in front of the other guys, would always deny ever thinking about or wishing, which of course was a lie.

In our eyes, Cindy Rezentes was very pretty. We all must have harbored a wish that one day she'd be a girlfriend; I know I did. And whenever we passed by her house, our hearts would start fluttering, we'd suddenly be quiet, or if we did say something our talk became nonsensical. And then Georgie one day in the mango tree broke out with a candid remark how he thought Cindy was pretty and that he wouldn't mind marrying her. We all jumped on that and kidded him until he almost cried but he didn't but he got really mad at us and left for home. We all knew that what Georgie said was what we all wished upon ourselves, though we never admitted that to each other, and that teasing Georgie was like teasing ourselves.

I remember those nights before falling asleep when my thoughts would wander to Chunky Kalama and Georgie's sister and about their deaths and about that disturbing gray feeling watching my parents watch the television and me watching the television, too, that gray Cuban missile crisis time. When my mind drifted to those dreary thoughts, I forced myself to think about Cindy and how pretty she was, and how, maybe, she would be my girlfriend and we'd be happy, holding hands and kissing like how Davey's brother did with his girlfriend. I'd think about that hot summer night when we were all in the mango tree and Georgie whispering that Davey's brother was coming with his girlfriend and we all became real quiet and watched them sit down below us and start making kissy-kissy and touchy-touchy.

Georgie came to my house early one morning with his eyes wide and excited. I was inside eating a bowl of cold cereal. Georgie came in and sat down with me at the kitchen table. He started helping himself to the dry cereal. Then he said, "Terry, try look what I found." He unfolded a soiled sheet of notepaper from his pants pocket.

I looked at it, spread out to the side of my bowl of cereal. It was a crude map of our neighborhood. I saw the square that was labeled "service station" and the streets with their names. There were all kinds of neighborhood landmarks penciled in like the big mango trees and the fire hydrant and the empty lot where Mr. Wong shot and killed the mad dog. Then there was one house marked with an "x" in a square, labeled, "my house," and a dotted trail that led from "my house" down a couple of streets, then up another street to an old abandoned botanical garden. The garden had the name "Friendship Garden," which we could never understand since entering the garden was like entering a heiau or an old Hawaiian graveyard. At least that's what was told to us, we had never gone into the garden. Willy said that his older brother had seen an old woman with long white hair and no legs floating around up there. It was a story he often told us, which made us never want to go there.

"Whose map is dis?" I asked.

Georgie looked at me hesitantly for a moment, then said, "Ah—is dah kine—ah dah kine—ah—Chunky's map."

"Chunky's map?!"

I stared at Georgie with disbelief and horror. Chunky's map? The first thought that came to my mind was that the bad luck associated with Chunky had come to my house and was here to stay. Maybe I was the next to die. I was scared—very scared—and very angry at Georgie for bringing the map to my house.

"Why you bring dis map ovah here?" I said.

"No—no. Is not Chunky's map. He nevah draw dis map. Is dah kine Damien who wen draw 'em."

"Damien?"

"Yeah—yeah. Damien."

"Den why you tell me is Chunky's map den?"

"Cause get his treasure ovah here." Georgie pointed to the end of the dotted line on the top of the map, deep in what was marked off as "Friendship Garden," and at the end of the dotted line was a big red X with the word "tresure."

"Whas dis?" I asked. "Whose treasure dis?"

Georgie smiled uneasily. "Chunky's," he said.

"Chunky's?"

"Yeah."

"How you know?"

"Cause I heard Damien talking 'bout dah map. I was down by dah ocean wit' Willy and Davey, dah time you had to go store wit' yo' muddah and fathah, and den we heard somebody coming down dah trail and sounded like Damien and so we wen go hide in dah bushes and was Damien and somebody else, we nevah know who dah othah guy was. But dey nevah see us. But den dey was talking loud and we could hear cause dey thought nevah had nobody around but dey was saying Chunky wen hide all his ball bearings and his money his grandmuddah always geeving him, his birthday money li' dat, and he get dah map cause he wen draw 'em out cause befo' Chunky wen die he tol' Damien 'bout dah treasure he wen bury up Friendship Garden."

"So how you got 'em?" I asked, referring to the map.

Georgie smiled. "I dunno. I think Damien must've ride his bike down dah trail and wen he and his friend wen go, must've wen fly outta his pocket. Cause wen we came outta dah bush, we saw dah piece pepah on dah ground. Den I pick 'em up and was dah map."

I looked at the map again. Chunky's ball bearings and his money. He had the best ball bearing collection, two of which were probably mine. That I was almost certain of. I had them in school in my cubbyhole and after recess when I came back in, my ball bearings were gone. I wanted to go up to Chunky and demand them back, but I was too scared to confront him. And we all knew that Chunky's grandmother was rich, she owned a store or a bar or something in Kanewai town, and Chunky always had the best-look-

ing bike and nice clothes and he always had money to buy candy and soda
water at the service station. He always treated his friend, Damien.

"But . . . so what?" I said. "What we going do?"

Georgie looked at me with a kind of helpless look. "I dunno," he
said. He looked at the map, turning it so he could see it straight. Then he
looked up at me and smiled. "We can go find dah treasure and take 'em."

I knew he was going to say that, and my body turned cold in protest
and in fear. "No . . . cannot," I said.

"Why?"

"Das . . . das . . . not our money . . . and ball bearings."

"You tol' me Chunky wen steal yo' ball bearings at school."

"Yeah . . . but . . . but . . . I . . ."

"Dah kine, Davey and Willy said if you go, dey go, too. If you like go
fo' dah treasure."

"You wen talk to Davey and Willy already?" I said with a chill in my
voice.

Georgie nodded his head.

And then, pulling out what I thought was the big stick, I said, "But if
we go deah and take dah treasure, den Chunky not going like dat and he
going haunt us wit' his ghost."

A worried look surfaced on Georgie's face. "Yeah, you right, Terry,"
he said after a brief thought. "No can take dah treasure. Dah kine, Chunky's
ghost . . . he going . . ."

Georgie didn't finish his sentence, but I knew what he was thinking
about.

Later that morning in the mango tree, the others agreed with our
decision. Surely, Chunky's ghost would come after us and scare us at nights
and maybe even beat us up if we took his treasure. The question then came
up of what we should do with the map. Willy suggested we give it back to
Damien, but I protested, saying that Damien would then try to get even
with us for taking his map. Georgie added that we all never liked him
anyway so why give it back. My cousin Davey said we should destroy it
then, burn it up so the ashes and smoke go back to Chunky. But Georgie
disagreed, saying that it was too valuable, but that maybe we should give it
to Chunky's mom and dad, that the map was rightfully theirs. And so we
agreed on that, that seemed right. We decided to go to the Kalama's house,
which was somewhere behind all the kiawe trees across the main road from
the service station. Chunky's family owned a lot of land on the down side of
the neighborhood next to the ocean. Willy said that before his grandma
died, she was a friend of Chunky's grandma and used to go visiting down
there.

So, shakily—since we had never gone even a looking distance close to Chunky's house, we being afraid of his reputed big brothers whom he had bragged about once as being ten times his size and would back him up in any fight—we climbed down the tree and started down the street to the gas station.

We stopped at the station, as Willy said, "fo' one pit stop." My cousin went to the phone booth. We all looked around and when we were sure that nobody was watching, Davey tapped the phone five times and out clinked two dimes in the change return slot. Then he did it again and two more dimes dropped out. Then we went to the sodawater machine and bought our bottles of Diamond Head sodas; my favorite was orange, I never got any other flavor but that. And as we approached the candy machine we all cast uncomfortable glances at it, taking a sidestep away as we passed it, hoping that we were far enough away so we couldn't catch anything bad and unlucky connected with it.

"You think we going get Chunky's bad luck?" Georgie asked worriedly.

I shrugged my shoulders uneasily. I couldn't offer Georgie any assurance. I looked over at the other guys and they, too, had worried faces.

We sat on the corner of the gas station lot and drank our soda water while we looked across the main road at the kiawe trees and buffalo grass in the direction of Chunky's house. Then Georgie said that he had gone there once while helping his older brother deliver the afternoon paper, but the mailbox was out on the road and so he didn't get to see what the house looked like, but that there was a narrow road that went inside Chunky's lot from the mailbox and that there was a lot of haole koa covering everything. My cousin Davey took the longest to finish his soda, but none of us complained because actually we were all taking our time, not really wanting to push it and get going to Chunky's house. When he finally finished his soda, we warily crossed the main road, silently, as if we were entering an old Hawaiian heiau.

Behind the thick bush, we came upon sections of the land where tractors had cleared the kiawe. (Later, we learned that his family had sold a lot of the land.) We saw several homes coming up and heard hammers whacking nails.

We had followed the narrow winding dirt road for a ways in when suddenly an old black dog came out of the bush and started howling at us. We froze. Then Willy picked up a stone and threw it at the dog, and then I picked up a stone and threw it, and then we all started picking up stones and throwing them at the old dog. The old dog trotted away with its tail between its legs, hobbled away actually, one of its hind legs looked hurt. And then Georgie threw a perfect shot: the stone sailed through the tail and cracked the old dog in its hanging balls. The dog gave a big long howl and ran off into the bush. We laughed, we thought it was so funny. And then I told a story of the time me and Davey went to our Uncle's pig farm and threw stones at the pigs' balls, which were big and pink and low hanging, and we all had another good round of laughs.

Then, after we went a little further down the road, Willy snuck up from behind and grabbed my 'olo'olos, shouting, "Grab balls!" I jumped and yelped weakly. I then tried to grab his ones, but he was already running away with his hands cupped over them. So I turned to get the others, but Georgie and Davey had already taken off down the road away from reach. I turned back to Willy and shouted, "I get you, punk!" And he said, "Whop yo' jaws!" And I said, "Whop yo' jaws!" And then I picked up a stone and threw it at him, but he was too far away for me to hit. So I turned and started walking down the road with a sour look on my face, the two ahead of me taking side glances back to see if I was sneaking up on them, and behind Willy kept his distance. I was all mad inside at Willy and vowing to get revenge. Momentarily, we kind of forgot why we were walking down the road; unconsciously, our legs were taking us towards Chunky's.

Then Davey and Georgie stopped at the side of the road and gave Willy and me this funny, what-should-we-do kind of look. I realized that we were at Chunky's house. All grudges were immediately forgotten.

Georgie and Davey waited for us to catch up with them. We studied the rusty, flagless mailbox, then nervously scanned the narrow road that led into the property, haole koa bushes hedging thickly on the sides. Speechless, we looked at each other.

Finally, Willy said, "What we should do, Terry?"

"Why we no leave the map inside the mailbox?" Davey suggested, his voice wavering.

"Das not good," Georgie said. "Den my bruddah going find 'em wen he come down deliver pepah. Plus that, I hate my bruddah. He wen punch my arm last night fo' nothing. No ways, José, I going let my bruddah get the map and go fo' the treasure."

They looked at me for leadership; I usually made most of the important decision-making for the group. But this time I was hesitant to voice my opinion.

I don't know how the words came out of my mouth, but finally I said, "We better take the map to his family cause das what we said we was going do." I guess I must have wanted to set a good example to the rest of the guys to show them that I was a good leader.

Then Willy said, "Com'on, Terry. You the leader. Go lead us in."

Inside, I kind of choked. But, without further hesitation, I started walking shakily towards Chunky's house.

We had gone a couple hundred feet down the dirt road, making a turn, when we heard a pack of dogs howling and barking wildly. We stopped in our tracks, listening nervously. Willy turned to me, worried and whispering, "Maybe is dah old dog wit' his friends." Then we heard a woman's voice shouting, "Kulikuli! Honey! Blackie! Shut up!" The dogs' barks and howls diminished to whimpers. The woman's voice gave us courage so we continued down the road.

We came to a flat grassy area. There was a line of coconut trees that separated the grassy area from the beach and ocean, and to the left of our view was Chunky's house. It was a small, squat house, it was dark in color, not brown or gray but somewhere in between. There was an old boat pulled up to the side of the house, leaning on its side, which a pack of old dogs and pups had seemingly taken as their home. The dogs came out of the boat and approached us cautiously, sniffing the air, then barking and howling again. The door of the house opened and an old Hawaiian woman came out on the porch, saying, "What I said, Honey? Blackie? Shut yo' mouths!"

And then the woman saw us, and she squinted her eyes with a confused look on her face. She said, "Yes? What you boys want?"

Nobody said anything; the others were waiting for me to say something. So I said, "Is dis Chunky Kalama's house?"

There was a long, very uncomfortably long pause from the woman, an almost sad pause, even the dogs stopped barking, or so it seemed. Just the coconut trees were rustling in the background. Then the woman said, "Yes, dis is Chunky's house." She looked at the ground, then at the dogs, then back at us and said softly, "You his friends?"

I was frozen, I didn't know how to answer that, but I began to nod my head. And the others did, too. Then I said, "We get something fo' him, something he—he—he forgot."

The woman motioned us to come forward. "Come . . . come heah," she said.

We approached her slowly, the dogs began to creep backwards, they began their barking again but with half the effort. The woman silenced them. When we came up to the wooden porch, the woman leaned on the railing and asked us in a kindly voice, "You folks like one soda water?"

Nobody said anything, nobody . . . but Willy. Willy said, "Yeah . . . I like."

"What kine flavors you folks like?" the woman asked, half turning to enter the door to get the soda.

We mentioned our favorites. The woman entered the house and returned shortly with the soda. She motioned us to sit on a picnic table that was to the side of the house. There she joined us with a cup of coffee and cigarettes.

"Which one of you boys is Davey?" she asked.

We were all surprised that she knew Davey's name. Davey said that that was he. Then the woman went down the list, asking who was who, mentioning all of our names, except Damien's.

The woman looked at us with smiling eyes as she smoked her cigarette. Then she said, "Chunky always used to talk about you folks, how you guys play so nicely together." Then: "Ohhh . . . my poor baby! Why dis had to happen?" And the woman began to cry, huge tears began dripping down her cheeks. We did not know what to do, we had never seen a grownup cry before. Then, as fast as she had started to cry, she stopped, wiping her eyes with the sleeve of her shirt. "I sorry I cry in front all of you. But I look at you folks, at yo' faces, and all I can t'ink of is my only grandson."

That made me start thinking: but I thought Chunky said he had big brothers who would back him up in a fight?

Then Chunky's grandmother started telling us—all stone-faced, speechless, not knowing what to do or think—that Chunky liked us all, that he often talked about us, his friends, giving him bamboocha marbles and shiny ball bearings. She told us that his father had died when he was a baby and that his mother worked downtown, how she and her husband, Chunky's grandfather, actually were raising him and were his father and mother, but now that Chunky's grandfather had died the year before and now that Chunky, too, was gone, there was nobody in the house but her.

She was silent for a long time. So were we. When we finished our soda water, we all told her thank you and she asked us if we wanted more sodas and Willy hesitated and was about to say yes, but I said no thank you and then the others said no thank you. Then she asked us to stay a little while more, and so we did, but just for a little while longer while she remained silent, smoking her cigarettes, and we silently watched her. Finally Georgie said he had to go back home, and so we got up and told her thank you again and began to leave. Chunky's grandmother, still sitting and lighting another cigarette, said to us, "You folks . . . you folks come back again. Okay?" And we nodded our heads and said we would come back, but we knew we would never come back.

It dawned on us after passing the sounds of the carpenters building the houses that we had forgotten to give his grandmother the treasure map.

Up on our high perch in the mango tree, we thought out loud about our visit to Chunky's grandmother's house and what she had told us.

"I thought Chunky had big bruddahs," Georgie said.

"Yeah," Davey said.

"Den how come dah grandmuddah said he was her only grandson den?" Willy said.

"Ah, Chunky must've wen lie to us," Davey said.

"Yeah," Georgie said.

"Yeah, he must've wen lie to us," Willy said, "and den he tell his grandmuddah how us guys his good friends." He paused, thinking, then said, "I wonder how come?"

"You know why, I bet," Georgie said, "is because he nevah had friends . . . Chunky."

"Damien," Davey corrected. "Damien his good friend."

"Yeah," Willy said. "Das right. Damien his good friend. But how come dah grandmuddah nevah say nothing 'bout him? And she knew all our names!"

Through all of their thinking-out-loud, I was silent, listening and trying to piece together everything. How did Chunky's grandmother know us when we weren't even his friends? I started wondering what was it that Chunky told his grandmother about us. Was it bad stuff? But the grandmother was happy to see us. If Chunky had told her bad stuff about us, then the grandmother wouldn't have been nice to us and given us soda water. What was it that Chunky told his grandmother about us?

Then I thought about Chunky, how he didn't have any father and his mother was never around, being raised by his grandparents, and how it must've been hard living like that and lonely all by himself, supposing that he didn't have any brothers and sisters. And then I thought how he wasn't really that popular around the neighborhood and at school, how Damien had other friends but he hung around Chunky maybe just to get candy and soda water from the gas station since Chunky always had money. I started feeling real sorry for Chunky, even though he used to push everybody around. Maybe he pushed everybody around because nobody wanted to be friends with him and maybe he wanted to be friends with everybody but nobody would give him a chance.

"Terry, what you think?" Willy asked.

I looked at him for a long time, still thinking about all of this, and I looked at the others and they were all silent, waiting for me to say something. And then I said, "We go get the treasure."

Everybody looked at me as if I was crazy. I knew they heard me and I knew they didn't like hearing what I said. I repeated myself.

Georgie said feebly, "But . . . but Chunky . . . das Chunky's stuff ovah there. Get his ghost going haunt us."

Willy kidded Georgie, saying, "What Georgie . . . you scared of ghost?" He laughed.

But I knew Willy was just as much against it as Georgie because his laugh wasn't convincing to me. And my cousin Davey was silent. He was turning a little pale, as if Chunky was down at the base of the tree, looking up, pounding the bark with his large hands, and threatening Davey never to come down or he'd pound his head into the ground, something that he had done at least twice.

"I not going fo' the treasure," Georgie said. "I not going."

"What . . . you scared?" Willy said. He laughed again.

"Not. I not scared," Georgie said.

"Den how come you no like go den?" Willy said.

"Not. I not scared. But I no like go."

"Ha! Ha! No lie. You scared."

"You scared, too!" Georgie said angrily.

"Not!" Willy protested.

"Yes—yes. I heard you say the time at your house that you scared Chunky's ghost come haunt you. I heard you. And you tol' me the othah day how you no like go down the gas station buy candy anymo' because Chunky's ghost."

"Not! I nevah said dat!"

"Terry, how come you like go get the treasure?" my cousin Davey asked, weakly.

I didn't have a reason. It had just popped into my mind that moment that Chunky wouldn't mind if we went and got his treasure. In fact, I was almost guarands-ball-barands sure that he would rather give us the treasure than give it to Damien. So I told the rest of the gang what I thought. Willy asked how did I know this, and I told him that I just had a feeling, especially after visiting with his grandmother. Willy now had a look on his face as if I had betrayed him. He probably thought I was at first joking about going up to Friendship Garden and getting Chunky's treasure, but now he knew I was serious, and since he had come off like he wasn't scared, he was jammed in a no-turning-back predicament.

Willy said, looking over at Davey for support, "Yeah, why you like go deah fo'? What you t'ink get?"

I shrugged my shoulders. I asked for the map from Georgie and he slowly got it out of his back pocket and passed it to me through Davey. I opened it up and looked at the map again, at the landmarks, in particular the one marked "my house." I noticed that the house was above the main road so it couldn't have been Chunky's house. And it was right on the street above the gas station so it couldn't have been Damien's house, since

Damien's house was two streets away, near Friendship Garden. And then I noticed the fire hydrant which was . . . that was the only one behind the gas station and . . . and . . . and . . . next to . . . my house.

I stared at the map in stunned silence. A creepy feeling came over me.

Willy said, "Whas the mattah, Terry? What the map say?"

I didn't know what to say. Or think. Willy moved over to my branch, and Davey and Georgie slid over next to me, and Willy took the map and started looking at it. And then I said, "You see the fire hydrant?" And Willy said, "Yeah." And I said, "Get only one, yeah? And das the one by my house, yeah?" And still Willy didn't catch on to what I was trying to say. So I told everybody what I saw in the map.

"Nah . . . how can be yo' house?" Willy said.

"You nevah draw the map," Georgie said. "I wen pick 'em up from wen drop from Damien's pocket."

"You sure das what the map say?" Davey said.

I took the map away from Willy and looked at it again. And I became more convinced of what I saw the first time. Why was my house in the map and why was it connected to the "tresure"? I couldn't think straight.

Georgie looked at the map and after studying it for a few moments said, "Yeah, look. Get the Ah Chew's mango tree ovah here. Look. And right next is the fire hydrant. And the fire hydrant right next to Terry's house." He pointed in the direction of my house. Then he looked at me and said, "What you t'ink Chunky wen hide in Friendship Garden?"

I told him that I didn't know, but that I had a hunch he had hid money and his ball bearing collection. Then I asked him if he was still sure that Damien had drawn the map and not Chunky. Georgie said, "Yeah." And then added, "I dunno."

I was trying to figure out why Chunky had connected my house with the treasure, if he had drawn the map, when Davey said bravely, "Com'n. Les go find dah treasure."

We looked at each other with faces doubtful but with a touch of adventure. Then we shrugged our shoulders and climbed down the mango tree and started off towards Friendship Garden.

We passed Cindy Rezentes's house and her dogs greeted us with angry barks. We looked towards her house and heard the strains of a Frankie Avalon song. But we walked on without thinking much about her, our minds were heavy with more important matters.

Willy looked at the map. "Dah stuff suppose to be buried by one fishpond."

"Where?" Georgie said, looking at the map. "No mo' one fishpond in Friendship Garden."

"How you know?" I asked Willy.

"Cause it say 'fishpond' on the map," Willy said. "Must be buried right ovah there."

"What fishpond?" Davey said.

"How you know no mo' one fishpond?" Willy asked Georgie.

"Cause, my bruddah said only get trees and rocks up there."

"But he nevah say had one fishpond or not, eh, ovah there?" Davey said.

"No," Georgie said.

"But no mo' fishponds up in the mountains," I said.

"Where it say get one fishpond?" Georgie asked. "Where?"

"It say right heah," Willy said emphatically, pointing to a word on the map in the area designated as Friendship Garden.

Georgie looked at the map. Then he started laughing. "Dat no say 'fishpond,'" he said. "Stay read 'Friendship'!"

We all started laughing up. Willy became irritated.

"How you know get treasure up deah?" Willy asked Georgie sourly.

"Das what the map said," Georgie said.

"But how you know? You dunno."

"I know," Georgie said. "You watch. I betchu all yo' marbles get treasure buried up there."

"Not."

"Yes—yes."

"Den how you know the treasure stay buried?" Willy said.

"Gotta be," Georgie said. "Treasures, dey always stay buried."

"Maybe dah stuff stay in one box and just on dah ground," Willy said. "You dunno."

"No," I said to Willy. "But you dunno, too."

"Dah stuff stay buried," Davey said. "I know."

"How you know?" I asked.

"I jus' know," Davey said. "Chunky, he would do something like dat. Bury his treasure so nobody find 'em."

We started up a road that climbed a hill; at the top of the road was Friendship Garden. But before getting there, we had to pass Damien's house.

"When we get ovah there," I said, referring to Damien's house, "we bettah be quiet, or else Damien going spock us and try make trouble."

The others nodded their heads.

As we cautiously approached Damien's house, we heard a loud scream, like that of a girl frightened by a big fat toad. We heard a deep voice yelling, "I tol' you no mess wit' my things!"

"I said I sorry!"

There was another scream, followed by a loud slap.

"I going tell Mommy!"

We realized it was Damien screaming and crying; the other voice was that of his older brother.

"Go—punk! Tell Mommy! And I going bus' yo' ass again! Go! Tell Mommy!"

Damien was crying loudly, then he screamed again; in our minds we saw Damien's older brother raising a big hand.

"No! No! I sorry! I not going tell Mommy! No hit me, Bobby! No hit me! I sorry! I not going play wit' yo' stuff!"

"You frickin' punk. I catch you messing wit' my things one mo' time, I going geev you one 'nother dirty licking. You heard?"

There was a pause. Meanwhile, unconsciously, we had slowed down to a snail's pace, our ears listening intently to what was happening. We had never heard Damien—or Chunky, for that matter—crying like a girl. They were the bullies and you never heard or saw those kinds of things. So it was a very sobering experience for us to hear Damien cry and get beaten up by his older brother.

"You heard—you punk? I cannot hear you!"

"Yeah, Bobby."

"I cannot hear!"

"YEAH, BOBBY!"

"All right den. Beat it! Scram! Out! Now!"

We heard a door open and shut. We realized we were stopped in front of Damien's house, so quickly we scurried on, afraid to have Damien see us and realize that we had heard everything that went on.

We continued on to the end of the road where Friendship Garden began. Nailed to a tree was a sagging sign, which read "Enter At Your Own Risk." Giant trees flanked the entrance, which had stone steps climbing in, and inside the Garden was dark and quiet. It was spooky.

We looked at each other blankly, not knowing what to do next. Then Georgie took out the map and looked at it. "Get one bridge inside we gotta go across. Den one 'swinging banyan tree.' Den dah treasure going be by one Japanee church."

"One what? What you talking 'bout?" I said.

"One Japanee church?" Davey said.

"Yeah, das what it say," Georgie said.

I took the map from him and studied it. One swinging banyan tree, before that one bridge to cross, then one Japanee church. That was what was written. And drawn in.

We looked into the Garden again. And for a moment, I wished I hadn't made that suggestion of going after the treasure.

No one was making a move, so I said, "Come on. We going or what?"

No one said anything. I didn't want to lead the group in. I was hoping one of them would refuse to go in, or suggest we leave. But none of them said anything. I was left standing not knowing what to do, the others watching me from the corners of their eyes for my first move. They were ready to go in, but they wanted me to lead them.

Then Davey said, "Les go in." And suddenly he took the lead and started in. And then Willy followed, and before I could make out what was going on, Georgie was in and I was at the back of the line, feeling a bit disappointed that they did not wait for me to be the leader.

Swarms of mosquitoes attacked us. We found ourselves ducking our heads under low-hanging vines and climbing a narrow trail that was covered with rotting leaves and followed alongside a dried-up stream. Parts of the trail had crumbled down to the stream, and we had to jump over those broken sections or swing across using the low hanging vines as handles. Then the trail flattened for a while, and we entered a grove of bamboo. We tried to break off some of the bamboo at the base to take home and use as fishing poles, but they were too green and too tough to break. We finally gave up, making a note to ourselves that if we came up here a next time we'd bring a knife to cut the bamboo.

The trail started to climb again. We passed tall paperbark trees; we tore off their flaking skins and tossed them around. Then, we started wondering: where is this bridge we are supposed to cross?

Willy looked at the map. "Says right heah," he said, pointing to the bridge. "Dah bridge. And get one stream running underneath. Look."

"Yeah, one stream," I said.

We looked around; we had left the dried-up stream behind.

"But where dah bridge?" Georgie said. "You t'ink we wen go dah wrong way or what?"

I shrugged my shoulders.

Davey took the map, saying, "Maybe . . . "

A wind blew into the Garden and we heard a chorus of moans coming from all around us. The sounds were probably branches rubbing against each other and leaves rustling, but to us, the sounds were frightening. We looked around, our eyes widening, thinking we were in the midst of ghosts; perhaps Chunky's ghost was about to pounce on us. I remember thinking about the story Willy told us about that old woman with no legs, floating around Friendship Garden. I became petrified; I remember telling myself that I was not going to say what I was thinking to the others. But looking at them, I had a funny feeling that they were thinking the same thing that I was thinking.

Then Willy did a bold thing. He picked up a stone and threw it deep into the bush. We heard it thrash through the trees. Then a thought flashed through my mind; I remembered my grandmother once telling me and my sister that if ever you come across a spirit and the spirit is making you real scared, the best thing to do is to make the spirit think you're not afraid of it. And so I picked up a stone, too, and threw it with all my might in the direction Willy threw his. And I yelled with the release of the stone. Willy picked up another and threw it. I picked up another and we both smiled boldly at the others and then they caught on and soon we were barraging the area with all the stones we could find or dig up with our fingers and nails, and even throwing broken branches and anything else that was on the ground.

We started laughing. Suddenly, we were the army fighting the invasion of the Martians, and we were winning. Georgie took a stick he found lying around and that became his rifle. Now the stones were hand grenades, and the wind sounds of the Garden were overwhelmed by our shrills and simulated explosions. Then Davey found something that started us back on track.

There was a concrete block that he had discovered while picking up a stone next to it. The block was covered with moss and mud and it was partially sunk at an angle into the ground. But it was squarish and had a flat surface, which were the reasons it caught his attention. He called us over. Georgie wiped his hands over the flat surface, clearing away the rotten leaves and dirt, uncovering an inscription. It read: 1937.

"What dis mean?" Willy said.

"I dunno," Davey said.

"Mus' be from one building or something," I said. "Dah old kine buildings, dey get dah old kine dates stuck on 'em."

"What building get up heah?" Georgie said with disbelief.

"I dunno," I said. "Maybe had one building up heah and dey wen tear 'em down."

"Who wen tear 'em down?" Georgie said.

I shrugged my shoulders.

"Maybe was something else," Davey suggested.

"Yeah, maybe was something else," Willy said.

"What?" Georgie asked.

"I dunno," Davey said. "But something else."

"1937 . . ." Willy murmured. "Wow . . . das real old."

"Yeah," Davey said.

"Dis Garden must be at least dat old," I said.

"Yeah," Willy said.

And then Davey made another of his remarkable discoveries. Looking down to the side of the trail, he saw what were once the low concrete-formed railings of the bridge. "Eh! Dis is dah bridge we standing on right now!" he said.

Sure enough, after brushing off some of the debris area we were standing on, we discovered a concrete slab. And we found a small tunnel underneath that had permitted the waters of a now non-existent stream to flow through.

"Dah bridge!" we yelled.

Georgie took out the map and we all looked at it. The bridge, then right after it the swinging banyan tree. Then . . . the Japanee church?

We continued on the trail. The trail climbed and took a turn, and right after the turn there stood a huge banyan tree with vines hanging down everywhere under its huge top. It loomed up on the side of a hill, silent and still, looking like a gigantic dark jellyfish-kind of monster. We didn't care to test the long straggly vines and play Tarzan; we passed the banyan tree quickly. If the tree had been in a less hostile environment, we would've run up to the tree and swung on the vines.

Then the trail started descending, it was covered with needles from shaggy ironwood trees and there was a mint-like scent in the air, probably from the guava bushes scattered about. We came upon a broken bird bath and further down the trail we found a miniature pagoda, made out of concrete.

"Das dah Japanee church!" Georgie exclaimed.

"Yeah, man!" Davey said.

We surrounded the pagoda. It was set on a square concrete slab, covered with bird crap and dark green moss and was as tall as me.

Davey said, "So where the treasure?"

Georgie looked at the map. "The map say suppose to be here. Look. The 'x' mark right next to dah Japanee church. Look."

The 'x' mark was to the left of the pagoda. We looked there, but all we found were a rotten guava, pine cones and a lot of pine needles. No treasure.

"You sure you no have the map upside down?" Willy said.

"Go look den," Georgie said.

"Das what the map says," I added.

We looked to the right of the pagoda, behind it, in front of it. We raked up the rubbish on the ground and gathered it all in one pile. We dug shallow holes with pointed sticks into the ground. Then we sifted through the rubbish. Still, nothing.

"I t'ink Chunky playing one big joke on us," Willy finally said. We were sitting around the pagoda, slapping away the mosquitoes.

"Yeah, I t'ink so," I said.

"But wasn't one joke on us," Georgie said, "was suppose to be fo' Damien cause was Damien's map."

We agreed.

"But we dah ones getting one kick in dah 'okole," Willy said. "Was yo' fault, Georgie. You dah one wen show us dah map."

"Eh, I nevah know," Georgie said bitterly.

"Yeah, was yo' fault," I said.

"Eh, I nevah tell you folks go find the treasure," Georgie said defensively. "Was you guys fault believe in the map."

Davey got up and looked at the pagoda. Then he kneeled and squeezed his hand into a narrow opening. He brought his hand out clutching a wad of wet paper.

"Whas that?" I asked.

"Huh?" Georgie said.

"That . . . what you got, Davey?" I asked.

We got up. Davey began carefully opening up the folded piece of paper, wet from the rain and a bit muddy. The folds of the paper broke apart. There was something written on the paper, we could see that ink was diffused in the paper by the moisture. Davey laid out the bits of paper on the ground, fitting the pieces together, and though the ink was blurred, we still could make out the words. The message read: "Whop yor jaws Damien."

"You see! Was one big joke!" Willy said, proud that he had stated his premonition before this.

"You see, wasn't me," Georgie said. "Dis was suppose to be fo' Damien."

But I was disappointed. We were all disappointed. We looked silently at the bits of paper that Chunky had written to his "good" friend, Damien. We looked around at the trees and bush, which were still and quiet, as if listening to our thoughts. Willy suggested we leave. We left the note on the ground. Georgie folded the map and put it back in his pocket. Single file, this time with me leading the pack, we went down the trail, our ears sensitive to the listening trees and to the silence and to an occasional leaf-rustling wind, but not as afraid as when we first came up.

We saw Damien sitting in the front yard of his house, throwing small stones into the road. He saw us coming and stopped throwing for a moment, then started again. When we came near enough to hear, he said sarcastically, "What you guys looking at?"

I told myself that I was looking at one big fat crybaby. But I didn't dare say that.

Damien started throwing stones at our feet. We continued walking, giving him stink eye, but making sure we didn't stare at him too long. He kept on throwing the stones at us. He started laughing at us. He threw a stone that struck Davey's head squarely. That's when Davey stopped, turned around, and shouted at Damien with the angriest words I ever heard him say. Right then and there, I thought my ass was grass.

"You sucken Damien!" Davey shouted. "You bettah quit that, or we going broke yo' head!"

Damien, stunned at Davey's sudden, unexpected outburst, got up, throwing down a handful of small stones. "What you said, you punk?" he said, with a terrible mad streak in his eyes.

"You heard what I said," Davey said. "Punk."

Damien ran to us. My legs suddenly turned like jelly; if I tried to run, my legs wouldn't have carried me. Terrified, I looked at Willy and Georgie and they, too, were scared. I saw Willy looking at Damien's house for Damien's brother, or brothers, to pile out and attack us with their big knuckles. I felt very small that moment, Willy and Georgie looked very small, too. Damien came up to Davey and said, "What you said, punk?" Davey's legs were shaking, and before he could answer, Damien gave him a tremendous shove and Davey flew backwards and landed on his elbows and 'okole on the asphalt. "What you called me, you punk Davey?"

Davey was near to crying, his eyes were moistening. Damien lorded it over him like the bully he was, he feigned a kick at Davey, making Davey wince with this helpless look on his face and shield himself with a scraped arm.

Then, something came over me, Georgie, and Willy. I can't explain what exactly it was. It might have been because our friend (my friend and cousin) needed help; he looked so desperately weak fallen on the ground, ready to accept one of the many beatings we suffered as a group. Or perhaps it was the anger and disappointment of finding no treasure, having to go into a dangerous and spooky place like Friendship Garden on a wild goose chase. Or maybe it was knowing that Chunky was not around to back Damien up. And maybe it was also because we had read that note and somehow realized that Chunky and Damien were never that tight as friends, they had a common denominator, being bullies, but that was it. And maybe it was also because we saw the other side of Damien, the cry-baby, something we thought we'd never see. Or maybe it was because we were sick and tired of being picked on again.

Maybe it was all the reasons above.

But whatever the reason, or reasons, Georgie and Willy and me all at once pounced on Damien, punching him and pushing him and knocking him to the ground. My fist connected on his mouth and I felt the bite of his teeth and the warmth of his saliva. He started to bleed from the mouth, though I don't think it was my fist that did it because I didn't punch him that hard; in his surprise, he must have bit himself on the lip or tongue. But the blood was pouring from his mouth and suddenly we all felt like victors. For a long moment, Damien was on the ground, looking up at us with the eyes of a scaredy-cat. Davey got up and came between us and started yelling at him that he'd better watch out or we'll bust his ass some more. Damien got up fast and shakily, retreating to his yard. He turned and started yelling at us, "You bettah watch out or I going call my bruddah come beat you guys up!"

Davey shouted, "Whop yo' jaws, Damien!"

We started yelling at him in unison while holding our jaws, "Whop yo' jaws, Damien! Whop yo' jaws! Whop yo' jaws!" We laughed. Then, from inside the house, came the deep voice yelling at Damien. "Damien! Get yo' ass in the house!"

We continued down the street, mimicking Damien's frail remark, laughing in pure abandonment, repeating our rallying cry over and over again, loudly, getting so wrapped up in our celebration that the driver in the car behind us had to wail his horn for a long burst before we realized we were blocking his path.

A couple of weeks later we started school again. But what started as a dreary, empty-feeling summer, ended on a nice high note for us. Damien never bossed us around again. He was a grade above us so we never saw him much in school anyway, and even around the neighborhood he never came around our territory anymore.

It wasn't until school was in its fourth or fifth month and in the beginning of the rainy winter season when we went back to Chunky's house. We thought we would never go back there, but we did because—though long months had passed—we harbored a guilty feeling that we had something of Chunky's that rightfully belonged to his grandmother. So we went down to the house—me, Georgie and Willy. (Davey had caught a cold from school and hadn't gone to class for a week.) And Georgie brought that piece of paper of a map.

The road was full of muddy potholes and we played a game of going between them and jumping over the biggest ones. Willy fell in one and soaked his pants in the yellowish clay mud. But we were all muddy anyway so that didn't really matter. When we got close to the house we became cautious for the dogs, but the dogs weren't barking, even when we got to the front steps of the house. In fact, we didn't see one dog there. The house looked deserted. We knocked on the door and waited. There was no answer. We knocked again, then decided to leave the map on the front steps and go.

Just as we were a dozen steps away from the front porch, the door opened and we heard the voice of Chunky's grandmother. "Chunky? Is you?" she said. Her voice was old and withered and thin and breaking. She squinted her eyes. Her hair was all white; she had gotten very old in the short time since we last saw her. She was almost unrecognizable. "Who's dat? Rose?"

"No," I said. "We . . . we . . . Chunky's friends."

She looked in our direction with a perturbed look. Then a dry weak smile came to her face. "Oh . . . you Chunky's friends. Yeah-yeah. Come heah." She waved us to come.

We moved slowly, confused about what she had said.

"Wait right heah," she said to us when we got to the bottom of the porch steps. She disappeared inside for a moment or two, then reappeared with a small cardboard box. She offered the box to us. Georgie went up the steps and took it from her. She said, "Chunky tell me geev dis box to you folks. He say he not going use 'em anymo'."

We thanked her without looking what was inside it. Then she closed the door without saying another word.

We left. We decided to open the box, which was heavy and all taped up, at my house since my house was the closest and we didn't want to open it up down there because of the mud. When we opened the box we found a note and the box filled with ball bearings—two of which I knew were mine—and many beautiful glass marbles. We looked further in the box and found ten dollars and a thick stack of baseball cards and five complete Martian card collections. There were a few comic books on the bottom of the box, too.

Then we unfolded the note and read it, and even till today, I don't know what it meant or why it was there. The note read: "Sorry."

BROKEN DREAM
Bronson Wayne Kealiikoa Rivera

My dad drives the hauler truck
for Waialua Sugar Company.
I want to drive a big hauler truck like my dad
when I grow up.
I like to hear it rumble by my house.
I like the sweet smell of burnt sugar cane.
But the sugar company will close down
in July, 1996.
I can never drive a big hauler truck
for Waialua Sugar Company
like my dad.
Ever.

YOU WOULD CRY TO SEE WAIĀKEA TOWN
Graham Salisbury

I'd never really thought much about my mother, I suppose because I never knew her. She died a month after I was born, from a small, unknown blood clot in her brain. Dad told me about it once when I was younger. Other than that, though, no one ever mentioned her. Except Aunty Pearl, and then only when she seemed to think I needed to hear about her. I knew her only as "your mama."

She wasn't a dead person. She was a myth, and sometimes a dream. But she wasn't *dead*. I knew nothing at all of death. I never gave it any thought, until I was twelve. No one I ever knew had died.

Then one day when I was walking up to Boy's house in the middle of a blistering hot road, jumping from one broken white line to the next, trying to keep my feet from burning, I found my mind racing with thoughts.

What is *dead*?

Who was *your mama*?

And then for no apparent reason I'd switch to thinking about Dad, or Uncle Raz, or Uncle Harley and Aunty Pearl, and even Boy.

And Grampa Lynn.

He was starting to get old. I knew that but never put much effort into understanding what it meant. Life simply *was*. But was it?

As the days went on Grampa Lynn, I think, could sense that I was wrestling with that question. He didn't give me any answers because there weren't any, but he kept an eye on me just in case my thinking took too tight a grip.

I didn't realize that something in me was changing until one summer night sitting alone in my room under the pale yellow glow of the lamp by my bed. It was the year after statehood, in the days we were all trying to get used to not seeing *Hawaii, T.H.* on the front of the mail. I was looking through a stack of *Life* magazines that Aunty Pearl had given me. "Here," she'd said. "See what the world is doing."

A moth was batting itself around in the lamp shade and the flickering shadow on the pages was beginning to bother me. Slowly it occurred to me that I should catch it and smash it. That's what Dad would have done. I put down the magazines and reached under the shade and captured the moth in the cup of my hand. The fluttering would stop when I squeezed.

But it didn't stop, because I carried the moth all the way out to the screen door and sent it off into the warm, Kona night alive. One of Dad's hunting dogs, who Dad kept roped near the front of the house, raised his head and we both watched the moth head straight for the outside yard light.

I went back to my room and put the magazines away and just sat there thinking about the moth. I could have rid the world of another insect as Dad had convinced me was the correct thing to do. And I would have, yet I didn't.

It's the girl.

It was because of what happened on May 23rd.

Without consciously pursuing it, I had slowly begun to concede that everything dies, that life ends at some point for everything. Even for me.

May 22nd was a Sunday. Uncle Raz was in Honolulu buying new Penn Senator reels for his boat, and Dad and Uncle Harley had gone to Hilo in the ice truck to sell fish. Since they'd planned to spend the night in Hilo I stayed at Boy's house. Aunty Pearl soaked a pile of meat sticks in teriyaki and Boy and I cooked them outside on the hibachi. We sat on upside-down fish buckets and watched the sky lose its color while we poked at the hot coals. The heavy cloud overcast of the afternoon was breaking up and in the gaps I could see stars beginning to come alive. And through the spaces in the trees I could see down the hill toward the ocean and out to Keāhole light, and I understood why Uncle Harley and Aunty Pearl sat out on the porch every night.

Back in the house Aunty Pearl was in a remembering mood. She sat at the kitchen table listening to the one Honolulu radio station we could get in Kona and looking at some photos in an old album.

"Boys, come see these old pictures," she said after we'd eaten and were getting restless for something to do. We sat opposite her at the table which was more like a booth at a restaurant. The chairs moved around but the table was nailed to the floor and to the wall just under the window. It was covered by a plastic blue and white table cloth.

"Look at this," she said to Boy. She smiled and shook her head. "Here's Daddy when he was just a little older than you. What a lolo that boy was."

She turned the album around and there was Uncle Harley waving at the camera with a stick fish in his mouth. It shot out from both sides of his face, about half a foot on each side. He looked darker then, though it was hard to be sure with an old black and white photograph. Boy laughed at his father.

"Was he really that crazy?" he asked Aunty Pearl.

"Crazy! That was *normal* for him. He was always showing off for me. I never loved anyone but that silly boy there with the stick fish."

She turned the album back around to face her.

"Show Sonny the one where he's swimming with the cow," said Boy.

"Hah! Gotta go way back for that one." Aunty Pearl flipped the pages back toward the beginning.

"Here it is. There's Daddy by the cow, and there," she said to me, pointing to a boy standing on the sand looking out at the swimming cow, "is *your* daddy."

It could have been any boy for all I could tell by the picture, but I took her word for it. There they were, like me and Boy, Dad and Uncle Harley watching the Parker Ranch cowboys swim the cows to the *Humuʻula*. Uncle Harley was swimming along with the cowboy and his cow, just a black dot of a head in the water.

"I didn't even know cows could swim," I said.

"They swim good," said Aunty Pearl.

I flipped through the pages and stopped when I found a picture of Dad with his arm around my mother. I'd seen pictures of her before, but Dad never kept any around the house, at least not that I was aware of.

"Your mama was a beautiful girl, Sonny. They were very happy."

They must have been about eighteen or nineteen when the picture was taken. They were on the pier. A sampan was behind them, and the Palace in the trees beyond was on the right, across the bay. Dad was thinner, but not as muscular as now.

Aunty Pearl must have sensed the wheels turning in my mind as I looked at the picture.

"Your daddy still misses her," she said. "It's hard even now for him to talk about her."

I felt bad for Dad but I couldn't feel his sadness. My mother was just a name and a few photographs that held no life. She was a part of Aunty Pearl's time, and of Dad's time. I felt that I should feel something, a hurt or a sadness. But I couldn't. I didn't.

Later, Boy and I went into his room and played Monopoly until we fell asleep.

When I awoke the next morning it felt as if something was off. I sat up and looked over at Boy across the room. He was still asleep. The sky through the small, rectangular window was full of grey clouds, a heavy-looking morning. There were no sounds—no dogs, no birds, no nothing. When I looked at Boy's electric clock I decided to wake him. It was frozen at 1:05.

Boy sat upright when I tapped his shoulder.

"Something's up," I said. His eyes were both wild and blank-looking at the same time. Uncle Harley had trained him well. No one in our family ever took more than a few seconds to get out of bed once awakened.

"What, what?" he asked, coming out of his sleep.

"I don't know, but the clock stopped in the middle of the night and the sky's dark. Maybe a big storm."

Boy tried the lamp, but it was out too. I followed him into the kitchen. It was strangely dark, and none of the switches worked there either. But what was strangest of all was that Aunty Pearl wasn't there. She was always up before us.

After a little more prowling around we found her sitting outside on the porch, listening to a small transistor radio. The voice coming through was small and covered with static. When she saw us she put her finger to her lips. We sat down on either side of her.

The reception may have been bad but there was no mistaking the news: a series of powerful tidal waves had hit the islands, but the worst had devastated the coastal areas of Hilo. My very first thought was of Dad at the fish market in Waiākea Town. It was right there at the mouth of the Wailoa River, as close to the ocean as it gets.

The reporter went on, sounding excited and a little shocked himself. The force of the big wave was tremendous, he said, and at least 26 bodies had been found. And then, coming sharply through the raspy speaker he said, "You would cry to see Waiākea Town . . . not one wall is left."

I jumped to my feet. He was there. Right there, in Waiākea Town.

Aunty Pearl and Boy sat side by side looking ashen. I started pacing, and fidgeting. I didn't know what to do. None of us knew what to do. The vision of Dad and Uncle Harley dead was too big.

Aunty Pearl finally spoke.

"Boy, take the Jeep. Go get grampa."

Now I was really worried. Boy was thirteen, only a year older than me, and never had Aunty Pearl consented to his driving Uncle Harley's hunting Jeep, even though she knew both he and I could handle it.

"Go through the pastures and stay off Hualālai Road," she said. We couldn't call Grampa Lynn because the phone was out. Everything was out.

It took a few minutes to get the Jeep going because it had been sitting so long. But Uncle Harley always parked it on a hill so he could kick-start it if the battery was down. I pushed and Boy kicked and got it going. We went uphill, through the tangled jungle of Christmas berry and towering mango trees. The road was rocky and overgrown, usually only getting foot use by cows and horses, and a couple of goats.

Boy drove in low gear and four-wheel drive through Sylva's pasture, and then Matsunaga's, and finally to the lower corner of Grampa Lynn's long, rectangular coffee orchard. Boy sat forward in the seat with both hands on the wheel, and chin pointing up to get his eyes high enough to see the road.

Neither of us spoke. I think we were both afraid to speak the things we imagined about our fathers. Life without Dad was something I'd never given an ounce of thought to. Now I was being forced into it, like when I was five and Dad dropped me over the side of the skiff and told me to swim.

Tutu Max filled the doorway when we drove into the yard, as if she'd known we'd be coming. She didn't say a word about Boy driving the Jeep. I got the feeling she had already heard about Hilo.

"Come inside," she said, holding open the screen door. "Grampa listening to the radio."

The news was still pretty much the same, except for a report from a pilot who said that the new cars stored at I. Kitagawa yard were tossed about like toys and that he saw two houses floating in Hilo Bay.

"Mama said to get you."

Grampa Lynn nodded and went to the back porch to get his rubber boots. It wasn't raining, but everything was still wet from the night.

Tutu Max gave us each a piece of coffee cake and a hug. As always, she seemed to know exactly what was on our minds. But this time it made me feel a little better. Tutu Max and Grampa Lynn were the fixed unchanging parts of the human landscape that surrounded me.

"Your daddys will be okay," she said. "They had warnings four hours before the first wave."

That bit of news gave me the first glimpse of relief I'd felt that morning. Still, I wanted to see Dad standing in front of me to be sure.

Grampa Lynn followed us out to the Jeep. He wasn't a whole lot taller than Boy, a thin, bony man as tough as ironwood, and as much the opposite in body from Tutu Max as a man could get. In his worn khaki shirt and khaki pants tucked into black rubber boots he looked more like he was getting ready to pick coffee than the man who was going to help us figure out what to do about the morning news.

Boy hesitated when we got to the Jeep, not knowing if he or Grampa Lynn should do the driving. This was a completely new situation.

"Well, what you waiting for?" said Grampa Lynn. For the first time that morning Boy smiled. Grampa Lynn kept his same old worn-out look and climbed into the front, letting Boy drive. I jumped into the seat behind them and bounced back to Boy's house with the engine growling and spitting, and seats squeaking all the way down.

Boy and I were uneasy in a deep-rooted way and Aunty Pearl wasn't much better off. Grampa Lynn wasted no time gathering in the situation and coming up with a plan.

"Only one way to know for sure—go find 'em. Could be days before they get the phones back. And if they're in trouble . . . ." It wasn't necessary to finish the sentence.

Within a half hour Grampa Lynn was driving Boy and me down to Kailua in the Jeep to see what we could find out before heading over to Hilo on the other side of the island.

Even in Kailua all the electricity was out, as, we soon discovered, was the electricity all over the island. In Kailua the waves had been more like an extremely high tide than a tidal wave. Most of the damage was done on the grounds of the hotels close to the ocean, the King Kam, the Kona Inn, and Wai'aka Lodge.

The fishing boats were all at their moorings in the bay, and their skippers were standing around in groups on the pier talking about the wave and what had happened in Hilo. No one had any first-hand news, not even by ship-to-shore radio.

In the King Kam dining room, which was just above the small beach next to the pier, a hotel crew was cleaning up the mess of tables and chairs and mopping out the water that had flowed all the way through and out into the main lobby.

We did learn some new things, though. The waves, *tsunamis* they were calling them, a word I'd never heard before, were set off by a big earthquake in Chile. There were four or five of them, one of them so huge that it ran through lower Hilo like a bulldozer scraping buildings off the face of the earth. No one knew how many, but there were a lot of people killed because they didn't believe a wave was coming.

We left Kailua and drove up Palani Road and headed north to the saddle road between Mauna Loa and Mauna Kea and the two-hour drive over the top of the island.

It was cloudy and wet in Hilo, which wasn't particularly unusual, but the streets were jammed with cars. The police and National Guard had the lower section of town completely blocked off. It would have been impossible to drive anything but a tractor through Mamo Street, which was little more than a muddy pile of rubble, like an open wound on a dazed victim.

Though we'd brought sweatshirts along we sat huddling forward in the Jeep with arms crossed, hugging ourselves. Except for Grampa Lynn. Nothing seemed to bother him. If it did, anyway, I couldn't tell. He was a lot like Dad that way, quiet and hard to read.

We were trying to get down to the fish market, but the way we usually went, along the shore line on Kamehameha Avenue, past the Cow Palace, was closed down. And the backstreets were too thick with cars and people caught up in the confusion. It took an hour just to go the two or three miles to the back end of the Wailoa River. We could have *walked* faster than we drove.

When driving became all but ridiculous Grampa Lynn pulled the Jeep off the road and drove into a field of knee-high grass to a clump of hao trees, about fifty feet from the road.

"We walk from here," he said. Boy and I jumped out of the Jeep without a thought. After a couple of hours on the road it felt great to move around. It was a little after noon, only six or seven hours after the wave had hit Hilo. The wave. Every time I thought of it a rush of dread would invade my stomach.

Grampa Lynn led us through a tangled mess of high, wet grass and out onto an old road, which went down toward the Waiākea Town area. But we didn't get very far. The street began to get vague, lost in mud and every imaginable kind of debris. What clinched it, though, were the soldiers.

Every street into the area was blocked off by men in Army ponchos, and patrols wandered the edges of destruction while others searched the rubble. Getting down into Waiākea Town began to look hopeless.

"Can't go in there," one of the guards told us.

"Listen," Grampa Lynn said calmly, "I got two boys here whose fathers were in Waiākea last night. We don't know if they're dead or alive. We gotta find them."

"If they were in there last night you ain't got much hope," said the guard, sounding tired, as if he'd been there for days. "But if they listened to the warning last night they're probably okay. Go check the intermediate school. They set up an emergency shelter there."

The two guards loomed over us with somber faces set back into the hoods of their ponchos. It looked as if it was as far as we'd be going.

We retreated into the long grass after being turned away.

But then Grampa Lynn cut back down toward the ocean, plowing through the wet California grass on a route that paralleled the road. He was never one to give up on a plan. If he wanted in, he'd get in. And he did, with Boy and me close behind.

When we finally ran into the Wailoa River the queasiness in my stomach became constant. We were still blocks from shore but the rubble in the river was incredible—splintered buildings, boulders, cars, bent and twisted steel beams, dead fish and cane trash. And a sampan as long as Dad's with its red hull to the sky.

We didn't get far before being forced out of the grass by the debris. There were men with shovels, axes, crowbars, hoes and ropes working in heaps of mud and boards. No guards bothered us once we were inside the barricaded area. It soon became apparent that they were as confused and overwhelmed as anyone else. Too little time had passed.

From four blocks away I could see where the fish market had once been. Waiākea Town, which had bordered it on three sides like the hands on an oyster around its pearl, was gone. Not damaged, gone. A whole town, flattened and pushed up into the heel of the river, splintered and shoved inland in pieces.

The mouth of the river, now barren on the edge of the choppy, grey ocean, and the shapes of the hills in the distance on the far side of Hilo Bay, now stood like unrecognizable landmarks, ghosts of another time. Only the crescent-shaped concrete bridge over the river assured me that the vacant cement pads where buildings had been, and the steel parking meters bent flat to the sidewalks were what we had come to find. Only now there was no fish market where we could look for Dad and Uncle Harley, no fishing supply stores or saimin shops where they might be.

"No need to go any further," Grampa Lynn finally said out of the silence that lay over us like merciful sleep. "Better we help, and ask questions."

Three men and a woman were nearby, the men pulling and prying tangled boards apart, trying to get down into the pile to something within it. The woman stood as if in a trance, eyes staring blankly into the mess, arms folded and still as stone. Grampa Lynn went over to help.

Boy and I followed slowly. Like innocent fools we'd come to Hilo completely unprepared, in all respects. But now the most present manifestation of our foolishness was our bare feet. Suspended in the mud, and tangled within it, were nails jutting from splintered boards, chunks of broken glass, and sharp objects. I tested each foothold slowly, pushing down into the muck looking for something solid to step on. Both Boy and I sliced our feet in several places but didn't know it until later, after we'd cleaned off the mud from a faucet at the intermediate school.

"He's okay," I said as if out of a dream, and went on in my mind thinking about Dad. If there'd been a warning, as the guard had said there was, he would have listened. He wasn't a foolish man, he would have listened.

Boy looked over at me, his face drawn and looking as anxious as I felt. In all the time we'd spent together growing up as cousins who might as well have been brothers, I'd never seen a more somber look on his face. It was as if he'd already given in to the worst, and now looked at me for a final shred of hope.

Then he looked away and continued picking his way through the debris.

Off to my left was a pile of cars, four of them, bent and intertwined into a silent steel sculpture. In one glance I could see the power of an ocean that had moved beyond its containment.

All that I saw and felt in those first few moments came to me in small, manageable scenes, broken down into simplified doses that I was able to accept. It was nothing I'd thought out on my own, but instinct moved me into a matter-of-factness, a way of being that allowed me to accept everything I saw and thought as simply being the way it was. Dad and Uncle Harley were *neither* dead nor alive, they simply were—somewhere, they were. But *where?*

Boy and I and Grampa Lynn shifted boards around alongside the three men in the silence they'd chosen to work in. One of them looked up and nodded, then put his head down and went on digging. Too much had happened, I thought later, for words to have carried much comfort.

But we had to ask questions. Grampa Lynn broke the silent trance slowly, and thoughtfully. Our need for information was as great as their need for silence.

"Did you have warning?" Grampa Lynn finally said to one of the men.

"Plenty warning," the man answered, offering no more.

We continued to pull trash from the pile. Then, minutes later, the man went on.

"Four hours, about, between the sirens and the waves. Some people never left. Some came back just before they hit, thinking it was a false alarm. We've had them before."

Grampa Lynn left it at that. There was no more they could say that would help us find Dad and Uncle Harley. The little they'd said, though, filled me with the belief that no harm had come to them. If Dad had known there was a tidal wave coming, he'd move. I was positive he'd move.

For the next hour we made slow progress through small groups of residents who were allowed within the barricaded area, asking questions here and there, learning a little more each time. From a policeman we learned that they were still finding people, dead and alive, in the piles of debris. I kept thinking of my feet. If he'd known that below the shin-deep muck Boy and I were barefoot he'd probably have sent us out of the area immediately.

As it was, he didn't like anyone our age in there anyway. Only Grampa Lynn's telling him of our search softened him.

As we retreated back in the direction of the Jeep the three of us drifted apart. I felt better alone with my thoughts, as, I suppose, did Boy and Grampa Lynn. In the river I saw three more half-sunk sampans. They should have taken them out and dealt with the waves at sea, I thought.

Then, in the midst of that thought, the myth I'd begun to build around the notion of everything being all right with Dad burst and fell away like sand in the tide.

Looking down for a safe place to step, I saw a small, muddy foot. I stood suspended over it in the same way Boy's electric clock stood frozen between seconds on the table by his bed. I stared at it, focused on it, and understood what it was. But I moved sluggishly, realization coming slowly from somewhere far away, like the sound of a dump truck coming down the hill in Kona somewhere out of view in the jungle and curves of the road. And then the truck blasts by, blowing dust and pebbles out both sides as it passes. When the reality of the foot hit me something inside me moved, changed. Escaped.

Foot. Small, human.

Child.

It rose just inches from the mud, as hidden from view as a black crab on the rocks by the sea. I looked down on it, unable to think.

Boy and Grampa Lynn moved on ahead of me unaware of my discovery. It must have been a full minute before I could find the word under the confusion I was feeling. It came out twice, once spoken, once shouted.

"Wait . . . Wait!"

Boy and Grampa Lynn turned in unison and looked back. I knelt down into the mud and started to move the rocks and cane trash and debris from around the delicate foot.

There was no merciful time interval, no soft voice and tender words, no nice way of telling me that the foot belonged to a dead child. My mind raced, going nowhere, then seemed to calm as I felt a connection to this young human that I had found. There's a child under this mess with its mouth full of mud. A person younger than me who is no longer alive. Somewhere someone is searching, hoping. Or maybe lying nearby, or under my feet.

Boy and Grampa Lynn came back and stood over me. I looked up at Grampa Lynn. His face, usually steady and expressionless, had softened. There was a warmth in it, and a sadness.

"Oh, no . . ." he said quietly, kneeling down at my side. That's all he said. There was no more to say.

The three of us moved the debris away and scooped aside the thickening mud around the body, handful by handful until we freed her—a small, thin girl, about seven years old.

I thought of the woman of stone staring coldly into the rubble as the three men dug into it and wondered if this is what they'd been looking for. Boy and I stayed with the body until Grampa Lynn came back with two policemen.

After they carried her away and we were once again alone, the memory of the small foot emerging from the mud began to consume me. I needed more than anything else in the world to see Dad. To stand beside him. To have him rest his hand on my shoulder, and to ask him why.

Thoughts raced around in my mind like disturbed ants, confused and without direction. My vision blurred as we made our way back through the deep grass to the Jeep. Grampa Lynn stayed back with me and walked with his hand on my back. He spoke only once, and with a tenderness I'd never heard before, from anyone.

"It is as it should be, Sonny. The living have no edge over the dead. She does not feel your pain."

When we got near the Jeep, Boy, who'd gone on ahead of us, looked back at me and Grampa Lynn. He smiled and started jumping up and down in some kind of celebration, but putting also a finger to his lips.

"It's Harley," said Grampa Lynn. He too seemed happy, relieved I think, that we'd finally made contact.

And it *was* Uncle Harley. He was sitting in the driver's seat of the Jeep with his arms crossed, asleep. He was alone. Still following Boy we crept like cats until we stood inches away. Grampa Lynn looked at Boy for the next move.

Boy pulled out a long strand of grass and toyed with Uncle Harley's ear. Uncle Harley batted away at it with his eyes closed, until Boy's laughing broke the spell. The lightness was as welcome as a white puffy shade cloud on a hot day, a huge release that helped to separate me from the sight of the dead child.

"Sonabadingding . . . . What the hell are you lolos doing here?" said Uncle Harley, coming alive in the Jeep.

"Looking for you," said Boy. He looked so relieved to have found his father that I, too, released some tension. Seeing Uncle Harley sitting there, so calm and familiar, gave me great peace. I knew Dad was all right.

"You buggers," he said, sounding angry, but clearly pleased to see us. "Raymond and I were walking up to the school when I saw the Jeep in the grass. I thought I was going nuts, it was *my* Jeep! But with everything else going on around here I said, why not? Sonny," he added, looking at me, "Raymond is okay. No worry."

"I knew that the minute I saw you sleeping in the Jeep," I said. "Where is he?"

"Meeting. Suisan and some people from Tuna Packers wanted to get together with the fishermen. Raymond went while I waited to see who'd show up here. Big problems. No ice to ice fish, the ice plant is gone. And they got to clean out the river so the boats can get back in. At least those that went out in the first place."

Grampa Lynn humphed.

Boy told Uncle Harley that we knew about the wave from the transistor. Kona was blacked out, and the phone was dead. He told him Aunty Pearl was worried. So were we.

Uncle Harley got out of the Jeep and put his arms around me and Boy.

"I know," he said. "I tried to call. We went up the hill when we heard the siren. Half the people just stayed in their houses waiting for another warning or something."

"Did you see the wave?" asked Boy.

"No, but we heard it. There was more than one wave, but the big one came in with a roaring sound, first like hissing, then rushing louder and louder. Then the whole town went black. Took out Waiākea completely."

"We saw," said Grampa Lynn.

For a minute it was as quiet as a lava tube. What could we say anyway? It was one of those times when only thoughts had a chance of making sense of it.

"Let's go get Raymond."

Uncle Harley drove us out of the grass in low gear, the Jeep jerking over the uneven ground, feeling as if we were climbing through the cow trails of Hualālai pig hunting, or picking our way over crushed lava to some secret fishing spot along the south Kona coast. I seemed to be reaching back into the past for something secure, something I could understand, wanting to shake the memory of the muddy body of the child from my mind forever.

Seeing Dad emerge in a long line of fishermen flowing out from their meeting, down the wooden steps of a classroom at the school, was a moment I'll never forget. Shorts and old sweatshirt, some papers from the meeting rolled up into a small tube in his hand, a Kona fisherman all the way, unlike the Hilo guys in their long khaki pants and jeans.

"Hi, son," he said calmly, as if nothing at all had happened. The word "son" sank far into my chest like an anchor sent into the deep, rich depths of a calm sea.

"We were worried," I said.

"Thanks." He put his hand on my shoulder and squeezed, the greatest show of physical love he was able to give. But just then, it was all that was necessary.

Dad and Uncle Harley said they were going to stay in Hilo for a few more days to help with the ice problem. Grampa Lynn fired up the Jeep. Uncle Harley slapped his palm on the hood and said, "Best damn Jeep on the island." We started back to Kona, taking it easy, saying little.

The old pock-marked saddle road was still damp, but the rain had passed and patches of clear sky worked their way into the mist and low clouds of the high country. Dusk was closing in and the air swirling around us in the Jeep was getting colder.

Just above Waiki'i Grampa Lynn pulled the Jeep off the road. It was dark by then, and cold. Boy had curled up in the back seat under a blanket Uncle Harley had gotten from the Red Cross in Hilo.

Grampa Lynn looked over at me. "Want to drive? Plenty dark. No police around here. No *anybody* around here," he added. And that was a fact. We hadn't passed a car since we left Hilo.

"Sure, . . ." I said, surprised, and a little hesitant. I think he sensed my wavering and added, "Get over here . . . do you some good."

I traded places with him and pulled Uncle Harley's old hunting Jeep back out onto the road, following the beams slowly into the night. I sat up on the edge of the seat holding the wheel with both hands, shifting gears in jerks, and feeling the warmth of the engine on the metal floorboard under my scratched and cut feet.

The clouds had cleared and a zillion stars filled the blackness around me, far from the lights of any human presence. I squinted over at Grampa Lynn when I reached the stop sign at the junction where the saddle road meets Māmalahoa. He was asleep, or just sitting there like Uncle Harley had been, with his arms crossed and his eyes closed.

I sat thinking at the stop sign with the engine idling, nothing in sight except the stars and the two beams of light in front of me. I was twelve years old, driving my cousin and my grandfather home on the main road in pitch black, I'd seen a dead girl, and feared for my father's life. Somehow being behind the wheel of the Jeep felt right, as if I could control something in my life, if only for an hour or so. And the open spaces, on all sides and above me, endlessly into the stars, seemed to have, like silence and the soothing vibration of the Jeep pushing through the night, the power to lift the weight I felt inside. Maybe that's why Dad was a fisherman. Maybe that's why the two of us spent so much time alone.

I drove around Mauna Loa and across the island highlands, now passing several cars and trucks, and all the way to Grampa Lynn's doorstep before he opened his eyes. At least as far as I could tell. I pulled into the yard and left the engine running. He sat there in the Jeep yawning and rubbing the stubble on his cheeks. His face was green in the light coming from the kitchen porch. He sighed and got out of the Jeep slowly, playing the part of an old man much more than I knew he needed to.

"You okay, 'Ōmilu?" he asked.

"I'm okay, Grampa."

He went into the house and closed the door without turning around to wave. The light on the porch went off and I drove down into the thick, black coffee grove as Boy climbed groggily into the front seat.

Grampa Lynn had called me 'Ōmilu, a term he used sparingly, and it meant a lot to me to be compared to the ulua, a fish that will give any fisherman a tough, two-fisted battle.

He knew, Grampa Lynn knew, what an hour behind the wheel of an old Jeep on a dark, winding road through an immense landscape of silent black sky and stars could do for a human spirit, and give a mind with too many thoughts.

ADAGIO
Cathy Song

She lifts her hands
like sea gulls above the keys,
the stubborn teeth of notes
she must sink and rise into,
giving herself to music.
Music met most days with resistance,
small fingers confined to a drill of steps.
Every good boy does fine.
All cows eat grass.

This is going nowhere,
I can hear her sigh.
I know.
I've been there.
I can see where I jumped
into air, mid-flight
up those stairs, places
where I played hooky,
shot pool, smoked a cigarette.
Passage where Mrs. Dorothy B. Chang scribbled
Adagio! Slow down!, underscored *Control!*
Another week without a gold star
to stick in the margins
like a pin on my father's lapel.

Silence, a sleeve I wanted to pull myself through,
my head, spun wire, a beehive,
reeling from the racket swarm of black notes,
undecipherable
as the algebra I was plagued with that year.

I want to play like you,
says my daughter: Fast and Furious.
Already I can hear it.

Heart and Soul, Chopsticks and Liberace.
Her schoolbag a heap on the floor,
her hair bow a limp corsage.
She wants to give herself to music
if the giving can be as uncomplicated
as the wanting will let her have it.

What do I want?
Someone to sing to me in the hour before supper?
Long hours I sang for my father.
The collapsed chords,
green and sour,
chilled a quiet room.
My father thumbed the pages of the newspaper.
My mother stirred the soup, and waited.

The late afternoon light,
in the still life of memory, burnished gold—
the pitcher of water, the simple
plates set on the table, the unblemished apple.
I take the apple out of the moment
as if to place it in my daughter's hand,
good girl, good little girl.

One day after years of lessons—
the treble clef trellised like a grapevine
along the musical wire,
the notes ripening into sound
pure and sweet and round—
my father put aside his reading
and shifting in his chair,
he closed his eyes and listened.

THE GRAMMAR OF SILK
Cathy Song

On Saturdays in the morning
my mother sent me to Mrs. Umemoto's sewing school.
It was cool and airy in her basement,
pleasant—a word I choose
to use years later to describe
the long tables where we sat
and cut, pinned, and stitched,
the Singer's companionable whirr,
the crisp, clever bite of scissors
parting like silver fish a river of calico.

The school was in walking distance
to Kaimuki Dry Goods
where my mother purchased my supplies—
small cards of buttons,
zippers and rickrack packaged like licorice,
lifesaver rolls of thread
in fifty-yard lengths,
spun from spools, tough as tackle.
Seamstresses waited at the counters
like librarians to be consulted.
Pens and scissors dangled like awkward pendants
across flat chests,
a scarf of measuring tape flung across a shoulder,
time as a pincushion bristled at the wrist.
They deciphered a dress's blueprints
with an architect's keen eye.

This evidently was a sanctuary,
a place where women confined with children
conferred, consulted the oracle,
the stone tablets of the latest pattern books.
Here mothers and daughters paused in symmetry,
offered the proper reverence—

hushed murmurings for the shantung silk
which required a certain sigh,
as if it were a piece from the Ming Dynasty.

My mother knew there would be no shortcuts
and headed for the remnants,
the leftover bundles with yardage
enough for a heart-shaped pillow,
a child's dirndl, a blouse without darts.
Along the aisles
my fingertips touched the titles—
satin, tulle, velvet,
peach, lavender, pistachio,
sherbet-colored linings—
and settled for the plain brown-and-white composition
of polka dots on kettle cloth
my mother held up in triumph.

She was determined that I should sew
as if she knew what she herself was missing,
a moment when she could have come up for air—
the children asleep,
the dishes drying on the rack—
and turned on the lamp
and pulled back the curtain of sleep.
To inhabit the night,
the night as a black cloth, white paper,
a sheet of music in which she might find herself singing.

On Saturdays at Mrs. Umemoto's sewing school,
when I took my place beside the other girls,
bent my head and went to work,
my foot keeping time on the pedal,
it was to learn the charitable oblivion
of hand and mind as one—
a refuge such music affords the maker—
the pleasure of notes in perfectly measured time.

CHILDHOOD
M. Suzuki

Up in the attic
I cringe
When I accidentally kick
An old Roach Motel
And it sounds like someone just shook
A half-full box of Raisinets.

In the corner,
The perforated surface
Of the air hockey table
Is coated with a layer of dust
Like the Barbie "Airliner"
Next to it—
A vinyl, miniature section of airplane,
Complete with carrying handle
And tiny stewardess supplies.

I remember playing dolls
With my brother,
Throwing the plane
From the swing set
Like in sequels of *Airport*.
GI Joe, Barbie,
And Kojak
(Ken with his hair shaved)
Were the repeated victims
Scattered in the yard from impact.
Although GI Joe
Had kung fu grip,
He always lost his arms
Since they were easily plucked
From his sockets,
While the others,
Found in the worn, dirt groove

Beneath the swing
Or on the slant of the doghouse roof
Were fortunate
Just to be unconscious.

MY HEALER

Jean Yamasaki Toyama

Born premature and weighing barely four pounds, I caused my family great concern. Believing me prone to early arrivals and departures, they listened to my every cough and wheeze with fearful worry. "Is she still breathing? Go look!"

It was thus that I was put into the care of my grandmother, the neighborhood healer. What she had done for others, she could certainly do for me.

The first order of business was my weight. Through a careful diet she saw to it that my mother produced enough milk and daily brought it to the hospital. "Drink up, Sachi. *Nonde*." It is thanks to this care that even today I am in no danger of perishing from weightlessness.

If my mother were the first earth in which I grew, my grandmother was certainly the gardener of my new world. She nurtured and pruned me, pulled the weeds around me and protected me from the elements.

I remember her hands, her warm, healing hands. Each time I had an asthma attack she was there to silence the wheezing. A toothache? Palms on my cheeks. A cold? Pressure on my chest. She even cured my baldness— I was born without hair—by applying her spit on my pate every day for one year.

I don't know where her powers came from, but they were real.

On the left side of our house facing the mountains was a chicken coop. We all had one in those days. No one complained. The incubator for the chicks was underneath the house. The houses were raised off the ground to allow the trade winds to flow all around and cool the inside.

One day I saw my grandmother in that fresh darkness sitting on an apple crate, her hands cupped around a small, yellow fluffy ball. "Poor thing, *kawai so*," she whispered to it.

Taking notice of me she said, "It's sick, Sachi, *itai*," and extended her cupped palms toward me. "*Motsu*? Come, take it."

I stretched out my hands to clasp that quivering ball and recoiled when I saw yellow oozing from between my grandmother's fingers.
"No, *Bachan*. Dirty!" I squirmed in the priggish tones of a child who had learned too well the lessons of hygiene. "Dooodoooo!"

"No, Sachi; it's sick, *Byoki*."

My grandmother hardly ever preached at me. After all, we barely spoke the same language. But I learned on that day that there are no absolute laws. The laws of cleanliness drilled in me with "Don't touch—dirty, dirty!" were now put into the perspective of other principles, those of healing and compassion.

Our neighbor, Mrs. Toyota and her husband, the Rico Milkman, had a bedroom window facing my grandmother's. Every night we would exchange good-nights and waves before I fell asleep at my grandmother's side. By that time my sister had been born, and she had come to occupy my crib. It was Mrs. Toyota who brought that couple to see my grandmother.

I remember this couple because they came for many months. That first evening the man wore a Japanese print shirt of *kabe* silk. I stared at the expectant eyes of the orange and blue fish swimming in a background of bright yellow. I saw rainbows in those eyes. The man's shiny black hair slicked down with pomade came to a little tail in the back. The woman wore a dark dress with buttons that went from her neck to the hem. Remembering all the trouble I had with buttons, I counted them in wonder.

They were Filipino; so I was more curious than usual. As they waited in the living room for my grandmother, I sprawled on the sofa and stared at them from all angles. "Hello. Me Sachi. Who you?"

They politely ignored me. Perhaps I seemed impertinent. Perhaps I was intruding. The lady fidgeted with her hair, pulling now and then at the ends just at the nape of her neck. Her hair was simply combed, limp and lifeless. She looked sad.

"Sachi can stay over there, if she's quiet," said my grandmother when she entered, pointing to the farthest corner of the room. Apparently, Mrs. Toyota had explained everything, because they said very little. Now that I think of it, they couldn't have said very much since all three knew very little English. I listened; I didn't need to understand.

"*Onegaishimasu. Onegai.* We try two years. Nothing happen. You help, okay?" said the man. He was sitting down on the floor like a Japanese, his feet crossed beneath him. He even bowed his head once in a while as he talked. His wife quietly sat down next to him on a cushion.

"Can do? Maybe? Maybe, no can do," replied my grandmother in a mixture of pidgin and Japanese.

She then told the man in word and motion to sit on the sofa and the woman to lie on the thick blanket that she had laid out on the living room floor. The woman understood that she should remove her dress, which she did, slowly undoing each button. She folded her dress and handed it to her husband. Then she lay on her stomach.

In the meantime my grandmother prepared her healing instruments. One by one she took the transparent cups out of the khaki bag and placed them in a row next to the woman's head. Then the bottle of alcohol, the candle and the matches. The towel lay in a basin of salt water.

I loved to watch my grandmother heal and was often tempted to leave my perch to participate. But her simple "No!" was enough to keep me in my place. I was no fool.

My grandmother would place her hands on the wife's back and wipe it with the towel, then she would look at its flesh as if she were measuring a piece of cloth to decide where to lay the pattern. The pale brown mole on her nose quivered ever so slightly, as she breathed through her stuffed sinuses. She placed the larger cups just to the side of the spine and the smaller ones along the edge of the curve of the woman's back. Then she took the cups off and placed them in a certain order, assured that she could maintain the pattern.

Everything ready, she lit the candle. She poured just a little bit of alcohol in a cup, swirled it around, and emptied it into another cup. She then wiped the edge of the first cup to make sure that the alcohol wouldn't drip, applied some salt water to a spot on the lady's back, and lit the alcohol with the candle. An orange flame leaped out of the cup. The first time, the man gasped in surprise.

She immediately slapped the cup on the damp spot, and the flesh rushed in to fill the glass.

"No worry, no worry, I no hurt your *wahine*," she said.

I moved closer. So did the man. His eyes got wide; his mouth opened. But he didn't say a thing.

Slowly the dark skin in the cup turned slightly red. Our eyes fixed on the sight of flesh forced into a mound, flesh that became now only color, texture, and shape.

In the meantime the healer lit another cup. Then another and another. Soon there were five cups on that back, each with a mound of rising flesh inside. The colors ranged from the shadowy red of Japanese prints to the dark blue of tattooed hands.

I waited for the part I liked best—the removal of the cups. Only the pressure of the index finger was needed to release the vacuum. As the air rushed into the cup, there would be the surprising sound of deep slurping, something I imagined like two giants kissing. Sometimes my grandmother let me participate in the healing. I'd place my finger next to hers and feel the whoosh of the escaping vacuum.

I would lie on the blanket next to the lady and listen to the *ssmmack* —*ssmmack, ssmmack*—*ssmmack* and fall asleep to that sound and wake up in the morning in my grandmother's bed.

The couple came every day for some weeks and then every week for a while. As time passed the woman's attire brightened along with her disposition. The dark brown of the first day changed to greens, yellows, even reds. She smiled more, spoke more. One dress in particular caught my fancy. It was bright yellow with two huge white pockets off on both sides in the front below her waist. During that treatment, instead of watching the ballet of cups, I played house with my doll in the woman's pockets.

Not only did the woman's clothing change, so did her hair. Now she wore it swept up, sometimes with a green barrette or a blue one, depending on the color of her dress. On her last visit she wore one in rhinestone.

I became confused by the opposite appearance of the man. I never saw those rainbow fish again. In fact he came only in T-shirts and faded pants. His hair never shined like before.

It was only when I heard Mrs. Toyota talking with my grandmother that I thought I knew the meaning of it all.

"So . . . what about the husband?"

"He tired, real tired. *Tsukareta*," my grandmother said, lifting her eyebrows high.

I thought I knew the meaning of all this. Women need to be healed to be beautiful; and men wear out, when they are.

Even the word "baby" was no mystery to me. We had a baby; she was a sister.

But what does a child of six understand of the yearning of a woman for a child? How can a child know of the distress of a flat, empty belly?

Six months later "Fumie" was born.

I never really knew my grandmother then, but now as I try to remember I can imagine the two of us keeping company, not needing to talk much. The silence held us together, a strong vacuum keeping us close. Like her healing cups her love kept me snug.

I left my grandmother's warm bed without regret, because my world too had grown beyond the neighborhood of those healing hands. At the end of our lane—how many times did I walk it, kicking up the dust, holding my grandmother's hand?—was Elm Street, royal palms and all. They're still there, those palms, but Rico Dairy isn't. Ke'eaumoku Street now runs over the old neighborhood. The asphalt has stopped the dust from flying. Tooting horns replace the sounds of chickens and the *ssmmack* of kissing giants.

Beyond that street, I have been told, lay watercress paddies and a water buffalo. These I never saw, since we didn't venture much beyond Elm Street. And I certainly wasn't allowed there alone.

Now time has forced me beyond those swaying fronds, beyond that dusty road without her, but that energy to heal springs from there, reaching out with the warmth of a grandmother's hand grasping securely the falling panties of a child, keeping her out of harm's way.

HOW TO COOK RICE from *A Little Too Much Is Enough*
Kathleen Tyau

Cook rice the way I show you and it will always turn out. Watch how I do it. This is the best way.

Did you wash your hands? And pin back your hair so it doesn't get in your eyes. Wash two cups, three if we're having salty fish for supper, four if we're having company. Buy the best rice in big sacks. Hinode is the best. Wash it good, like this, so the talcum powder comes off. You don't want to eat what we put on the baby. Just swirl the rice good with your hands, like this. See how white the water gets? Pin your hair back, sister, so it doesn't get in your eyes. Take Daddy his slippers and give him a kiss when he gets home from work. Rinse the rice until the water is clear. Save the rinsewater for the orchids. And pick out all the rocks and bugs.

Save your papaya seeds too. Dig a hole in the ground like this and stick them in. Water them every day and soon you will have a papaya tree and all your papayas will be sweet and you can have as many as you want. Eat a papaya every morning and it will keep you regular. Wear bright colors. Red is good.

Kiss Daddy every day when he gets home from work and he will love you. Let him talk and just don't listen if it bothers you. Water your orchids every day. Your daddy was shanghaied, so he can't help it if he talks. Black and white are colors of the dead, so wear bright colors. Red is a good color for you. Water your orchids every day and plant your papaya seeds just like I showed you.

Cover the rice with water and put your middle finger in the pot, like this. See the water come up to the first joint of your finger? No matter what size your pot is or how far you are from home, use your joint to measure and your rice will always turn out right.

Pin your hair back, Māhealani. How many times do I have to tell you? This is why I want you to wear your hair short, so it doesn't get in your way. Long hair is for loose women, so short is always better. Don't sit in a boy's lap. And don't let him touch your personal. Wash your personal good so you don't smell bad. Did you wash your hands?

Wear old clothes to the dentist, so we don't have to pay his bill right away. We can shop for new clothes for school while your brothers are at the dentist. Don't wear black and white. Buy bright colors—red is good. Hide the new clothes in the car trunk so Dr. Chun won't see them or he'll make me pay up today. Go, hide now, and don't let your daddy see them.

After the water boils down, cover the pot. Pretend you are listening. Turn the heat down. Just don't listen if he bothers you. Let the rice simmer until it's done.

Always wear clean panties, pretty things. A woman always wants to feel good underneath. You can wear leopardskin, polka dot, lace, anything. Just look like a lady on top and walk like this. Pin your hair back, Sister.

Black and white are for the dead, just like chrysanthemums. April is the month of the dead. That's when I was born—in the month of the dead, on Bad Luck Friday, Friday the 13th. We must go to the graveyards in April and bai san for Popo and Goong Goong in heaven. I hate to go, but we must. Kneel and bow your head like this and make your hands go up and down like this. Three times is good enough. Don't eat the food on the grave. That's for Popo and Goong Goong to eat. And don't walk on their heads. Did you wash your hands? And don't give me chrysanthemums for my birthday.

Water your orchids every day. Wash your personal. Wear red dresses. Plant your papaya seeds. Buy the best rice. Wash it good.

Don't think about things that make you sad and they will go away. Save your money, even if it's only a quarter a day. By Christmas you will have enough to buy something good. You can buy a red dress. Wear lace panties. Hide them. Don't sit on a boy's lap. When you go away to school, I'll send you orchids and panties.

Save the rinsewater for the orchids. Pretend you are listening. Hide. Pin your hair back, Sister. Cook your rice this way and it will always turn out right.

MIXING POI from *A Little Too Much Is Enough*
Kathleen Tyau

My father, Kūhio, was mixing poi for the lū'au. Sweat ran down his arms into the stainless-steel tub full of pounded gray taro.

No worry about the sweat. Sweat makes the poi taste mo' bettah. I've been mixing poi for a long time now. First time when I was five. My mama let me. It was the luau before I got shanghaied. Some things you never forget. I didn't eat poi again until I came back from China.

As he closed his hands, the poi oozed through his thick chocolate-brown fingers, over creases and bumps.

Mixing poi is not as easy as you think. Sure, you just add a little water, then reach in and squeeze. But how much water? How long to squeeze? You have to mix it so it's just right to eat. That's why I'm doing it, because I know how. This time I'm making two-finger poi. That means not too thin and not too thick. You want the poi to stay in your mouth a little while before going down. Otherwise it's gone too quick, before you can taste.

I used to think China was just an outer island, like Ni'ihau, where my mama was born. She sang to me about Ni'ihau, how she couldn't go back home. My papa was the same way. Talking all the time about China. He wanted me to go back with him, so I did. I didn't know he was going to leave me there. The whole time away, all I could think about was home. The beach, the ocean, the fish, the poi. All the things you miss when you go away. It's not easy to hold on to poi. The harder you squeeze, the more it runs away.

My father plunged his arms deeper into the poi. The taro lake rose above his elbows.

Rice, that's all they fed me. Rice and salt fish, rice and pickled cabbage. We ate a little bit of fish and a big bowl of rice to fill us up. I still love my rice, but, oh, I missed my poi like you don't know how. I asked my popo in China, When is my papa coming back for me? I talked to her half in hakka, half in sign language. I scraped my two fingers in my bowl and put them in my mouth. She gave me another scoop of rice.

He shook his head and stopped mixing. The poi swallowed his arms like quicksand.

Poi is very hard head. Sticks to your hands, sticks to your mouth, hard to wash off. But taste real ono with kalua pig and lomi lomi salmon. All the salty food. Poi is like staying home. You get tired if you eat out too much. When I came back to the islands, I couldn't eat enough. Where is my poi? I asked my mama. Where is my squid, my mango, my breadfruit? I ate up everything before they could take it away. Sure, I love my rice. But poi is what I was hungry for.

My father's arms rose out of the vat. The poi fell off his muscles like sheets of gray rain. He scraped the poi down his left arm, off his palm, off each finger, one by one. He did the same with his right arm, then reached for a bowl.

You have to hold it in your hand like a baby. Lift it up easy, squeeze, then twist. See how the poi stops falling for a while? That's when you stick the bowl underneath. That's all the time you have, so you better be quick, just one second before it falls.

PUKA KINIKINI
Elizabeth Wight

When I was a child, no one spoke to me in Hawaiian, recited my genealogy, told me stories of the old gods or my 'aumākua. Although I grew up surrounded by Hawaiian music, I wasn't taught any of the words to Hawaiian songs. No one even taught me to surf or to paddle; in those days not many women were active in sports. People with some Hawaiian blood hid it if they could; it was not OK to be too "ethnic" or too dark, like my father was.

"Daddy, tell me about the past, about my Hawaiian side. Tell me about my family. Tell me about gramma, she spoke Hawaiian I know, but I don't remember her. What was she like?"

I couldn't stop asking. It was not just curiosity, or merely wanting to know. It was a desperate need for training, for weapons to fight off the over-powering allegiance to Western ways, the intentional forgetting of roots and culture. My need came from a deep alienation from the "haole way" that my parents tried so hard to instill in me. It was something born in me, felt in my bones, an indistinct whispering, unintelligible, yet as real as any living voice, a presence that was as much a part of me as the shadows of clouds constantly changing the dark greens and blues of the mountains in my valley home or the peace I felt wandering in the "pakapaka ua," the pelting rain drops that would settle the disquieting foreboding in me, the uneasiness of being pulled between two cultures, Hawaiian close to being crushed into oblivion by the importance of conforming, of being "American," of being "progressive."

My parents did give me "hula lessons." A neighborhood friend came to teach us hapa haole hula such as "There Goes My Tūtū Ē," "Little Brown Gal" and "The Hukilau Song." I hated them with all the intensity of a child's passion. I hated them for a complexity of reasons which I could not have put into words. One of the reasons had to do with being a pre-teen in an age of sexual vulnerability where no protests were raised against acts that have come to be labeled date rape, spouse abuse, child molestation. I hated being trained to display my body to please men, an underlying but unspoken assumption of those lessons. Another reason was my strong sense that these songs were selling out my cultural heritage. What about ancient chant and dance? Those were hidden, unknown, or considered too "foreign" for

Growing Up Local   151

tourists to be comfortable with. I was being allowed to dance only songs that, intentionally or not, belittled the beauty of brown skin, the dignity of elders, the tradition of sharing work. Yet another reason was my shame at being so uncoordinated and awkward, doubly shamed at being the daughter of a race for whom grace of movement flows in the blood. At *lū'au*, my father would occasionally be inspired to "hula" after many drinks. He would get up with a silly drunken delight and "go around the island" with an 'ami that was uninhibited and as graceful and manly as any large male dancer could be. I would have had to be as drunk as he was to lose my "shame" and enjoy the dance.

And so, at age ten, I searched and searched for someone to teach me a Hawaiian song. Teach me a song of my heritage, a song that I can sing, a song to fend off the cellophane hula skirts and the coconut shell bras, the Tahitian belly twitches and the selling of young brown flesh to fulfill the fantasy of the "hula maiden." Teach me a real Hawaiian song, to fend off the comic hulas that rob us of our dignity, little "brownies" clowning around for the tourist trade.

Teach me an ancient chant to celebrate the connection I feel between me and my land and my ancestors, those that encircle my spirit. Let me hear the hills echo the sounds that will tie me to this place, this time, ground my hā, my breath in this body, now. Teach me a song to hold on to, to let me know that I can be in this dark age, that all the things that are Hawaiian in me can live.

Teach me a song to hide my awkwardness, my clumsiness, my big *lū'au* feet, my shame at being so unskilled a dancer. I can't dance, for shame. For shame. So teach me a song that I can sing. Not "Oh we're going to a hukilau, a hukihukihukihukihukilau." Years after I learned that "huki" means to pull and that "hukihuki" means to have arguments or problems with others, literally pulling back and forth. No wonder I feel I'm being pulled apart.

And yes, I did learn a Hawaiian song. An old Chinese lady who was visiting my parents taught me both words and movements to a child's song of three lines long. She spent about a half an hour teaching me, patiently saying the words over and over until I got both words and hand motions.

> *Puka kini kini, Puka kini kini,*
> *'a'ohe 'ao 'ewa, 'a'ohe 'ao 'ewa,*
> *he 'upena, he 'upena.*

Many, many doorways, many, many doorways,
but none I can get out of, but none I can get out of,
it's a fish net, it's a fish net.

She had given me a gift, a bigger treasure than she ever knew. I have never forgotten that moment and the joy I felt at having this small piece of my Hawaiian heritage to cling to. I sang that song for days and days, putting index finger and thumb together for the "eye" of the net, making fish swim with my hands, throwing the shoulder net in the last line. A child's song, one appropriate for my age. It wasn't until years later that I would look back and see how appropriate it was for my situation, a little part-Hawaiian fish trapped in a soul-smothering net of Western ways.

For me, that simple song was a start. It was one of the first times my thirst for Hawaiian knowledge was quenched just a little, a small empowerment for who I was. It was a small impetus forward in my lifelong search for learning my culture and traditions, the language and literature that have such depth of beauty and complexity and which even today remain unapproached by most of us.

And I will always sing the ancient songs that I have come to learn, the chants that echo from my beloved mountains, and I will tell those whisperings that still call to me now, ever more clearly. And this I promise to that little child who disappeared so long ago, that although I may never dance, I will sing out my Hawaiianness, *a mau a mau,* forever.

BOSS OF THE FOOD

Lois-Ann Yamanaka

Before time, everytime my sista like be the boss
of the food. We stay shopping in Mizuno Superette
and my madda pull the Oreos off the shelf
and my sista already saying, *Mommy,*
can be the boss of the Oreos?

The worse was when she was the boss
of the sunflower seeds.
She give me and my other sistas
one seed at a time.
We no could eat the meat.
Us had to put um in one pile on one Kleenex.
Then, when we wen' take all the meat
out of the shells and our lips stay all cho-cho,
she give us the seeds one at a time,
'cause my sista, she the boss
of the sunflower seeds.

One time she was the boss
of the Raisinets.
Us was riding in the back
of my granpa's Bronco down Kaunakakai wharf.
There she was, passing us one
Raisinet at a time.
My mouth was all watery
'cause I like eat um all one time, eh?
So I wen' tell her, *Gimme that bag.*
And I wen' grab um.
She said, *I'ng tell mommy.*
And I said, *Go you bird killa; tell mommy.*

She wen' let go the bag.
And I wen' start eating
the Raisinets all one time.

But when I wen' look at her,
I felt kinda bad cause I wen' call her bird killa.
She was boss of the parakeet too, eh,
and she suppose to cover the cage every night.
But one time, she wen' forget.
When us wake up, the bugga was on its back,
legs in the air all stiff.
The bugga was cold.
And I guess the thing that made me feel bad
was I neva think calling her bird killa
would make her feel so bad
that she let go the bag Raisinets.

But I neva give her back the bag.
I figga, ehhh . . .
I ain't going suffer
eating one Raisinet at a time.
Then beg her for one mo
and I mean *one mo*
fricken candy.

LICKENS

Lois-Ann Yamanaka

I neva like when she hit me with the iron hanger
'cause was so-wa. Mo so-wa than the wooden one.
So when she told my sista, *Go get the hanger,*
I always hope she would get one wooden one.
In fact, I wen' hope she would get the hanger
that I wen' put crochet on top in Miss Takata's class
for madda's day 'cause was soft.
I wen' try for make all the iron hangers crochet
but I wen' run out of yarn.
I neva have money for buy some mo.

Sometimes my sista was piss off at me
so she go bring the iron one
but I figga better cover my ass and no worry
about what kind hanger she brought.
Then my madda would say, *Move your arm.*
Move your arm. But I couldn't think fast
which was mo so-wa—
lickens on the arm or lickens on the ass.
So my madda hit my arm
'cause I covering my ass.
Lickens on the arm is mo worse
than lickens on the ass.

My madda, she tell my sista, *Go get the iron hanger.*
Then I know my madda real mad.
When she tell my sista, *Go get the wooden hanger,*
then I know she ain't that mad.
My stupid sista, everytime my madda tell her
go get something for lick me with, she run.
I guess she neva like get lickens too.

Ho boy, one time my small sista wen' say *fut*
which we no could say 'cause the word

us had for use was *poot*
and she got lickens with the green brush
which was mo so-wa than the fly swatter
but both was less so-wa than the iron hanger.

My small sista everytime get lickens
'cause she always act dumb in public.
My madda wen' catch her looking
under the dummy's dress
in Edith's Dress Shoppe, downtown Hilo side.
So my madda wen' grab her
and ask her, *Whatchu doing?*
and my sista said,
Mommy, this lady no mo panty, and guess what?
My sista got lickens when we went in the car
'cause you cannot make shame in public.

No tell nobody, but one time,
my small sista wen' show her ching-ching
to one boy and she wen' get lickens with the golf club.
I dunno who wen' tell my madda.
I figga was the sista
that always run go get the hanger.
Must have been so-wa,
the lickens with the golf club.
But I dunno 'cause I neva do nutting that bad yet.

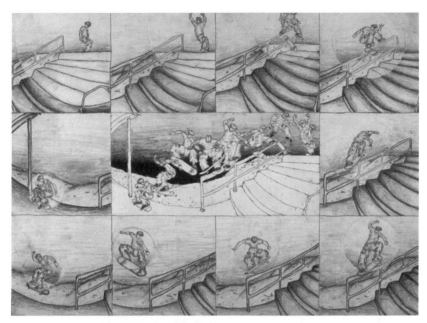

untitled by Carmichael Doan, 'Aiea High School

RECOLLECTIONS
Anjanette Balinbin

January 28, 199–

Honokowai, Maui. His apartment.

He looked at me and I knew what he wanted. "I have something for you," he said. "Happy birthday." And he smiled.

I felt faint because what did I know about him really? He left me in the dark, in the living room, with the CD changer playing . . . a low-sung gangsta rap flowing . . . . He went into the back rooms, where I'd never been.

"It's just a little something I picked up." He smiled at me again . . . softly. "I hope you like it."

And I smiled back, faintly. "You didn't have to. . . ." My voice trailed off. "I wasn't expecting anything."

"I know, I just wanted to get you something," he said, holding out a little black box: a jewelry box, small, velveteen.

I reached out for it.

"It's nothing, really," he said. I looked up at him, looking oh-so-handsome and slightly nervous.

I took it from him and sat down. He joined me . . . and I stared at it before I opened it up.

The CD changer switched; the sweet, clear voice of Sistah Robi and the Hawaiian Style Band came on: "Love and Honesty."

It glittered slightly in the low light that came from the kitchen. Hawaiian Heritage . . . a small, heart-shaped gold pendant, with the initial "A" in black ebony enamel on it.

I stared at it, then fingered it lightly. All quiet.

He shifted slightly next to me.

"It's nice . . . thank you . . . ," I said softly, disjointedly. "Thank you . . ." and my voice trailed off.

January 29, 199–

Hanakaoʻo (Canoe) Beach Park. In *his* truck.

Watching the waves roll in . . . it's nearly moonset.

"Does it bother you?" he asked. "The age thing, I mean." He looked at me, eyes dark brown, as he leaned in close. I felt the corner of my lips turn down: not a frown, just thinking . . . .

"I'm not sure," I shrugged. "How old are you again?"

"Twenty-five," he said.

"Seven years apart then," I replied.

"For five months," he continued, "then eight." He asked, "What are you thinking?"

"Nothing," I replied.

There was silence . . . but it was filled. Sweet melodies, Keali'i Reichel's "Kawaipunahele" drifted in from the radio.

I was silent . . . and so was he.

Our fingers touched and intertwined.

"Are you still thinking?"

"No," I replied.

And he lifted his other hand to cradle my chin.

I looked up at him, neither seeking nor avoiding, feeling like a child looking wide-eyed and unafraid at something she doesn't like or understand . . . but for the life of her, won't look away.

I looked up at him unmoving and closed my eyes as he leaned in close, still holding my chin.

"Twenty-five," I thought again, and then refused to think.

"You kiss so well," he murmured against my lips.

And I blinked "twenty-five," thinking about his hand on my chin, "twenty-five."

February 2, 199–

Honokowai. His apartment, again.

He held my fingers to his lips, a chaste kiss . . . and looked at me. He trailed his fingers along the inside of my wrist . . . and looked at me. He held his hand to frame one side of my face and ran his fingers through my hair. He looked at me.

I could see *something* in his face, but I couldn't read his thoughts through his eyes. He leaned forward to kiss me, and I shut my eyes.

I felt his lips as they began to move, soft and warm, and his tongue claimed mine as our lips parted and I let it in, searching. . . . I responded in kind and let myself go without time in this sightless, seeking *yearning*. . . .

Lips on lips and tongues touching tongues: moving . . . *curving* . . . searching, always searching . . . for something drawn just beyond the next breath . . . hungry . . . gentle . . . *burning*.

February 15, 199–

Lahainaluna High School: established 1831.

Advanced Placement Calculus.

Morning. Announcements are on.

24-7 . . . twenty-four seven . . . 24-7 . . . that's how often I think of him. I like it . . . but I don't.

He never calls and I only see him on weekends when he's off work and I'm off school.

He's got all the time in the world for me then.

I don't like it . . . but I find myself counting the days till I can see him again. I don't like it . . . but I can't refuse to see him. I can't stop myself from calling him, leaving messages on his machine—"hi, it's me"—not often, just enough to make sure he doesn't think I forgot.

Or let myself think that he's forgotten me. I know. I know it's just a game.

It started out that way; for me, too.

But you can't pretend for very long before you're pretending to pretend.

February —, 199–

Lahaina Surf Apartments. I missed the bus.

I'm not pregnant.

I'm at home staring at nothing, but I'm not pregnant. Nothing's on. Not the radio, not the TV, nothing moving, nothing sounding; no noise but the outside noise of leaves being raked and the voices of the men that rake them.

Cars are passing by on the street beside my house-apartment. A gecko clicks; his laughter comes clattering in from the window sill. The curtains blow, lifting, swelling under the morning breeze. Will I swell like that?

No. I'm not pregnant.

I'm eighteen, now. I'm going to college next year. I'm not pregnant, I can't be pregnant. Not pregnant. Not me.

I *won't* be just another single, teenage, welfare mother in Paradise. I won't. I'm not just another statistic. *I* have a future. I'm not pregnant.

So why the taste of salt on my lips? My cheeks are wet . . . my eyes are stinging. I just got something in my eyes . . . that's all. I'm not pregnant.

KONA SIDE
Arlene Biala

Junior kneels
leaning forward
against me
Nanette
swabbing alcohol
on cuts
all over his back

surfing
pulled under waves
he hit reef
dinged his body

claw marks
bright red warning
on brown skin
wide scrape
on shoulder blade
nail stroke
spine scratch

Junior flinches
eyes shut tight
Nanette starts
wiping
the deepest cut
gouged white
not yet bleeding
meanwhile
swell coming in
reef rash
crashing
over his back

squeezes my hand
jokes
he's glad
this morning
reef wasn't
so hungry
feeling lucky
takes one long drink
guava juice

OF WALLS AND WHEELBARROWS
Eric Alfred Boteilho

It was a cold day. The rains were steady and constant as they had
been for a number of days. My family had just moved into our new home in
Makawao. Coming from sunny Pā'ia, where the beaches are accessible all
year, Makawao was a complete culture shock for all of us. The rains began
shortly after we moved in and it rained continuously for over a week there-
after. The past two days of rain were particularly heavy and I was certain we
had moved during the monsoon season.

My father was working for Maui Electric Company at the time. He
was on call twenty-four hours a day. This had been an extremely long day
for him. He came home tired, hungry, and more than a little wet. The bad
weather did not help his job or his disposition at all. There were electric
poles knocked down from Haleakalā to Kā'anapali, and my dad had spent
the entire day hiking to places he did not know existed to fix electric lines
he couldn't find. He really wanted to curl up in front of a warm fire and
sleep. But as with life, what we want and what we get are often two differ-
ent things.

My mother, alias "Wanda the Worrier," met him at the door. She had
been watching the rain all day and had worked herself up to a new level of
hysteria. "You're not going to like this," she began ever so cautiously. "But I
don't think the wall is going to make it through the night."

"The wall," as we had come to refer to it, was my father's monument
to the world. There was a major slope from our yard into the neighbor's yard
and Dad had decided that what was needed to level out the slope was a
wall. He said so himself: "What we need here is a wall." A ten-foot hollow
tile wall was built between the neighbor's yard and ours. Then the rains
came and Dad did not have the time to backfill it with dirt. The rain had
turned our backyard into a muddy version of the Aswan Dam and the wall
was bulging. Wanda the Worrier was afraid "the wall" was going to blow.

Dad sprang into action. With the speed of a gazelle he readied him-
self for battle. It was Man versus nature. The wall was the prize. The goal
was simple: fight the elements before they claim your hard work, your lega-
cy, your monument to the world. He sprinted down the hall, put on his old
blue jeans, slipped into his old shoes, slapped goggles over his eyes, draped

himself in a yellow rain slicker, and, bearing a slight resemblance to Neil Armstrong ready to land on the moon, he bolted out the door.

Mom and I watched through the back window. Dad was in rare form. He surveyed the situation and planned his attack. The muddy water that was filling rapidly behind the wall was deep. He yelled to us that he couldn't see the bottom. This was going to be a good fight. I looked at Mom, she looked at me, we silently recognized the futility of the situation.

Muscles rippling, clothes soaked to his skin, Dad filled the wheelbarrow and raced to the wall. He emptied the mud into the bottomless pit. Mom and I watched with eyes straining. The rain looked like we were witness to this fight through a veil of cheesecloth. Back and forth he ran, filling, dumping, shoveling, filling again. If he was winning this battle, it wasn't evident. Once more he flashed across the mud flats back to the mud pile, filled his wheelbarrow, and like a cheetah ran across the muddy field to the wall. Only this time he ran a little too fast.

It has been said that the human body is an amazing work of art, capable of performing wondrous tasks. What my mother and I saw through that window was nothing short of miraculous. Dad's foot slipped in the mud; he lunged forward, pushing the wheelbarrow with his entire body. Both feet slipped out from under him, and the wheelbarrow began to pick up speed, cutting through the mud like a ship out of control. Dad held onto the handles but, unable to right himself, he was dragged behind, slicing through the muck and mire like a marlin in tow behind a speeding boat. The wheelbarrow was full and heavy, and once it hit the slope toward the wall its speed on the slippery mud was incredible. Valiantly, Dad hung on, trying to scream but creating only a subhuman sound that woke every four-legged creature in the northern hemisphere. The wheelbarrow sped on toward the wall, Dad hung on, there was a sharp crescendo in Dad's gurgle as he realized his fate, wheelbarrow and human soared through the air, then a crash, a splash, and silence . . . . Only the sound of the rain against the roof.

"Wow!" I cried. "Dad's gone!"

"Daddy go swimming?" my one-year-old sister asked.

Mom looked alarmed. Dad had truly gone over the mud, and down into fifteen feet of liquid dirt. That's when the panic hit. He was really gone.

It seemed like an eternity that my mother stood by that window screaming her lost husband's name. The thought of going out into the rain never occurred to her. After a few minutes of this useless screaming, we saw it. It looked almost biblical. Man rising from the muck to reach his full potential. First, one muddy hand. Then another! The Messiah had come! My sister clapped.

Slowly he pulled himself up. He was black from head to toe, the mud hiding his facial features, grass and twigs sticking to his body, and his hair matted and flat against his head. The Creature from the Black Lagoon had emerged. He stumbled to the garage like Quasimodo, where Mom and I met him. I could tell that my mother wanted to hug him, but besides being "Wanda the Worrier" she is also known as the "Goddess of Clean," and she couldn't bring herself to touch him. Ever so slowly, Dad reached up, grasped his goggles, and raised them over his head. The areas around his eyes were white and clean and he looked more like a raccoon than my father. Mother could not control it any longer, and broke into hysterical laughter. I soon followed as we led Mud Man into the house.

After Dad had cleaned up, we sat down to dinner. Dad had given up on the wall, and no one dared mention it. As we ate, neither Mom nor I could look at my father without seeing the image of his fall and resurrection. It was my sister who broke the silence. In total innocence she asked, "Tomorrow, can I play in the mud like you, Daddy?" The laughter came in waves, each of us recounting our perception of the event, at Dad's expense. It took a long time for the family to calm down, but somehow we knew that everything was going to be all right. Dad vowed to have the wall pumped out by professionals the very next day, Mom vowed not to tell anyone about the incident, and I explained to my sister why she still couldn't play in the mud.

As for the wall, it still stands, a monument to my father and a burial place to a once demonic and possessed wheelbarrow with a mind of its own.

feescol ajukeshen
bradajo

nyn... grayd

kauai hai skool

yugadatek

feescol aju keshen
yugada wea dakyn
joe shtrap

enden dey gee yu
da beggy rayd shawls
mia lyk wea
ma choppa pents ah
vachuno ken

enden coach tal
okei boys
luday... yugoin born
calless... tannics

to... avey badey
feelopino... poda gee
bodeengkay... haole
jebenee... pake... kaneka
ena coppol popolo
weeda... begay rayd shawts
jaaampin op endaun
ontop da gress
feescol aju keshen

bada wrrs paat kamin op
bikaws nao
yugadago eensai
  tek sha wa
so avey ba dey
feelopino poda gee
  bodeeno kay haole
  jebenee pake kaneka
    ena cop pol popolo
raaanin eensai dalaka room
tek offda begay rayd shawls
  endadem joc shtrap
  eng go eensai da sha wa
dats wenyufai naut
  avey ba dey
    say m

nax...day
yugadago...seedaun
eensai-da-kwonset-hot
enden..coach-tal
okei..boys........luday
yugoin...born
sax...aju..keshen
enden...he..onrollom
da...beeg..peesha
he..tal
dees...eeg.da.lassleecol
na.......
endenyugadaluk
da..moovay

awl
dees
tym

da..saan
he..shynin
da...wayv
he..brayshin
enymgadaseedaun
eensadea

won aujol
she hedajo
wai anae hai ah
she tal me
wendabeeg wayr
he bray kin
da hol skool
amp tey
oneda ticha
stey eensai
aano keedyu

HAWAI'I PONO'Ī

Puanani Burgess

On Friday, August 7, 1987
Forthy-three kanakas from Wai'anae,
In a deluxe, super-duper, air-conditioned, tinted-glass
        tourist-kind bus,
Headed to Honolulu on an excursion to the Palace,
        'Iolani Palace.

Racing through Wai'anae, Ma'ili, Nanakuli—
Past Kahe Point, past the 'Ewa plain—
In the back of the bus, the teenagers—35 of them
Rappin', and snappin', and shouting to friends and strangers
        alike: Eh, howzit, check it out, goin' to town . . .

(Along the way, people stop and stare, wondering,
        What are those blahs and titas doing in that bus?)

Cousin Bozo, our driver, (yes, that's his real name)
Spins the steering wheel, turning the hulk-of-a-bus,
Squeezing and angling it through the gates made just
Wide enough for horses and carriages and buggies.

Docent Doris greets us:
"Aloha mai. Aloha mai. Aloha mai.
"Only twenty per group, please.
"Young people, please, deposit your gum and candy in the
trash.
"No radios. No cameras.
"Quiet. Please."

"Now, will you all follow me up these steps.
Hele mai 'oukou, e 'awiwi."

Like a pile of fish, we rushed after her.

At the top of the steps,
We put on soft, mauve colored cloth coverings over our
        shoes and slippers,
        to protect the precious koa wood floors
        from the imprint of our modern step.

Through the polished koa wood doors, with elegantly etched
        glass windows,
Docent Doris ushers us into another Time.
Over the carefully polished floors we glide, through the
        darkened hallways: spinning, sniffing, turning,
        fingers reaching to touch something sacred, something
        forbidden—quickly.

Then into the formal dining room, silent now.
Table set: the finest French crystal gleaming; spoons,
        knives, forks, laid with precision next to gold-rimmed
        plates with the emblem of the King.
Silent now.

La'amea 'U.

Portraits of friends of Hawai'i line the dining room walls:
        a Napoleon, a British Admiral . . . But no portrait of
        any American President. (Did you know that?)

Then, into the ballroom,
Where the King, Kalākaua, and his Queen, Kapi'olani, and their
        guests
        waltzed, sang and danced and yawned into the dawn.
        (No one daring to leave before His Majesty)
The Royal Hawaiian Band plays
        the Hawaiian National Anthem and all chattering
        and negotiating stops. As the King and his shy Queen
        descend the center stairway.

And up that same stairway, we ascend—the twenty of us.
Encouraged, at last, to touch . . .
        Running our hands over the koa railing,
        . . . we embrace our history.

To the right is the Queen's sunny room . . . a faint
       rustle of petticoats.

To the left, we enter the King's study:

      Books everywhere. Photographs everywhere.
      The smell of leather and tobacco, ink and parchment—
      The smell of a man at work.

      Electric light bulbs (in the Palace of a savage,
      can you imagine?)
      Docent Doris tells us to be proud, that electricity lit
      the Palace before the White House.
      There, a telephone on the wall.

      Iwalani longs to open those books on his desk,
      Tony tries to read and translate the documents,
           written in Hawaiian, just lying on his desk.

La'amea 'U.

Slowly, we leave the King.
And walk into the final room to be viewed on the
      second floor.
The room is almost empty; the room is almost dark.
It is a small room. It is a confining room.
      It is the prison room of Queen Lili'uokalani.

Docent Doris tells us:

"This is the room Queen Lili'uokalani was imprisoned in
for nine months, after she was convicted of treason.
She had only one haole lady-in-waiting.
She was not allowed to leave this room during that
time;
She was not allowed to have any visitors or
communications with anyone else;
She was not allowed to have any knowledge of what was
happening to her Hawai'i or to her people."

Lili'uokalani. 'U.

I move away from the group.
First, I walk to one dark corner, then another,
      then another. Pacing. Pacing, Searching.
      Trying to find a point of reference, an anchor,
      a hole, a door, a hand, a window, my breath . . .
I was in that room. Her room. In which she lived and
      died and composed songs for her people. It was
      the room in which she composed prayers to a
      deaf people:

      "Oh honest Americans, hear me for my downtrodden
      people . . ."

She stood with me at her window;
Looking out on the world, that she would never rule again;
Looking out on the world that she would only remember
      in the scent of flowers;
Looking out on a world that once despised her,

And in my left ear, she whispered:
'E, Pua. Remember:

This is not America.
And we are not Americans.

Hawai'i Pono'ī.

Amene.

ATTACK FROM WITHIN
Stacy Chang

Bump. Dad maneuvers the old, beaten-up Honda right into the deep groove between the cracked, water-raised asphalt road and our smooth concrete driveway. The force lurches me forward, jolting me from a dream of delectable, quadruple-decker chocolate dobash cake. Five forty-five, blinks the dashboard clock.

I race through the front door, dash up the stairs to my room, and rummage through the brown oak dresser for socks, shorts, tank top, and a jogging bra. By the time I emerge from my room and veer for the front door, only a quarter of the sun still hovers above the Ko'olaus outside my window. I bounce my steps into a little half-jog warm-up.

"You can do it. No matter what the obstacle, you can hurdle it. No matter what the goal, you can reach it," drones (drippy) Ida of "(Drippy) Ida's (Drippy) Personal Plan for Success" through my headphones. Hey, you take it any way you can.

"You can *make* it through this diet. You can *make* it through this run. You can *do* a veggie burger."

Huh. Do a veggie burger. Did good ol' Ida get whacked in the noggin?

"Is? *Isabel!* Aren't you gonna eat?" Mom appears, holding out a neon orange tray overflowing with rabbit food. God, look at the size of those veggie burgers! And those potatoes, too, and rice—and soybeans.

"I'm going jogging. Leave it on my desk."

"Humph." She shoves the tray at me. Gosh, this thing weighs a ton. Who does she think I am? Eating Poombah of York, with a stomach the size of Montana?

"FAT . . . FAT . . . FAT . . ." pulses the soybeans. "FAT . . . FAT . . . ."

Mom'd like me to be fat. Then I'd be "So cute!" and they could roll me to school and back every day, without ever worrying about sexy, horny guys corrupting their little angel.

"You can do it," Ida informs me. "Reach out and take hold of your goal." The veggie burgers sit mere inches from my hand . . . .

You know, my school sucks. It's overflowing with beautiful little bingers, all skinny as hell. Jesus, haven't they heard of the one-in-four obesity rate in America? And then there's my best friend:

Chomp, chomp. Thar goes ye fried-me-hearty chicken sandwich!

"Jeez, Krys, how do you stay so skinny?"

"Oh please, Is. You're sk—. I mean, you . . . eat healthily." The triple-fried chicken sandwich disappears magically down her all-encompassing throat, vaporizing in that nonexistent stomach.

Help me out here. This puny thing is doing her speech oratory on "the beauty myth." How in the world would you feel if some slim, gorgeous, wide-eyed girl with a boyfriend list two miles long told you, "You don't have to be thin and beautiful to be happy"?

Besides, eating healthily doesn't cut it. The healthier I eat, the more I eat. I can't leave anything on that damned plate, whether I'm hungry or not. Not a bit of the ultra-humongous Vegetarian Burrito from The Big Burrito, not a speck of rice in Tsuruya's smooth black lacquer bowl. God, I hate it.

I don't want to be fat. I know, I'm not obese, but there's still that mega-stomach deal, and the disgusting tapioca pudding that wiggles around your thighs and bottom. There's still the snickering and sneering from guys in art class:

"Hey, Dav, how do you go sailing without a boat?"

"Slap a fat woman and ride the waves!"

Of course, I get Jeff's "I don't care about that, Is. You're always pretty to me. Can I change the channel?"

But that's what they all say. And as soon as those size 3's cut red marks into your ample flesh, it's bye-bye lump, and off to the girl races! Pick and choose, folks! This 5'4" beauty weighs in at 93 pounds, has a 24-inch waistline. Sold!

This five-footer weighs 110 pounds, 27-inch waistline. Any takers? Anyone?

It's for a good cause . . . .

Dammit, guys shouldn't talk. It's so easy for them. They don't have the tight-fitting tops and dresses. They don't have tight-fitting anything— not even their stupid underwear, if they want! They're not judged by their size or weight so much as their accomplishments and personality.

You know, during the summer my waistline loved me. I judo-ed myself out ten hours a week, jogged an hour and a half each day, and ate like a bird. Eighty-five pounds, I'm telling you.

Would Mom quit asking if I'm anorexic or bulimic? God, I could only wish. Why can't there be a perfect eating disorder, bingeing like a bulimic, but looking anorexic? Probably because then everyone'd be like the girls in my class. Everyone already is—except me.

The food keeps calling and I run toward it, and it pulls me in. Is it like this for anyone else? It cheers me on, and numbs my pain, and then becomes me. What am I now? All food, all fat, all flesh. The skinny girl I used to be drowned long ago under all this lard. I love food—and I hate the mirror. I hate the mirror and hate the food. I hate the food and what it's made of me. What I've made of myself.

I pull open the front door and step out into the night. Long, coarse hairs rise on my arms as the icy Kona wind whips at my flesh, trying to push me over, threatening to slice through me. The last sliver of sun smatters the clouds with a final breath of pink-orange light, then retracts its long tendrils of warmth and happiness. Black night creeps around me, envelops my lumpy body, cloaking me, choking me.

The tall, rusted street lamps glow like cats' eyes in the night, shading dark corners darker, and the ways around them into deep black holes. In the eerie yellow light, thousands of sinuous black night-devils offer their hands, and pull me in.

I hack through the lightless abyss, gasping for air, heart hammering wildly in my throat. The wind whispers in my ear, egging me on. I stumble across the hard pavement, push harder and harder, until the freezing cold whips away all my feeling. The fat on my legs, the ugly flesh bouncing with each step, disappears. The tape measure squeezing my waist finally lets go, blinking away into nonexistence. The rubber grips of the scale fade gradually beneath my sore feet. I run faster and faster, away from home and Mom, away from school, and Krys, and the boys in my class, and all the skinny girls in the world. Away from food, and comfort, and happiness, and depression. Away from myself.

WAY BACK TO PĀLOLO
Stuart Ching

The Kalihi boys were a greasy pack of rats, creeping from the storm drain behind Pālolo District Park. In the dark yard, we were waiting, Kawika, Fred, Felipe, and me. That night Kawika absorbed the left hook of the Kalihi boys' best man, Bobby Castro. It was said that Bobby sparred with professionals at Kalākaua Gym. When Bobby landed his right cross, Kawika spat and grinned. "That's nothing!" he said. "You hit like one fly-weight!" They traded punches until we heard the sirens. No one had ever knocked out Kawika.

Three months later on Halloween, I did. We were twelfth-graders. Kawika was a strength man—thick neck, burly arms. Every year Mr. Ginoza, Kaimuki High School's football coach, tried to recruit him. After school, the four of us caught the bus to Pālolo, climbed into the gutter, and started into the valley. We passed the backyards of homes; threw rocks at the dogs barking at us through the chain-linked fences; and stepped over fallen coconut fronds, patches of moss, and half broken beer bottles. When we neared the projects, we waited for Fred to show us his Halloween surprise.

"What you get?" said Kawika. "One joint?"

Fred grinned.

"I not sniffing glue," I said, recalling the time Fred had soaked the rag with glue from shop class. "Glue make you stupid," I said.

"Why, you smart?" said Fred.

"Chun told me for go college," I said. "She said college guys no get drafted."

"You dreaming," Felipe said. "You going be like me, humping through the jungle or digging one ditch."

"Had one guy on the news," Fred said. "He went chop off his baby toe. One stroke with the butcher knife. After that the Amy never like him." Fred unrolled his dirty gym shirt, revealing a bottle of Mateus wine. We passed the bottle around. Then Fred reached into his pocket and pulled out a plastic bag holding four small pill-like tablets.

"What's that?" I said.

"Holy communion," said Fred. "Acid." He placed one on his tongue, then swallowed some Mateus. Kawika and Felipe did the same. We sat down and drank all the wine.

"Come on, Stanley," said Fred.

It was the first and only time that I tried acid. The alcohol and LSD took about an hour to work. Suddenly I was watching a mushroom sprout from a pimple on Kawika's cheek. Then mushrooms began popping out all over his face. He leaned toward me, waving his hands in circles. I pushed him away.

"No fuss," I said.

"What, Stanley?" he said. "You seeing ghosts?" He stood up and put on the Halloween mask that he'd worn to all six periods during school. Now his face became half troll and half fish, and was peppered with warts and leeches. He reached down and pinched my cheek. His thumb and forefinger gaffed my skin like giant fish hooks. I stood up. He came at me again. I punched low. "Hnnhh," he grunted, stooping, holding his ribs. He straightened. "Fricken Stanley," he said. He began punching with both hands. His fists pelted my face like rocks. I stumbled backward. Kawika lunged. I swung blindly, turning my shoulder and hip instinctively into the punch as I'd learned at the Pālolo Boxing Club. I got lucky. I looked down. Kawika was sprawled on his back, his white eyes sunken behind his plastic, green skin, a flower of blood already blossoming through the crack in his forehead.

Despite home-visits from Mr. Toma, Kaimuki High's outreach counselor, Kawika didn't attend school for a month, so one day, Felipe cut class to see him. Kawika lived with his father, a decorated Korean War veteran, recipient of the silver star and purple heart. On his back he had two large shrapnel scars that looked like nipples. At the end of the valley Kawika and Mr. Nobriga lived in a clapboard shack with corrugated roofing. Flanking the shanty were a pig pen and a chicken coop. Shack, pen, and coop—all three were illegally built on state land zoned for public housing. Tall grass and overgrown weeds crowded one side of the house, and the other side opened on a wide patch of dirt and gravel, where a rusty truck was parked. The lot was separated from the paved road by a narrow dirt lane shaded by a mango tree and crowded by rusty oil barrels and an old, tireless car with a dented hood and a gnarled fender. Felipe walked into the lane. He approached the fence made of wooden frame and chicken wire at the edge of the yard and read the message painted on the weather-beaten sign: "Stay out or I going shoot." Telling us the story later, he said that he was feeling slightly light-headed and brave—earlier he had finished a six-pack behind Manono's Grocery Store—so he pushed open the gate and walked across the yard. He knocked on the door. No answer. "Kawika!" he called. The barrel of a shotgun poked out from a chink in the boards. *Pawh!* The buckshot sprayed the top of the mango tree. "No shoot!" Felipe shouted. "This Felipe! Felipe Ortiz! No . . . !" A second blast split a tree limb, and the branch crashed to the ground. Felipe fled, high-stepping and bobbing, stumbling, falling and skinning his knees, then scrambling to his feet and zigzagging, staying low. *Pawh! Pawh!* He ducked behind the car in the lane and peeked around the gnarled fender. The shotgun barrel was gone.

"He think he John Wayne," Felipe told us later. "This Pālolo Valley, not the Wild West!"

Sunday that same week, I went with my parents and my sister, Tiani, to the seven o'clock evening mass. Tiani was wearing the pink dress that Mom bought at the Momoharas' garage sale. Tiani tugged at Mom's hand and pulled her to the glass door. Mom smiled into the reflection. "Come, Ben," Mom said. "Look your girl." Dad walked over and took Tiani's hand.

Inside, the church was crowded. There was Mrs. Ho, who always gave the neighborhood kids *lichee* when her tree blossomed red. There were the Garmas, the Suzukis and the Kamakaus, the Hookipas, the Lorenzos, the Arrudas, and the Bautistas. And walking toward me was Leimomi Costa. In her last trimester of pregnancy, her stomach bulged beneath her muʻumuʻu. Beside her, Eva, her younger sister, winked at me and whispered, "Meet me after." All through the service, I smelled Eva's sweet perfume wafting through the sanctuary.

After Father Ricardo gave the communion and told us to go in peace, I turned to Fred and his mother in the pew behind. "Bye, Mrs. Pule," I said, leaning over and kissing her cheek. Several rows back I saw Mr. Nobriga sitting with Kawika near the aisle. I started toward them, but when Kawika saw me coming he stepped out the side door. I followed him. "Kawika," I said. He waved me off, lit a cigarette, and kept walking.

I told my parents that I'd be coming home late and met Fred in the parking lot. We waited for the cars to pull out, and then we smoked a joint in the empty lot behind the church.

"Kawika still mad," I said.

"Nah, he shame," said Fred. "You lucky that time he was stoned. Good thing he never come back for you. Eh, what Eva said?"

"I supposed to meet her." I said. "You like come?"

"Nah," said Fred.

"Maybe she get one friend," I said.

Fred and I hopped the fence and slid into the drainage ditch. We planned to follow it for several blocks up to Eva's backyard. Then we heard voices, saw cigarettes glowing in the black air—the Kalihi boys.

"Run!" I said. Fred was already scrambling out of the ditch and pulling himself over the fence. He landed on the other side. He was running, running fast.

Halfway up the wall, I felt someone grab my leg. I kicked my leg loose and grabbed the fence. I pulled myself over. I landed and rolled. The Kalihi boys, maybe six of them, swarmed on me, punching and kicking. Then suddenly, the mob cleared. I looked up. Kawika was standing over me, a tree branch in his hand.

"Five seconds," he said. He swung the branch like a bat. "Five seconds before I knock all you guys out! Where Castro? I looking for Bobby Castro! Where he stay! Tell Castro that Kawika Nobriga looking for him! Tell him I going kick his ass!"

The Kalihi boys backed off. I heard the fence rattle, rubber slippers and tennis shoes landing on asphalt. Then I felt my body rising. The last image I saw before closing my eyes was the big white cross hovering over St. Mary's Church. When I awakened, I realized that I was moving quickly down Pālolo Avenue, appearing and disappearing in the passing headlight beams of speeding cars, held in Kawika's arms.

Dad reset my nose. Mom iced my swollen eyes and bandaged my bruised ribs with strips of an old bed sheet. She closed my cuts with adhesive and gauze.

I stayed home from school. My jaw and teeth were sore, so for two weeks I mostly ate soft food like Campbell's Chicken Noodle Soup and rice. Sometimes I ate vegetable soup or eggs and rice and *shoyu*. Dad would come home in the evenings, smelling like tar from patching roofs all day. Some evenings he smelled like freshly cut grass from beating back bushes and weeds along some beachfront property or empty lot—these jobs he did after work for extra money. After changing into clean overalls, he often drank a glass of Crown Royal and passed the bottle and cup to me. "Good painkiller," he said. "Drink up." I swished the Crown Royal in my mouth, and the liquor burned, numbing my gums, which still bled when I chewed. I held the liquor as long as I could, and when I swallowed, I traced the fire plunging down into my body, wincing when it ignited my stomach.

Kawika visited once.

"Hi, Mr. Maluna," I heard him say at the door. "How Stanley doing?"

"Come inside," Dad said.

"Nah, I supposed to be home."

"Kawika," Mom called from the kitchen. "I hope you staying for dinner."

"Nah," said Kawika.

"Sure," Dad said. "Come inside."

Kawika entered the livingroom, where I was lying on the couch. Dad filled three shot glasses.

"Thanks for helping Stanley," Dad said.

"Nah, me and Stanley go way back," said Kawika, looking at me. "From small kid time."

My father nodded, opened the screen door and stepped outside. We heard him strumming his ukulele.

"You lucky," Kawika said. "Your father take care you. Me, I take care my father. Sometimes I like run away, but . . . but if I go, who going watch out for him?"

After three weeks, I was back in school and roaming the streets of Pālolo. One warm spring night I found myself standing on Eva's doorstep.

"Eva," her mother said. "One boy asking for you."

Eva came to the door. She was wearing a yellow blouse and white shorts. The light inside the apartment turned the soft edges of her black hair light brown, almost the same color of her skin. I heard a baby crying.

"Leimomi's second one," Eva said. "I think different father. This baby get green eyes. You like see?"

"Nah. Maybe later on," I said. "I was thinking, you like go someplace?"

We walked to the nearby intermediate school. The sky was clear, the stars visible. We crossed the yard and sat in one of the stairwells. She caressed my back, then took my hand.

"Your hand cold," she said. She guided my hand under her blouse. She leaned over and kissed me. I tasted the gum she was chewing. Her breath was mint. Kissing me again, she passed the gum into my mouth, her tongue gliding behind my teeth. Surprised and embarrassed, not knowing what to do, I swallowed.

"You supposed to give it back to me," she said. "You know what happen when you eat gum?"

"No."

"You get constipation," she said.

"Not," I said.

"Nah," she said. She ran her hand through my hair. Then, whispering, "I the first girl you kissed?"

"No."

"Tell the truth," she said, nibbling on my ear.

"Not really. Maybe, I guess."

"I going make this special," she said, kissing me again. "You going remember me."

Word of the eviction was buzzing among the adults of St. Mary's Church on Christmas Eve. During the service, I glanced periodically at Mr. Nobriga sitting stoically beside Kawika. After mass, as we were leaving, Mr. Nobriga leaned on the pew in front of him and propped his fists on the backrest.

"We go, Dad," said Kawika. "Church *pau* already." Mr. Nobriga shook his head. "Now I know how Jesus feel," he said. "I give my body to this stinking country. All I asking is one place for live, and they crucifying me!" After we passed them and entered the vestibule, I looked back and saw Father Ricardo resting his hand on Mr. Nobriga's shoulder.

The first Monday after winter vacation, I cut school with Fred and Felipe and watched the eviction. Waiting for the police to arrive, we crouched on a small, rocky outcrop on one side of the valley, some forty yards above the house. Mr. Nobriga was sitting on an old wooden chair with a blanket draped over his knees. When the three squad cars arrived and the officers opened the gate, he pulled out his rifle.

Mr. Nobriga pointed the barrel toward the sky. *Pawh! Pawh!* The reports filled the valley. Two officers ducked behind their cars and drew their revolvers. The other officer pulled a rifle from the trunk of his car and ducked behind the car's open door and began talking on the radio.

Kawika ran out of the house and wrestled the gun from Mr. Nobriga's hands. Mr. Nobriga fell to his knees. A gust of wind blew. Dust swirled. Mr. Nobriga shielded his eyes with his forearm. Kawika reached down and grabbed Mr. Nobriga's arm, helping him up. The police officers converged on them. They secured the gun, handcuffed Kawika and Mr. Nobriga, escorted them off the property, and pushed them into the back seat of the squad car.

One officer walked into the house. After he stepped outside, he circled around back to the chicken coop, then walked to the front yard. He checked the truck's license plate and scribbled something on a notepad.

"Somebody should do something," Felipe said. He stood up, clutching in his fist a mossy rock the size of a baseball. He cocked his arm, stepped forward, and hurled it. There was a small explosion of dust ten feet from the officer. The officer scanned the mountainside. He spotted us. Felipe hurled another rock, and another.

"Hey!" shouted Felipe.

"You crazy," said Fred. "Get down."

"Up here!" Felipe yelled. The officer drew his revolver.

We took off into the mountainside, grabbing ledges and plowing through *haole koa* bushes. We stayed low, crouched, kicking loose rocks and breathing hard. My thighs burned and my lower back tightened. After we climbed some thirty yards up the mountain, we stood on an open ledge and looked down. Now two officers were standing in the middle of the yard, looking up at us. I picked up a rock and threw it. The stone disappeared in the air. Far below, there was a miniature explosion of dust just in front of the officers. We scrambled farther up the mountainside until we reached the top. Here the sky opened into blue space. We paused to rest, sucking in air.

"You hear that?" said Fred.

We all listened, and then we heard the distant flapping of a helicopter. We looked up and saw the chopper arcing above us over the Ko'olaus.

"That's one military Chinook," I said.

"How you know?"

"Chun's class," I said. "Can tell by the two propellers and the size. Can fit one Jeep inside. Probably came from Kāne'ohe . . . from the Marine base."

The helicopter flew toward Barber's Point. I motioned toward the trail leading into the next valley. Fred was already moving ahead of me. Felipe was walking and still looking at the chopper. We stopped at a clearing. "Check it out," said Felipe, nodding toward the ocean. Opening before us, Honolulu appeared vast and sprawling, the hotels massed on the waterfront, the subdivisions to the west pushing at the city's edges into Ewa, and condominiums and apartments rising like pillars over downtown.

"How people can live like that and other guys no more even house?" said Felipe.

I knew from Mrs. Chun that it had something to do with the Great Mahele, the legislation of the 1840s which severed the Hawaiians from the land. Later plantations appeared—manager on top in the big house with open verandas and huge, grassy lawns; field workers, mostly immigrants, living at the bottom in shacks. Mrs. Chun was not like other teachers. She told a version of history beyond books. Her grandfather from Kwangtung, China, used to fix irrigation ditches above Hakalau on the Big Island; her grandmother, a part-Hawaiian, harvested the fields, grew old and worn and withered until, finally, she became the dust of those fields. Mrs. Chun knew the value of land. Those who didn't have it suffered. I wanted to say all this, but instead I said, "Shee."

Then I waved them on, and the three of us disappeared over the top of the mountain and escaped into the upper trails of Saint Louis Heights.

That morning was the last time that I saw Mr. Nobriga in Pālolo Valley. Nowadays, while driving my car in Honolulu, I sometimes see him sitting at the bus stop outside the Nuuanu YMCA. Once I saw him fishing with his bamboo pole on the River Street Bridge. The day of the eviction, according to Kawika, Mr. Nobriga was arrested and finger-printed. Kawika was released without charges.

"What going happen to your father?" I asked him three days later in school.

"They sending him to the state hospital for testing."

"And where you staying? Come live with us."

"Nah."

"For real. My father said for tell you."

"I doing okay, me and Leimomi. Leimomi Costa. You know who's that, eh? I staying with her."

"She get two kids," I said.

"They mine," he said.

"How you know? How can?"

"What you talking?"

"I mean, how you know you not too young for start one family? How you going make it?"

"I going take the fireman's test. I went see Toma. He helping me. He said firefighters get good benefits from the city, medical plan, too. He going write one letter for me. You should take the test too, Stanley."

"Nah, I going college," I said. "Maybe even mainland."

"This my home," Kawika said. "Leimomi, the kids, my father, I going take care them. Yeah, Hawai'i my home. This where my family stay. Pālolo."

Later that month there were rumors that the Kalihi boys were planning to raid the projects. We decided to take the fight into their neighborhood. That night, we caught the bus and spread out among the back rows. We wrote our names in ink on the seats. Fred wrote in big letters on the window: PALOLO BOYS RULE. When we stepped off the bus in Kalihi, Kawika practiced swinging his Willie Mays Slugger—he'd carved Willie Mays's name into the bat with a steak knife. We walked four blocks and waited in the dark alley across the street from Kalihi Billiards.

From down the street came one of the Kalihi boys, a lanky kid wearing jeans and a white t-shirt. He stopped in front of the pool hall beneath the red neon sign, looked at himself in the window, and ran a comb through his hair. He lit a cigarette and walked inside.

"Batting practice," said Kawika.

The sounds of loud music and revving car engines came from the parking lot behind the hall. Kawika crossed the street. We followed. We ducked behind the building, slipping into the shadows of wooden crates, cardboard boxes and a row of trash cans. Fred and I moved up, flanking

Kawika. Felipe was just behind, crouching. He edged up beside me. For a few seconds, we were all very quiet, together, feeling each other's presence and the reassurance that came with that presence, the only sound among us, our breathing.

In front, at the farthest corner of the parking lot where the pavement became gravel four boys were leaning against parked cars. One of them was wearing a windbreaker; the other three were dressed in shorts and t-shirts.

"Four on four," said Kawika. The back entrance opened, and eight more boys walked into the parking lot. Kawika cracked his knuckles and ran his hand over his bat.

"Let's come back later," said Fred.

"You scared?" said Kawika.

"No."

"Chicken," said Kawika.

"Shhh," hissed Felipe.

Then a boy over six feet tall wearing jeans and an undershirt walked out the door. He was easily over two hundred pounds, muscular. "Bobby Castro," said Kawika. "Last time he went false-crack me."

"We come back later," I said.

I started retreating slowly along the wall. Fred and Felipe followed.

"Where you going?" Kawika said. "Come here. Eh, you need slaps."

I looked toward the parking lot. Three boys were walking briskly toward us. I motioned to Fred to move back around the building. He bolted out from the shadows, rounded the corner and was gone. Felipe and I sprinted after him. Behind us, Kawika followed. Running down the road, I heard the Kalihi boys jeering and glass bottles breaking. A car engine started. I looked back. Two headlights were bearing down on us. We cut through an alley, hopped a brick wall, and landed in a yard with a large mango tree. A woman screamed from inside the house. We darted into the street. A bright beam hit us and threw our shadows onto the pavement. We hustled through a lane, exited on the other side, and slipped into an abandoned garage beside an old mom-and-pop store. The bus stop was fifty yards away at the stoplight. Kawika stood in open view near the curb, twirling his bat.

"Kawika," said Fred. "Kawika, you jackass, get in here."

Then Kawika was caught in the beam of a headlight. The car screeched and stopped, and six boys jumped out. The fight spilled onto the sidewalk. We leaped out of the shadows and joined the brawl. In the confusion of flailing arms and feet, I managed to knock someone down. Then I faced a giant, Bobby Castro, I threw two straight punches. He slapped the first punch down; the second one hit him in the mouth. He walked straight in, his head tucked behind his fists, taking three blows to the face so that he could land one. He began landing at will, driving me back until I was off the sidewalk and back-pedaling into the garage. I dropped to one knee. I saw his groin a foot away from my face. I rammed my open palm straight up between his legs and squeezed hard. He screamed, buckled.

I looked up. The bus was approaching. Fred and Felipe had momentarily beaten down their attackers and were running toward the bus stop. I started down the street, pulling Kawika, who was kicking someone on the ground. Before boarding, I glanced back. A second car was pulling up alongside the first, and five boys were jumping out.

We asked for transfer tickets and moved quickly to the rear of the bus. Except for the seat occupied by an old woman sitting near the driver, the bus was empty. Felipe's left cheekbone was swollen. He opened his window and let the night air blow his hair back. Kawika sat in front of me, clenching and unclenching his fists on the handrail over the backrest in front of him. Fred slumped down in the corner of the back seat. His shirt was gone; his lip was split.

"Wake me up at the transfer stop," he said.

"Panty," said Kawika, turning. He swung one leg into the aisle and looked back.

"Always running."

"What?"

"You heard me."

'Shut up."

"You fricken jerk," said Kawika.

"Cool it," I said.

"Nobriga, you one real jackass, yah, you," said Fred. Kawika stepped into the aisle.

"Stand up," Kawika said. "Come on, right here."

I grabbed Kawika's shoulder. He slapped my hand away. The bus stopped and the back door opened. "Eh, settle down back there or you going be walking," the driver called, looking into the rear view mirror. Kawika's eyes darted back and forth at the bus driver then at me. "I going get Bobby," he said. "Who coming? Who going watch my back?" He looked at me. "Stanley," he said. I didn't answer.

"Pālolo boys wimps," Kawika said. We were two miles outside of Kalihi, in Chinatown. Kawika propped the Willie Mays Slugger on his shoulder and stepped onto the pavement. Before the doors closed, he turned. "You owe me one, Stanley. I going meet you in the drainage ditch," he said. Outside, a drunkard stumbled out of a bar. A man in tattered clothes slumped against the entrance to an alley. Down a side street, two sailors were approaching a woman in a slinky dress, and from somewhere along King Street came the sound of Hawaiian music. As the bus pulled away, I watched Kawika through the windows. "After I finish Castro!" he yelled. He pointed the bat at me. Then he turned and began to trot. I almost rang the bell and got off the bus, but instead I stood in the aisle and looked out the back window. Kawika was running across the street, weaving between the traffic, his body now only a shadow. He turned a corner and was gone.

The next day, I watched doors—the doors of buses, classrooms, restrooms—waiting for Kawika to step through. "You and me, Stanley." And I rehearsed again and again in my head, lowering my hands and taking every blow. After school, I climbed into the drainage ditch, and waited. I waited until dusk. Finally, he came.

I stood up. He slid down the wall and closed on me. His face was badly beaten, one eye completely shut. The other eye peered at me through ripe, swollen skin. Years later, I still remember the way that one battered eye looked at me, and I realize that Kawika had seen much more than I did at that moment. "You okay?" I asked.

"What you think? I was going pound your face. But you not worth it. Beat it, Stanley. You no belong here no more."

I turned and left, and that summer, I worked at the cannery to earn money for tuition. Felipe flew to Georgia for basic training. Fred took a knife to his hand when he received his notice. "The government like my life. Aah, forget 'em. The only thing going rot in one box is my finger." In the fall, I left Pālolo. I began classes at UH, moved into a room on University Avenue, and took a job stocking shelves nights at the Mō‘ili‘ili Star Market. By April, troops were coming home in mass. I graduated in '74 with a degree in journalism and landed a job at the *Star-Bulletin*. Soon after I bought a condominium along the Ala Wai Canal. On the fourteenth floor, my balcony opens on Mānoa Valley and Saint Louis Heights. One Valley over, beyond the shimmering city, Pālolo.

MAKING DA SCENE
Eric Chock

In '66, our hair
was hitting da tops of our collars
and doing da surfa flip,
we neva tuck in da tails
of our button-down paisley shirts,
and you could still wear Beatle boots
and make da scene.
All summer we cruised Ala Moana,
Conrad and me, new wrap-around
sunglasses making everything green,
rolling along with da Stones and
getting no satisfaction
in his brother Earl's '63 Dodge Dart,
lifted, quad carburetor, could do 90
on da new H-1 Freeway, but
we neva even think we was mean.
Everytime around,
we just leaned down in his
blue vinyl seats, hoping
somebody would notice us
as we rumbled through da park,
those wrap-arounds like protection
and a tease
for those cute chicks
who was out there every day,
doing the same thing.

THE TEMPURA WAR
Shayna Ann A. Coleon

Pzzzzz! Pspzzzzz! Pshtttt!

I watched the gel-like bubbles rise to the top and spit out the cooking oil with a small sizzle each time my mom dropped a yellow battered shrimp into the giant red wok.

"So, is Jeremy coming to New Year's dinner?" She dipped the chopsticks into the wok, snatching out the tempura when they turned golden and fluffy.

"Who? Mariko's haole boyfriend?" Aunty Lynn interrupted before I could answer as she stuck her hands into the vegetable tempura and mixed the gooey mixture.

"He is soooo haole, yeah?" my cousin Alisa, who was a year younger than me, teased me. "But that's okay, Mari. You like him plenty, yeah?"

My mom and aunty laughed. I could feel my face heating up and it wasn't because of the sizzling wok. I looked down at the batter and noticed slivers of fish cake with their hot-pink edges jutting out.

"He's coming," I sighed. "Don't bother him, okay?"

"Yeah, but he going eat anything or what?" Mom glanced up from her cooking and stared at me.

"And what is that supposed to mean?" I asked, but I already knew the answer.

Jeremy was hapa. His mom was Japanese and his dad was from Montana. Jeremy, however, ended up pulling the haole side. But that didn't matter to me. We had already been going out for eight months and I loved him. Dad constantly joked about how I gushed over a "white boy," but he liked Jeremy. Mom, on the other hand, was apprehensive about Jeremy because he seemed, as she said, "different."

Since I spent New Year's Day with his family, he would have New Year's dinner with my family. But what my mom said was true. What was he going to eat?

Jeremy was particular when it came to eating. One time, he came to my house and Mom offered him some sushi.

"No thanks," Jeremy shook his head. "I don't eat sushi." Mom's eyes widened, but Jeremy continued to explain, "I never really tried it."

"What? You mean you lived here all your life for seventeen years and you've never tried sushi before?" She pushed the tray of sushi towards him. "Why don't you at least try a bite. It's not like it has raw fish or anything in it."

"Uhh, that's . . . all right," Jeremy hesitated.

"You sure? It's good." Mom offered the tray again. "You don't like my cooking?" She smiled as if to indicate she was joking.

"Ma! He doesn't want to eat it, okay?" I nudged her to the living room. "Mom, when he says he doesn't want any, you can't exactly shove it down his throat!"

"What kind Japanese is that?" Mom shrugged. "Mariko, you sure about him?"

"Mom, I don't even understand you. Just leave him alone." I stormed out of the room.

Ever since then, Mom made snide comments that I always ignored. I just prayed that she wouldn't hound Jeremy at dinner tonight.

"Mariko, did you hear me? Your boyfriend—" She hesitated and placed her hand on my shoulder. "Jeremy—he's here."

I met him outside and he hugged me. "Hey, I'm warning you. Lots of relatives and all that food you just *love!*"

"Mari, I don't even care, okay?" He laughed, baring a mischievous smile. "There's always Stove Top Stuffing, right?"

"Yeah, right." I grabbed his hand and took a deep breath as we walked back into the house.

"Eh, Jeremy!" Dad waved him over to meet everybody. Some of them were already chomping away.

"What, come get food first." Mom ushered us towards the dining room. My aunties and uncles huddled about the table, spooning macaroni salad, sushi, and *nishime* onto their plates.

My eyes flitted to Jeremy and then to Mom and then again to Jeremy. My heart pumped faster as we approached the table. Fully aware of the situation, I realized Mom was testing Jeremy. She eyed him carefully as he picked up a paper plate and examined the dinner table.

The dishes lay neatly on the table. The fleshy red sashimi sat on a bed of shredded cabbage. Bold green and red fish flakes, broiled eel, and earthy brown mushrooms nestled in the middle of the tightly wrapped rice and nori. Steam curled into the air above the plates of sliced turkey, kalua pork, and Korean spicy chicken.

Mom and I hovered above to see what he would choose, at ease and totally unaware of the contentious situation he was in.

We watched as Jeremy proceeded to pick up a couple slices of turkey and kalua pork. He started to scoop salad and stuffing onto his plate when Mom interjected.

"Jeremy, why don't you try some tempura? We made it this morning."

I looked at him as he shook his head. My ears began to burn and my cheeks reddened. "That's okay," Jeremy smiled. "This is all I need right now."

"Are you sure?" she pushed, as she used the metal tongs to pick up a vegetable tempura. "Here, this one doesn't have any shrimp. It's only sweet potato and carrots."

"Um, no thanks . . . ," Jeremy trailed off.

"Mom, he doesn't—"

"Mariko, just let him have this one." She nodded and placed the tempura on his plate.

"He doesn't want to eat it, Mom," my voice cracked. "Don't force him to eat it, all right?"

"Nah, that's okay. I'll take it," Jeremy said uneasily.

"See now, Mariko. Jeremy not only haole boy, ah?" She winked, but I was furious.

"I'm gonna wait out there, okay?" Jeremy hesitated, then went back into the living room.

"Does it make him a good boyfriend just because he eats local food?" I hissed madly.

"Mariko, calm down," she said impatiently. She ignored my question and handed me a couple of bowls. "Here, we better take the rest of this to Dad guys."

Our family had sprinkled themselves around the living room as Mom and I sat down to eat. The room buzzed with conversation when a foul stench filled the air. Mom proceeded to open the lid of her *natto* and, with her chopsticks, picked up the beans. A string of slime clung to the beans as she lifted it to her mouth.

"Karry! That stinks! How can you eat that?" Dad cried in disgust.

"Why don't you try it?" she teased him and waved the bowl in front of his face.

"No way! I hate *natto*, I'd never try that!" He laughed as Mom walked back into the kitchen for more food.

I told Jeremy I'd be right back and followed her into the kitchen.

"Mom, do you love Dad?"

"Of course. Why you ask me that for?" She smiled and looked at me.

"Because he doesn't try your *natto*, right?"

"Well, true," she said carefully. "But I just wanted him to try his Japanese side."

"But isn't he just like me, right? I mean you're Japanese and Dad's Filipino, right? Or is it because he's just haole?"

"I know what you're getting at, and I'm sorry." My mom nodded slowly.

We looked up in the doorway in surprise as Jeremy walked into the room with an empty plate.

"Jeremy, I just wanted to apologize—"

"Those yellow things are *ono*," Jeremy interrupted, his mouth full of food.

Mom and I began to laugh hysterically as he plopped more tempura onto his plate and grinned back at us.

CARNIVAL QUEEN
Mavis Hara

My friend Terry and I both have boy's nicknames. But that's the only thing about us that is the same. Terry is beautiful. She is about 5'4" tall, which is tall enough to be a stewardess. I am only 5 feet tall, which is too short, so I should know.

My mother keeps asking me why Terry is my friend. This makes me nervous, because I really don't know. Ever since we had the first senior class officers' meeting at my house and my mother found the empty tampax container in our waste basket she has been really asking a lot of questions about Terry. Terry and I are the only girls who were elected to office. She's treasurer and I'm secretary. The president, the vice-president, and the sergeant-at-arms are all boys. I guess that's why Terry and I hang out together. Like when we have to go to class activities and meetings she picks me up. I never even knew her before we were elected. I don't know who she used to hang around with, but it sure wasn't with me and my friends. We're too Japanese girl, you know, plain. I mean, Terry has skin like a porcelain doll. She has cheekbones like Garbo, a body like Ann Margaret, she has legs like, well, not like any Japanese girl I've ever seen. Like I said, she's beautiful. She always dresses perfectly, too. She always wears an outfit: a dress with matching straw bag and colored leather shoes. Her hair is always set, combed, and sprayed; she even wears nylon stockings under her jeans, even on really hot days. Terry is the only girl I know who has her own Liberty House charge card. Not that she ever goes shopping by herself. Whenever she goes near a store, her mother goes with her.

Funny, Terry has this beautiful face, perfect body, and nobody hates her. We hate Valerie Rosecrest. Valerie is the only girl in our P.E. class who can come out of the girl's showers, wrap a towel around herself under her arms and have it stay up by itself. No hands. She always takes the longest time in the showers and walks back to her locker past the rest of us, who are already dry and fumbling with the one hook on the back of our bras. Valerie's bra has five hooks on the back of it and needs all of them to stay closed. I think she hangs that thing across the top of her locker door on purpose just so we can walk past it and be blinded by it shining in the afternoon sun. One time, my friend Tina got fed up and snatched Val's bra. She wore it on top of her head and ran around the locker room. I swear, she looked like an albino Mickey Mouse. Nobody did anything but laugh. Funny, it was Terry who took the bra away and put it back on Val's locker again.

I don't know why we're friends, but I wasn't surprised when we ended up together as contestants in the Carnival Queen contest. The Carnival Queen contest is a tradition at McKinley. They have pictures of every Carnival Queen ever chosen hanging in the Auditorium corridor right next to the pictures of the senators, governors, politicians, and millionaires who graduated from the school. This year there are already five portraits of queens up there. All the girls are wearing long ball gowns and the same rhinestone crown which is placed on their heads by Mr. Harano, the principal. They have elbow length white gloves and they're carrying baby's breath and roses. The thing is, all the girls are *hapa*. Every one.

Every year, it is the same tradition. A big bunch of girls gets nominated to run, but everybody knows from intermediate school on which girl in the class is actually going to win. She has to be *hapa*.

"They had to nominate me," I try to tell Terry. "I'm a class officer, but you, you actually have a chance to be the only Japanese girl to win." Terry had just won the American Legion essay contest the week before. You would think that being fashionable and coordinated all the time would take all her energy and wear her out, but her mother wants her to be smart too. She looks at me with this sad face I don't understand.

"I doubt it," she says.

Our first orientation meeting for contestants is today in the library after school. I walk to the meeting actually glad to be there after class. The last after school meeting I went to was the one I was forced to attend. That one had no contestants. Just potential school dropouts. The first meeting, I didn't know anybody there. Nobody I know in the student government crowd is like me and has actually flunked chemistry. All the guys who were coming in the door were the ones who hang around the bathrooms that I'm too scared to use. Nobody ever threatened me though, and after a while, dropout class wasn't half bad, but I have to admit, I like this meeting better. I sit down and watch the other contestants come through the door. I know the first name of almost every girl who walks in. Terry, of course, who is wearing her blue suede jumper and silk blouse, navy stockings and navy patent leather shoes. My friend Trudye, who has a great figure for an Oriental girl but who wears braces and coke bottle glasses. My friend Linda, who has a beautiful face but a basic *musubi*-shaped body. The Yanagawa twins, who have beautiful hapa faces but pretty tragic, they inherited their father's genes and have government-issue Japanese-girls legs. Songleaders, cheerleaders, ROTC sponsors, student government committee heads. I know them all. Krissie Clifford, who is small and blonde, comes running in late. Krissie looks like a young version of Beaver's mother on the TV show. She's always running like she just fell out of the screen, and if she moves fast enough, she can catch up with the TV world and jump back in. Then she walks in. Leilani Jones. As soon as she walks in the door, everybody in the room turns to look at her. Everybody in the room knows that Leilani is the only girl who can possibly win.

Lani is *hapa*, Japanese-*haole*. She inherited the best features from everybody. She is tall and slim, with light brown hair and butter frosting skin. I don't even know what she is wearing. Leilani is so beautiful it doesn't matter what she is wearing. She is smooth, and gracefully quiet. Her smile is soft and shiny. It's like looking at a pearl. Lani is not only beautiful, when you look at her all you hear is silence, like the air around her is stunned. We all know it. This is the only girl who can possibly win.

As soon as Leilani walks in, Mrs. Takahara, the teacher advisor, says, "Well, now, take your seats everyone. We can begin."

We each take a wooden chair on either side of two rows of long library tables. There is a make-up kit and mirror at each of the places. Some of Mrs. Takahara's friends who are teachers are also sitting in.

"This is Mrs. Chung, beauty consultant of Kamedo cosmetics," Mrs. Takahara says. "She will show us the proper routines of skin cleansing and make-up. The Carnival Queen contest is a very special event. All the girls who are contestants must be worthy representatives of McKinley High School. This means the proper make-up and attitude. Mrs. Chung . . ."

I have to admire the beauty consultant. Even though her makeup is obvious as scaffolding in front of a building, it is so well done, kind of like the men who dance the girls' parts in Kabuki shows, you look at it and actually believe that what you are seeing is her face.

"First, we start with proper cleansing," she says. We stare into our own separate mirrors.

"First, we pin our hair so that it no longer hangs in our faces." All of the girls dig in handbags and come up with bobby pins. Hairstyles disappear as we pin our hair straight back. The teachers look funny, kind of young without their teased hair. Mrs. Chung walks around to each station. She squeezes a glop of pink liquid on a cotton ball for each of us.

"Clean all the skin well," she says. "Get all the dirt and impurities out." We scrub hard with that cotton ball, we all know that our skin is loaded with lots of stuff that is impure. My friend Trudye gets kind of carried away. She was scrubbing so hard around her eyes that she scrubbed off her scotch tape. She hurries over to Mrs. Takahara's chair, mumbles something and excuses herself. I figure she'll be gone pretty long, the only bathroom that is safe for us to use is all the way over in the other building.

"Now we moisturize," Mrs. Chung is going on. "We use this step to correct defects in the tones of our skins." I look over at Terry. I can't see any defects in any of the tones of her skin.

"This mauve moisturizer corrects sallow undertones," Mrs. Chung says.

"What's shallow?" I whisper to Terry.

"*Sallow*," she whispers back disgusted. "Yellow."

"Oh," I say and gratefully receive the large glop of purple stuff Mrs. Chung is squeezing on my new cotton ball. Mrs. Chung squeezes a little on Terry's cotton ball too. When she passes Lani, she smiles and squeezes white stuff out from a different tube.

I happily sponge the purple stuff on. Terry is sponging too but I notice she is beginning to look like she has the flu. "Next, foundation," says Mrs. Chung. She is walking around, narrowing her eyes at each of us and handing us each a tube that she is sure is the correct color to bring out the best in our skin. Mrs. Chung hands me a plastic tube of dark beige. She gives Terry a tube of lighter beige and gives Lani a different tube altogether.

"Just a little translucent creme," she smiles to Lani who smiles back rainbow bubbles and strands of pears.

Trudye comes rushing back and Linda catches her up on all the steps she's missed. I got to admit, without her glasses and with all that running, she has really pretty cheekbones and nice colored skin. I notice she has new scotch tape on too, and is really concentrating on what Mrs. Chung is saying next.

"Now that we have the proper foundation, we concentrate on the eyes." She pulls out a rubber and chrome pincer machine. She stands in front of Linda with it. I become concerned.

"The eyelashes sometimes grow in the wrong direction," Mrs. Chung informs us. "They must be trained to bend correctly. We use the Eyelash Curler to do this." She hands the machine to Linda. I watch as Linda puts the metal pincer up to her eye and catches her straight, heavy black lashes between the rubber pincer blades.

"Must be sore if they do it wrong and squeeze the eyelid meat," I breathe to Terry. Terry says nothing. She looks upset, like she is trying not to bring up her lunch.

"Eyeshadow must be applied to give the illusion of depth," says Mrs. Chung. "Light on top of the lid, close to the lashes, luminescent color on the whole lid, a dot of white in the center of the iris, and brown below the browbone to accentuate the crease." Mrs. Chung is going pretty fast now. I wonder what the girls who have Oriental eyelids without a crease are going to do. I check out the room quickly, over the top of my make-up mirror. Sure enough, all the Oriental girls here have a nice crease in their lids. Those who don't are wearing scotch tape. Mrs. Chung is passing out "pearlescent" eyeshadow.

"It's made of fish scales," Terry says. I have eyelids that are all right, but eyeshadow, especially sparkling eyeshadow, makes me look like a gecko, you know, with protruding eye sockets that go in separate directions. Terry has beautiful deep-socketed eyes and browbones that don't need any help to look well-defined. I put on the stuff in spite of my better judgment and spend the rest of the time trying not to move my eyeballs too much, just in case anybody notices. Lani is putting on all this makeup too. But in her case, it just increases the pearly glow that her skin is already producing.

"This ends the makeup session," Mrs. Chung is saying. "Now our eyes and skins have the proper preparation for our roles as contestants for Carnival Queen."

"Ma, I running in the Carnival Queen contest," I was saying last night. My mother got that exasperated look on her face.

"You think you get chance!"

"No, but the teachers put in the names of all the student council guys." My mother is beginning to look like she is suffering again.

"When you were small, everybody used to tell me you should run for Cherry Blossom contest. But that was before you got so dark like your father. I always tell you no go out in the sun or wear lotion like me when you go out but you never listen."

"Yeah, Ma, but we get modeling lessons, make-up, how to walk."

"Good, might make you stand up straight. I would get you a back brace, but when you were small, we paid so much money for your legs, to get special shoes connected to a bar. You only cried and never would wear them. That's why you still have crooked legs."

That was last night. Now I'm here and Mrs. Takahara is telling us about the walking and modeling lessons.

"Imagine a string coming out of the roof of your skull and connected to the ceiling. Shorten the string and walk with your chin out and back erect. Float! Put one foot in front of the other, point your toes outward and glide forward on the balls of your feet. When you stop, place one foot slightly behind the other at a forty-five degree angle. Put your weight on the back foot . . ." I should have worn the stupid shoes when I was small. I'm bow-legged. Just like my father. Leilani is not bow-legged. She looks great

putting one long straight tibia in front of the other. I look kind of like a
crab. We walk in circles around and around the room. Terry is definitely not
happy. She's walking pretty far away from me. Once, when I pass her, I
could swear she is crying.

"Wow, long practice, yeah?" I say as we walk across the lawn heading
toward the bus. Terry, Trudye, Linda, and I are still together. A black Buick
pulls up to the curb. Terry's mom has come to pick her up. Terry's mom
always picks her up. She must have just come back from the beauty shop.
Her head is wrapped in a pink net wind bonnet. Kind of like the cake we
always get at weddings that my mother keeps on top of the television and
never lets anybody eat.

"I'll call you," Terry says.

"I'm so glad that you and Theresa do things together," Terry's mother
says. "Theresa needs girlfriends like you, Sam." I'm looking at the pink net
around her face. I wonder if Terry's father ever gets the urge to smash her
hair down to feel the shape of her head. Terry looks really uncomfortable as
they drive away.

I feel uncomfortable too. Trudye and Linda's make-up looks really
weird in the afternoon sunlight. My eyeballs feel larger than tank turrets
and they must be glittering brilliantly too. The Liliha-Puunui bus comes
and we all get on. The long center aisle of the bus gives me an idea. I put
one foot in front of the other and practice walking down. Good thing it is
late and the guys we go to school with are not getting on.

"You think Leilani is going to win?" Trudye asks.

"What?" I say as I almost lose my teeth against the metal pole I'm
holding on to. The driver has just started up, and standing with your feet at
a forty-five degree angle doesn't work on public transportation.

"Lani is probably going to win, yeah?" Trudye says again. She can
hide her eye make-up behind her glasses and looks pretty much OK. "I'm
going to stay in for the experience. Plus, I'm going to the orthodontist and
take my braces out and I asked my mother if I could have contact lenses and
she said OK." Trudye goes on, but I don't listen. I get a seat by the window
and spend the whole trip looking out so nobody sees my fish scale eyes.

I am not surprised when I get home and the phone begins to ring.

"Sam it's Terry. You stay in the contest. But I decided I'm not going
to run."

"That's nuts, Terry," I am half screaming at her, "you are the only one
of us besides Lani that has chance to win. You could be the first Japanese
Carnival Queen that McKinley ever had." I am going to argue this one.

"Do you know the real name of this contest?" Terry asks.

"I don't know, Carnival Queen. I've never thought about it I guess."

"It's the Carnival Queen Scholarship Contest."

"Oh, so?" I'm still interested in arguing that only someone with legs like Terry even has a chance.

"Why are you running? How did you get nominated?" Terry asks.

"I'm Senior Class secretary, they had to nominate me, but you . . ."

"And WHY are you secretary," she cuts me off before I get another running start about chances.

"I don't know, I guess because I used to write poems for English class and they always got in the paper or the yearbook. And probably because Miss Chuck made me write a column for the newspaper for one year to bring up my social studies grade."

"See . . . and why am I running?"

"OK, you're class officer, and sponsor, and you won the American Legion essay contest . . ."

"And Krissy?"

"She's editor of the yearbook, and a sponsor and the Yanagawa twins are songleaders and Trudye is prom committee chairman and Linda . . ." I am getting into it.

"And Lani," says Terry quietly.

"Well, she's a sponsor I think . . ." I've lost some momentum. I really don't know.

"I'm a sponsor, and I know she's not," Terry says.

"Student government? No . . . I don't think so . . . not cheering, her sister is the one in the honor society, not . . . hey, not, couldn't be . . ."

"That's right," Terry says, "the only reason she's running is because she's supposed to win." It couldn't be true. "That means the rest of us are all running for nothing. The best we can do is second place." My ears are getting sore with the sense of what she says. "We're running because of what we did. But we're going to lose because of what we look like. Look, it's still good experience and you can still run if you like."

"Nah . . ." I say, still dazed by it. "But what about Mrs. Takahara, what about your mother?" Terry is quiet.

"I think I can handle Mrs. Takahara," Terry finally says.

"I'll say I'm not running, too. If it's two of us, it won't be so bad." I am actually kind of relieved that this is the last day I'll have to put gecko eye make-up all over my face.

"Thanks, Sam . . ." Terry says.

"Yeah . . . My mother will actually be relieved. Ever since I forgot the ending at my piano recital in fifth grade, she gets really nervous if I'm in front of any audience."

"You want me to pick you up for the carnival Saturday night?" Terry asks.

"I'll ask my Mom," I say. "See you then . . ."

"Yeah . . ."

I think, "We're going to lose because of what we look like." I need a shower, my eyes are itching anyway. I'm glad my mother isn't home yet. I think best in the shower and sometimes I'm in there an hour or more.

Soon, with the world a small square of warm steam and tile walls, it all starts going through my head. The teachers looked so young in the make-up demonstration with their hair pinned back—they looked kind of like us. But we are going to lose because of what we look like. I soap the layers of make-up off my face. I guess they're tired of looking like us: *musubi* bodies, *daikon* legs, *furoshiki*-shaped, home-made dresses, *bento* tins to be packed in the early mornings, mud and sweat everywhere. The water is splashing down on my face and hair. But Krissy doesn't look like us, and she is going to lose too. Krissy looks like the Red Cross society lady from intermediate school. She looks like Beaver's mother on the television show. Too haole. She's going to lose because of the way she looks. Lani doesn't look anything like anything from the past. She looks like something that could only have been born underwater where all motions are slow and all sounds are soft. I turn off the water and towel off. Showers always make me feel clean and secure. I guess I can't blame even the teachers, everyone wants to feel safe and secure.

My mother is sitting at the table peeling an orange. She does this almost every night and I already know what she's going to say.

"Eat this orange, good for you, lots of vitamin C."

"I don't want to eat orange now, Ma." I know it is useless, but I say it anyway. My mother is the kind of Japanese lady who will hunch down real small when she passes in front of you when you're watching TV. Makes you think she's quiet and easy going, but not on the subject of vitamin C.

"I peeled it already. Want it?" Some people actually think that my mother is shy.

"I not running in the contest. Terry and I going quit."

"Why?" my mother asks, like she really doesn't need to know.

"Terry said that we running for nothing. Everybody already knows Lani going win." My mother looks like she just tasted some orange peel.

"That's not the real reason." She hands me the orange and starts washing the dishes.

There's lots of things I don't understand. Like why Terry hangs out with me. Why my mother is always so curious about her and now why she doesn't think this is the real reason that Terry is quitting the contest.

"What did the mother say about Terry quitting the contest?" my mother asks without turning around.

"I donno, nothing I guess."

"Hmmmmmm . . . . . that's not the real reason. That girl is different. They way the mother treats her is different." Gee, having a baby and being a mother must be really hard and it must really change a person because all I know is that my mother is really different from me.

Terry picks me up Saturday night in her brother's white Mustang. It's been a really busy week. I haven't even seen her since we quit the contest. We had to build the Senior Class Starch Throwing Booth.

"Hi, Sam. We're working until ten o'clock on the first shift, OK?" Terry is wearing a triangle denim scarf in her hair, a workshirt and jeans. Her face is flushed from driving with the Mustang's top down and she looks really glamorous.

"Yeah, I thought we weren't going to finish the booth this afternoon. Lucky thing my dad and Lenny's dad helped us with the hammering and Valerie's committee got the cardboard painted in time. We kind of ran out of workers because most of the girls . . ." I don't have to finish. Most of the student council girls are getting dressed up for the contest.

"Mrs. Sato and the cafeteria ladies finished cooking the starch and Neal and his friends and some of the football guys are going to carry the big pots of starch over to the booth for us." Terry is in charge of the manpower because she knows everybody.

"Terry's mother is on the phone!" my mother is calling to us from the house. Terry runs in to answer the phone. Funny, her mother always calls my house when Terry is supposed to pick me up. My mother looks out at me from the door. The look on her face says, "Checking up." Terry runs past her and jumps back in the car.

"You're lucky, your mother is really nice," she says.

We go down Kuakini Street and turn onto Liliha. We pass School Street and head down the freeway on-ramp. Terry turns on K-POI and I set-tle down in my seat. Terry drives faster than my father. We weave in and out of cars as she guns the Mustang down H-1. I know this is not very safe, but I like the feeling in my stomach. It's like going down hills. My hair is flying wild and I feel so clean and good. Like the first day of algebra class before the symbols get mixed up. Like the first day of chemistry before we have to learn molar solutions. I feel like it's going to be the first day forever and I can make the clean feeling last and last. The ride is too short. We turn off by the Board of Water Supply station and we head down by the Art Academy and turn down Pensacola past Mr. Feiterra's green gardens and into the parking lot of the school.

"I wish you were still in the contest tonight," I tell Terry as we walk out toward the Carnival grounds. "I mean you are so perfect for the Carnival Queen. You were the only Japanese girl that was perfect enough to win."

"I thought you were my friend," Terry starts mumbling. "You sound like my mother. You only like me because of what you think I should be." She starts walking faster and is leaving me behind.

"Wait! What? How come you getting so mad?" I'm running to keep up with her.

"Perfect, perfect. What if I'm *not* perfect. What if I'm not what people think I am? What if I can't be what people think I am?" She's not making any sense to me and she's crying. "Why can't you just like me? I thought you were different. I thought you just liked me. I thought you were my friend because you just liked *Me*." I'm following her and feeling like it's exam time in chemistry. I'm flunking again and I don't understand.

We get to the Senior booth and Terry disappears behind the cardboard. Valerie Rosecrest is there and hands me a lot of paper cupcake cups and a cafeteria juice ladle.

"Quick, we need at least a hundred of these filled, we're going to be open in ten minutes."

"Try wait, I got to find Terry." I look behind the cardboard back of the booth. Terry is not there. I run all around the booth. Terry is nowhere in sight. The Senior booth is under a tent in the midway with all the games. There are lots of lightbulbs strung like kernels of corn on wires inside the tent. There's lots of game booths and rows and rows of stuffed animal prizes on clotheslines above each booth. I can't find Terry and I want to look around more, but all of a sudden the merry-go-round music starts and all the lights come on. The senior booth with its handpainted signs, "Starch Throw—three scrip" looks alive all of a sudden in the warm Carnival light.

"Come on, Sam!" Valerie is calling me. "We're opening. I need you to help!" I go back to the booth. Pretty soon Terry comes back and I look at her kind of worried, but under the soft popcorn light, you cannot even tell she was crying.

"Terry, Mr. Miller said that you're supposed to watch the scrip can and take it to the cafeteria when it's full." Val's talking to her, blocking my view. Some teachers are arriving for first shift. They need to put on shower caps and stick their heads through holes in the cardboard so students can buy paper cupcake cups full of starch to throw to try to hit the teachers in the face. Terry goes in the back to help the teachers get ready. Lots of guys from my drop-out class are lining up in the front of the booth.

"Eh, Sam, come on take my money. Ogawa's back there. He gave me the F in math. Gimmee the starch!" Business is getting better and better all night. Me, Val, and Terry are running around the booth, taking scrip, filling cupcake cups, and getting out of the way fast when the guys throw the starch. Pretty soon, the grass in the middle of the booth turns into a mess that looks like thrown-up starch, and we are trying not to slip as we run around trying to keep up with business.

"Ladies and gentlemen, McKinley High School is proud to present the 1966 Carnival Queen and her court." It comes over the loudspeaker. It must be the end of the contest, ten o'clock. All the guys stop buying starch and turn to look toward the tent. Pretty soon, everyone in the tent has cleared the center aisle. They clap as five girls in evening dresses walk our way.

"Oh, great," I think. "I have starch in my hair and I don't want to see them." The girls are all dressed in long gowns and are wearing white gloves. The first girl is Linda. She looks so pretty in a maroon velvet A-line gown. Cannot see her musubi-shaped body and her face is just glowing. The rhinestones in her tiara are sparkling under each of the hundreds of carnival lights. The ribbon on her chest says "Third Princess." It's neat! Just like my cousin Carolyn's wedding. My toes are tingling under their coating of starch. The next is Trudye. She's not wearing braces and she looks so pretty in her lavender gown. Some of the guys are going "Wow," under their breath as she walks by. The first Princesses pass next. The Yanagawa twins. They're wearing matching pink gowns and have pink baby roses in their hair, which is in ringlets. Their tiaras look like lace snowflakes on their heads as they pass by. And last. Even though I know who this is going to be I really want to see her. Sure enough, everybody in the crowd gets quiet as she passes by. Lani looks like her white dress is made of sugar crystals. As she passes her crown sparkles tiny rainbows under the hundreds of light-bulbs from the tent and flashbulbs popping like little suns.

The court walks through the crowd and stops at the Senior booth. Mr. Harano, the principal, steps out.

"Your majesty," he's talking to Lani who is really glowing. "I will become a target in the Senior booth in your honor. Will you and your Princesses please take aim and do your best as royal representatives of our school?"

I look around at Terry. The principal is acting so stupid. I can't believe he really runs the whole school. Terry must be getting so sick. But I look at her and she's standing in front of Lani and smiling. This is weird. She's the one who said everyone knew who was supposed to win. She's smiling at Lani like my grandmother used to smile at me when I was five. Like I was a sweet *mochi* dumpling floating in red bean soup. I cannot stand it. I quit the contest so she wouldn't have to quit alone. And she yells at me and hasn't talked to me all night. All I wanted was for her to be standing there instead of Lani.

The Carnival Queen and four Princesses line up in front of the booth. Val, Terry, and I scramble around giving each of them three cupcake cups of starch. They get ready to throw. The guys from the newspaper and the yearbook get ready to take their picture. I lean as far back into the wall as I can. I know Trudye didn't have time to get contacts yet and she's not wearing any glasses. I wonder where Val is and if she can flatten out enough against the wall to get out of the way. Suddenly, a hand reaches out and grabs my ankle. I look down, and Terry, who is sitting under the counter of the booth with Val, grabs my hand and pulls me down on the grass with them. The ground here is nice and clean. The Carnival Queen and Princesses and the rows of stuffed animals are behind and above us. The air is filled with pink cupcake cups and starch as they throw. Mr. Harano closes his eyes, the flashbulbs go off, but no one comes close to hitting his face. Up above us everyone is laughing and clapping. Down below, Terry, Val, and I are nice and clean.

"Lani looks so pretty, Sam," Terry is looking at me and smiling.

"Yeah, even though the contest was juice she looks really good. Like a storybook," I say, hoping it's not sounding too fake.

"Thanks for quitting with me." Terry's smile is like the water that comes out from between the rocks at Kunawai Stream. I feel so clean in that smile.

"It would have been lonely if I had to quit by myself," Terry says, looking down at our starch-covered shoes. She looks up at me and smiles again. And even if I'm covered with starch, I suddenly know that to her, I am beautiful. Her smile tells me that we're friends because I went to drop-out class. It is a smile that can wash away all the F's that Mr. Low, my chemistry teacher, will ever give. I have been waiting all my life for my mother to give me that smile. I know it is a smile that Terry's mother has never smiled at her. I don't know where she learned it.

It's quiet now, the Carnival Queen and her Princesses have walked away. Terry stands up first as she and Val and I start to crawl out from our safe place under the counter of the booth. She gives me her hand to pull me up and I can see her out in the bright Carnival light. Maybe every girl looks like a queen at one time in her life.

SHORT TONGUE
Lisa Linn Kanae

My little braddah, he not mento.
So you bettah stop teasing him,
all da time making like you can talk
more bettah dan him,
more bettah dan all da kids
going da regular-kine schools,
not da special-kine schools
where da teacha clamp
one rulah-looking kine' ting on your tongue
just so you can *ar-teek-coo-late*.
My braddah wen gag so much,
he hate fo talk.

I hold my maddah's hand
everytime da bus drivah take Harold-Boy away.
Inside dat yellow bus get funny-kine looking childrens.
One boy look like he stay wearing one bird cage
over his head, only his eyes can move.
Get one girl wit magnifying glasses—
da kine fo kill ants—
strapped to her head.
Get one noddah girl who no can stay still,
she use to pull out her hair
befo da bus drivah wen force her
for wear white seatbelts
across her chest and her legs.
And get one skinny boy, he just stare at my braddah.
What you looking at? I yell,
Baddah you or what?
He no say noting.
Gala gala dribbles from his crooked lip,
collar stay all wet.

Piss me off.
Harold-Boy neva do nutting wrong.
Only me can understand what he trying fo say.
Is-tah, Is-tah—Sister;
Wuh-yold—World;
Too-too, Too-too—Popeye da Sailor Man.
We smile up
when he squeeze da can,
eat da spinach, beat up Brutus.
Olive Oyl, she kiss Popeye all ovah,
heart wit wings fly all around deah heads.
My braddah,
he love to sing along wit da Popeye song.
You like undahstand him or what?
Try let him sing.

A SCOLDING FROM MY FATHER
Juliet S. Kono

To R.H., D.K., M.M.

What kind Japanee you?
Nothing more worse in this world
than one Japanee
who like be something
he not.
No matter how much you like—
no can!
No can be haole.
Who the girl? You know, the Michael girl.
The doctor's daughta, good-looking,
live in the big house Wailuku Drive.
Big eyes, nice car, blonde hair.
You like talk like one haole?
You like big eyes?
You try live their house.
No can *be* Chinee.
Rich. Wong-family-rich.
Daughta go Honolulu, dorm at Punahou.
We no more their kind money.
Me? I only one mechanic.
Your mother, Baker II
at Waiākea Waena Elementary School Cafeteria.
And no can *be* Hawaiian.
Like Keli'i family daughta.
You know which one—the smart one.
Good hula dancer, fast swimmer, going mainland.
You like dance like her?
Nice nose too she get—some tall.
You like one nose like her?
You dreaming, girl.
Come from her mother side.
You one flat nose Japanee
because your mother get flat nose.
So why you like ack different for?

Why you like be something you not?
You no more shame or what?
Eh, you no figa too,
that maybe these guys
they no *like* you
suck around them?

FROM A . . . BOX BUILDER
Lanning Lee

> A teacher affects eternity; he can never tell where his influence stops.
>
> Henry Adams, *The Education of Henry Adams*

It was a Saturday morning, two Decembers ago. I was sitting in almost the exact same spot where I'd sat that Saturday morning back in the fall semester of 1970, after I'd broken into the art room through a window. Back then I'd wanted to spend the day handbuilding a huge pot I'd started during my ceramics class earlier in the week. This time I was working on a kind of organic sculpture vaguely resembling something between a human body and a mass of vine-like foliage.

I looked up from my work when he walked silently, as always, into the ceramics room. He smiled that soft smile of his, barely whispered a hello, and began loading articles from his ancient, green, metal desk into a small cardboard box. It looked as though he hadn't shaved that morning, which was unusual for him. His hair wasn't combed. I watched his swift, silent packing. There was no conversation. He finished quickly, turned to me and said, "And don't forget—" That quick, gentle smile spoke volumes—"to lock up, Chris." I nodded. He turned away, then disappeared down the hallway. I didn't know it then, but that was the last time I would see him at the school. He had retired, without telling anyone, and he was gone for good to Maui.

It was August, 1970, the first day of my eleventh-grade year. Most of my closest friends had already taken ceramics, some since ninth grade. Not a single one had ever said a negative word about the class. They all seemed to love it. I was bored. I can't even remember what electives I'd had in ninth and tenth grade. This art class looked like a good choice.

I suppose because I was known to make a good-humored wisecrack or two on occasion, a few of my friends wanted to warn me to hold back a bit in this class.

"Eh, Chris," Gerald advised as we went down the concrete stairs past the kiln area and into the glazing room, "watch out for Yamada. He's a nice guy, but he's kind of . . . well, strict."

"What, Gerald, no sense of humor?"

Gerald rubbed his chin. "Ah, nah, well, yeah, but . . . "

Patrice laughed. "What he means, Chris, is that Yamada isn't going to put up with all of your lame jokes and let you be a butthead. You'll find out the hard way if you act wise."

"Eh, guys, my jokes aren't that bad, are they?"

No comment.

We turned in to the ceramics room. In one corner there were three rows of stools lined up, stadium style. Standing very tall at a table in front of the stools, Mr. Yamada was nodding and smiling at both the old and the new faces. He didn't look too mean to me, but I was curious now.

"Okay, all the old students, get working on whatever projects you want. All the new students, please take a seat on these stools." The Japanese man gestured to the elevated rows of gray metal stools.

I don't really know why I felt so nervous all of a sudden. "New students? That's me," I thought, feeling odd twinges of real dread for having consigned myself to this class. "Rules and regulations, maybe?" I wondered.

I sat in the back row. Gerald and Patrice had helped hatch a strange fear in me. I mean, Mr. Yamada seemed like a pretty nice guy, but I was worried. Something weird, some kind of bizarre vibrations were running through the novice group. Even the most notorious troublemakers, like Ron, were quickly settled and silent. We all could feel whatever it was.

After a big smile—it seemed real—and a hearty hello, Mr. Yamada pinched a handful of clay off a large, cone-shaped mound that sat on the table. He then proceeded to mold it, quickly, into a perfectly smooth, round ball. This ball he held out to us. "I want to welcome you to Beginning Ceramics. This," he tossed the ball lightly in the air, "is the medium you will be working with. If you look over at those shelves," he pointed to a display area for finished projects, "you will see that we can create many different shapes—almost any shape you can imagine and then successfully engineer." Another enormous smile.

"Do any of you know what property it is that allows us to create this wide variety of shapes?"

Silence. Blank stares. The typical student response.

"Well, let me put that another way. Do any of you know the word we use to describe the quality of clay that makes it so easy to shape?"

I was still quite nervous, but I raised my hand, very slowly.

"Yes . . . what is your name?"

"Chris. Christopher Lau."

"Okay, Christopher, what word do you think it is?"

Everyone had turned around to watch me. "Ah, is it 'flexible'?"

"Flexible. That's a very good word, Chris. Flexible is close, but that's not quite the word we're looking for."

He looked around at the other students. "Anybody else have a word?"

I raised my hand again. "Yes, Chris," he chuckled. "Do you want to have another go at it?"

"Ahm, how about 'pliable'?"

"Pliable. That's another good choice, Chris, but it's still not quite the word we're after."

My hand went up again. "Is it 'malleable'?"

"That's a fine guess too, Chris, but we tend to use malleable when we talk, oh, say, about metals that are easy to work."

"Elastic?" I questioned.

"Hmmmmm, you're getting very warm, Christopher. You're almost there." He gave me what looked like a very kind, very encouraging look. But I'd run out of words. "Okay, I don't want to wear Mr. Lau out, so I'll tell you the word. It's 'plastic.' Clay is extremely plastic. Watch how easily I can mold this into any shape I'm after."

He stopped speaking and began to work the clay. In a matter of seconds his powerful hands and veined arms had turned the ball of clay into what he called a pinch pot. He held up the finished product. "Of course, this is a little bit easier for me because I've been practicing a while. But if you practice hard, too, you'll be able to do this just as easily."

He set the pot down on the table, picked up a piece of fishing line, and swiftly sliced the pot in half. He held the cut edges toward us. "See how thin the walls are. And notice that they are very even, though thickening slightly toward the bottom. Your first project will be to make a simple pinch pot, like this one. Are there any questions?"

There weren't. "All right," he said, smashing the pot back into the big cone of clay, "come with me and I'll show you where to get your clay and how to wedge the air bubbles out of it."

We followed quickly, in silence. I wanted to dig right in and whip out my pinch pot, but trying to figure out how to wedge the clay properly took the rest of the period.

During that week, and even the next week, I tried very hard to make the "perfect" pinch pot. Mr. Yamada would sit with each one of us, offering advice on technique. He smiled all the time and rarely spoke as loudly as he had on that first day. With no effort at all, he had gained total control over the classroom. He dominated it. And although he appeared gentle, no one looked very anxious to cross him.

Every day I sweated blood over my latest pinch pot. Every time I thought I'd done the job, Mr. Yamada would either weigh the pot in his hand and tell me it was not proportioned correctly, or he would cut it in half and show me how uneven the walls were. My frustration mounted, but I kept trying to get it right.

"Don't be afraid to destroy your work and start over," he told me—every single time. Then he'd grin while he watched me mash my latest failure back into its little "plastic" lump.

After pinch pots, we were supposed to "master" simple coil rolling. Everyone moved busily on to making tiny coiled objects—except me. I continued to struggle with my pinch pot, the only one in the class who still did not have what Mr. Yamada would call a "keeper." By the time he finally allowed me save my first lousy pinch pot, that still wasn't as nice as plenty of the others—and most of those were borderline pathetic—almost everyone else had finished their stage-two coil projects.

The class moved on to slabs then, but not me. "Try to get your coils more even, Christopher. Try to make them more uniform." It wasn't easy. "Thinner, Chris, make them thinner." Yeah, right, I'd think, gritting my teeth.

Something was happening to me. I spent more and more time sitting there doing nothing that seemed important. I was sick of the effort it took to roll out first the "perfect" coil, then the "perfect" slab. Why did everything have to be so "perfect"? I'd thought this class was going to be easy. Why in the world did all my friends think this guy was so great anyway? He was definitely turning me off to art, as far as I was concerned.

I let myself slide. I started fooling around, wasting clay on the most peculiarly useless little projects. One day I rolled out some very thick, very uneven slabs, plastered them together into a mountain, and planted a tiny clay tree and a little clay cabin on top of it. Tom laughed at me each time he looked over at my "sculpture." I asked him to kindly shut up.

At the end of class I was about to crush the whole thing into a "nonkeeper" ball when Mr. Yamada came over to inspect my minor masterpiece. "You have to weld that tree together a little better," he said. "It won't make it through the firing like that."

"The firing?" I asked, not quite comprehending what this voice from heaven meant.

"Yes, the firing." He walked around to the other side of the table, taking in the full effect of viewing my humble piece in the round. "You know, Chris . . ." The considering pause was quite lengthy. "That's the first thing you've ever really done. It's definitely a keeper."

He walked away. Patrice came over to me. "Wow, Chris, Yamada really likes this, huh?"

"Really?" I couldn't quite figure it out. I thought I'd been wasting time. I thought I was fooling around. I was surprised he hadn't been upset.

216 Lanning C. Lee

Welding the tree together took some time; I was late for my next class, but Mr. Yamada wrote me a note of excuse.

From then on, Mr. Yamada rarely talked to me. One day in late November he walked into the room. It was lunchtime, and only a few of us were spending that sacred lounging period working. I was piecing together what I seriously referred to as a "stylized goblet." Everything I did now was taking me one step farther, each time, into the realm of the strange, the stranger, and hopefully, one day, the strangest. Mr. Yamada observed me for a while, his arms folded contemplatively across his chest. Finally he spoke. "You know, Christopher, if you keep this up, you could die famous." Then he turned around and walked back out the door.

It was a Saturday morning in December, 1970. School would be out in just under two weeks. I'd begun work on what I projected would be an enormous coil-built vase. I figured that class time and lunch time alone wouldn't be enough to complete it. After parking my car way up on Metcalf Street, quite a distance from the art room, I walked casually down the stairs of the mountain side of the building. I tried forcing open several of the lower windows without any luck. The last window budged a little, so I put more pressure on it. Someone hadn't secured the latch, and the window popped open. I wriggled in through the opening.

I took one of the gray metal stools off the table and then began a production line roll of coils, all of them as long and as thick as possible. With the other stools up on the tables around me, I figured I was pretty well screened from view of the security guards and other passersby. I hadn't turned on the overhead lights either, though it was overcast and fairly dark in the room. After twenty minutes or so, I began to feel pretty relaxed and fairly sure that I was secure.

You know, Mr. Yamada had always moved silently, like a ninja in fact. He could come up right behind you, but you'd never know it until he either said something, or slid stealthily into your peripheral field of vision.

That particular morning he turned the key in the lock and walked into the room before I even realized he was there. I was hidden from view, thanks to all of the stools, but I could neither get over to the window nor out the front door without him noticing me. I sat there petrified, wondering whether he had it in him to kill me. I watched him closely, hoping for an opportunity to escape.

I had never seen Mr. Yamada move the way he did that Saturday morning, now that he believed he was alone in the classroom. He appeared to be somehow possessed. After tossing his wallet and keys on his desk, he ripped off his shirt and quickly put on his long, blue denim smock. That smock had always hung on the hook next to his desk, but I'd never actually seen him wear it. It never seemed to get dirty. Now, dressed for what looked like some very serious work, he took long, forceful strides to the galvanized garbage can which contained the clay. In two or three muscular scoops, he piled up what looked to be about fifty pounds of clay. While he manhandled the huge mound at the wedging table, he whistled, loudly, some tune which was unfamiliar to me. He hoisted the perfect cone of clay effortlessly, though I could see the muscles in his back and arms bulge. Still whistling, he walked over to the Robert Brent wheel and slammed the clay square in the middle of the bat. He went to the sink, filled a large bowl with water, then returned to the wheel with chamois, sponge, and teasing needle in hand. The wheel engine hummed louder as the spinning mound accelerated. While he centered the clay he wiped perspiration from his forehead on his bare shoulder from time to time. I could feel the intensity of his concentration; I realized that he'd stopped whistling. All of his energy became centered in the clay. I'd never seen anyone throw such a huge mass at one time.

And then it happened. He suddenly stood up and took several forceful steps in my direction. He stopped. We were looking each other in the eye. He smiled. "Oh," he said softly, "hello, Chris. Working hard, are we?"

I nodded, at most, a weak yes. I wondered what he'd do to me. He walked by me, picked up several empty boards, and returned to the wheel. He went back to work, throwing perfect tea bowls, one after another, maybe fifty of them, or more. After I realized our conversation was over, I went back to building my vase. I didn't feel very relaxed for some time, but gradually I lost myself in the work. Like he had, the instant he stopped talking to me.

My vase had grown by about two feet when I noticed him putting his shirt back on. "Christopher, I've set the lock, so all you have to do is slam the door when you leave. And," he smiled, "make sure all the windows are latched . . . tight."

"Okay, sure. Yes, Mr. Yamada, I will." That afternoon, after double-checking all the windows and before slamming the door securely shut, I inspected the blue smock. It was still spotlessly clean.

On Monday morning, Mr. Yamada gave me a set of keys to all the art rooms in Castle Memorial Hall. He also gave me a letter, addressed to the security guards, stating that any Lab School students who were working after hours and on weekends were authorized, by him, to do so. By the time senior year rolled around, many of us were in the art wing at all hours of the day and night. Mr. Yamada taught everyone how to operate the kiln. Production was up so much that he, alone, couldn't possibly manage to bisque and fire all our work.

When I graduated from the Lab School in 1972, I asked Mr. Yamada to sign my annual. My slab technique must have improved quite a bit. This is what he wrote:

> Aloha to a Super Box Builder:
> Christopher, it was rough going, but I think
> I've succeeded a little in toughening your hide.
>
> Shige Yamada

But the story doesn't quite end there. I've come back to the Lab School, a teacher now. When I first ran into Mr. Yamada, I called him "Mr. Yamada."

He smiled that same, old, mysterious smile, and said in that same, gentle voice, "Chris, we're colleagues now. You don't have to call me Mr. Yamada. Please, call me Shige."

"Okay, Mr. . . . Shige," I said. I nearly choked on the words.

Before that final Saturday morning, two Decembers ago, I must have seen him day after day after day. But I could only ever manage to call him "Shige" that one time. Every time afterwards, I addressed him as "Mr. Yamada." Each time I said it, he would smile. And then he was gone.

It's a good thing that my hide is so tough these days.

THE VISIT
Tori Lono

We are driving along a road when I catch sight of a big gray building. It is the place I have come all the way from Maui to Oʻahu to visit. My father is somewhere in those dull, cold, concrete walls. It is time I visit my dad. The thing is: I am not walking to his room downstairs to say good morning; I am not walking up the dirt path to visit him; I am visiting a prison.

My dad has gotten himself into trouble: my kind, intelligent dad whom I love so much. I trusted him. We used to have so much fun. Sometimes it's hard to believe that someone who once seemed so good could have done something so dumb.

My knees feel like water as we, my brother, mom and I, walk to the door. My heart seems to bulge out of my chest. I begin to chew my finger. *What am I supposed to say to him?* I try to think of things we can talk about. I want to grab his hand and run the rough trail to the beach, or jump into the cool ponds of ʻUlaʻino. I want to sleep in the sweet smelling ginger patch and know that my dad will come to wake me and take me home, but I can't do any of these things . . . anymore.

We can try and play games. I grab a paper and pencil out of my mom's purse and put it in my pocket. Just inside the door, my mom is giving information to the woman who sits behind the collapsible table set up for visiting hours. I manage to braid my hair and fish a rubber band out of my pocket. The lady just asks for facts: nothing more, nothing less. She wears a drab uniform that seems to blend in with the depressing walls. Her hair is short and dull just like her uniform and the building in which I stand, the building that keeps my father from home and family.

Mechanically she asks, "Can I see your passports or birth certificates?" My mom hands the lady all three passports. "Who are you here to visit?"

As my mom answers, I stop listening. *Yes, if we play games that should take up a lot of time.*

My mom is done talking to the lady behind the table, who motions to another security guard. Now we are headed towards the women's bathroom to be searched. All she does is run her hands along our clothes. Then she asks us to remove our shoes and she checks to see if we have taped any drugs or contraband under our feet or shoes. She says that I can't take a paper and pencil with me or wear the rubber band that is holding my braid together, and my poor brother has to change because his knee-length shorts are too short.

We go back out to the car so my brother can change. My mother unlocks the door, and I find a pair of pants for him to wear. We lock the car and decide on hiding the key above one of the tires in the fender. We are all so nervous that we waste time on trivial things instead of rushing in to see my dad.

We walk towards the gray building once again and I am feeling anxious yet excited. Forget the games. *Now the visit is really going to be weird.* We will probably sit there feeling uneasy and not do anything. Oh well.

To get to the next floor we first must go through some strange doors. We press a button, wait till it clicks and push them open. The loud hollow "BOOM" bounces off the walls over and over again. It echoes around me like a desperate and miserable cry on the other side of an enormous cave, dark and empty. We do this four times until we reach the elevator. We finally pass through two more doors. There is my dad. He sits in a chair wearing brown clothes like most of the other prisoners in the room.

As soon as he sees us, he stands and smiles a tentative smile as my brother rushes to hug him. I walk hesitantly, and hug him stiffly. We all sit in plastic chairs lined evenly in rows against the walls.

My dad looks a little different. He is a little skinnier and taller. He is also much whiter. We compare hands and my brother's hand is now the darkest in the family. My dad's hair is short and he doesn't have a beard anymore. I assume he cannot let his hair grow because everyone else here has short hair.

There are guards at every door, but they seem more human than the lady downstairs. My mom, me, my dad, and my brother sit stiffly trying to begin a conversation. My dad tries to ask us questions, but my brother and I answer in just "Yeses," "Nos," and "Kind ofs." Eventually my mom and dad end up doing most of the talking.

Over the loudspeaker a voice vibrates through the room, "Number ten, your visit is over. Number ten." In my dad's pocket is a laminated yellow card with the number ten written on it. I sigh, in relief or disappointment, I don't know. Our "good-byes" are as awkward as our "hellos."

Retracing our steps in silence, we go down the elevator, through the same four doors, and head towards the car. We find the hidden key and get in. We drive away from the dull gray walls that hold my father; we drive onward.

I am glad to have seen my dad and no matter what, I will always love him. I find it hard not to. I cannot walk away from him and forget all the fun we used to have. I do know that we will never have that kind of fun again. *Nothing will ever be the same.*

ORPHAN ANNIE: COLORING IN THE EYES
Darrell H.Y. Lum

My favorite comics was Little Orphan Annie cause she had one big guy Punjab as her bodyguard and she had da rich guy, Big Daddy Warbucks who wasn't her real Daddy, but was rich and kind. Sometimes I used to draw eyeballs in each of the pictures of Little Orphan Annie cause Orphan Annie no mo eyeballs. She jes get circles fo eyes. Sunday was easy cause da pictures was bigger and in color; you put in one small dot in each eye. First one, den da uddah one. J'like how Mrs. Hosaka, our next door neighbor, used to color in the eyeballs of one Daruma doll everytime: first one side when she make one wish and den da uddah side when come true. When Mr. Hosaka went hospital fo operation, she went color one eye. When her son Kennet went Vietnam, she went color one eye. When dey came back okay she went color da uddah side.

She went show me da one fo Kennet. "Da war made him little bit pupule," she told me. "He talk to himself, no go work or nutting. Live by himself. I donno where. Ah, but das all right. At least he nevah come home in a box." She look at me kinda sad. She probably had one nudda Daruma fo wish he come bettah.

Coloring Orphan Annie's eyeballs was j'like wishing fo all da tings I wanted: one nice dog, Sandy, one rich Daddy, one big strong bruddah fo proteck me. Das why I liked dat comics.

Russo's favorite was Dick Tracy, especially da guy, B. O. Plenty, cause he da hauna guy, all dirty and stinky. J'like Alfred in school, ho, da hauna! Russo like Prince Valiant too but I tawt dat comic was junk cause wasn't dat funny and you gotta read um from da beginning or you no can catch da story. Da pickchas was nice though. Da worse comic was Mary Wurt. Russo call um Mary Wurtless. He tell me Mrs. Hosaka j'like Mary Wurt cause she always nosing in uddah people's business.

Russo and Brynie da next door neighbor boy used to call Mrs. Hosaka da witch lady and couple times dey made me call her dat too. I donno if she went hear us but one time Brynie went tell real loud, "She one witch, right? Right, Dan-yo. She one witch, yeah? When you go her house you watch her do her witch stuff. She like you come one witch, too, so you can take ovah when she die. Or you might come all nuts like Kennet!"

My mout like say, "Not. She jes like her good luck cats and her
Daruma dolls and watch out or she going make one voodoo Daruma on
you!" But I no can say dat and pretty soon my mout saying, "Yeah, I guess."
I donno if she went hear me, but if you like stay wit Russo and Brynie, you
gotta talk like dem or else dey going call you anykine stuff. I know dey no
like me play wit dem except Mama tell Russo he gotta watch me, so he no
can send me home even if he always tell me if I no do what he say I no can
play wit dem and he going send me home. I know he no can but I donno
why I so stupid. I let dem tie me to da clothesline pole and be da prisoner of
war; when dey play cowboys, I gotta be da Indian; when dey play war, Russo
is Sgt. Rock and Brynie is da Captain, I gotta be da Japanee.

Mrs. Hosaka tell me, "Daniel-san, why you let dem do dat?"

I tell her, "I donno."

She say, "Da Ching boy, Bryant, all same bad boy. Only smart wit da
mout."

I called him Brynie from small kid time cause I couldn't say Bry-ant.
Brynie smart wit da mout, smart wit da slap to da head too, if you no watch
out.

Mrs. Hosaka said her grandfahdah was one samurai. She get da sword
someplace. She would show um to me bumbye cause I get samurai heart.

"You get good heart, kind heart," she tell me. "Jes like Kennet." Das
da time she was cutting carrot sticks and pointing da knife at me. She said
bumbye she going show da sword to me. I tink everytime she tink about
Kennet, she no pay attention so when she started cutting again, she went
cut her finger little bit and had blood and she went wipe her eyes and den
suck her finger and I went tink about what Russo and Brynie told me about
how witches drink blood.

"Not," I told dem, "only Dracula do dat."

"No, witches too," Brynie said. And I was tinking about dat when I
seen her sucking her finger. She went look at me and ask me if I like have
one Daruma and color one eye.

"Yeah," I said.

"What going be for?" she ask me.

"I donno. Maybe so Russo and Brynie no pick on me."

"Da Daruma not fo one wish, dis not one magic lamp. Dis fo some-
ting you want to accomplish."

"What about you?" I told her. "You always make wishes."

"I'm diffrent. I'm too old to accomplish tings, so I gotta jes wish," she
laugh.

I no catch but I color da eye and she put um on top da TV. Mines is
da one wit da blood fingerprint by da eye.

I used to go to Mrs. Hosaka's house everyday summertime cause she told me she would gimme dollah every day if I came ovah help her around da house. She had dis whole collection of good luck cats and Daruma dolls in her house. She could tell me what each one was for. Kinda spooky when you walk inside her living room cause she get like fifty of dem and j'like all da dolls stay looking at you. If you look at da cats too much, dey look spooky; da white ones look like obake, and da black ones, da eyes shine right at you and follow you around da room. And she went draw some of da Daruma eyes crooked so look like dey looking at you cockeye. Gimme da hee-bee gee-bees. But so sad when she tell you da story of each one. She can remembah too, you know. Da one fo her daughter to have good marriage. She couldn't color um in cause she got black eye from her husband right away but finally she went color um in when she went divorce um. Da one fo Kennet coming back from Vietnam, she went color um in cause he nevah come back dead. And she had anykine good luck cats, maneki neko, big kine, small kine. She even had da local kine wit sunglasses and holding one boogie board, giving da shaka sign. She tell me, "Da black one is fo good health. Da white one is fo plenny money. See da cat get da gold coin, eh. Supposed to put dis by your door cause you like da coins come inside your house. Da cat waving at you Daniel-san, 'Come, come.' Japnee dey wave backwards. J'like dey shooing you away but means 'come, come.' So da good luck cat waving da money to come inside your house."

"And what, Mrs. Hosaka, da surfah cat telling da waves, 'Come, come'?"

She laugh. You supposed to burn da Daruma dolls aftah you pau get your wish but Mrs. Hosaka, she keep um all. Some eyes stay fading so must've been from long time ago, yeah? I open da door and make da go-come wave.

"What you doing, boy-san?"

"I waving all da good luck and good health and plenny money inside." She laugh again.

She tell me, "Tanks to God, I so lucky. So good you come visit me. Uddah children don't come visit me. Only you. When I die, I going remembah. I going come visit you."

I wasn't sure how she was going visit me or if I wanted her to visit me, but I jes said, "Okay."

Mrs. Hosaka told me when Mr. Hosaka died, I wasn't born yet. Da priest told her, "Don't be sad. Mr. Hosaka in Buddha-land now and he is very happy. He have no pain. He want you and da children be happy. If you live your life in a good and compassionate way, you will see him again."

"So, I going see him again," she told me. "But I have to do all dis," she wave at all her good luck tings, "to make sure I make it."

Das when my fahdah said Mrs. Hosaka came mo bossy. He said dat she was going help all us guys go heaven cause I guess she tawt if she nevah help us, she wouldn't make it either. She always telling people what to do, how to do tings.

My fahdah complain, "If you sick, she tink she one doctor. She tell you what to eat, what not to eat. She say, 'No drink too much milk, too much coffee, too much tea, too much ice water.' Everytime I try grow vegetables she tell me I giving too much water to da tomatoes. Water da ground mo bettah, no get da tomatoes wet, bumbye going get spots. Da lettuce give plenty water, bumbye wilt. No good plant da papaya next to da lemon tree, da papaya going come out sour. And if you like have baby, you gotta eat plenty eggs and if you have gas that means you eating too much cabbage. I no even ask her, she tell me what to do!"

So one time I went ask her how she know so much stuff. She say, "I donno. I jes learn tings. I listen to da radio, I read da newspaypah." But I nevah seen her read da newspaper except fo da Longs ad and to cut coupons. If get sale on Spam and get coupon too, das double lucky. She probably would color in one Daruma eye fo dat.

Anyways, she started doing stuff and making like she know everyting. Like she was in heaven already and showing us how fo get dere too. She always tinking about what da priest, da Bonsan, went say when she went church dat week and she tink he stay talking direck to her. She figgah da Bonsan from Japan and da Buddha from Japan too so was j'like da Buddha was talking to her, telling her what fo do. Das when she started fo put out da mayonnaise bottles fill up wit water in her yard. I tawt was fo chase da dogs away from her yard, you know, fo stop dem from making doo-doo.

"How come you do dat? Dogs not scared of dat," I went tell her.

"Yeah," Mrs. Hosaka said. "Dogs smart. Dese bottles fo catch da tawt waves direct from da Buddha, who live Japan. Japan far you know, so da signal weak. Das why you look da Japanee temples, all get antennas on top fo catch da signal."

"Like TV?" I went ask her.

"Yeah, like TV. And da Bonsan jes one regular guy except he know how interpret da signal."

"J'like da guys at da United Nations," I told her. "When da main guy stay talking, everybody else gotta listen on earphones. Dey not listening radio, you know. Dey listening to da interpreter."

"Yeah," she said. "So what if da translator guys was only making up stuff, telling boo-shet kine stuff. No good, eh? Das why da Bonsan gotta train fo long time, gotta learn all da prayers la dat fo test him if he one good translator, dat he not boo-shet. One day he going tell me what fo do about Kennet."

"So what Mrs. Hosaka, das what you like be when you grow up?"

"Ha!" she laugh. "I'm old already. Already grown up. No place fo me to go except heaven. No, my job is to train you so you can learn how listen. So you can learn how to catch da signal."

"But I no like be one Bonsan, Mrs. Hosaka."

"Yeah, yeah. You no need be one Bonsan for learn da secrets. Once you learn dese tings, you can be anyting. Even President of da United States."

"Nah, no can. Only haoles can be President."

"You donno. Look our districk, Richard Kageyama, Frank Loo, get plenny Oriental politician."

"But my fahdah said dat dey da ones who boo-shet." I went tell "boo-shet" kinda soft so she no scold me for using bad language.

She told me da story about da Daruma. "Long time ago, had dis monk, so devoted he sit in one cave fo nine years. Meditate. Pray, yeah? Pretty soon his arms and his legs dry up and fall off cause he no use um fo so long. He become a cripple, eh? So how he stay sitting up? He meditate so much, he no can fall ovah. My mother used to say, 'Daruma, seven time knock down, eight time get up.' You, boy-san, gotta be like Daruma, errytime get up. No let anybody knock you down."

"J'like Muhammed Ali," I told her.

"Nah," she told me, "he nevah get knock down." She laugh, "Maybe Floyd Patterson. Or da big haole one, Ingemar Jojohnson." She went show me Kennet's Biddy Boxing trophy. "Nevah been knock down," she tell me.

Mrs. Hosaka know anykine stuff about boxing and Fiftieth State Wrestling and she know everybody on da Hawaii Islanders baseball team. Her favorite was Carlos Bernier, rightfielder and homerun hitter. My fahdah always tease her from our back porch when she watering, "Hey, Annie, your boyfriend Bo Belinsky going pitch tonight. You going da game?"

"Naw, dat two-timing playboy going out wit Mamie van Doren. Wassamatta wit him, I'm available. I going stick wit my Borinque, Carlos. Hee, hee."

Christmas vacation I go ovah help Mrs. Hosaka. She make me ride bus wit her fo go fishmarket. Most times she treat me lunch at Kress or Woolwort so I no mind but ho, she like to talk to all da old fogies on da bus.

J'like listening to da Japanee radio station except she translate um fo me
and da guys who no undahstand. Anyways, Mrs. Hosaka, she stay telling
everybody on da bus no eat da mochi in da ozoni soup cause dey might
choke, "How many peoples in Japan die every New Year cause dey went
choke on mochi, ne?" Nobody like listen, but she went say um already and
already get one old man in front chewing his false teet like already get
someting stuck down his throat. And now, whenever dey eat mochi fo da
rest of their life, dey going tink of Annie Hosaka sitting sideways in da front
of da Alewa Heights bus, j'like one puka shell tour guide telling all da sights
on da way to heaven. She tell da whole show from KZOO radio: train
crash—sixty dead, oden recipe. Da sumo results from Channel 13 wit full
sound effects: she make her voice high like da referee at da beginning of da
match, "Kamaete. Jikan? Das like, 'Ready, set, go' yeah?" Den she stamp her
feet, chrow da salt, den slap her hands togeddah fo when dey charge and she
shouting in Japanese like da ref, "Nokotta, nokotta, nokotta." She give us
da subtitles, "He saying 'Inside, inside. You still inside, inside da ring.'" She
bend ova, wit her head push out in front like she giving stink eye to da
wreslahs when dey stay stuck, not moving, you know, and she yell, "Yoi,
hakke yoi!"

    Da driver beep his horn and yell, "Move yo fat ass!" to da car in front
and Mrs. Hosaka ack all shocked like and say, "Ai!" But I heard her say dat
too couple times when I was watching TV wit her. She put her hand by her
mout and make geisha-kine giggle, so fake.

    "Yeah," she tell us, "Hakke yoi is get a move on. Fight with some
spirit." Da driver laugh and tell, "Yeah, das what I said, 'Move your ass!'"

    She switch to da interview wit Takamiyama, "Das Jesse Kuhaulua
from Happy Valley, Maui boy, you know. He talk wit one hoarse voice cause
one time he got hit in da troat and damage his voice box, no time fo
surgery. Gotta get back to da tournament. Evah since den he talk like dis
. . ." And she make in one sore troat voice, " 'Ganbare masu! He going try
his best, yeah Daniel-san? You too, all da time you have to try your best.
Kennet when he fight, he always try his best. Das why he win."

    Da bus driver heard dis one before so he tell her, "Pretty soon your
stop, Missus. No foget any packages, now. Got your sweater? Get all ready
now, I not going stop too long. I'm late today."

    And Mrs. Hosaka check her watch and say, "You not late. Get plenty
time. Wassamattah you?" Da driver smile into the mirror to the rest of the
bus. We all can see him wink at us and shrug his shoulders. Mrs. Hosaka no
can see, she go on to da obituaries.

    By now I know New Year's time Mrs. Hosaka going call me come her
house eat mochi in da soup. Me, I no even like mochi but she going give me

one bowl ozoni and I going eat little bit and den watch her eat. She use da spoon cut up da mochi real small like one pea and she chew real slow, her false teet going click, click, click. Da radio stay on and she get pencil and paper ready and I can tell by da music, slow and sad, dat da obituaries coming on and I know she tinking about how many people in Japan went choke dis year but you gotta eat mochi for good luck so I take one small bite and I watch her so she no choke. I tink about how I goin' save her. I seen in da magazine what fo do if somebody stay choking. You gotta grab dem from behind and push their stomach in. J'like you putting da bear hug hold on dem.

Sometimes I go her house watch Fiftieth State Wrestling. Ho, she ack kinda nuts when get wrestling. She know all da holds and she can tell you how fo do a reverse out of one sleeper hold, how fo break da grip first den apply one hammerlock. She know anykine so I was worried what if she was choking on mochi and I try save her but she gimme da wristlock wit one arm bar. How you get out of dat?

When get Chief Billy White Wolf, da good guy, in da Indian Death Match against Rippah Collins, da bad guy, she stay yelling at da TV, "Watch out! Watch out! Wally, Wally!" She calling to da ref on da TV, "He pulling hair. He cheating!" Rippah Collins get Chief Billy White Wolf in one headlock and he turning, turning, turning so dat Wally no can see all da dirty stuff he doing like poking da eye, pulling da hair, blasting um wit his knee. She know dat Chief Billy White Wolf going get um back cause he da good guy and da good guys always win except when da bad guys cheat. When he finally get out, he start spinning Rippah Collins around until he come all dizzy and da Chief sweep his legs out and drop a knee on his throat. Rippah Collins is flat on his back wriggling around like one dead cockaroach and Chief Billy White Wolf make big chest and slam himself down on Rippah Collins body and Mrs. Hosaka stay slapping da arm of the couch in time wit Wally. Blam, blam, blam! One, two, tree! And Mrs. Hosaka stand up, breathing hard, holding her hands up "da winnah!" J'like she went wrestle da match.

Rippah Collins stay talking to Lord Tally Ho Blears aftahwards about how he going wrestle next week in "High-low" and "Moi" and Mrs. Hosaka tell me one mo time, "Dat haole boy still donno how to say, 'Hilo' and 'Maui.'" And she always cheer for Dean Higuchi even if he so junk. She like him cause he Japanee boy and he always try his best even if he lose errytime. "Tsk, ahh . . . shikataganai . . . no can help, yeah?"

Sometimes she sigh and say, "Kennet, shikataganai. No can help, yeah?"

Daddy said she foget who she tell what sometimes so we always get da rerun about her daughter and her grandchildren and where dey stay on da mainland when dey coming home. Sometimes da story change. She mix up yestaday wit ten years ago. Sometimes she call me Kennet, sometimes she foget Kennet's name and gotta call him, "whachucall," and I gotta tell her, "Kennet. You mean Kennet, Mrs. Hosaka," and she tell, "Yeah."

Sometimes she jes stop, cause she foget what she was talking about. Daddy tell, "She put me to sleep."

Mama say, "She jes lonely. Nobody stay home, only take care orchids. Ride da bus." Das my job, every vacation time. Everyday, I go feed da dog, get da mail, water da yard, rake da leaves, carry stuff fo her. She gimme dollah. Sometimes, I scared go her house though, cause I tink, what if she went ma-ke in her sleep and I gotta find her? Or what if she went get heart attack and ma-ke? Sometimes she talk about dying. She say, "I'm old. Bumbye ma-ke. But I still going take care you, you know. So you bettah behave or else, I going come sit on you. You going feel me sitting on your chest j'like one heart attack, and I not going go away until you behave. You hear?" And she give my arm one squeeze. Fo one old, shriveled up lady, she get strong hands. All bumpy from artritis but she strong, boy.

One night aftah she told me dat, I went feel one heavy weight on my chest. J'like somebody went body slam me and was trying fo pin me in my bed. Wally was trying to count me out. Blam! One! Blam! Two! I wasn't scared though. I know she was just testing me, fo see if I knew what to do. You know what I did? I seen Nicky Bockwinkle do um dat day on TV. I went slam my two hands on da mat hard and make neck bridge, den crab-walk sideways and twist my legs out and jump to my feet. I knew dis one.

Mrs. Hosaka stay circling now, hunched ovah, hands out and we grapple. Break. Grapple. Break. You gotta watch da eyes cause if she looking down, she going try da leg take down but she wearing her free cardboard sunglasses from da eye doctor and da samurai headband from Bon Dance. No can see her eyes but I know must be her, testing me.

Dis Christmas, my muddah told me no need go ovah to Mrs. Hosaka's house cause da daughter came home from da mainland to help her out. Shet, no can get my dollah, I tawt. But den I nevah even see her outside watering long time so she must've been sick or someting. Da daughter only do kapulu job watering, only little bit water and pau.

"Da orchids going die," I told my muddah. One time I seen Mrs. Hosaka sitting outside pointing at da orchids wit her teacup. Da daughter talking to her, fast, waving her arms, "Go call Kennet, den!" She sounded mad.

Da next week Mrs. Hosaka call me up to go ovah because her daughter had to go back mainland early. When I went ovah, she gimme one Daruma and da marsh pen and said, "Go color one eye fo me."

"What dis one fo, Mrs. Hosaka?"

She jes said, "One wish. Maybe come true." She talking to herself, "Go, den. Kennet going come bumbye. He help me. You watch, Kennet going come."

From Chrismas time Russo and Brynie start making their firecracker plan. Brynie's fahdah always buy plenny firecracker and our fahdah only buy us little bit so mostly Russo help Brynie figgah out how to burn his stuff: what to burn first and whether to burn one whole pack or take um apart and burn um one by one. Dey had nuff bottle rockets fo shoot off twenty per hour starting from nine o'clock.

Nine o'clock dey start shooting um off at "da witch lady's house" counting down, "10, 9, 8, 7, 6, 5, 4, 3, 2, 1, fire!" Brynie get his camouflage uniform on, he look j'like one real Army guy. Russo put on his helmet and his Boy Scout canteen belt. Dey making like G. I. Joe, calling out, "Coordinates. Hot house, eleven o'clock." Mrs. Hosaka come outside her house wit her hair all pin up in pincurlers and she get one scarf wrap around her hair and tie under her chin, make her chin stick out, and Brynie stay pointing at her, "Not by the hair on my chinny chin chin." Dey stay cracking up. She no mo hair on her chin. I donno why dey so mean and I wishing dey stop but I too chicken fo say anyting cause bumbye dey going start teasing me. And I tinking, she kinda do look like one witch, one old Russian lady wit one babushka. And she go out in back by her orchids wit her hose and try shoot down da rockets dat coming by her house.

"No shoot at my house," she shouting, but dey no can hear her. "No shoot. Wassamattah you kids, no shoot my house! I going tell your fahdah!"

Brynie only laugh cause he still playing war, "Enemy at tree o'clock. Fire torpedo one!" *Whoosh!* "Fire torpedo two!" *Whoosh!* And *whoosh, whoosh* two mo rockets go by da hothouse. Brynie told Russo he was going shoot da Roman candle.

"Das not da plan!" Russo tell him. "We was going save um fo midnight. No waste um!" Russo getting scared of what Brynie was going do. But Brynie, he no care and he light da Roman candle and jes hold um in his hand and da ting go *phoomp, phoomp, phoomp* and little by little each shot getting closer to Mrs. Hosaka's roof. I donno if he getting tired or he starting to aim da ting, but couple shots land on her roof and by now get anykine rockets shooting all ovah cause coming closer to midnight so no can really tell if was Brynie's Roman candle but Mrs. Hosaka's roof start smoking and she stay yelling, "Fire! I going call da cops, boy!" She stay pointing and calling, "Kennet, you goddamn no good kid! Sommabitch." And j'like she was talking to me, calling me "no good," and I tinking when she die she really going come get me. She going sit on my chest and get me wit dat samurai sword I never got to see and all da Daruma going only get one eye and she not going color um in until me and Russo and Brynie all dead and all da good luck cats stay poking finger, *stoo-pit, stoo-pit, stoo-pit* at me. Russo stay yelling and crying, "Daddy! Mrs. Hosaka's roof stay burning! Call da fire department." Mama dialing, Mrs. Hosaka trying to shoot her roof wit water but her water too weak, no can make it. Her roof smoking only little bit, but she start bringing out her Daruma dolls and good luck cats out from the living room putting um two at a time in her front yard. I go ovah to help her. She talking to herself, "Kennet, you see what dose kids did? You don't be like dem, now."

I no say nutting. My fahdah and Russo trying to connect our hose to her hose. We donno where Brynie stay.

Next ting you know, two bottle rockets went off from our garage, *whoosh, whoosh!* One went right past us in da yard. Da uddah one went go nuts and turn and come right back at Brynie and land inside da beer box wit his firecracker stash and, *boom,* da whole ting went light up and all da fire-crackers and rockets and Roman candles and sparklers was exploding in da garage, da whole box on fire. *Pock, pock, pock, pock! Tweee . . . boom! Tweee . . . boom! Boom, boom, boom! Praaack!* Da firemen come running down da driveway wit one fire extinguisher.

Mrs. Hosaka yelling at dem, "Not dem, my roof. Damn Kennet burning down my house! Nemmine dem. My roof!" But by den da fireworks all pau already and da roof not smoking anymore and Brynie's fahdah find him hiding under da stairs and he slap his head and call um "stupid." Mrs. Hosaka saying, "Baka, baka!" over and over. She look at me an call me, "Whachucall, come ovah here and help me put my tings back inside."

I no say nutting. Daddy stay sweeping up da rubbish in da garage. He tell me, "Go, help her." And I see Mrs. Hosaka in her front yard, holding one Daruma. She still looking fo Kennet. In da dark only can see da reflection off her glasses. J'like she no mo eyeballs. I going color um in. So she can see.

NO MO' FISH ON MAUI

Barry Masuda

You old-timers like fo' complain.
No mo' moi nowadays, no mo' pāpio
No mo' nothin'.

Kahului Harbor polluted.
Da 'ōpelu no run anymoa.
Makena get too much tourists.
Da tako no come in already Olowalu-side.

Bombai, afta' complaining, you guys
Go in da backyard fo' hibachi 'opihi and
Drink Milla Light and reminisce.
We use' fo' fill-up eight 48-quart coolah-full moi,
Laying net down by Big Beach.
We use' fo' poke stringa-full kumu, 4-5 pound kine,
Diving outside Baldwin Park.

And den you load-up yo' 4WD Ford Broncos
And head to your secret spot past Kaupō with da
Rusty exhaust pipe coughing smoke into
Da ozone.
You come back with three coolahs menpachi
And 'aweoweo, and ask me fo' help you
guys clean 'um.

So I tell you guys screw you and give you
Da fingah.
Yeah, right, no mo' dis no mo' dat no wonder.
Clean yo' own fricken fish.

And den you guys mutter
Goddam keeds nowadays no mo' respect.

WONDER WOMAN AND MY JUNIOR PROM
Wendy Miyake

My mother wanted a normal girl. One who dressed in pink ruffle dresses and played nicely with her Donny & Marie Osmond Barbie dolls. As a five-year-old, I was more ambitious. I would parade down our quiet street in red rain boots, a red flannel slip-on robe buttoned around my neck in cape fashion, plastic clip-on earrings and Crayola decorated paper crown and power bracelets. I thought Wonder Woman was a fascinating character to live in but the neighborhood boys thought it was odd. My mother thought it was very odd. I guess sleeping in the costume was too much for her. Needless to say, I outgrew the Wonder Woman attire but I failed to out-grow a certain backwardness of my ways. Even something as traditional as a junior prom turned out unusual. Now that I look back on it, it was down-right embarrassing.

In our narrow high school world, there were certain pre-prom scenar-ios that were acceptable. For example, boy meets girl, asks her friends to ask her to the prom, and then exists in eternal bliss and relief. My scenario unfolded into girl buys dress, earrings, shoes, gloves and bids in pure opti-mism of snagging a date. Unfortunately, in my mad rush to purchase all these items, I had forgotten about the existence of the Hierarchy of Social Greatness. Basically the system worked if you were very skillful with pom poms, exuded a consistent aura of perkiness or were born with incredible bone structure. You sat in the coolness of the pyramid's summit. Few made this level. Few strayed from this level. I was somewhere in the middle of the pyramid where it was starting to crack under the weight. Although this would severely limit my choices, I told myself, "I am not worried."

I leisurely dialed the number of one of my guy friends. He was a good Japanese boy: intelligent, tall, and a lot of fun. Notice the past tense verb. I thought he was all these things until I heard the tactful version of "no" spelled out to me over the phone. He said he was scheduled to work. Right. I wished I could have ripped off my golden truth lasso and squeezed his pudgy body until he fell over begging to tell the truth. However, in the spirit of optimism, I told myself, "I am not worried."

A few days later my best friend Eileen called. Ryan, another decent Japanese young man and our mutual friend, did not have a date yet. Wonderful. Unfortunately, Ryan means "No, don't ask me" in some distant

European language. He said he didn't think it would work out. I wasn't looking for a four-month commitment but rather a fun night. Was it a part of my anatomy—too small here, too large there? What? The questions kept coming. Could you choose a part? Pinpoint the problem. At this point, I buried my nose into Leo Buscaglia "love yourself" books to keep my self-esteem up. I mumbled to myself, "I am not worried."

As the days dragged along, my dress began to sag in the closet as if trying to empathize with me. The bids were crinkled from my constant fingering of the pages. Now my father, my brave father, was disgusted at seeing me deep in the trash barrel of life. He asked me, "Do you want me to ask Scott?" I was on the couch staring blankly at the darkened television screen. I turned to him with red, swollen eyes and said: "I don't know."

This was my dream to avoid the heart wrenching rejection and all I could say was "I don't know" because at this point I did not care. My father took that as a "yes" and marched over to our neighbors, the Marumotos, like a determined superhero. As I watched him approach their rust house on the corner, I saw his shoulders droop as if all that super power had been sucked out of him by the impending deed. Scott was watering the front yard. "Hi Mr. Iwamoto."

"Um . . . ya . . . hi . . . uh I don't know how to ask you this . . . and he he . . . and . . . uh I—I don't usually ask these uh questions . . . but . . . well, you see . . ." His voice trailed off and he began wringing his hands like an intimidated child.

"Yes, what is it?"

"Well . . . my daughter . . . y-you know the one who lives in my house. Yah, well . . . she uh bought this beautiful white dress, see, and ah . . . these bids you see . . . and I-I'd hate for it to go to waste and . . . ."

"I'd be glad to take her."

"And she has these pretty gloves that go with the dress . . . and oh I don't know how to say this . . ."

"Mr. Iwamoto, I'll take her."

"You will?" My father's eyes were wide like a child's at Disneyland.

"I'll give her a call later, okay?"

"Thank you. Thank you so much." And with that my father practically skipped all the way home. He pushed open our front door and said, "Praise Buddha." I knew that he had said "yes."

Scott was twenty at the time and he had been very popular at Mililani High School. He sat atop that pyramid with all the other nice football players. He did not gain his popularity by being a rebel or a major athlete but rather he gained it by his gentleness toward women. He's been a gentleman all his life. In fact, I do not remember him laughing at my Wonder Woman costume when I was young.

That night when we stepped into that enormous ballroom, people looked and they smiled. I smiled back. Scott smiled. The place looked like a wedding reception with candles, peach napkin fans and tons of flowers. It made me wonder if anything could be this blissful in my entire life. We ate, we danced, and the whole time we were the life and energy behind this night. We even led the whole dance floor in a rendition of square dancing.

When we drove home that morning, a cool aura draped over me like a shawl. For the first time in my high school life, I could feel the cool breezes of the pyramid's summit. I may have mistaken the air conditioning for this feeling but even in the warm morning air, I felt like I had reached this peak. We got to my front door. Scott stood holding my hands. "My Wonder Woman," he said as he kissed me lightly on the lips. I smiled, covering the peephole with my hand. My mother wouldn't need to know he kissed me again.

AN INFINITELY SUBTLE SHAME
Bill Miyasato

In a notebook I made for her in the fifth grade, my mother keeps a list of Significant Deaths. The cover is filled with loopy fluorescent flowers, with "Happy Mother's Day" chicken-scratched in large, childish letters. She scans the obituary column daily, then neatly enters the name, date of death, date and time of funeral services and, if known, cause of death in evenly spaced columns and rows on the clean white sheets of the notebook. The last column is reserved for miscellaneous comments. "Hilo High Class of '45," it might say, or "Sachi's brother-in-law's wife." She faithfully cross-references each name with the guestbook from my grandmother's funeral, and sometimes the entry would read, "Give $5—didn't attend Grandma's." I thought this list, kept meticulously up-to-date like an accountant's ledger, was morbid and grotesque.

She thought it important for me to attend Sharkey's funeral. Wasn't it tragic, the way he died? So young, such a pitiful waste. But what timing, she said, that I was back in town for a visit. Sharkey's parents had helped my grandparents in the plantation camp, and since I was a classmate of his, it would be a good idea for me to go to the services.

I refused. I had treated him badly in school, I reasoned, and I hadn't seen him in thirteen years, or even thought of the guy. I was not going to be a hypocrite.

"No, you don't understand," my mother told me, in an all-too-familiar tone that signaled the start of a lecture. "If you go to the service, you show respect not only for the person, but for the family, too. Death is an honorable thing, you know, so you honor his life, as well as respect his death. You honor him. He won't be just another traffic fatality."

"Besides," she added, after a pause, "they had to ship the body all the way from New Mexico, and it'll probably be a closed casket anyway, so you won't have to worry about feeling sick, like the last time, looking at a stiff."

Mothers.

"They keep track of such things, you know. Then, when you die, they come to your funeral, just like returning a favor. And," she concluded, saving the best for last, "you might even see some of your old friends there."

His legal name was Yoshiaki, but that was too ethnic, too Nisei, to our Sansei-sensitized ears. The rest of us had names like Craig, Brian and Mark, names gleaned off programs from our parents' newly-acquired television sets. We called him Sharkey.

In the ritualized, tribal society of childhood, Sharkey was a natural target, with his squishy, roly-poly, chi-chi dango body, severe crewcut and his resigned, yawning personality. He had a look that reminded me of a dog bracing itself for a spank. Sharkey's sheepish grin and all-accepting disposition riled us to no end, and we constantly devised plans to get him out of what we thought was his retardation slump. He was always "It" in runmaster and hide-and-seek, but it was no fun since he could never catch us. When we played war, he was always "The Japs," always the first to die. It frustrated us that he never fought back or tried to get even. After the first five or six times, he wouldn't come back to life after counting to 20, the requisite time of death in our war. "What for," he asked, "when you guys only gonna kill me again?"

Merciless as we were, however, the older kids in the camp were even more merciless, smearing goat droppings on him, bombing him with rotten guavas or leaving him stranded at the river. We didn't dare come up to bat for him, for fear that they would turn their wrath on us. Sharkey ignored us and stayed home or played with the younger children after Dennis, an older boy in the camp, broke Mr. Ferreira's plumeria tree and blamed it on Sharkey. His parents never complained to ours, or if they did, we never heard of it.

On the first day of school Sharkey entered the classroom that smelled of construction paper and clothes-for-Christmas and Wildroot, wearing short pants and cowboy boots, while the rest of us, now full-fledged students, dressed up in our brand new khaki trousers, button-down shirts with collars that scratched our necks and clean black-and-white Keds. No one wanted to sit next to Sharkey or be his walk-in-line partner, so Miss Suehiro, the teacher, became his partner. Every day he had to hold her hand and walk with her at the end of the line down to the playground or the cafeteria. He didn't seem embarrassed at all. She treated him well, but instead of raising our estimation of Sharkey, it only lowered our impression of the teacher. How can she be so blind, we asked each other. When Susan Hamano dropped her lunch plate, we called her Sharkey's sister, and Michael-Michael-Motorcycle became Sharkey's brother when he pissed in his pants. The ultimate insult. Sharkey merely smiled, never said a thing. His nicknames ranged from a tepid Thing, to Germ, to Radiation, Dodo-head and Porcupine (though we didn't know it at the time, it was our first double entendre, because of his size—Porky Pig, get it?—and his pokie-pokie hair).

Sometimes we included Sharkey in our group, only because he had money handily available. It wasn't as if he was buying our affection; we extorted it: "Sharkey, buy me dis!" "Eh, Porcupine head, gimme money!" He lavished us with candy, gum, soda, comics, baseball cards, marbles and toy soldiers. He made us feel smarter and stronger than we really were.

Once, in first grade, during Juice Time, someone bumped Sharkey, causing him to spill his guava juice over the crotch of his pants. He didn't have an extra pair in school, so Mrs. Mowat made him change in the broom closet into his denim sleeping bag until his mother could come to school with a change of clothing. Clad in his sleeping bag with his belt holding it up at the waist, Sharkey hopped out of the closet. The class roared with laughter, even Mrs. Mowat. That was the only time I saw Sharkey cry. After that, no one wanted to exchange papers with him to correct arithmetic or spelling because we didn't want to be the next Cry-Baby or Shishi-Boy.

My family was part of the great migration, in the '50s and '60s, from the plantation camps to the suburbs. We moved from my grandparents' house to a standard Hicks Homes three-bedroom, two-car garage, redwood model on a neatly parceled lot, with a hollow-tile wall fortressing the yard. Most of my friends and their families moved into subdivisions close by, into similar homes that smelled of wood shavings and fried chicken, not like the camphor-and-lacquered-tray smell of the houses in the camp. For whatever reason, Sharkey's family stayed behind. I attended another elementary school, so after the third grade, I saw Sharkey only once, at my grand-mother's funeral, until we entered Hilo High School.

Even in high school, with a larger and more diverse population, Sharkey was still the guy jumping out of the broom closet in his sleeping bag, pudgy and retiring, quiet and secretive. He hung around the fringes of the Pirates' Corner when school first started, but The Pirates ignored him. He was "too panty" to be one of them, they claimed. Then he tried The Wreckers, but they drained him of his money in the crapgame-bathroom for five consecutive days. After that he usually stayed by himself in the library, reading newspapers from mainland cities and looking through magazines and reference books. We joked that Sharkey could be the leader of his own gang, the L-Sevens.

Because he was one of the first guys in our class to get his driver's license, sometimes Sharkey would take us to football games in his father's pickup truck. We ditched him at the game, and met up with him afterwards in the parking lot. We'd pile in the back, arguing over which one of us was going to ride up front with Sharkey, and he'd cruise through Banyan Drive or Honoli'i, or we'd chase the mahus on Mamo Street. Later we'd go to Jimmy's Drive-Inn for a late night snack which, Sharkey insisted, was his treat, over our meek and phony protestations. Then he'd buy Ripple or beer for us from his uncle's liquor store, and we'd go to Wailoa State Park and get ripped.

At the start of our senior year we noticed Sharkey had slimmed down and his hair was a straggly black mophead held in place with a yellow-peace-sign-on-black headband which, from a distance, looked like a grotesque third eye. He wore an army jacket with the American flag sewn upside down on the back, and faded Levis with "Love" and "Peace" patches over the back pockets. Instead of Clark Kent eyeglasses, he now wore John Lennon-type wireless specs. He walked with a strident confident pace, wearing his Italian toe-sandals and smelling of essence of patchouli. He befriended the haole kids, those whose parents worked for the federal government at the Volcano National Park or the military. In many ways those kids were outsiders, too, moving from place to place every couple years, and they probably saw more in Sharkey than we, who grew up with him, ever could.

He ran for Senior Class President, on a platform of Honesty and Significance (he proposed doing away with such insignificances as Homecoming Week and the prom). He was booed off the stage at the election rally and lost decisively, of course. For the Senior Class Variety Show, he auditioned by accompanying a tape of Ravi Shankar's music with "harmonic elements" on a garden hose. He circulated a petition calling for an end to the Vietnam War, and wanted the student body to go on strike to protest Nixon's bombing of Cambodia. He stopped driving his father's pickup so he wouldn't contribute to the environmental crisis, except for the time we first got stoned and went to see *Woodstock* at the Mountain View Theatre, since the Palace Theatre in Hilo wouldn't let us in to the R-rated movie. He listened to Jefferson Airplane's *Surrealistic Pillow*, while the rest of us were quoting lines from The Carpenters.

It must've been the drugs, we reasoned. In the early '70s drugs hit even sleepy old Hilo like a hazy tidal wave, though it consisted of nothing more sophisticated than Baggies full of stem-and-seed infested marijuana, five dollars a bag. We experimented awkwardly. We thought ourselves to be so cool, so hip, though we used it sparingly. If not, we laughed nervously, we would become hippies like Sharkey.

At the commencement exercises, no one came to see Sharkey graduate. His father was in the hospital, and his mother had gone there to feed him. His uncle and auntie had to work at the liquor store. When Sharkey went to the stage to pick up his diploma, he gave the Black Power salute, a defiant fist thrust straightforwardly into the air. The audience gasped, some even booed. The other graduates shook their heads and chuckled, but it pissed me off. Why do a stupid thing like that and spoil it for all of us, I wondered. Why buck tradition?

After the ceremony everyone was caught up in the excitement and euphoria of kissing and hugging the girls, giving pseudo-hip black hand-shakes like on *Mod Squad*, congratulating each other, the laughter, the leis. We did it, we kept telling ourselves, we really did it. As if we were the only ones in the world that accomplished this milestone. Outside Sharkey took off his single blue-and-gold crepe paper lei given to each graduate by the alumni association and placed it and his cap and gown in a brown paper bag he retrieved from a dumpster, then started walking home. We passed him by about six blocks later. We offered him a ride, though secretly I wished he wouldn't accept because I was still mad at him for what he had done earlier.

Sharkey shook his head. When one of the guys in the car asked him why he did what he did at the ceremony, he said we would never under-stand, and he wasn't taking any more crap from anybody in this hellhole town. He wasn't going to get in the car and pollute the air by participating in the act of mechanical transportation, nor pollute his space with a bunch of smalltown hicks who hadn't given him anything but crap all his life. A stunned silence. Sharkey's little diatribe lasted less than a minute, but it sounded just too perfect, practiced and rehearsed to be spontaneous.

We weren't in the mood to feel guilty or sorry.

"Asshole!" Kent snarled. The guys wanted to beat him up right there, but we roared off to the parties and booze instead, leaving Sharkey walking in the dark echo of taunting laughter.

Later that summer we heard that Sharkey took off for the mainland.

"And how did he get there?" I asked sarcastically. "Swim? Or did he 'participate in the act of mechanical transportation?' Or don't airplanes count?"

To my mother's chagrin, I refused to go up to the front of the hall at the funeral service. Since this was no place to argue, she and my father went up there without me, burned incense in front of the (closed) casket, then proceeded down the line to shake the hands of Sharkey's relatives. My mother pointed me out to Sharkey's mother. Wearing a simple black dress, her salt-and-pepper hair neatly pinned in a bun, she turned around and nodded slightly. She had the same tired eyes as Sharkey. I waved desultorily.

The room smelled of lilies and incense. The heat of the late after-noon was being swirled around by a noisy overhead fan. Tacky piped-in organ music permeated the room. Black houseflies buzzed about, and the squeaky scraping of the metal folding chairs on linoleum jarred the nerves like fingernails on blackboard. There were people there who acted somber in front of Sharkey's family, only to see someone in the back they hadn't seen in a while, race up the aisle, smiling, enthusiastically shaking hands and patting each other on the back, whispering good-naturedly. I went outside for a cigarette, joining two high school friends who were chatting. We talked about what we'd done since school: our work, our salaries, marriages, divorces, the children we saw too little of, how the town had changed. As an afterthought we talked about Sharkey.

"He was a cool guy," Mark-the-engineer-now-living-in-Chicago-where-they-filmed-*Ordinary People* said. "Kinda ahead of his time."

Wes—"a Xerox sales rep/fifty grand plus commission and bonuses/married a Punahou grad/we live in Kaneohe/my kids go to Punahou/have you thought of investing in mutual funds?"—agreed. "Yeah, we were kinda rotten to him, but he must've known that we were only kidding. He must've known that deep down we really liked him. I mean, he took care of us small kid time, and we gotta take care our own, after all, right?"

There was nothing to say. What a poor excuse—"Kinda ahead of his time." A limp justification. I shudder at the many times, though, I myself have thought just that. It took my own leaving and being on my own to be on the outside, like Sharkey, incidents strung together like a stagnant, straggling lei of misunderstanding: the constant queries from well-meaning but ignorant whites, in all seriousness, about "what's it like to be Japanese," or the math instructor at UC-San Diego who proudly showed me a photograph of his grandparents, "Russian-Jews who, just like you, know all about discrimination and oppression," or the black woman recruiter for Third World Students for Revolution to "get the muthas up against the wall and, hey, I seen that *Yojimbo* picture four times and, whoa, that My-Fune guy? He is one foxy dude!"

Or the Sunkist inspector who marveled at my fluent English and "the camera equipment you carry around every time you guys tour the plant," or the doctor at the emergency room who served as a medic in World War II and saw "all the damage you people did to our boys, but don't worry,"—chuckle, chuckle—"I don't hold grudges. I'll fix you up REAL good."

But this realization is merely academic now. This hollow acknowledgment means nothing to Sharkey, offers no absolution. It took some poor schmuck on a motorcycle slamming into the dumb sonofabitch in a crosswalk in Taos, New Mexico, and my mother, the death chronicler, to get me here. My presence doesn't offer any comfort to his family. It doesn't honor his life, much less his death. It only gives Wes and Mark and myself and all the rest an empty feeling of fulfilling our obligation, and therefore making things all right. We'll go on. Wes and Mark and I make plans to meet at The Green Door, where we'll brag and BS over beer, and maybe talk more about Sharkey. Will it be another thirteen years before I think of him again?

Maybe. Maybe not. Guilt, not love, is "the strongest poison and medicine of all."

The best revenge, too.

THE MONK AND THE MILLIPEDE
Jina Oshiro

"*Namu myoho renge kyo,*" chanted the black-robed monk. "*Namu myoho renge kyo.*" He rang another bell. A comfortably warm breeze blew through the field. The air was filled with annoyingly cheerful bird songs. It was drizzling lightly, just enough to make you wonder whether it was raining or not—supposedly a good omen. It was morning in the National Cemetery of the Pacific, inside Punchbowl Crater. And I was burying my father.

Dad died on July 7, 1987, at about two o'clock in the morning. He was fifty-five years old. He had been a boxer in college, as well as in the Air Force. He had taught elementary school for thirty years, and had received a pen-and-pencil set for this accomplishment. I had depended on him all of my life. Now suddenly he was gone, and it was up to me to pick up the pieces, sort them out, and figure out what I was going to do with them.

A gong struck brazenly, and I tried to pay attention to the ceremony. "*Namu myoho renge kyo,*" the monk chanted on in Japanese, and since I did not understand a damned thing he was saying, I ignored him and thought some more.

At the funeral the night before, there had been about seven hundred people, and most of them had been crying. I had cried for three days straight after that awful first night, the night that Dad died, and then I had shut myself off. I did not cry at my father's funeral. I would not let myself. I was almost eleven years old, and I was not about to let all of my relatives see me turn into a crybaby. Even though I was the youngest, even if my mother cried freely, unashamedly, I would not break my own personal pledge. I handed out tissues to weeping women who said I was a "dear, sweet child." I knew that I was no such thing, but I smiled and nodded anyway. I shook hands. I looked at my father's body, clothed in his best suit (and, underneath the suit, the hearts-and-flowers undershorts that he always felt embarrassed wearing). I talked. And I waved good-bye as they drove the coffin away in a black hearse.

Back at the cemetery, seven Air Force sergeants fired three times. The sharp crack of rifles cut through the air. A single man standing on the hill above us softly played "Taps."

I looked at the little bronze urn that held my father's earthly remains. So this is it, I thought. The monk continued his chant, droning on and on until I thought I would fall asleep. I squeezed my mother's hand. She smiled, and pretended to pay attention to what the monk was saying. I withdrew into my mind for a little while, staring at the cement under our feet.

It was then that my mother and I noticed the millipede.

It was a perfectly ordinary, small brown millipede, slimy-looking and many-legged. And it was crawling up the monk's foot.

The monk continued his chant, but his voice suddenly seemed shaky. I wondered if perhaps he was ticklish. I started to giggle. My mother elbowed me, but she was smiling. The millipede crawled up the monk's leg, disappearing up his pants leg. I was choking back the laughter now. My face felt red. My shoulders were shaking. The people behind me must have thought I was insane, but I didn't care. I could tell that my mother wanted to laugh too, but she was a little better than me about hiding it.

The rest of the ceremony passed with a merciful quickness, and we received the flag that we would later donate to Punchbowl Cemetery. The monk looked a little flustered, but still retained his dignity as he nodded a good-bye to us.

The millipede incident introduced me to something that I had never thought could combat grief: humor. This lesson was reinforced a few months later, when Mom received a notice in the mail from the Straub Clinic, the very place where Dad had died, addressed to him, asking why he had decided to terminate his health plan there. There was a space, under all the usual excuses, labeled "Other (explain)." She checked that, filling in the space with the simple explanation, "I died."

The late comedian Lenny Bruce said that tragedy plus time equals comedy. This is true, because when Mom and I think about my father, we laugh. We laugh, and now we heal.

WHERE TO PUT YOUR HANDS
Lee A. Tonouchi

Everytime I went my grandma's house she always gave me da same lecture. Wuz Valentine's Day so I went fo' visit her drop off candy li'dat. Plus I had fo' drop off da orchid my ma guys bought cuz her and pa wuz going Pearl City Tavern fo' dinner. Usually my faddah no let me drive all da way town side, but so long as I came back before dahk he sed can. Naturally grandma wuz all happy fo' see me. I walked down da driveway, waved both hands in da air and yelled "Grandma!" so she knew dat I wuz coming. She looked through da kitchen jalousies and she sed, "Is dat you, Aaron?" She opened da screen door and I dunno why but wen I handed her da stuffs her hands wuz acking all shakey ah. At first I tot maybe wuz cold, but actually wen I walked into da house wuz kinda hot. Ever since dey wen cut down da mango tree da house always come hot now. Today da house wuz supah stuffy too so I toll her I wuz going open some windows li'dat, but she sed, "No. Mo' bettah leave 'em close, bumbye people can see inside." I tot dat wuz strange cuz she always grumble wen we go my oddah grandma's house dat their house no mo' air, but I nevah say noting. And da house wuz kinda quiet too today. Usually da TV stay on or my grandpa stay listening to his Japanese radio station. Strange dat my grandpa nevah say noting today too. Usually wen I come I yell "Hi grandpa," too, but I tink he wuz sleeping cuz I nevah hear him yell, "Eh who dat come!?"

My grandma tanked me fo' da candy and she toll me tell my ma guys tanks too. She wanted me fo' hug her ah, but I nevah like. Embarrassing. I nevah hug her since small keed time. Feel weird hugging people. I dunno muss be a teenage guy ting I guess. Gotta be macho ah. So I jus did da fass kine pat pat on da shoulder. My grandma axed me if I wanted to stay fo' dinner. I toll her, "Okay, but I gotta eat early." I wuz kinda hoping she would offer cuz oddahwise I would have to go home cook myself one Tyson Turkey TV Dinner. Last time I wen cook dat my friend wen call and I forgot about 'em and came all ko-ge.

Anyway, soon as I came my grandma wuz giving me da lecture about how I gotta fine one good kine wife who going take care me. Wife? I tot. Gee grandma, I gotta kinda get girlfriend first try like. She wuz all, "Hakum you no mo' date tonight?"

"Cuz grandma, I gotta fine da right girl. I no like choose any kine girl you know." Das wot I sed, but da troot wuz, I wuz too sked most of da time fo' talk to girls.

Since intermediate school time I wuz sked fo' talk to Joy. She wuz like my ideal. Since intermediate I always had her in at least one class. I wuzn't sure wot she wuz really. Maybe little bit Japanese, Hawaiian, Filipino, and maybe little bit haole too. Woteveah she wuz she looked full on Local. So Local dat fo' da second straight year she wuz May Day Queen. I dunno why but everytime I wanted fo' talk to her I got all nerjous. And I came all sweaty too. So I figured da bes way not fo' get all anxiety attack is jus not fo' talk to her. Joy wuz pretty smaht. She always scored high on tests and stuff, but I wouldn't say she wuz a nerd or noting. Cuz one pretty nerd is like one contradiction in terms, ah. So mentally she wuz up there. And ho, physically she wuz pretty uh . . . developed fo' one sophomore. But you know wot wuz da one ting dat impressed me da most—She wuz always supah friendly. Even though me and her, we nevah had one conversation dat lasted mo' than couple minutes and not like we evah did anyting outside of class, but she still always sed hi to me wen we passed by in between classes. And not jus "Hi" and pau, but da kine "Hi" and da wave. And not one quick wave too, but da kine wave within da wave where all her fingers stay up den slowly starting from da pinkey dey go down until at last da index finger goes down and den she do 'em one mo' time. Take like tree times as long as one regular wave, her patented five finger linger wave. Ees like she wanted fo' make sure dat everybody saw dat *she* wuz waving at *me*.

My grandma always sed, "Anykine girl you choose, me no like. Make sure you no marry popolo girl now. Grandpa no like blacks. And no can be Filipino. My friend son from Lanakila go marry Filipino; now they divorce. Only two months you know. And no can be Chinee. Remembah your Uncle Richard, look he marry Chinee and look she take all his money and go leave him fo' marry haole man. Japanee maybe, but depen on da family."

My grandma so choosy. Going be one miracle if I evah do fine da right girl. Usually wen my grandma give me da lecture I jus zone li'dat until she pau. Sometimes I tink in my head—But not like everybody pure someting li'dat. Take Joy fo' example. She all kapakahi. Jus by looking you dunno wot she is. And not jus her ah, I mean plenny people hapa, ah. So sometimes I felt like saying, "Oh but grandma, wot if she half Japanese, half haole, and half Hawaiian?" I nevah like get into all da wot-if scenarios so wen my grandma wuz pau and went into da kitchen I decided fo' cruise in da living room watch little bit WWF wrestling. Sometimes my grandpa watch WWF wit me cuz almost like his sumo. I wuz going ax him if he wanted fo' watch, but ah I figgah he sleeping ah. Plus, I wuz kinda zoning ah, not really into da matches. Usually my grandma's girl lecture no boddah me, but today wuz Valentine's and I wuz hoping I wuz going get one in da mailbox wen I went home. I wuz kinda worried.

Cuz wuz jus dis pass week I went to da Leo Club dance in da school cafeteria and I wen dance mostly wit da girls who wen ax me. Eh, I not ugly k, if das wot you tinking. Had some girls wen ax me. I remembah I wanted so bad fo' dance wit Joy. I nevah like ax her cuz I admit, I wuz too chicken. I remembah da cafe wuz so crowded. I wuz getting so hot. I couldn't figgah out how fo' stand so I jus stuck my hands in my pocket. Wuz getting mo' sweaty in there, but at least could wipe 'em off small kine.

I had my eye on Joy da whole night. I saw all da different guys she danced wit. I kept track of who she axed and who axed her. Not like I toll anybody I liked her ah, but cuz dey wuz invading my turf I had fo' put some of my friends on my doo doo list. I made da kine mental comparison fo' see wot all da guys she axed had in common fo' see if I had chance. Had chance. Everytime one song came on I sed, "K dis goin' be da one," but everytime had one fass song and me I like take tings slow ah so I jus waited. I missed some opportunities wen da slow songs came on and before I could make my move some oddah girl came up to me. Before I could even make my move. Das my cool way of saying I nevah get any moves fo' make. But I wuz learning, making 'em up as I went along. I learned where da bess place fo' stand wuz. Not by da wall cuz in case get one chic you like avoid. Need room fo' maneuver ah. Not by da punch bowl, cuz mo' chance you might spill on top you li'dat. Get all nerjous da hand start shakin' ah. Mo' worse you might spill on top her. In fack, James did dat and like da gentleman he wuz he offered fo' wipe 'em off her chess. Da stupid pervert. Da best place fo' stand wuz by all da Math club people cuz you can look good, ah. Hey I pretty smaht you know. Some girls I could ax. I wuzn't dat chicken like some of my friends who made *me* go ax fo' dem. "Oh, Carrie, James like you dance wit him. Nah c'mon, he really like you, you know. I promise he not going spill again. Aw c'mon. C'mon. C'mon. Pleeeeeeeeeease. Shoots you going chance 'em den." See, easy fo' beg wen you not axing fo' yourself. See, I know all da secrets.

I no tink my grandma would give her vote of approval for a lotta girls at dis dance. K, my grandma would probably say dat Leslie is too fat. I mean I not da kine superficial kine guy dat I only judge by looks. Wot I saying is dat da girl gotta be healthy-looking. Eh, I like my potential wife live long time, ah. And take Charisse. She too skinny my grandma would say. I can dig dat. I like curves. I tink my grandma would like hips cuz gotta have plenny grandkids, ah. My grandma would probably like breasts too cuz mo' healthy, ah, fo' my kid if he get breast milk. Da mo' plenny he get da mo' bettah, ah. I no dig doze artificial kine formulas. Gotta tink all natural. Noting beats da real deals, dude. Joy would be perfeck if wuzn't fo' dat ethnicity ting. I mean mo' bettah, ah, if she all mix up anykine. Cuz like dogs fo' example, those pure bred kine, dey die young. But da kine poi dog, dey live long time, ah. Ho, conflict now dis kine rules.

Maybe wuz only to my eyes, ah, cuz dey say beauty is in da eye of da beholder, but to me Joy wuz definitely a beauty to behold. Wuz almost twelve o'clock and wuz da lass dance of da night and had da Kool and the Gang song, "Cherish." Ho, of all da songs fo' pick, dat wuz my favorite song. Wuz kinda ol' already, but still I liked dat song. I could hear da sea gulls gulling. And my body started swaying side to side. I wuz all in la-la land tinking of how perfeck would be jus me and her on da dance floor. Dis night would be da firs of many nights as tonight would be da night dat we would fall in love. As da chorus started playing I looked all ovah da room, looking, looking fo' Joy. She wuz gone. No tell me she went shi-shi break. Not now. Wuz da lass song. No mo' songs aftah dis. No mo' songs tonight. No mo' songs evah. As I wuz getting all frantick, I started sweatin'. I could feel myself getting all hot. And wuzn't da kine good kine hot, but da kine nervous kine hot. Da kine hot dat dis-going-be-one-vital-crossroads-in-my-life kine hot. Da kine if-I-screw-up-tonight-den-I-going-be-one-geek-fo'-da-ress-of-my-life kine hot. Ass why I wen go jump outta my Faddah's shoes wen somebody wen bump butts wit me from behind. Literally I wen jump, ah, cuz my Faddah's shoes wuz big. I nevah get dress shoes li'dat. I wen go bend down fo' fix my shoes and as I wuz tying da laces somebody wen go bang into me. Wen I looked up, staring right at me, wuz Joy. She sed, "Oh excuse me." And wen I stood up again, she smiled and sed, "Hi." I couldn't tink of anyting fo' say back, so I just sed, "Hi." But wuzn't da kine simple kine "Hi," but one extended, gradually fading "Hiiiiiiiii" extending da "i's" hopefully long enough fo' me to add on someting at da end but unfortunately before I could come up wit anyting witty or clever to say, I ran out of breath.

I remembah my grandma sed dat wen she and grandpa got together she wuz only nineteen. At first grandpa's dad nevah like her, but aftah awhile he came to like her. Wen grandpa's dad died grandma wuz by his bed. She had fo' clean up his shi-shi pan and stuff. He toll her tanks li'dat. She sed, "Remembah, befo' time you no like me, remembah Otoosan?" He nodded weakly and sed, "Befo' time me no likey, but now me likey," and he put his hand on her hand. Da next day he jus nevah woke up. So I dunno why dey nevah like my grandma. I tink someting about dey from different village back home or someting. I dunno, these ol' fashion people not so smaht I tink. Cuz c'mon, you gotta figgah if you only can marry people in your village den pretty soon everybody going be all related and you going get all mutant kine babies.

My grandma called me over to eat. She axed me where my mom guys went. I toll her dey went PCT. My mom liked da monkeys. Usually my grandma's food wuz pretty good, but today fo' some reason nevah get taste, but I nevah say noting. Fo' long time wuz quiet. Den she wen ax me one weird question. She sed, "Aftah you marry, wea you going buy house?" I toll her, "Uh, Kahala, grandma. No worry I going fine one big mansion." Den she wuz silent. I dunno, my grandma wuz acking all weird. She toll me dat wen I buy house, she no like me stay townside cuz too much crime. She sed she no like me stay country side cuz too abunai. So finally I toll her, "Den wea you like me live grandma? No mo' no place else fo' go. Mainland? Ass worse." Den all of a sudden I wuz confuse wen she toll me *she* wanted fo' move. But she cannot move, I tot. Dis house get memories. Wen I wuz a leedle boy, every weekend I used to go my grandma's house cuz she used to babysit me. Until I wuz like twelve around. Her house wuz always pretty cool cuz had da big mango tree outside. I used to love dat mango tree. My grandpa used to pick 'em wit his stick ting and pass 'em down to my grandma who wen stick 'em in bucket. Every mango season we used to give all da neighbors. Sometimes people jus used to come by and ax for mangoes and my grandma used to always give even if we nevah get dat much. Usually had plenny though. But da lass few years hardly had any and da few dat had people used to come and jus steal 'em li'dat. Had fo' pick 'em wen green cuz if we waited till wuz ripe would be gone. Lass year da tree had termite so dey wen chop 'em. Now she wanted fo' move. "Olaloa," she sed. She explained dat Olaloa stay Mililani side. Da suburbs? Olaloa supposed to be one gated community fo' old people or someting. There everybody look out fo' each oddah. More secure she sed. Mo' safe.

Wen Joy sed "Hi" to me wuz like major danger cuz dis wuz like new uncharted ground. Tings wuz easy wen me and Joy kept our distance. "Hi" from afar, never up close. Now we wuz talking in one social context. I cannot ax, "Oh, you wen do your homework? . . . You wen study fo' da test or wot? . . . Wot's da chemical symbol for krypton?" Somehow I knew we had a certain chemistry though. Could she possibly like me too? I mean I not da most good-looking guy in da world, ah. Maybe by relative comparison to da dorky math guys around me, but definitely not da most good-looking in da room. I mean I not da smahtest, well maybe top ten percent. But maybe cuz I funny. Plenny people say I funny.

"Huh?" I sed as I realized dat she wuz talking to me and I wuz tinking too much to myself again. "I was asking you if you wanted to dance?" Wow, so wuz like she wuz saving dis last dance fo' me? Das so sweet yeah. I mean who could turn down one line like dat? She wuz saving da lass dance fo' me. Meaning dat all da oddah guys she danced wit da whole evening before nevah really mattah. Michael Furoyama, Rommel Ofalsa, Ashley St. John, Langford Logan, Kyung Taek Kang, Brian Chong, Tyrell Gospodarec, Chad Maialoha, Matt Takamine, Eric Young two times, and Mr. Hirata all nevah mattah cuz while she wuz dancing wit all dem she wuz really only tinking about me. I dunno how long I took fo' answer but seemed like wuz, wuz, wuz one really long time. Dat whole night I dreamed of dancing wit Joy. But now I wuz having second tots. My hands wuz getting mo' sweaty now dat she wuz actually here. Pretty soon my pockets going get so wet going look like shi-shi stain. Dis wuz like too fass fo' me. Me and her nevah even fass dance before and now I gotta make physical contact. Hands on hips? Hands on da arch of her back? Or would we go all da way, hands completely around? I had no idea where fo' put my hands wit her. Wot if I danced too close? Wot if my sweaty palms got her dress all wet? Wot if I stepped on her feet? Wot if I screwed up so bad dat everybody wuz going talk about me. Da entire sophomore class would probably gossip and make fun li'dat and razz me fo' da rest of my high school career. Wuz I ready? Wuz I prepared to take such a big risk? Finally aftah much contemplation I toll Joy, "Uh, I no feel like dancin'. . . Uh, but you like talk? Maybe too noisy in here ah, uh . . . you like go outside talk story leedle while."

Outside wuz kinda quiet. Maybe too quiet. I jus leaned against da wall and formed a smile wit my lips as I looked at her. She apologized for banging into me. I explained wuz cuz da shoes. Den had plenny silent moments and I nevah know wot fo' say so I jus started bobbing my head and smiling wit my lips hoping she would say someting. Soon. Da silence wuz broken wen all of a sudden, fo' no reason, she just started giggling. Must be my shoes I tot. I toll my dad wuz too big fo' my feet and dis only wuz going be one cafe dance. I gave her my puzzled face and I axed why she wuz laughing. She sed she wuz tinking of da way I sed "hi" before. My "hi" sounded like a deflating balloon.

"Well das cause you knocked all da wind outta me," I sed.

"That's because I didn't see you."

"Why wuz you looking fo' me?"

"I almost didn't recognize you in your nice clothes."

"Why, you saying I usually dress all bummy?!"

"No, I like that aloha shirt."

"Ah, ees okay. Wuz on sale. Did you see James' aloha shirt? His one is cool."

"Was it a blue shirt?"

"No, purple."

"Oh, I didn't look good."

"But . . . you always look good."

"Hah?"

"But you always *look good*."

And she looked puzzled fo' like two seconds before she finally caught on. Den she laughed so hard dat she made one piggy noise. Wit dat she had me all laughing too and she covered her mouth and tings settled down fo' awhile and den we jus started full-on laughing togethers. Finally she calmed down and she offered me a compliment back, "And you're not so bad yourself."

"Why tanks, I've been saying my prayers and taking my vitamins."

"You mean like Hulk Hogan?"

"How you knew dat? You watch wrestling?"

"Yeah, why? Is there someting wrong?"

"Oh no, you're weeeeeeeird."

And we jus talked and talked fo' supah long. About wrestling. About how funny I wuz. About how weird she wuz. About if she could make any other animal noises wen she wuz laughing. About all kines of stuffs. We jus talked and talked aftah dat and before I knew it we talked fo' like almost an hour already. My ma and pa wen buss me wen I got home. My first time taking out da car by myself and I break curfew. Pretty stupid ah. But wuz worth. She gave me her number dat night and I called her da next day and we talked fo' almost da whole day.

I dunno how I could have so much fo' say den, but noting fo' say now. My grandma wuz showing me her brochure for Olaloa and all of a sudden she jus started crying. I started fo' put my arm around her, but nevah feel like wuz da right ting fo' do. I mean she should be telling my mom dis, not me. Not my place fo' say anyting. But I knew I needed fo' say someting so I sed, "No need go Olaloa grandma. I come take care you." I dunno why I sed dat cuz not like I wuz ready fo' transfer school. Whatabout Joy? And not like I can take care my grandma. Not like I can cook. Not like I know how do laundry. I wen try one time and my fluorescent green T&C jacket came all Hypercolor. Not like I know how fo' do anyting. I jus got my license and

I no tink I can take my grandma anyplace cuz townside I dunno da roads so good.

Aftah awhile my grandma calmed down leedle bit. She toll me dat grandpa wuz moving to a nursing home. Ho, I wen look in fass kine wen I came in, but he looked da same. I jus assumed he wuz sleeping as usual. My grandpa had hod time walking ever since his stroke. My grandma sed dat fo' da pass couple weeks he wuz having problems eating so dey might have to feed him from one tube so he probably gotta go Maunalani Nursing Home up Wilhelmina Rise.

Wuz quiet fo' kinda long den she sed, "Tell your mom call me wen you get home, k." I nodded. She looked like she felt kinda awkward and I guess I did too. Cuz not like I evah saw my grandma cry before. Only once wen I wuz shmall and she wen go give me spankings den I wen go pass by her room and I saw her crying on da bed. Now I felt like crying too, but grandpa wuz kinda sick fo' long time already so we all kinda knew dat he wuzn't going get any bettah.

I jus sat there wit my hands closed together between my legs. Finally she sed, "You would come stay wit grandma?" I nodded and she laughed. "You cannot take care grandma. You still boy yet, you still going school." I wuz gonna argue dat I could transfer, but I knew she wuz right. She den changed da subject and axed me if I sent anyone a Valentine's. I toll her I jus sent out to one girl. She axed wot her name wuz. I toll her Joy. She den axed, "Wot her last name?" Den she gave me da lecture again. But midway thru she looked at me and stopped and she sed, "I guess nowdays cannot tell from lass name, no?" I nodded and she continued, "Maybe no make differ-ence. So long as you fine good kine girl, nahf. So long she take care you, grandma happy." Den she axed me how my dance wuz. I toll her how long I talked to Joy on da phone. Approximate kine. Around eight hours. Forty-tree minutes. And twenny-two seconds. And I toll her how da firs ting I wuz going do wen I went home wuz check my mailbox. My grandma sed, "No rush go drive wen you go home now." Den she sed, "Good you find girl. No fun wen you alone." Den it struck me. Wot if I wuz at da dance and no one axed me to dance. Wot if all da oddah guys in da Leo Club had da bubonic plague and I wuz da only guy in da room and Joy and all da oddah girls went lesbo and only danced wit each odder? Wot if no one cared for me den? Wot if no one cared for me ever? Wot a frightening tot it wuz fo' be all alone. I wanted say someting fo' stop my grandma's watery eyes, but I came all teary eyed too as I wrapped my arms around her, hands clasped tightly.

KONA GLITTER, A GHOST STORY
Kobai Scott Whitney

I wonder what that dumb, gum-chewing high school girl behind the counter at Dave's thinks of me: The fat, old maid white lady who comes in (all too often, I might add) and swoons through her one scoop of lychee sherbet—eyes crossed under closed, fluttering eyelids, lost in her mid-life fantasies?

How could I ever explain to her what the taste of lychee sherbet does to me, how immediately it brings me back to the Kona of 1964 when I had my first taste of Calvin Ah Siu.

This is the year of our thirtieth high school reunion; that's why all this has come so vividly back to mind.

For the life of me I can't remember what word we used for "hunk" in 1964. It seems to me that hunk did not appear until the '70s or '80s and that the girls of Konawaena High in 1964 must have said things like: "he's a dream," or just plain "wow."

Whatever word we might have used in those days, it would certainly be connected to my prom date that year, Calvin. He was taller than most of the other country boys in our class, more muscular, more poised. The dream of not just yours truly.

I was one of four haole girls in that senior class. Even today, my habit is to think of the word haole as being a routine descriptive designation. Often we didn't know each other's last names so, for instance, Dexter Ito was "you know, the Japanese boy with the eyes," (poor Dexter's eyes crossed or stalled unpredictably in their tracking) or Ellison, "you know, the rascal Japanese one who hangs around with the jocks."

I was known as: "you know, Lisa, the haole girl with the Buick." It wasn't my Buick, of course; it was Daddy's—a sleek baby blue show boat with the innovative transmission called "Dyna-Flow." In later years, when the Buick started showing signs of age, Daddy used to refer to the transmission spitefully as "Dyna Flush." But that Buick, plus my haole-ness, was simply the way I got identified.

Although our family never thought of ourselves as rich, I know that my classmates did put me into that category. This social class distinction started in elementary school, where wearing slippers to school was a sign of affluence. The ordinary kids—I don't think anyone thought of themselves as "poor" in those days—the ordinary kids just came to school barefoot. Because of this classification system, and much to the frustration of my mother, I was continually managing to lose my slippers between home and school.

If you didn't know Calvin's last name, he was "you know, Calvin, the *pake* boy with the Mother." Calvin's mother was famous, and feared, by the rest of us. It was because of her, and despite a dramatic personal appeal and home visit by Coach Ikeda, that Calvin was not on our football team. He was more coordinated, and more confident than the other boys on the team, and the coach wanted him badly. Yet Mrs. Ah Siu would not budge in her conviction that football was a barbarian American invention—something too risky to allow her son to play.

She didn't like surfing either, but occasionally Calvin snuck away to ride the waves with his friends. Yet he would never complain about her strictness, nor would he ever dream of defying her in any direct way. Stealth-surfing was the only minor rebellion he ever allowed himself. So, with the exception of surfing, he was totally loyal to Chow Fun Lady—as I used to call her in the peevish privacy of my adolescent mind. (In Elementary, Calvin always had chow fun in his bento box, instead of rice, but since he was universally loved by his peers, he rarely got teased about it.)

The coup of my senior year was landing Calvin as my date to the prom. What he never knew—even to this day, thirty years later—is that I had also slated him to become my husband.

I had watched Calvin with the cunning of a huntress since eighth grade. I knew his every movement, stance, posture, habit of speech. Fortunately, first love—a love which is that intense and tragic and idiotic—only comes once. My love for Calvin was the kind of love that breaks your heart on a daily, or even an hourly, basis.

I would see some other slut flirting with Calvin and my heart would break. ("Excuse my French," as we used to say so urbanely in 1964, but I'm a mature, single professional woman who has no need for euphemisms anymore.)

Such glimpses of the competition would launch me off into dark fantasies of abandonment, and solo jumps from the sides of steaming, desolate volcanoes. Suffice it to say that for nearly five years Calvin was the pivot, the center, the axis of my swirling schemes and feelings.

*   *   *

Here is prom politics in a nutshell: Get yourself on the Dance Committee. The Dance Committee gets to choose the "team." (It was not until I was in my first English Composition class at U.H. that I realized that there was an English word spelled THEME.) Our "team" was to be MOON-LIGHT FOR LOVERS, but Mr. Clark, the principal, finally made us change it to "Moon River." Does anyone remember Andy Williams anymore? I think they trotted him out on a stage last Christmas for a television special, like some mainland Don Ho, crooning his long-ago memorized medley.

So I got myself on the Dance Committee, and I got the love-of-my-life to agree to take me to the prom. I was at the pinnacle of senior year politics.

There was one committee battle I lost, though. I didn't like glitter, even in those days, but for the rest of the committee it was just too irresistible: all that silver glitter on the cardboard moon, with a blue-green glitter river (down which we'd all float, I supposed, with our dates, into an ocean of spangled bliss).

I went along with the rest of the decorating scheme for the gym—no hotel ballrooms in those days. The main thing was to hide the two basketball backboards and to create enough of an illusion of glitz that only the sense of smell would reveal the true identity of our dreamy, sophisticated ballroom.

We accomplished the hiding of the backboards with a false bamboo ceiling—which turned out to be a bit too low for some of the taller boys, including Calvin. Several thousand yards of colored paper streamers and several hundred acres of freshly picked Kleenex tissue flowers completed the gym's disguise.

When I talk with school friends now about these details, it all seems so tacky—and we do nothing but laugh at ourselves. But it was so serious then, so huge and romantic and other-worldly. For most of us that shoddy prom was as important as our graduation; for some of us, probably more. And though we can't remember what we did the day before or two days later, our collective memories can fill in every detail of that bewitching night on Moon River.

As the sons and daughters of my classmates prepare for their five hundred to thousand dollar proms in 1994, we remember our own preparations for that big, but much cheaper, night. No limos. We were lucky if the boys washed down the coffee Jeeps before they picked us up. No dinner out. Where, for instance, would one go? Tashima Restaurant?

If the sixties were supposed to be a time of sexual license, you wouldn't have known it by Kona. Ignorant farm boys and naive would-be Annette Funicellos, that's what we were. Maybe others were getting some in the cane roads at night, and I heard rumors of some clumsy groping in the back rows of the Kona Theater, but certainly the Kona Coast was not exactly the free love capital of the world. In my own home, sex was never mentioned, except for some brief and evasive medical mumbo jumbo when I first started my periods.

Our house was filled with the Christian haole women of my mother and grandmother's generations. They were women who referred to themselves as *kamaʻāinas*, as if it were a designation of royalty—as if they were baronesses with right of succession. It had nothing to do with being "children of the land." It had to do with entitlement and imagined grandeur and a place in society that would never have been possible in the New England of their (much humbler) origins. In this lily-white world, sex was never on the agenda—except as some vague and euphemized danger to young ladies.

But I did, once, have a taste of Calvin. And I mean that quite literally. We kissed one evening about a month before the prom—where else but in Daddy's Buick. I had picked him up one late afternoon at the school and we parked off the road between the Greenwell House and the main road. For what seemed like hours we talked and watched the sky go dark. I escalated things by reaching for his hand and holding it while I dreamed up more things to say.

Finally at a loss, I pulled him toward me and we kissed. For him, it must have been the first time he had kissed anyone but his mother or his aunties. I taught him as best I could, and in that teaching I got my first, elusive taste of him. The closest I can come to describing the taste of Calvin's body is the flavor I have since discovered at Dave's Ice Cream: Lichee Sherbet. It has that same vanishing sweetness that I tasted on his body that night so many years ago.

For a long time I thought of it as the Man Flavor, but with more experience I began to realize that it was a uniquely Calvin flavor. Since discovering its replica at Dave's, I've been extremely careful only to have one scoop on the premises. (Much like the dangers of off-premise liquor sales, I fear total loss of control should I ever have an unlimited supply in my own condo. I can't risk it.)

*   *   *

Before our thirty year reunion, I had last seen Calvin at Ellison's funeral in 1986. That memorial became an unofficial class reunion too, since every one of us had watched our televisions and seen (over and relentlessly over again) that lonely rocket split in horrid, smoke-trailed pieces . . . and we each must have thought to ourselves: "There goes Ellison—you know, the rascal one."

For the people of the Kona coast, especially the older ones, the Challenger disaster became a kind of cautionary tale, Kona's own version of Icarus as local boy. For many of our elders, Ellison's daring demise was proof, once again, of the dangers of life on the Mainland, or, alternately, a parable about the perils of haole-made hardware.

It seems a frivolous thought, but all of us who were his classmates knew that no one of us would ever die in such a dramatic, showy, or unimaginable way. Like speeding off a road at 100 miles an hour, it was an adolescent way to die.

But if he was Icarus to the older people, he was James Dean as local boy to us. Because of that, our own late childhoods also went up in smoke, 21,000 feet above Florida, with brave, rascal Ellison.

*   *   *

Here is what happened in 1964 to my perfect prom politics: let's call it, Revenge of Chow Fun Lady. About a week before the prom, when Calvin had finally gotten the nerve to tell his mother who he was taking to the Prom, the pork hash hit the fan. Mrs. Ah Siu apparently interpreted the prom as a serious precursor to marriage, and Calvin was ordered to go to the prom alone.

I must admit too that my own mother was not overjoyed at the thought of my going to the prom with a Chinese boy. The miscegenation fear of her age and class were never stated verbally, but that brief tightening of the right side of her mouth told the story all too clearly. (I had actually rehearsed for a direct prohibition from her. It culminated with the line, "There aren't any haole boys to go with!" But I realized that this would have been too much of a temptation for her—and I was sure she would have taken up the challenge, unearthing some pale-faced cousin, descended perhaps from the Maui planter aristocracy she so admired.)

Now it must be said that going to the prom alone was no big disgrace in those days. A lot of people, especially the fat girls, went to the prom alone. Well, actually, the fat girls usually got one of their *mahu* boyfriends to go with them. This worked out perfectly since the *mahu* were the only boys who loved to dress up. They were also flashy dancers—and they were the only ones who could give their dates tips on makeup and hairstyles. (Secretly, I think the parents were also relieved, since they knew their daughters' virginity would go unchallenged during their gay night out.)

But I was NOT a fat girl—not then, at least—and the idea of showing up at Moon River without a date sent me back into my tragic-maiden, volcano-jumping fantasies.

I tried to convince Calvin to meet me outside the gym that night so we could walk down the concrete stairs together into the ballroom and be announced as a couple. Quite sensibly pointing out the smallness of the Kona community, he refused, convinced that his mother would find out.

So I went alone, driving daddy's Buick into the parking lot like some rich, spoiled mainland girl, in hooped crinoline and a ratted-beehive-hairspray-helmet that pushed up against the inside lining of the Buick ceiling. (This left an indelible chemical stain that neither I nor my father ever spoke of.)

Holding back the tears which would have told of my tragic aloneness, I entered early through a side door and threw myself into last minute decorating details with the other girls on the Dance Committee.

Calvin showed up an hour or so later, also entering through the stag side door. I pretended not to see him. I pretended to be absorbed in the business of the glitter. One boy, poor Dexter Ito, ("you know, the one with the eyes") had already guided me out on the dance floor. His breath was sweet with what I now know was Sloe Gin and his fickle eyes were bloodshot. "You are so beautiful," he whispered carefully into my left ear as he lurched his crotch into my crinolined left hip, quite impressively demonstrating his arousal.

"Poor Dexter," the old ladies of Kona used to say, "such a nice Japanese boy—too bad, yeah, about his eyes." Dexter's cousin, Lily, a fellow dance committee member, saw my plight on the dance floor and redirected her cousin outside the gym—where he later up-chucked streams of purple projectiles. (I know now I should have given myself over to Dexter's advances. After high school he was able to get corrective lenses for his eye problem and he has now become one of the richest men on the Big Island.)

Calvin did, though, come over to the sidelines and ask me to dance about midway through our Special Night. That seemed brave enough to me at the time. It was a slow dance too. (How weighted that term was in those days: "Slow Dance"! We pronounced those two words with the same caution and awe that surrounded phrases like "Heavy Petting" or "French Kiss.")

So for just a few minutes my Prom dreams came true. I closed my eyes and leaned my head against Calvin's neck as we swirled down Moon River. It was then I decided on one more taste. As I opened my eyes—fully intending to lick his earlobe or taste his dreamy cheekbones—my line of sight panned the side entrance where the chaperons were huddled.

Like the little square in the center of the viewfinder (that video game target-finder we got so used to during the Gulf-Oil/ CNN War) my vision zeroed in on Mrs. Ah Siu standing in the doorway—her own serious range-finders fixed right on me.

I immediately shut my pre-moistened lips and guided the two of us toward some glitter camouflage. "Calvin," I whispered, "your mother is here." I could feel his muscles tense, and we broke off our duet, parting from each other, fading into the sidelines as far from her iron stare as possible.

I guess I have greatly romanticized Calvin's bravery in my convenient recollections of that evening. The visuals of Calvin and I dancing under the bamboo sky are still filed in my memory as a scene from *Romeo and Juliet*—brave Romeo defying his family, and hers, to woo the girl he loves.

But, let's face it, I was no Juliet, and Calvin didn't exactly defy Chow Fun Lady.

The evening was wrecked, of course, and I don't remember much more after that, except that I stayed to help with clean-up and ended up getting drunk with the fat girls and the *mahu* under some coffee trees. Someone drove me home in the blue Buick as the dawn light diffused above the waters of Kona. I'm sure I got in trouble with mother, but all I remember is a tragic hangover.

*   *   *

Calvin has since married a Chinese girl, just like his mother wanted, and is a big-time lawyer in L.A.—with all that implies: poofy silk shirts, pants with pleats for days, gold chains, and a cellular phone. He's become a very 90s kind of guy.

Mrs. Ah Siu died in 1981. Calvin and his brothers and their one sister all appeared in Kona for the funeral. I know; I watched them carefully from a distance.

Now, thirty years later, our reunion was to be held at the Kamehameha IV Hotel, not in the gym. There was no glitter, thank God. It was an elegant and expensive evening and I hoped, at least, that the interior lighting would be dim enough to hide our aging faces.

I went alone of course, as the only Old Maid that class produced—excepting, of course, for Sister Mary Cordeira who still teaches at a Catholic school on Maui.

I had enough gumption to sit next to Calvin and his wife. She was actually quite nice to me, and fun to talk to. At least I didn't have to arouse her suspicion by saying that Calvin and I had gone to the Prom together.

As my second white wine began to kick in, however, it was all I could do to keep from leaning toward her nearest ear and asking, in a whisper, how Calvin tasted after all these years.

I danced with him only once that night, after asking my new friend, his wife, for permission. As we talked on the dance floor it became clear to me that he did not remember his mother's prohibition—or her prom-night appearance at all. He seemed to recall that we had both gone to the prom alone and he didn't acknowledge that there had ever been any other plans.

Somehow I was deeply shocked at this discrepancy in our separate memories.

In a fit of boldness, I closed my eyes briefly and licked my lips—and I was about to have myself a taste of Calvin when he whirled me around in sync with the music.

As my vision grazed the side entrance to the ballroom, there she stood, floating phantom-like next to the white-coated busboy: Chow Fun Lady with her eyes fixed on me—no legs visible below the knees, just like the Hawaiians say. Just those burning eyes.

I gasped and separated myself from the puzzled LA lawyer. I mumbled something about too much wine and fled outside to the hotel parking lot.

Standing in the night air, afraid to glance over my shoulder for fear that Ellison too might appear, I thought: *Where are they tonight—the fat girls and the* mahu—*when I need them again?*

*   *   *

The next morning, I took the plane back to O'ahu. While airborne I wouldn't let myself think about anything that had happened the night before. For awhile, I closed my eyes and took refuge in my habitual fantasy about the perfect brown legs of Honolulu's UPS drivers.

I took the bus home from the airport, and as I walked along the last block between the bus stop and my condo, I noticed a new abandoned car—now almost totally stripped and trashed—where nothing had been before. There was also some new graffiti on the wall of the warehouse across from my building.

LONELY GIRL LOVES KENNY, it read, and I was overwhelmed with the impulse to wish her well.

TITA: BOYFRIENDS

Lois-Ann Yamanaka

Boys no call you yet?
Good for you.
Shee, everybody had at least
two boyfriends already.
You neva even have *one* yet?
You act dumb, ass why.
All the boys said you just one little kid.
Eh, no need get piss off.

Richard wen' call me around 9:05 last night.
Nah, I talk *real* nice to him.
Tink I talk to him the way I talk to you?
You cannot let boys know your true self.
Here, this how I talk.
Hello, Richard. How are you?
Oh, I'm just fine. How's school?
My classes are just greeaat.
Oh, really. Uh-huh, uh-huh.
Oh, you're so funny.
Yes, me too, I love C and K.
Kalapana? Uh-huh, uh-huh.

He coming down from Kona next week.
He like me meet him up the shopping center.
Why, you like see him?
He one fox with ehu hair.
I know he get ehu hair
'cause he wen' send me his picture.
What you said?
Of course he know what I look like.
Eh, what you trying for say?
That I one fat cow?
Yeah, he get one picture of me.
I wen' send him the one of us by the gym.

The one us made you take for the gang
'cause us neva like you in the picture.
Nah—I was in the back row
so I wen' look skinny, eh.
Only had my face.

I get this guy wrap around my finger
'cause of the way I talk on the phone.
I told him I get hazel eyes and I hapa—
eh, I pass for hapa ever since I wen' Sun-In my hair.
Lemon juice and peroxide too.
Ass why all orange and gold.
Plus when I glue my eyes
and make um double,
my eyes ain't slant no mo
and I swear, everybody ask me,
Eh, you hapa?

So what if not all true?
How he going know from that picture I gave him?
I was so far in the back.
He said he get um in his wallet.
And no be acting all cute when he come.
Just shut your mouth
and let me and him do whatevas.
I warning you now, no get stupid.
And no follow us if he like go cruising
'cause something might happen
in the car. I get um.

I get um good.
'Cause I know what boys like to do
and it ain't hanging around the gym
or swimming laps after school
or sitting around the shopping center eating slush
with losers like you,
I tell you that much.

So you keep writing Elmer's name
inside your folders and prank calling him,
and dedicating songs to him

and writing him stupid letters signed ano-namous
and shoving um in his locker.
Eh, think I stupid?
Everybody knows you like Elmer.
And everybody know you the dumb ass
doing all those dumb things.
How they know? 'Cause maybe I told um.
Why. You going make something of it?
I would *love* to have to kick your ass right now.

Yeah, I told um. I told um all.
And you like know what?
You better give up all that crap
and grow up 'cause everybody,
all the boys think you just one small kid
and no boy going eva be your boyfriend
'cause you dunno how
for make your voice all nice,
your face all make-up,
your hair all smooth and ehu,
your clothes all low cut,
and your fingernails all long.
You dunno how for act.
And you, you just dunno how for please.

untitled by Dezmond Gilla, 'Aiea High School

POINT OF CONTACT
Alohi Ae'a

Kalākaua Avenue was always busy, from the late evening into the early morning. Makani moved through the crowd with the absent-minded experience of one who is familiar with the turf and the art of dodging people. Without realizing it, he moved past the ABC Stores, Jack-in-the-Box, an expensive leather goods store that belched cold air into the sidewalk. The ten-thirty night clans flowed around him, seeping out of eating places and stores, oozing around the t-shirt vendors that charged twenty dollars for ten thin, low-quality, touristy t-shirts.

A table covered with sarongs caught his eye for a second, and his attention was riveted on the blond-haired girl that stood contemplating a dark purple sarong tied around her waist. She decided to take it, and the white moons and pale blue stars of the sarong disappeared as she folded it and dropped it into the plastic bag the vendor held. Blond hair . . . the way she stood, hand on hip, left foot forward . . . . He didn't notice Julie until he felt his surfboard hit something. A light point of contact, but contact nonetheless.

"Sorry about that." He was still thinking about the blond girl he'd been looking at, so he didn't look at Julie at first. She was just another face in the crowd, another figure to brush his eyes over blankly, seeing the image but not registering the person. She shook her head, and it was the birdlike motion that caught his attention.

She reminded him of somebody, the same person that the other girl had reminded him of. A face that he knew very well . . . . He stared at her for two seconds, trying to recall who moved like that. It was right at the edge of his mind, a motion that he knew so well . . . . He gave up, then realized that the girl was staring back at him.

Her hair was fine and yellow, a dark rich yellow that made her fair face look even whiter. Glossy lips curved up and then back down, a pouty bow slightly parted over white teeth. He kept on staring at her, and was both attracted and repelled at the same time. He wondered why she was alone; it wasn't because of her looks. She shifted uneasily, still looking at him, and then tugged her skirt down toward her knees. It was then that he noticed her faded clothes, the old shoes she wore, the ragged backpack at her feet.

This only added to her attraction, though, the mystery of what she was doing and where she came from. And then, the person that she resembled . . . . This mystery both excited and depressed him. There was nothing sinister about her life or her roots, yet it was easy to imagine her coming from a sordid background. It was the hunted look in her eyes.

It was an awkward moment for both of them as their eyes locked and then found nowhere else to go. His were red from the sun and dark brown from his mother, hers were a deep blue she'd inherited from her grandmother and full of a savage wistfulness that her life had produced. She looked so lost and worn and alone, and he was still coming off his high from surfing, and those were the only reasons that he could think of to justify what he did next.

"Hey, do you need somewhere to go?" They both started a little at his words. There was no turning back; he had committed to something that he could not, would not, get out of. "I've got some room at my place." She was silent for a long time, then she shook her head again.

"I can't believe you just asked me that." There was no clue as to how she felt about it.

"I'm sorry. I—I just assumed . . . I mean, you looked so lost . . . . Your, you . . . ." All of a sudden he was warm, and he felt incredibly rude. To just assume that she was homeless, or, at the very least, needy, just because she was standing alone on the sidewalk with faded clothes and a tired-looking backpack. It was one of the highest forms of insult that he could have given a person. It brought him down from his leftover high. "I'm sorry. I'll, uh, leave you alone."

"No, wait." She paused, then looked down at the sidewalk. "I mean I can't believe that you just offered me a place to stay. Either you're a sick weirdo, or the kind of guy I've been looking for all my life." She laughed nervously, trying to joke about it. "You look like a nice guy, and I'd really love to stay at your place tonight. You can't know how much it means to me."

"And if I am a sick weirdo?" He asked it because it was the thing to do. Her answer surprised him.

"Well, it's no big loss to the world. No one will miss me." Her voice didn't hold enough laughter to be a joke, but there was a sullen note of fury under everything that she said. She picked up her backpack and would not look at him. Waikiki hummed around them, and they walked in silence and wondered at their actions.

His house was in Makiki, a small old-fashioned home with paint chipping off of the eaves. He parked his '82 Honda in the garage and unstrapped his board from the surf rack. Mosquitoes swarmed around their legs as they walked up the stone paved walkway. "We've got a little room next to the kitchen; some of my friends crash there sometimes. It's nothing special, but it's the coolest room in the house. I'll get Ruth to lay out a futon for you." His initial attraction towards her he pushed aside, and he intended to treat her like any of his other friends that came home with him on the nights when they had nowhere else to go.

"Ruth?" It was a polite question, but he felt a twinge of regret at what he had to answer.

"Ruth—my wife. She'll like you." It was probably a lie, he thought, but he would work things out. He pushed the front door open and set his surfboard on the rack next to the door. The lights in the kitchen were on, and he could hear the sound of his wife rummaging through the drawers. "Ruth? I'm home."

"Well, hon, it's late enough." Her voice floated in the air, a rich musical sound. He knew that she was probably smiling to herself, and although she wouldn't show it, she was relieved that he was home safe. He smiled also, and forgot about the girl for a moment. The anticipation of see-ing his wife again sent warm shivers up his neck, and his smile grew broader. The girl shut the door behind her, and he remembered.

"Ruth, I've brought someone home with me." He motioned to her, and she slid the shoes off her feet before she followed him into the kitchen. Ruth's voice was laughing again as they made their way across the living room.

"Which one of the bums have you got with you tonight? They don't need my permission to stay—the lack of it hasn't stopped them before. Just make sure he's clean before he sleeps on my sheets. He can use the dog's towel." Her back was to them as they entered the kitchen. She was cutting something in a pan, and her long hair dripped water onto the floor.

"It's not a bum this time. Julie, meet Ruth. Ruth, this is Julie." He saw her pause in her movements. Then, slowly, she turned around.

"Julie. Nice to meet you. I'm sorry—I thought you were another one of Makani's buddies. Make yourself at home. Would you like something to drink?" Ruth's voice was low and smooth, and she looked up into Julie's face with calm dark eyes.

The contrast between the two women was so strong that Makani wondered how it was possible that there could be so much difference in the world. Julie was tall and fair and looked out of place in the tiled kitchen, while Ruth was small and dark and perfectly at home. Julie's eyes were full of something that caused those around her to ache in a small hidden part of their hearts, while Ruth's face was serene and content, her eyes earth-col-ored pools of light. Even their voices were totally unalike.

"I'm fine, thanks. But—you don't know how much this means to me." Julie sounded strained as she twisted her fingers, and pain flitted into her eyes. Makani wondered what it meant.

Ruth noticed also, and her face softened. "Are you all right, hon? It's no big deal. We're glad to have you. I love having visitors." There was a warmth in her voice, but a dangerous edge also. Julie didn't know it, but Makani did. He was uncomfortable for a second, and searched for something to do.

Julie tensed at the compassion in Ruth's voice, mistaking it for pity. "I'm fine. Nothing's wrong that I can't handle." Her voice was terse now, and the fury Makani had heard earlier bubbled to the surface.

"Well, no one should have to handle things alone. If Makani brought you home, it seems as if you need a bit of help. Just as long as you know that pride isn't a bad thing to lose." Ruth's voice matched Julie's, but Makani knew that Ruth's anger was not directed toward the girl, but toward the circumstances that must have driven her to where she was.

"I'll get you a towel, Julie. The bathroom's off the living room; you'll find it. The extra room is right through that door. Just dump your stuff there." All of a sudden he was tired, and his eyes felt hot and dry as he gave her a towel. In the kitchen, Ruth was still cutting the food. He dropped another towel on the floor and mopped up the water from her hair.

Ruth didn't turn to him. "She reminds me of Christine." He stopped what he was doing.

"That's who it is. I've been trying to figure it out ever since I saw her. I knew that there was something about her that was very familiar to me."

"How did you meet her?" The question was neutral, flat, but Ruth wasn't moving.

"I hit her with my surfboard. Not in the water; I just walked into her on Kalākaua. But there was something about her that seemed familiar. The way she shook her head. It was totally Christine. I just didn't realize it until now. But she looked so desperate and lost there, I had to invite her home. I don't think she's very happy. It's like she's waiting to die, and she'd do it herself if she could." He spoke slowly, voicing what he'd felt the minute that he saw her.

"At first I didn't even look at her. But then when I did, it was weird. I mean, she was beautiful, but there was something more. Like, I looked at her and I realized that there was a person under all of that skin and hair and makeup. Like I'd finally realized that she was actually a person. You know what I mean? When you finally realize something that you knew but didn't actually know? I don't know how to explain it."

The floor was dry now, and he draped the towel on the counter. "She's even more beautiful than Christine was," Ruth said. Her voice had dangerous undercurrents, but he didn't know what was going on.

"Christine . . . Christine was beautiful in her own way." He was silent, thinking about the first woman that he had been engaged to. She was eighteen when they met, a soft pale girl with eyes that made him want to bring her everything that he owned. Dark blue eyes that saw more than she ever told him about, a nose that almost tilted upward, and perfect white teeth. As lovely as she was, though, there was a sorrow and mystery around her that fascinated him and made him fall in love with her.

Something had grown inside his heart as he grew older, a compassion for those who were hurting. A local boy with salt in his hair and sand between his toes, he had never imagined the type of things that this fair mainland creature had lived through. Two months after they met, they became engaged. Two weeks after that, she was an empty shell, her body crippled from the self-inflicted wounds it had endured. She'd gone a little too far, indulged a little too much. His grief at losing her was only enhanced by his unawareness of what had been going on. Everything that he'd thought about her was proven false.

When he became close to Ruth a year later, he held her off. They dated for five months, but he refused to get close to her. Because she knew of Christine, she was patient. Born and raised local, she had all of the silkiness and none of the roughness of the islands. His friends loved her because she treated them with all of the care that she would have given them if she had been married to them. His parents loved her because she treated them as if they were her own. Finally, he put aside the haunting specter of Christine and asked her to marry him.

The night that he proposed was warm and humid, and he remembered the sweat beading on her upper lip as she looked at him. "I thought you'd never ask me. I thought I'd have to settle for your friend Jim." He'd laughed and held her and wondered why he'd waited so long. In his arms, he felt her tremble. He didn't realize that she was relieved beyond measure. But he felt her love enfold him as he wrapped her in his arms.

The two years since then had sped by, and he forgot what it was like to live without her. She was now a part of him, so much a part that on the nights when she slept over at a friend's, or stayed in Makaha with her sister, he would wake up in the middle of the night feeling as if he was missing something. His body would seem incomplete. Then he would remember the cold empty space next to him, and he would lie awake until the chilly gray light of dawn came through the windows and the neighbor next door started his car and drove away at five in the morning.

All of this he thought as he stood in the kitchen, and something cold clutched at his heart. Her voice wasn't right. Even when they fought, she had never sounded this distant. Her words, so innocent, sent shivers through him. "This one is beautiful like Christine. But more so. I think it's because she seems sadder than Christine ever was." Ruth covered the pan that she'd been working on, and threw her knife into the sink. "I'm going to bed."

He watched her move away, her thick hair swinging with the motion of her hips. He noticed a bruise on her left leg: a dirt-biking souvenir. A cold feeling settled over him. His wife, so open and receptive all of the other nights that he'd brought people home, had suddenly refused to accept. The house was too warm; he went out to the backyard.

The night was dark and quiet, and he squatted down in the grass. The girl came out to join him. He looked up at her, and again saw the look in her eyes. Yes, she was like Christine. "Julie, are you happy?"

She looked down at him, and there was a look in her eyes that made him turn away. "I thought I'd never be happy. I've never known what it was like, I think. Or I made myself believe that. But when I saw you tonight . . . ." She looked up at the sky. "When you turned and actually looked at me, I felt as if you were really looking at me, Julie, the real Julie. My clothes, my looks, the fact that I was alone: none of it mattered to you. And your eyes were so full of—of—contentment. You were happy with your life. I saw it in your eyes, and I realized that I could have it. All I need—" she laughed softly "—All I need is a man like you."

The attraction that he felt at first flared up in him again. Ruth was angry with him, and this desperate woman standing next to him reminded him so much of the first woman that he'd really loved. He stood up and bent down to her. He had no idea what he was doing, or why, but he thought that he could have kissed her then. Except that something held him back. Her blond hair curled around her face, and the light fragrance of ginger reached him. It was the same scent that lingered in his bedroom, the scent that he dreamed of when he buried his face in Ruth's hair.

He turned to go into the house. "Makani . . . ." In the night lights, he could see the shining in her eyes. Her hand was on his arm, he felt the sweat on his forehead. Turning away, he saw the lights go off in his bedroom. He left the door open for Julie, but it was many minutes before she came in.

Inside, Ruth lay awake, listening to the sounds of the house. She heard him wash the knife and scrub the kitchen sink. The front door was locked, the drapes pulled shut in the living room. He padded around, putting away books and newspaper. The linen closet creaked open, and he put a blanket on Julie's futon. The back door clicked shut, and she heard their voices rise and fall for a short time. Tears started down her face.

He brushed his teeth and flipped off all the lights. The toilet flushed, and she heard him jiggle the handle. He was in the shower now, the water running noisily. She let herself cry, and reached for the Kleenex box under the bed. By the time he was through showering, she had stopped. Now the only sound she heard was her own breathing.

The house was dark, but she saw his form as he came into the bedroom. He dropped his towel onto the floor and pulled on a pair of boxers. Then he turned to look at her. "What's wrong, Ruth?"

"You didn't have to bring her home."

"Would you have me leave her? Would that have made you happy?" His voice was soft, but she was not fooled.

"No, I wouldn't have you leave her." She had to admit it, even to herself. "That's one of the reasons that I love you. Because you can't help bringing people home. But you didn't have to want her." She was through with crying, but her voice still quivered.

He sat on the bed with his back to her. Then he lay down on top of the covers and stared up at the ceiling. "Ruth, I love you." He would not deny the fact that he had been attracted to Julie. It would be a lie, and they both knew it. But the attraction that he felt for Julie had been nothing compared to what he felt for this sorrow-filled woman lying next to him.

He turned and looked at the woman whom he loved more than anything in the world. There was nothing he knew of that he could say. She looked at him, and he saw wet spots on her cheeks. "Makani, you wanted her. But you need me." She took everything that he had been thinking and threw it at him with those eight words. He rolled over on his back again, and could not speak.

Finally, he slid under the sheets and looked at her. She stared back at him, and even without the light she knew the color of his eyes and the arch of his lips. His face was etched in her memory, and his voice in her heart. "Ruth, I love you." It was all he could say.

"I know it, Makani." She touched his cheek softly, then closed her eyes. She was asleep, and still he watched her. His heart broke with the knowledge that it would be a long time before the hurt she felt would be forgotten.

He got out of bed and opened the blinds over the windows. Dim streetlight filtered in and he could see the tear stains on her face. When he got back into bed, she curled toward him automatically. She moved to match the curve of his body, and he rested his hand in the familiar dip of her waist. Sighing in her sleep, his name danced on her lips. But he did not hear her; he was already dreaming.

In his dreams, they were diving from the falls in Waimea. Holding hands, they sliced the blue depths of the water and went down forever. Then they were shooting upward. They resurfaced, laughing, and climbed again to the top. As they jumped, he could feel his heart soaring, and this time he held Ruth close to him, his arms around her waist. She looked up into his face, and the measure of his love was greater than the depths of the pool and stronger than the rush of the waterfall.

NO MINDLESS DIGGING

Kathy Dee Kaleokealoha Kaloloahilani Banggo

For Jeff

He used to call me pua, said he had been blessed with rain.

> One time . . . many times . . . long before classic
> Rolls Royce lipstick and stilletto heels,
> when white owls past midnight meant my father's
> ghost warned me home, my first love and I
> claimed Hālawa valley. We picked flowers, ate
> guavas, hiked barefoot,   let the mosquitoes bite,
> examined insects, wrote poetry, ran our hands
> over bark, got high, smelled leaves, b r e a t h e d,
> listened to bird calls and answered back, planted
> seeds, whistled, recited poetry, stripped and
> kissed and made love, dozed, ate more guavas, hid
> from the rifle-shouldering boys come to harvest
> their pakalōlō crops, dreamed of plump babies and
> papaya trees, the rows of sleeping willows, the
> kalo patch, the ocean just beyond the window,
> the skateboard ramp out back . . .

Some days I want to turn around, turn my back on black stockings
and fax machines, the sticky adhesive of the city, lost love, new loves, cold
cream, offices, therapy.

> We drove right on in past the barricades on
> most nights. Other times, the boys bothered
> to step out of the car to push those red-orange
> striped barriers aside. No trespassing? Who
> but a handful of misfit kids in worn out flannel
> and torn denim would be interested in an
> unfinished freeway?

> We parked in the bushes, out of sight of HPD;
> the boys drank beer and tossed their empty
> Hinano bottles into the ditch running alongside

H-3. I scolded, being sober, and an environmen-
talist of sorts.

It could mean a return to a time before my own burial—digging, I mean.
Thoughtful digging. Ethical effort. Every measured meter of dirt uplifted
and cleared away could mean uncovering an old and forgotten simplicity.
My friend Kammie, a young nouveau-hippie with spacious eyes and a china
plate smooth forehead, told me about the job. She's working Hālawa
with an archaeology group contracted to excavate the valley. The pay is
good and I'm a penniless wanna-be poet burned out on poor, wanna-be
poetry. The real stuff is out there, means walking those trails again like we
did 8? 9? 10? years ago. Hell, I'll dig. If it means feeling the walls again
(2 feet high at the most), built beside the stream.

> "Some old hippie dude built that wall," he says,
> "Wanted to live like Thoreau."
> "Crap." I'm kicking the shallow water with my
> toes. "Little people did this."
> "Littler than you?"
> I snob slowly, the way a chameleon blinks but
> without the drugged laziness, and say, "See
> how low the walls are? And look at the way
> the rocks are placed."
> He grins.
> "Carefully and with craftsmanship. One by one.
> By hand." I nod. "Yup. Menehune."
> "Yup," he mimics, "Menehune."
> I am tired from speaking and lean against him.
> My jaw hurts and I have cotton mouth from
> all the effort it takes to pronounce my
> English properly. He and his long-haired
> buddies had teased the pidgin right from my
> tongue so only traces of the melodic island
> lilt remain.

I didn't know. I thought finding artifacts would save Hālawa. Isn't there a
law—? Like I said to my ma, it'll help to preserve the culture. She had been
up in arms against my wanting to dig. Not because of H-3—my mom, she
thinks in terms of white owls. So I told her, I told her, I said without really
saying that she was being superstitious. You see, I had forgotten. Somewhere
between oceans I'd dropped the old blueprints, somewhere a long time ago.

One time at high noon. Right on the hood of
his Duster, with a helicopter hovering and
buzzing overhead like some insane dragonfly.
I've never been so warm.

At night he drove mauka down H-3, flicking the
headlights off   then on   to the base of the
mountain where construction stopped. I didn't
know which was worse, driving with the lights
on or off. There's something ominous about
being the only hissing engine on a half-built
freeway. Slows the breath. All that bleached
concrete illuminated in the headlights thins
the air. It's paved desolation, a silence too
difficult to understand. We didn't try. Instead
we closed our eyes and kissed.
       "Someday when we're old and this thing's built
we can tell our kids how and where and when—."
We stripped and kissed and made love because it
was easier. Because freeways cutting through
sacred valleys, like blue shadows darkening under
the eyes, was too burdensome a subject for the
churning, the arrogance of youth. *Why? Why?*

CHOOSING MY NAME

Puanani Burgess

When I was born my mother gave me three names.
Christabelle, Yoshie, and Puanani.

Christabelle was my "english" name.
My social security name,
My school name,
      the name I gave when teachers asked me
      for my "real" name, a safe name.

Yoshie was my home name,
My everyday name,
      the name that reminded my father's family
      that I was Japanese, even though
      my nose, hips, and feet were wide,
      the name that made me acceptable to them
      who called my Hawaiian mother *kuroi* (black),
      a saving name.

Puanani is my chosen name,
My *piko* name connecting me to the *ʻāina*
      and the *kai* and the *poʻe kahiko*
      my blessing; my burden,
      my amulet, my spear.

I COME FROM A PLACE
Ho'oipo DeCambra

I come from a place
where pale golden fields
and sharp mountains
surround a hālau.
A hālau crying to be recreated
for po'e hawai'i.

I come from a place
where menehune trails
are silhouetted
against the horizon's colors
of blue, green and silvery grey.

I come from a place
where black lava rocks
melted together over time
embrace the coastline
while ehu-colored limu
cling to the deepest recesses
close to the ocean's bosom.

I come from a place
where people love old cars.
They like fixing them,
making them well,
and the challenge
of getting to town and back
just one more time.

I come from a place
where people are satisfied
with the bare minimum
income and
living conditions.

I come from a place
where Puanani dreams mouse poems
and a kukui nut leaf mirrors her beauty.
Where Diane remembers seeing
Lono calling the rain
and Robbie is willing
to say
"Kaneaki Heiau is our sacred site."

I come from a place
where DeWitt dreams and works
for Makua to be
given back to the po'e hawai'i
and Isabel swims in front of
Rest Camp, all the while dreaming
of the soon to be
the greatest marine science school for our kids.

I come from a place
where it is dark
and Kamaka teaches us about
the light in the heavens
and dolphins dance on water for your birthday.

MY FATHER'S GARDEN

D. Māhealani Dudoit

Outside my screen door, the wind is blowing through my father's garden. Sunlight like the softest rain penetrates the tangled branches of the acerola tree and falls upon the dark-green bromeliads and feathery asparagus ferns growing beneath. Tiny white acerola blossoms swirl into the open faces of leaves and scatter in whirls over the ground. My father planted the tree twenty-five years ago, when we moved into this house. I planted the bromeliads last year, after returning to the end of a hot summer in these islands. The ferns found their way here on their own.

As gardens go, this one is not a raving beauty. The family who lived here before us patched things together as they went along, out of their common sense and limited experience. As a result, exquisite lava rocks are cemented beside broken fragments of cinder blocks in terrace walls, the stairs leading to our house from the public street above are uneven, and mounds of stones have been left to work their way back into the dry soil.

Over the years, I've covered the mounds of stones with philodendron, gotten used to the unevenness of the stairs (number twenty-two is the tricky one), and found a certain kind of poetic symmetry in the walls.

In a good year, like this one, when the winter rains are evenly spaced and plentiful, the garden will flourish. In a dry year, however, the plants hang on pitifully to the rocky soil unless watered daily, a chore I don't have the luxury of time to attend to. Summers when I go away are the worst. No one wants the task of watering, and the most I can get out of my family are a few grudging promises to "try to remember." I don't blame them. The job sometimes seems thankless, and the effort in the face of the persistent lack of rain futile. Many of my plants, lawn grasses included, die. But those that survive despite the lack of rain do so with a vengeance. Adversity makes them strong.

As gardeners go, I'm not a particularly good one. Like the family who lived here before me, I do what seems natural: I water, scatter chicken manure now and then, and prune excess foliage and weeds. But since I have a taste for the jungle, the garden tends toward the dense and varied. Wild ferns cling tenaciously between cracks in the stonework. Long, thorny branches of scarlet-colored bougainvillea drape themselves over the rubber tree. Leathery-leafed stephanotis insinuate their tendrils between the supple stems of the coffee bush. The flowers of the Chinese-lantern tremble in the wind above pots of bay, basil, rosemary, dill, mint, Mexican oregano, sage, thyme, and a particularly hardy breed of chives that—like a lone bull in a field of cows—has inseminated every niche within reach.

When my father was alive and sole keeper of the land, his garden seemed constantly in bloom. Orchids flowered, acerola cherries multiplied, ti leaves glistened. I'm still convinced the garden could not have flourished as it did without my father's daily ritual. No matter what the weather— rainy or dry—when he returned home from work each evening, he would immediately unravel the water hose and for the next hour, standing in white undershirt and navy-blue work pants, he would shower each plant with a light spray.

First he watered the terraces to the right of the stairs—a jumble of palm, jade plant, Angel's Trumpet, pīkake, dryland taro, lemon grass, and about thirty other varieties of plants. Then he would water the terraces to the left, including the spreading branches of the plumeria tree, the crotons under them, and the bittermelon vines growing wild around the base of the tree's trunk. Next he would turn to the small oval of lawn and the acerola tree that shaded it. The steps to the lower part of the house—where I lived—began under the tree and led down to a row of long-stalked ti, an orange tree, a coconut tree, several banana trees, a patch of heliconia, and an assortment of tropical plants. Back up the other side of the house were his coffee tree, more ti, and a papaya tree that has now grown higher than the first floor of this house.

My father, who was otherwise a talkative and often angry man, always retreated into thoughtful silence while he was watering the garden, as if he too were experiencing a cleansing from all the day's cares and dis-cords, as if he too were being nourished.

Many years after the care of my father's garden had passed from his hands into mine, I saw a lifesize paper stencil of a man much like my father in the Honolulu Academy of Arts. I had gone there with a Panamanian friend and her seven-year-old daughter to see the exhibits devoted that week to El Día de los Muertos, the Hispanic version of All Saints' Day. In a scene that ran nearly the entire length of a gallery, the man in silhouette was watering his garden. The paper had been cut in detail so fine one could get lost in the multiple blades of grass and the individual droplets of water falling on the open petals of roses and daisies. Unlike my father, the man wore a sombrero and suspenders; but he too, it appeared, had just returned home from a day's work somewhere else, with aching body, to the evening comfort of his garden. The scene, the sign said, had been created by a daughter's hand.

A table stood in front of the paper garden. Upon it had been placed a hairbrush, pipe, favorite cup, hand mirror, doll—each item laid out lovingly before a portrait of the one to whom it had belonged in life. From out of the picture frames, a girl smiled, a young man tilted his meticulously combed head, and an old woman stared with heavy eyelids. Along the remaining three walls of the gallery, rows of death masks stared down at us, each covered with pastel-colored paper and decorated with paper flowers.

In a small adjoining room stood three glass cases containing papier-mâché figurines. In one case, a mariachi band of human skeletons wearing sombreros danced as they played. In another case, bowls of fruits and plates of meats and sweets presented a luscious feast. In the last case, a green serpent entwined itself among the branches of a tree. At the tree's base stood a naked woman, her tresses covering her like a light veil. A naked man, with a fig leaf between his thighs, stood before the woman. His hand was extended not, it seemed, toward the apple she held out to him, but toward her breast instead. The serpent's bright red tongue slithered near the tip of the woman's tiny earlobe.

"Who is that?" my friend's daughter asked as she stared at the scene. I looked down at the top of her head, wondering how the story of Genesis had managed to escape her childhood. The girl's mother was meanwhile engaged in Spanish conversation with a middle-aged woman also visiting the museum. "Your mother will tell you," I said. I dreaded the responsibility of being the one to introduce her to the first great Christian myth, a myth that had puzzled me for as long as I could remember. But the little girl was insistent. "No, you tell me," she demanded.

How was I to answer? I had rejected Catholicism at the age of fifteen, the first adult act of my life, the act that had initiated the wandering course of my life's subsequent long spiritual journey. The Bible, for me, was a combination of art and history. Such a belief did not put me at odds with Christians; but where we differed was in which parts were which. To me, the sacred Scriptures were sacred only in their intent, not in their authorship. They were not unlike the paper stencil dedicated with unquestionable love to a father now gone.

God created man in the image of himself, in the image of God he created him, male and female he created them. God blessed them, saying to them, "Be fruitful, multiply, fill the earth and conquer it. Be masters of the fish of the sea, the birds of heaven, and all living animals on the earth." God said, "See, I give you all the seed-bearing plants that are upon the whole earth, and all the trees with seed-bearing fruit; this shall be your food."

"A long time ago," I explained to the persistent little girl, "there was a garden, and in the garden lived a man and a woman."

"Did they have children?"

"No, they had no children yet. But they lived with many animals, all kinds of animals—"

"Zebras, too?"

"Zebras, elephants, monkeys, every kind of animal you could think of. And in the garden grew all kinds of plants for them to eat and enjoy—mango trees, banana trees, orchids, figs. God made the garden and everything in it. He even made the man and the woman. And when he made them, he told them that the garden was for them to be happy in. He told them that they could play with anything they wanted and eat anything they wanted. But there was one tree they couldn't eat. It was a special tree."

"Why was it special?"

What did the authors of Genesis have in mind when they conceptualized the tree of the knowledge of good and evil? That such knowledge demands responsibility too great for a human to bear? That it inevitably leads to corruption? That it's only one step short of eternal life? That it must be wrested from a jealous God? Had I been the first woman, would I have eaten from the tree?

"It was special because God said it was special." Obedience to authority. I thought of how the girl's mother and I had earlier spent half an hour in the parking lot convincing the girl it was perfectly appropriate to wear her pink leotards and tutu in the Art Academy. We had come straight from dance class and had no clothes for her to change into. In the interest of expedience, I had sided with her mother, even though I knew that neither of us adults would have dreamt of strolling through those polished halls—or practically anywhere else—in similar clothes.

But this time the girl, standing there in her pink tutu before the nearly naked images of the world's first sinners, did not challenge me. "And then what happened?" she asked.

"She ate the fruit anyway."

"Why?"

That question had always been the most difficult part of the story for me, even when I had been the same age as this little girl—or perhaps most especially when I had been her age. Culpability. Hadn't the serpent told her it was okay? How was she not to choose the moist breath, hot in her ear, over the stern, unseen voice?

I remembered the day High Mass on the eve of Lent was given in the auditorium of my Catholic high school. Those of us receiving Holy Communion were required first to make a confession to ensure that we would be in a state of grace when we received the host. When my turn came, I began with the usual formula: "Bless me, Father, for I have sinned. It has been six months since my last confession. These are my sins . . ." I paused, searching my mind and my soul, and then I said with confidence, "I have no sins."

There were a few moments of heavy silence, then the priest said slowly, "What do you mean 'no sins'? You must have sinned at least once in six months!"

"No, Father, I have no sins."

The priest shifted in his seat to face me, his features easily recognizable through the loose mesh of the screen separating us. "You must have sinned at least once!" he insisted.

"No, Father. I have no sins."

"I can't believe it!" he whispered hard. "You must have some sins! You're under oath, remember?"

Under oath? I wondered. Was my confession legal testimony? Was a priest with disbelief in his heart my judge? Fifteen years of unexplained contradictions, inflexible dogma, and what I had long felt were outright lies came flooding back to me. I knew an important moment had arrived.

I took a deep breath. "I lied," I finally said, knowing that my lie was my claim to a lie.

The priest sighed and began to breathe evenly again. "Good." In Latin he absolved me of my new sin and then sent me on my way with, "God be with you." When I heard those words, I stood up, threw open the curtains of the confessional as if they were the gates of Eden, and strode straight out into a new world, never to return to the Catholic Church.

Why indeed had Eve eaten the fruit? "Because she wanted to," I finally said to the little girl. That answer, although perhaps not what the Scriptures had intended to imply, was something both the girl and I could at least understand, and what I felt had truly been in Eve's heart. Not a desire to know anything in particular, or to disobey, or to possess power, but simply to experience, a desire that was as pure and natural as the state of grace whose existence that priest had denied.

God said, "Let there be lights in the vault of heaven to divide day from night, and let them indicate festivals, days and years. Let them be lights in the vault of heaven to shine on the earth." And so it was. God made the two great lights: the greater light to govern the day, the smaller light to govern the night, and the stars. God set them in the vault of heaven to shine on the earth, to govern the day and the night and to divide light from darkness. God said that it was good. Evening came and morning came: the fourth day.

The names of the sun and the moon, because they were worshipped by neighboring peoples, were omitted from the Hebrew Bible, and they were subsequently treated as mere lamps to light the earth and regulate the calendar. When I was born, my parents gave me the name Māhealani, "full moon," because of my father's love for the heavens. On the night of Māhealani in the Hawaiian calendar, it is good to plant taro. The taro will thrive, be strong. Taro was the firstborn—an unformed fetus—of Wākea the Sky Father and his daughter, Hoʻohākākalani, "the one who generates stars in the heavens." The couple named the child Hāloa, "long stalk," and buried the body in the earth. From Hāloa, the first taro plant appeared.

One Christmas Eve when I was still a child, my father, a believer in taro, Wākea, and Hoʻohāhākalani—not in Adam, Jesus Christ, and Holy Communion—decided to make my Catholic mother happy by attending Midnight Mass. I don't know when the last time had been since my father had set foot in church—certainly not in my lifetime up to then—and I don't know why he chose to relent for my mother's sake on that occasion. Perhaps he had been caught up in the general mood of things; perhaps the warm glow of the nativity scene invited him in.

My family arrived early and walked quietly to the front row, where we each sat down carefully on the beautifully polished bench. We were all wearing our best clothes. We girls had new lace dresses and white patent-leather shoes, still perfectly unscuffed. My brothers were dressed in brightly flowered shirts. My mother wore the red-and-green dress my father had given her. And my father had on his one pair of dress pants. I had been waiting all year to hear the singing of Christmas carols, music whose exquisite harmonies always made me cry, and to smell the heady, acrid smoke of incense.

As more people arrived and the church began to overflow, the press of bodies made me think of the crowded manger where the Christ Child had been born. In the silent darkness of midnight, the church with its stained-glass windows seemed a sanctuary among the stars. Even without the light of day shining through them, the blues and scarlets of the windows radiated warmth and welcome.

Suddenly, just as Mass was about to begin, a man in a white suit approached us and whispered in my father's ear while motioning toward the man and woman who had come up behind him. My father looked at the man, then at the couple. His face turned hard. He rose from his seat and

turned to us. "Let's go!" he said. Since my father was not one to be dis-
obeyed, we silently followed after him. It was only when we were outside
that he began to curse and we understood what had happened. The man in
white had asked him to give our seats to the distinguished couple because
they were "important people."

We missed Christmas Mass that year, a venial sin if I remember cor-
rectly. And my father denounced Christianity forever and accepted eternal
damnation.

God said, "Let the earth produce vegetation: seed-bearing plants, and
fruit trees bearing fruit with their seed inside, on the earth." And so it was.
The earth produced vegetation: plants bearing seed in their several kinds,
and trees bearing fruit with their seed inside in their several kinds. God saw
that it was good. Evening came and morning came: the third day.

This winter was a good one. The rains were evenly spaced and plen-
tiful enough to germinate seeds that had been long dormant. In the herb
pots, dill came up among the bay leaf, wild anise among the sweet marjo-
ram, Chinese parsley among the oregano. In a container that had once held
basil, but which I had let go to weeds because I loved their tiny, bright-yel-
low flowers, a profusion of violets bloomed. I had twice failed to raise violets
from store-bought seedlings, but now they blossomed forth with a hardiness
that came from their having found their natural niche.

Beside the steps leading to the back yard, a banana tree had miracu-
lously appeared. Bananas usually propagate by sending up shoots near their
base, commonly called keiki (children). But this one had appeared as if
from nowhere. It's not impossible that it started from a detached keiki, but
our banana trees were all downhill in the back yard. Perhaps a shoot had
washed down from the street above, carried by the rain. I knew that in the
spot where it had sprouted, crowded on the shady side of the house, the tree
wouldn't thrive and grow sturdy. But somehow I wanted to leave it there, to
let the tree adapt in whatever way it could to the place it had been born.

The other day another little girl said to me, "I had a dream last night.
I dreamt my Daddy's garden was growing again like when I was two." She
was now six; her parents had divorced when she was four. I asked her what
was growing in her dream garden, wondering if it was just a vague notion in
her mind, or something much more real. She thought for awhile, then said
with certainty, "Potatoes. Pumpkins. Okra. Lots of lettuce . . ." I recalled
with sadness the garden that had flourished at her home once, but that now
was a wild tangle of weeds covering the occasional survivor of some of the
best vegetables that had ever tantalized a palate.

In the beginning God created the heavens and the earth. Now the earth was a formless void, there was darkness over the deep, and God's spirit hovered over the water.

God said, "Let there be light," and there was light. God saw that light was good, and God divided light from darkness. God called light "day," and darkness he called "night." Evening came and morning came: the first day.

Last night was the night of Māhealani, the full moon. Looking at her in the sky, I thought of Wākea the Sky Father, who had also mated with his sister, Papa the Earth Mother. From them, the Hawaiian islands were born. I also thought of Hāloa, the taro child of Wākea and Hoʻohāhākalani. After Hāloa, a second child was born and was given the same name as the first child. This child grew strong and flourished, and became the ancestor of the Hawaiian people.

In my family of many brothers and sisters, I am thought of as the first daughter. But, in fact, there was a daughter before me, born prematurely in her seventh month. She was named Violet, after my mother, and she died after only one day of life. She is buried beside my father in Pūowaina crater, Punchbowl.

Today is Easter Sunday and outside the screen door the children have left their cups and napkins scattered on the table under the acerola tree and have gone off to church. The wind is blowing through the branches of the tree, scattering its blossoms upon the empty branches, the steps leading down to my door, the banana tree that appeared as if from nowhere. The wind blows through the leaves of the coconut tree, the orange tree still heavy with fruit, the avocado tree I started from seed. In an hour or so, my family will return and together we will go to place flowers on the graves of my father and my sister. I will take some heliconia, a couple of ti leaves, and some stephanotis blossoms from my father's garden.

Yesterday I saw something that would have made my father happy— a taro plant growing in my compost pile. I thought about replanting it in a place more accommodating, but when I tried to remove the plant, I discovered that its stem went down deep into the mound, and that to free it I would have had to tear out the roots. I covered the roots up again, and let the taro remain there among the papaya skins, potato peelings, coffee grinds, and egg shells. Perhaps one day, I thought, the compost having been spread over some other part of the yard or in some pot where seedlings were being coaxed, other taro like that one would flourish again of their own accord and in their own time.

MAX WAS HEA

Cathy Kanoelani Ikeda

Stolen Gargoyle glasses
Hide your bloodshot eyes.
We sit in your '64
Lime-green Bug.
A faded blue and white tassel,
Hanging on your rear-view mirror,
Trembles as the rap,
Onyx with heavy bass,
Spills into the glare of noon.
Your vacant eyes stare at the surf.
I think you're dead,
Just sitting there
As a cigarette threatens to burn your fingers.
"What's wrong?" I ask.
You say nothing for what seems like forever,
More like three sets.
I have nothing better to do,
I count the waves
And try not to go deaf.
Then your petroglyph tattoo moves.
You turn the tape down,
And your voice, so serene in the
Violent ringing of my ears, tells me,
"Life's screwed!
I thought everything was going be so simple,
Surf, cruise, party, surf again
Just the way we dreamed about, remember?
But I neva dream about this.
You saw Joey Wong's picture in the paper?
The one that talks about the doctors they get
At their hospital?
Kaiser or something?
Joey, the one Andy wen corner in the bathroom
5th grade time

And Joey wen get so scared he piss his pants
'Ass how come we used to call him
Shishi Boy in high school.
He one fricken obstetrician.
Then get Randy, he playing pro ball
Up the mainland someplace,
And Tammie, the one we used to call giraffe
Stay modeling in Paris
And I see her in the Liberty House
Catalogs sometimes, Zooper Sale, li' dat.
And then get Lei,
The one who asked Michael to the prom
Then Paka boy, then Scotty
And she wen get rejected by all of them,
How the hell we knew she would be Miss Hawai'i?
She neva look like that in high school.
Andy, he the lucky one, though
'Cause when his car wen huli
Wrap around the banyan tree,
Crash and burn,
At least was one week after graduation,
And everybody wen come out
And we knew he was gone
Scattered his ashes in the ocean
J'like he was one Viking or something.
But nobody told me that
I would still be living in Waimanalo,
Same house, same room
My mother doing my laundry
And bitchin at me about finding one job
And keeping em.
Nobody told me
All my dreaming wasn't going be enough
And after ten years of this
It ain't enough
And I stay lost
Like I going disappear in the foam
And nobody going give a rip,
No one going know I gone."
I want to say something funny,
Or something profound

Something that will make you snap out of it,
But all I can think about is you,
20 years ago,
You were in warp speed, telling us
About the newest Kikaida show
With spit flying you jumped on the table,
Showed us how Kikaida threw his death kick
Arms taut in the death chop,
Your bare feet flying high in the air
Shattering the glass door
Your rusty blood spilled on the yellow sidewalk,
And I cried for you, the pool spreading
As I took my finger, stirred it in your crimson blood
And wrote "Max was hea"
On the once virgin glass.
You fumble for another tape,
Bring me forward 20 years,
Two friends sharing a smoke.
Through the haze,
The swirl of dust, you tell me,
"I scared
Get nightmares of being my pops,
Beer gut hanging out the bottom of his shirt
His pants so low
You can see his crack when he standing up.
I see him under the mango tree
Drinkin beer with all the other losers
All day, all night
And mom no say nothin to him
'Cause at least he get his workman's comp check.
Plus I think she just bitched out already
'Cause bitchin at him j'like yelling at the ocean
You get drowned out by his snores,
So she workin on me,
Hopin I neva go deaf yet.
Too late.
I can think about all the things I shoulda done
All the times I had the chance
And neva take 'em
But everything is past already,
Too late,

And if all I get in front of me is my pops
Wearing the same undershirt
Every damn day
The thing so thin can see right through,
Too late,
And that perfect wave,
The one we dreamed about,
The tube we said was like heaven
And sex
Sucked me under
And I neva even know until stay
Too late."
I don't know how to bring you back
Or tell you what you mean to me.
I take out some lipstick,
Brandied Berry 71,
And write
"Max is hea."

SHAME AND THE FIRST DAY OF COLLEGE

Darlene M. Javar

Auditorium,
More big than Pahala Theater.
Too much green leather chairs,
Too much people,
Japanese and Haole intellects,
For one history class.
More people than
Our whole school,
High school and elementary
Put together.

I no can open my mouth.
My words,
My sentences,
Not going make sense.
Too much pidgin.
Pudgy, pilipino, pidgin speaking pygmy.
I no like make shame.

I sit in front,
I listen real good,
I write down every comma I hear.
But I scared look up.
If the professor look at me
I look away.
I no can talk good English.
And I shame.

Big history class
Get small lab class
For share,
For talk.
I still shame.
I raise my hand

Only for share
What I write.
I write real fine.
I spend hours
Writing
To make up
The difference.

History class get exam.
I study
All day,
All night.
I pour caffeine
Into my blood
To make up the difference.

Cause I not stupid.
I just no can talk
Good English
Yet.

A BITE OF KIMCHEE
Nora Okja Keller

I was weaned on kimchee. A good baby, I was "able to eat anything," my mother told me. But what I especially loved was the spicy, fermenting, garlicky Chinese cabbage my mother pickled and bottled in our kitchen. Not waiting for her to lick the red peppers off the won bok, I would grab and gobble the bits of leaves as soon as she tore them into baby-size pieces. She said even if my eyes watered, I would still want more.

Propping me in a baby carrier next to the sink, my mother would rinse the cabbage she had soaked in salted water the night before. After patting the leaves dry, she'd slather on the thick red pepper sauce, rubbing the cloves of garlic and green onion into the underarms of the cabbage, lifting the leaves, bathing it as she would one of her own children. Then grabbing them by their dangling leafy legs, she'd push the wilting heads into five-gallon jars. She had to rise up on tip-toe, submerging her arm up to the elbow to punch the kimchee to the bottom of jar, squishing them into their own juices. We kept an extra refrigerator in the garage just for the kimchee.

Throughout elementary school, our next door neighbor Frankie, whose mother was the only other Korean in our neighborhood, would come over to eat kimchee with my sisters and me almost every day. After school, we'd gather in our garage, sitting cross-legged around a kimchee jar as though at a campfire or a seance. Daring each other on, we would stick our hands into the mouth of the jar and pull out long strips that we would eat straight, without rice or water to dilute the taste. Our eyes would tear and our noses start to run because it was so hot, but it seemed as if we couldn't stop. "It burns, it burns, but it tastes so good!" we would cry.

Afterwards when we went to play the jukebox in Frankie's garage (we would pretend we were nightclub singers, karaoke performers before our time) we had to be careful not to touch our eyes with our wrinkled, pepper stained hands. Sometimes it seemed as if the hot, red juice soaked through our skin and into our bones; even after we bathed, we could still feel our fingers tingling, still taste the kimchee on them when we licked them with our tongues. And as my sisters and I curled into the night, nestling together like doves going to sleep, I remember the smell lingered on our hands, the faint whiff of kimchee scenting our dreams.

We went crazy for the smell of kimchee—a perfume that would lure us to the kitchen table. No one in our home had to eat alone; the odor of kimchee beckoned for companionship. When my mother hefted the jar of kimchee out of the refrigerator, opened the lid to extract the almost fluorescent strips of cabbage which she placed in soup bowls at the center of the table, she didn't have to call out to us, though she always did. "Girls, come join me," my mother would sing and even if we weren't hungry we couldn't resist. "My stomach says no, but my mouth says yes yes yes!" My sisters and mother and I lingered over snacks that lasted two or three hours.

I smelled like garlic, like kimchee, like home.

I didn't realize that the smell, carried within my intestines like a parasite, followed me to school. One day, walking across Middle Field towards the girl's locker room, a girl I recognized from the gym class before mine stepped in front of me.

"You Korean?" she asked. She narrowed eyes as brown as mine, shaped like mine, like mock-orange leaves pinched up at the corners.

Thinking she could be my sister, another part-Korean, part-haole hapa girl, I nodded and welcomed her kinship with a smile.

"I thought so," she said, sneering. Her lips scrunched upwards, almost folding over her nostrils. "You smell like one."

I held my smile, frozen, as she flitted away from me. She had punched me in the stomach with her words; the wind knocked out of me, I tried to catch a breath like a gaping fish. Days later, after replaying this confrontation endlessly in my mind (in one fantasy version, this girl mutated into a hairy neanderthal that I karate chopped into submission), I thought of the perfect comeback. What I should have said, I thought then, was: "Oh yeah? Well, you smell like a chimpanzee." I also tortured myself with the thought that I should have said something that day. Anything—a curse, a joke, a grunt—anything at all, would have been better than a smile.

I smiled. And I sniffed. I smiled and sniffed as I walked to the locker room and dressed for P.E. I smiled and sniffed as I jogged around the field, trying to avoid the ball and other girls wielding field hockey sticks. I smiled and sniffed as I showered and followed my schedule of classes.

I became obsessed with sniffing. When no one was looking, I lifted my arms and, quick, sniffed. I held my palm up to my face and exhaled. Perhaps, every now and then, I caught the odor of garlic and cabbage in sweat and breath. I couldn't tell; the smell of kimchee was too much a part of myself. I belonged to a tribe of kimchee eaters, marked by primordial scent.

I didn't want to smell like a Korean. I wanted to smell like an American, which meant being odorless. Americans, I learned from TV and magazines, erased the scent of their bodies with cologne and deodorant, breath mints and mouthwash.

I erased my stink by eliminating kimchee. Though I liked the smell and the sharp taste—garlic and pepper biting my tongue—I stopped eating my mother's food and purged it from my system.

I became shamed by kimchee, by the shocking red-stained leaves that peeked out from between the loaf of white bread and carton of milk, by the stunning odor that, as I grew to realize, permeated the entire house despite strategically placed cartons of baking soda. When friends I invited to my home pointed at the kimchee jars lined up on the refrigerator shelves, squealing "Gross! What's that?" I'd mumble, "I don't know, something my mom eats."

Along with kimchee, I stopped eating the only three dishes my mother could cook: kalbi ribs, bi bim kooksoo, and Spam fried with eggs. (The first "American" food my mother ever ate was a Spam-and-egg sandwich; even now, she considers it one of her favorite foods and never gets tired of eating it. At one time in our lives, Spam was a staple. We ate it every day.)

I told my mother I was a vegetarian.

One of my sisters ate only McDonald's Happy Meal cheeseburgers (no pickle), and the other survived for two years on a diet of processed cheese sandwiches on white bread (no crust), Hostess Ding Dongs and rice dunked in ketchup.

"How can you do this to me?" my mother wailed at her American born children. "You are wasting away! Eat, eat!" My mother plopped heapings of kimchee and kalbi onto mounds of steaming rice. My sisters and I would grimace, poke at the food and announce: "Too fattening."

When we were small, my mother encouraged us to behave like proper Korean girls: quiet, respectful, hard-working. She said we gave her "heartaches" the way we fought and wrestled as children. "Worse than boys," she used to say. "Why do you want to do things like soccer, scuba, swimming? How about piano?"

But worse than our tomboy activities were our various adolescent diets. My mother grieved at the food we rejected. "I don't understand you girls," she'd say. "When I was growing up, my family was so poor we could only dream of eating this kind food. Now I can give my children meat every night and you don't want it."

"Yeah, yeah, yeah," we'd say as we pushed away the kimchee, pushed away the Korean-ness.

We pushed my mother, too, so much so she ended up leaving Hawaii. After she moved away, wanting to travel and explore the America she had once—as a new bride barraged with foreign language, customs, foods—been intimidated by, I ate kimchee only sporadically. I could go for months without a taste, then suddenly be hit with a craving so strong I ran to Sack-n-Save for a generic, watery brand that only hinted at the taste of home. Kimchee, I realized, was my comfort food.

When I became pregnant, the craving for my own mother accentuated my craving for kimchee. During the nights of my final trimester, my body foreign and heavy, restless with longing, I hungered for the food I myself had eaten in the womb, my first mother-memory.

The baby I carried in my own body, in turn, does not look like me. Except for the slight tilt of her eyes, she does not look Korean. As a mother totally in love with her daughter, I do not care what she looks like; she is perfect as herself. Yet, as a mother totally in love with her daughter, I worry that—partially because of what she looks like—she will not be able to identify with the Korean in me, and in herself. I recognize that identifying herself as Korean, even in part, will be a choice for her—in a way it wasn't for someone like me, someone recognizably Asian. It hit me then, what my own mother must have felt looking at each of her own mixed-race daughters: how strongly I do identify as a Korean American woman, how strongly I want my child to identify with me.

Kimchee is an easily consumable representation of culture, digested and integrated by the body and hopefully—if we are to believe the lesson "You are what you eat" that episodes of *Mulligan Stew* taught us in elementary school—by the soul as well.

When my daughter was fifteen months old, she took her first bite of kimchee. I had taken a small bite into my own mouth, sucking the hot juice from its leaves, giving it "mother-taste" as my own mother had done for me. Still, my daughter's eyes watered. "Hot, hot," she said to her grandmother and me. But the taste must have been in some way familiar; Instead of spitting up and crying for water, she pushed my hand to the open jar for another bite.

"She likes it!" my mother said proudly. "She is Korean!"

When she told me this, I realized that for my mother, too, the food we ate growing up had always been an indication of how Korean her "mixed-blood" children were—or weren't—at any given time. I remember how intently she watched us eat, as if to catch a glimpse of herself as we chewed. "Eat, eat. Have some more," she'd say, urging us to take another serving of kimchee, kalbi, seaweed soup, the food that was linked to Korea and to herself.

Now my mother watches the next generation. When she visits, my daughter cleaves to her, follows her from room to room. Grandmother and granddaughter run off together to play the games that only the two of them know how to play. I can hear them in my daughter's room, chattering and laughing. Sneaking to the doorway, I see them "cooking" plastic food in the Playskool kitchen.

"Look," my mother says, offering her grandchild a plate of plastic spaghetti, "noodles is kooksoo." She picks up a steak. "This kalbi." My mother is teaching her Korean, presenting words my daughter knows the taste of.

My girl joins the game, picking up a head of cabbage. "Let's make kimchee, Halmoni," she says, using the Korean word for "grandmother" like a name.

"Okay," my mother answers. "First salt."

My daughter shakes invisible salt over the cabbage.

"Then garlic and red pepper sauce." My mother stirs a pot over the stove and passes the mixture to my daughter who pours it on the cabbage.

My daughter brings her fingers to her mouth. "Hot!" she says. Then she grabs the green plastic in her fist, holds the cabbage to my mother's lips, and gives her halmoni a taste.

"Mmmmm!" My mother grins as she chews the air. "Delicious! This is the best kimchee I ever ate." My mother sees me peeking around the door.

"Come join us!" she calls out to me and tells my daughter, who really is gnawing at the fake food, "Let your mommy have a bite."

SISTER FROM ANOTHER PLANET

Christine Kirk-Kuwaye

In this one, Pearl stands behind the McDonald's counter in her ill-fitting white-pin-stripe-on-navy lapeled jacket patiently awaiting orders. She is the very picture of forbearance, a face wiped clean of impatience, haughtiness, boredom. It was the face of a good girl.

But then Pearl was in her junior year of high school in this picture, the year she still believed that she was, alternately, immortal and destined for an early, beautiful death. The most poignant detail in her costume is the way her visor is slightly off-center and has begun to be dotted with traces of vegetable shortening (that is all McDonald's uses, Pearl has insisted upon numerous occasions). It may be interesting to note that immigrant children in America's past worked in mines where coal hung thick in the air and blackened their lungs, in factories where lint threatened to stuff them alive, in fields where dust filled their noses, ears, and eyes, stopping their thoughts, choking their wills. But this child, the great-great granddaughter of immigrants on both sides, dwells in an atmosphere of particles of suspended fat. It clings to her clothes, her hair, her skin. She inhales it. What will this work make of her?

This is a somewhat dated image. Pearl is today safely into her 20s, although still at a McDonald's, still breathing fat. But she no longer just labors, she manages others now: interestingly enough, immigrants and first-generation workers, even deeply rooted descendants of some of the earliest, albeit reluctant, settlers to America. She oversees what is called "drive through."

Not far from where Pearl lives and works are "drive by" shootings. Much has been said about Americans' love for their automobiles and their endlessly innovative uses of them. Come to think of it, there must have been some American who was conceived, then born, and finally died in an auto. Today it is possible to destroy life without losing your own, without damaging your vehicle, and without ever having to move from your bucket or, in earlier models, bench seat. The drive-by shooting.

But drive through is taxing, Pearl has said, and perhaps much worse than simply inhaling fat into your lungs. It is arduous, aggravating, sometimes dangerous. People do not articulate or speak loudly enough or know what they want. While comfortably seated in their cars, customers keep her

standing in her glass booth, food teller that she has beco˙
headset arching, resting gently on her hair, she is like some ⌣
energetic working class beauty queen. She comes from a long liˍ
workers, and although a career at McDonald's is really no career at aˍ
can't help but admire her dedication.

To add a finishing touch to a jaunty demeanor, Pearl often refers affectionately to McDonald's as "Mickey Dees." Oh daughter of Rosie the Riveter, flex thy tensioned biceps, cock thy nobly stained visor, and hoist that carton of frozen fries! (See enclosed button.)

Pearl's dedication is store-specific. The Branch-Welles, owners of the Nuevo Rancho McDonald's, are the parents of her long-term and long-distance boyfriend, Marc. The Branch-Welles are like a family to her. In fact, they are her family, her California family, which is, in reality, her year-round, all-the-time family except when she is home on vacation in Hawai'i. Hawai'i is her birthplace, where she grew up, but it has become in the past few years a vacation spot where she reunites briefly with her mother and step-father. Hawai'i isn't home in the daily sense and has become home in the Thomas Wolfe sense. At least that is the way it appears.

This, too, is poignant because Pearl is, from her father's side, part-Hawaiian. Please note that the last U. S. Census reported that there are more Hawaiians in California than in Hawai'i. I have wondered what that says about American society, about Hawai'i. About the Hawaiians themselves? Many are alarmed by this and call it a diaspora. Others say that it is healthy. Perhaps it is simply the global way here in the late Twentieth Century.

The Branch-Welles are extremely successful partnerpreneurs. Unless you have read the book Pearl's mother co-authored (as a "with") with the female half of an entrepreneur couple, you have been no doubt unaware of this word until this moment. Grace took on this project to make a lot of money and set herself free, economically. She is not free.

But the Branch-Welles. They have two children, well spaced in age. Marc is nearly finished with college, Skyler has just begun high school. The parents are hard-working middle-class folks with no college but apparently lots of smarts. They are church-goers, seem to have a solid marriage, and possess an enthusiasm for life, just the very picture of ideal partnerpreneurs according to the book for which Grace provided the words. Mrs. Branch-Welles owns a Jaguar with personalized plates: "Sally's Sass." The husband has some minor health problems due to a typically American diet (high fat, high salt, too much protein) and typically American sedentariness, but nothing terribly serious thus far. They work hard, and, as a result, inspire people like Pearl.

Of greatest inspiration has been the level of demonstrable material wealth that they have acquired, and, of no less importance, the fact that they seem to enjoy their lives. Would it be a surprise to learn that the Branch-Welles are an African-American family? What kind of family did you picture before you learned this most significant point? Also, what does this do to your notions about African-Americans?

And what are you thinking about the hyphenated name? Although more common these days than in the past, hyphenated names still cause some comment, particularly if a man is, as they say, hyphenated as well. Interestingly, historians, sociologists, and the like talk about the phenomenon of the hyphenated American, referring, that is, to the way Americans describe themselves in terms of race-nationality or ethnicity-nationality, not to mention their pre-nuptial versus post-nuptial identities. What are people thinking when they hyphenate themselves? Are they trying to be more inclusive or, paradoxically, more exclusive? Perhaps someone at some point under some circumstances will refer to herself as a female-American or himself as male-American. And when s/he does, what do you think will be the point?

When Pearl was visiting Hawai'i she told this story about "drive through." One evening she was in the box, taking orders. Although she could not see the car nor, of course, the customers in it, she knew by the sounds that came through her headset that she was about to serve a couple who was not having a good night. Pearl couldn't explain how she knew this to be, but she knew this nonetheless.

There was some confusion about the order. Pearl felt playful that night, she said, and lightly teased the man: "Was that an orange *drink* or an orange *juice?*" (Very subtly playful, it would seem.) Nonetheless, he seemed to get it and laughed, then clarified the order. She assured him that, sir, he would get his order. Something like that. It's difficult communicating in mere words on this page how communication happens. There's so much subtlety. Small movements of hands, almost imperceptible adjustments to facial features. Slight passes of air in and among words seem to be powerful. It is much like Pearl knowing things that, nonetheless, she can't explain.

And then the remarkable happened. As the car idled at the window and the man held out his money and smiled up at her, the woman leaned over the lap of the man and said to Pearl, "You leave my man alone, you bitch."

"Pardon me?" Pearl said, having heard perfectly well what the woman had said but wanting to give her the chance to issue the challenge again or to retract it by pretending to clarify it and somehow steer away from what was shaping up to be an impending event. "You heard what I said." The woman paused and then, as many a pulp fictionist has described it, spat out, "Bitch."

Pearl squared her shoulders, told the woman she did not appreciate being called that when what she was doing was simply her job. She had no interest, none whatsoever ("uh hunh"), Pearl said, in "your man," drawing out the vowel sound to somehow suggest that he might not be much of one anyway. Accepting the money for the drink, Pearl turned toward her cash drawer. It was then that she simultaneously felt and heard the orange drink hitting her up side the head.

Then comes the best part of the story. Things happened quickly. She rips off her headset, explodes from the glass box, strides up to the woman who is now out of the car, puts up her fists (Sees-tah! Sees-tah! imagine an invisible crowd chanting), and says, "We can do it right here, right now. Whatever you say." And the woman leaps at her and Pearl clips the woman on the jaw. The woman falls but springs up and starts scratching and punching. The man finally intercedes and pulls the woman off and into the car and drives away.

Pearl has surface scratches that leave no visible scars. But she has learned something permanent, she says: "You can kill people with kindness." She speaks these words as if she is the first intelligent being in the universe to discover perhaps one of the greatest tools the weak can use to control the powerful. It's worth recalling here that Martin Luther King, Jr. called this the "moral offensive."

But she might as well have been the first because of the great and enduring importance of the lesson for her. "She comes in the store every once in awhile," Pearl says of the woman, "and when I see her I'm as nice as can be." Isn't that a wonder? How can two women have a fist fight ostensibly over a man but really over nothing that is personal and then in all subsequent contacts be docile and quiet customer, courteous and cheery waithelp? This story of Pearl's offers a range of possibilities to contemplate about human behavior; it also plumbs the elemental.

This story has physicality, too. Imagine petite Pearl going after a woman who clearly outsizes her by 3 inches and 40 pounds. Note that Pearl's fingers are long and slender, her wrists delicate, her arms shapely but thin. And yet they can send and deliver a punch. See that any bulk that Pearl has is from the waist to the knees, a low center of gravity, one that keeps her firmly planted and is perhaps the place from which her power emanates.

The throwing of this punch may prove to be the significant factor in Pearl's development. It is this physicality that has finally come to begin to define her. Pearl was a child who was not so much invisible as frequently translucent, not so much ignored as periodically forgotten, not so much insignificant as, well, minor. She has worked, all these years, toward giving herself substance.

Pearl, in fact, has been feeling something awakening inside her. "Something important is going to happen," she said on a long distance call. "I can feel it." She paused. "I think it will happen when I visit home." Yes, she said home but it was mere shorthand for Hawai'i. This would be an exciting story: Child of Hawai'i returns and connects with the past, with the culture, with the 'āina, with herself, a perfect circle connecting.

As the trip to Hawai'i approached, Pearl tried to explain the feeling she was having: irritable, as if her skin was too tight and scratchy, like the inside of a leotard that is full of nettles. "I've been yelling at people. For no reason. I hate everyone I work with." She sighed. "I never feel this way."

It was during her trip to Hawai'i that she told the story about Jamaican Delphine who works at the Nuevo Rancho Mickey Dees and how she, Pearl, can't stand her. Delphine, Pearl said, thinks she is better than everyone else. Delphine, by all appearances, is black. But Delphine's identity for Delphine is Jamaican, an identity she clearly feels is superior to those in America (and presumably anyone else on the planet) whom she may resemble. Furthermore, Jamaicans, again per Delphine, are superior island people. No doubt Delphine's island chauvinism is a double personal affront to Pearl, whose blood boils at this. But so is it infuriating, Pearl said, to the assortment of workers at Rancho Nuevo. Workers, you will remember, who are trying so very hard to be American and to reconcile personal, class, ethnic, racial identities with being "an American." In the context of Mickey Dees, Delphine has become an island unto herself.

It is evident that Pearl has not sorted through how she feels about being Hawaiian. She does know that she is more comfortable in California, because when she is in Hawai'i she is less her new self, more her old self. This is difficult to bear for her because she has been working, slowly working, toward substance-ness, toward—as the saying goes here, "just spit it out"—success. In Hawai'i Pearl, aware of the negative stereotyping of the Hawaiians, has always found herself in conflict—defensive and ashamed one moment, brimming with pride the next.

In California she is often taken for anything but that which she is. In a Mexican border town people approach her speaking Spanish. In parts of L.A., they rattle her with Lebanese, Arabic, Hungarian! Queerly, she is chameleon-like, except that it is not she who changes. As she moves into various surroundings, she is, although unchanged herself, perceived by those who observe her to be a projection of who they think should be in the foreground of that backdrop. That is a complicated thought that is not well expressed. Here: would you not expect an ancient shield face-side down at a dinner place to be a very large plate and not the implement of war that it is, simply out of context? That is what it is like.

When people approach her in these ways she is often rendered speechless and angry. When asked why she isn't flattered to be, gratis, a citizen of the world, she acts confounded, shamed by the question but still angry about what she feels has been an insult nevertheless. She is thrilled when people are impressed to learn she is Hawaiian. Only mainlanders and those from abroad seem impressed anymore. In California she is the Pearl of her own making and yet completely true to herself; in Hawai'i she blends in with the scenery. In fact, in the context of tourism Pearl probably is the scenery.

Several weeks ago, actually the weeks following her uneventful sojourn in Hawai'i, things began to unravel. Of course, the unraveling was not detectable at first. Like a low-grade infection, a subtle disruption of communication took place in the Branch-Welles household. All couples, all families experience this but for Pearl, who believes the Branch-Welles to be superior, this unusual quiet became a sign of impending disaster. Even Marc, away at school in upstate California, stopped calling her or being home when she called:

"Marc? You wanna talk to Marc? Hold on. Hey, Marc, you home?"

"Who is it?"

"Pearl."

"Nah, I'm not home."

But at some point Marc and Pearl did have their talk.

Marc was home for the spring break and needing to tell his parents why he would need yet another extra semester in school. This time basketball season had been too successful, which resulted in his classes being far less successful than they needed to be in order to fulfill the requirements for earning a degree. To graduate is what he has been aiming to do for a long time. Mr. Branch-Welles has never understood why Marc wanted to go to college since his McDonald's store is doing so well: all Marc needs to do is step in at the assistant manager level, put in a couple of years or whatever it takes, then simply take over. According to Pearl, this is an oft-played tape in the Branch-Welles's repertoire of family performances. Marc's mother, Sally, thinks college is a fine idea. Marc, according to Pearl, often doesn't know whether he's comin or goin.

Pearl has continued to love him anyway and has freely admitted, when she called "home," that she likes Marc a whole lot better when he's upstate and she's down and he's home for only two weeks at a time. She confided recently that she wasn't looking forward to the summer because

Marc would be home for all of it. (But, in retrospect, that all that might be camouflage to protect an oft-wounded heart.)

That must seem particularly ironic to her now that she has realized that she won't be having a summer at Mickey Dees or with the Branch-Welles, that she and Marc are not a couple, long distance or otherwise, that she is out of a home and must look for a new one.

What Marc was also home to tell Pearl was that he and Pearl had no future plans anymore because there simply wasn't room for marriage to more than one woman at a time. It was a long way of telling a simple thing.

Pearl was distraught; she also wanted to kill Marc and spent some time considering methods. "I feel like I'm from outer space," she said. That is, she felt weird inside and not a part of her immediate environment on the outside. She couldn't imagine staying where she was much longer but was unsure where to go. Is this the feeling that all emigrants feel right before they book passage? Is there a biological, physiological, psychological mechanism that kicks in in order to make the journey seem possible, then inevitable, eventually even desirable? Perhaps this feeling of disengagement was the cause of "the accident."

There is some debate about whether indeed what happened to Pearl, Marc, and Skyler was indeed an accident since the driver of the car who hit them insists that the car the three were riding in simply came to a halt for no reason that anyone could detect. This is how it happened.

Pearl was driving her red Tercel on one of those thunderingly massive gray freeways that were built to link the far-flung areas of Southern California when "I Will Always Love You" as sung by Whitney Houston came on the car radio. Marc hated that song, was sick of it. It was not a favorite of Pearl's either but, for various reasons, she turned it up and began singing along. Skyler joined in. Skyler, Pearl has said, has a perfect voice. In fact, she sings in the church choir and hopes to have a career in the theater. Skyler's voice was so lovely in fact that it and the words and the plot of the movie in recollection caused Pearl to start crying. Sobbing, really. So much so that she couldn't see quite as well as she should while driving that Southern California freeway.

Like a chain reaction, Pearl thought about losing Skyler, a teenager with whom she had grown quite close. Skyler had been the younger sister she had never had. "And never would have," was how Pearl finished that thought. She blinked, clearing the tears, and noticing Marc's knees nearly touching the dash even with the seat pushed back as far as it would go. "Sky," Pearl said, "put on your seat belt. Right now." The girl obeyed. Moments later Pearl hit the brakes and stared into the rearview mirror to watch the silver BMW sedan grow larger and larger.

Pearl was insured, so was the driver of the Beamer. "Lucky break," Pearl's step-father told her, "that you were hit by a yuppie." Pearl agreed. "Just don't sign anything," he said, making sure she understood the great importance of this advice by also typing it up and sending it to her by mail. He even gave her the name and telephone number of his secretary who would happily verify her horrible experience of being broadsided. The secretary, unfortunately, had signed something.

"The accident" aggravated a previous back injury of Pearl's, a job-related condition exacerbated by having had sexual intercourse with a loving but hefty boyfriend. Skyler, protected by her seatbelt and her youth, miraculously escaped unchafed. In fact, moments after the collision she crawled out the back passenger window, flagged down a driver with a cellular phone, and got help. Skyler is terribly upset about Pearl and Marc's break up, particularly now that she sees Pearl as having saved her life. "My brother is rotten," she told Pearl. "Always was. Always will be."

Marc got it the worst. His knees, not good after years of holding up great height and weight as well as being asked to play basketball, required surgery. Basketball can only be a memory now; and he will be on crutches for several weeks. Pearl has said she sees him when she can.

In her last phone call Pearl mentioned that she'd gone to a movie with Kaleo recently. Kaleo, who is a stock clerk at Ralph's supermarket in the Rancho Nuevo shopping complex and a bit younger than Pearl, is another transplanted Hawaiian, she said. Except his whole family uprooted itself to California after he graduated from high school in Hawai'i. "He's very goodlooking," she said, "and he's starting to talk about attending college." That was followed by a small noise, a breath blended of resignation and longing.

"I've started packing," Pearl said. "Now all that's left to do is decide where I'm going to call home next." She laughed for a long time after saying this, so long that it seemed as if she might never stop. But humans find humor wherever they can. Just as they are driven to create and recreate places for themselves even from swaths of nothingness. Perhaps there is hope for us yet, Sister.

BEFORE TIME

Juliet S. Kono

They said to marry only Japanese,
and only *some* of our own kind;
not zuzuben, batten, kotonk,
hibakusha, eta, Uchinanchu—
night-soil carrier, big-rope people.
Before time, they said not to marry
keto, gaijin, haole—hair people, foreigner, white;
saila boy, Chinee, club foot, one thumb, chimba, mahu, glass
        eye,
harelip, bolinki, pigeon-toe, Pologee, Uncle Joe's friend,
        Kanaka, cane cutter, mandolin player, night diver,
        Puerto Rican, tree climber, nose picker, Filipino,
        thief, bartender, jintan sucker, Korean, paniolo,
        farmer, bearded,
mustachioed, Teruko's brother, daikon leg, cane hauler, left-
        handed, right-handed, smartaleck, Christian, poor
        speller, commie, Indian, leper, Hakka, cripple,
        drunk, flat nose, old, Jew Pake, chicken fighter,
pig hunter, moke, ice cruncher, opium
smoker, one-side-eyebrow raiser, fat,
olopop, skinny, Punti, thick lip,
albino, kurombo.

JOJI AND THE ICEMAN

Juliet S. Kono

I'm just there, watching
people bring in the bodies
from the ocean,
the line of them growing
like so many Buddhas
in the front of Dodo's Mortuary.
So many bodies to prepare.
The iceman taps me on the shoulder,
and walking away, he yells
at me to watch the truck, the cab he pops into,
as he backs toward the bodies
sprawled on the army surplus
cots and stretchers.

He sloshes about in rubber hip boots,
black apron pants, leather gloves
and blows blossoms of cigar smoke
in front of his frozen face
as if to kill the smells.
He gives everyone orders.
Like blocks of ice
or marbled beef slabs,
he swings the bodies up,
and I'm told to slide them
deep into the bed of the truck—
the bodies to be stored
in the town icehouse.

Bopping his horn,
he comes for me in the morning.
He takes me to the icehouse.
On the vaulted doors,
someone has placed a bouquet of flowers,
which he whips off as he grunts

and swings the doors open.
Overnight, the bodies have frozen together.
I circle the blocks.
I top them off with the flowers he had thrown aside
and peer into the ice of eyes and faces.
I take the pick he hands me.
I chip the ice away;
sometimes pierce flesh:
an arm, a face.

LATE PRAISE
Juliet S. Kono

Japanese fathers give praise
thin as toothpicks, limp as saimin noodles, rough as bone meal.
My father couldn't say anything nice.
He'd rather jump off Honoli'i Pali.
Just not his style. His style? Attack the head.
He called me "stupid," "dumb," "bakatare."
And best to do this in front of people,
to make shame,
break the proud daughter bone
that straightened the back
and hauled in the immovable
will of the mouth. And it's the mouth,
after all, he just had to get to—
like mud wasps on the housewalls
in summer.
It was too smart for its own good,
that ugly sphinctered mouth.
It got his goat, cut his bait and hurled its turd
like no Japanese girl's should.
He knuckled the head,
connected to the angry face
and the O ring of the mouth
that was ready to snap—
mean with the teeth of disappointment.
There was always the taste of something bitter,
like melons and medicine,
year after year.
Now, my father's old.
He cups his ears to hear,
pees with bad aim and walks with a cane.
In his wallet he keeps
a yellowed newspaper clipping of me.
Wrapped in Saran Wrap,
it looks like an old Shinto talisman.

He shows it to his friends.
"Das my daughta," he says,
rapping the picture with a knuckle.

TAI CHI MASTERS OF DIM SUM CHECKS
Peter C.T. Li

Like two Tai Chi masters practicing the art of the sticking hand
my father and my mother-in-law pushed each others' arms in various
circular motions while fighting for the prize of the *dim sum* check.
The check would be passed from hand to hand,
back and forth,
up and down,
round and round,
in sync with the Yin and the Yang motions of the universe.

Both dueled to save face in the name of family honor.
Armed with ancient secret techniques such as
"Crane Plucks Check from Tiger's Claw" and
"Buddha's Benevolent Palm Tipping the Waiter for Check."
It was no surprise that my father would defeat
my mother-in-law each outing and pay for the lunch.

The only time my father lost was when my mother-in-law
snuck away from the table while he was busy eating the last
  siu mai of the meal.
I named her technique "Fox Stealing from Sleeping Monkey."

It was an unwritten Chinese tradition of the dining martial arts
passed down through centuries from one generation to the next.

Dim sum and my in-laws at the China House Restaurant.

CHILDHOOD MEMORIES
Wing Tek Lum

She sewed my bunny costume
and watched me tap dance at Chinese school.
She held me in her lap when I confessed,
downcast, that Santa was a sham.
Both of us sat silent at dinnertimes
during my father's tantrums.
She called up Sheryl's mom once
to arrange my date for a sophomore dance.
With one hiss she used to scold me
for staying up too late to watch TV.
In the car she told me how
she told her friends that Jesus was her Lord.

These are the memories I have of her—
a mother and her young son,
one giving love, the other always receiving,
though not without protest.
We had no long discussions
about the woman that I would marry,
about the days I wore my hair long,
or about China and its revolutions.
I did not share with her my opinions
on whether there is a life after death,
or whether the real estate market in Hawai'i
will continually go up.
She never got a chance to hear me
speak to her in Cantonese
or to hug my skinny daughter.
I never found out why she loved my father so.
When I visit her grave
I am a child again, forever.

I would not have it any other way.

KIDS DO THINGS THEY DON'T MEAN
Wing Tek Lum

I knew this guy since elementary school
and he's all right now
but when he was a kid
he used to be real chunky
and could throw the football.
He was athletic all around
but sometimes also was a bully.
Like I remember one time
outside in his driveway
he got me in a headlock and I cried
because no matter how I tried
I could not get loose
and I had to say I gave up.
I still remember the hard dirt and the shame
but I don't hold it against him now.
Kids do things they don't mean.
He's a nice guy, not that cocky anymore
—and probably doesn't remember
what he did that day.
If I brought it up
he might get embarrassed
at what kind of kid he was.
Either that or he'd be embarrassed for me
that I was once such a wimp
such a long, long time ago.

UP MAUKA
Michael McPherson

I come back alone in the rain
up Chain of Craters, open this while
and soon to be covered again.
This once in my life I drive
the whole length from Kalapana
to the caldera through fog and rain,
and beyond the sea cliffs one shark
follows in blue till I turn inland
over black rock sliding down Hōlei,
wind upward on the slick and barely visible
road so seldom open, past stark black
figures in indiscernible distance
standing and waving in the rain.
'Ōhi'a. Lehua. Aloha. This
greeting like none other anywhere,
landscape of darkest dreams.
At the store across from Peter Lee's house
I stop for a pint of gin,
tuck it in my pocket and drive
again to Halema'uma'u silent in the rain.
I walk the trail with a bandanna over my face
like Jesse James, jacket pulled flush
up under my chin, gin warm in my belly
and cold evening wind beating on my ears,
no one for miles, alone and home again.
So long so far away. Footsteps crunch.
Wisps of sulfur in the gathering dark.
I'm under the wire, out over one
deep crack and standing at the edge
where I can see the bottom to the far side,
the rain beating on my back
and down to the dark floor,
remembering how once my father
held me up to see this same floor

churning red and molten, fountains leaping
in the air we shared, night
so dark beyond that moment's glow.
I take one long pull from the bottle
for us all, my bandanna loose and flapping,
close it up and throw it as far as I can.
One for you, Auntie,
listen how long it falls.

THE WAKING STONE
Michael McPherson

The sharks here cannot be trusted.
Poisons in their meat make them crazy,
they feel no bond of loyalty or kinship
nor any longer honor the ancient ways.
Living seas near shore are stained
with runoff from the burning fields,
effluents open like brown dark flowers
and coax the grey swimmers to frenzy.
Spirit warriors are returning to land,
they stand and cast a spectral gaze
over plains now littered with debris.
On the seventh green of a golf course
an old one rises from under the cup
and scatters caddies like reef fish,
a trail of balls and putters and bags.
Another comes after hours and stands
among white columns in a restaurant,
watching where dolphins swim circles
in a lagoon cut from ancestral ground.
Canoes slide silent before the dawn,
their wakes trail long white phosphors
dancing over the backs of dark waves
like fires to light the coming day.

THE VALLEY OF THE DEAD AIR
Gary Pak

The day after Jacob Hookano died, that old hermit who had lived at the very end of Waiola Valley, a bad air from the ocean came in and lingered over the land. The residents of the valley thought that a Kona wind had brought in that rotten smell from the mangroves and mud flats of the coastal area, and they waited impatiently for another wind to take the smell away.

As Leimomi Vargas said succinctly, "Jus' like old Jacob wen fut and dah fut jus' stayin' around."

And stay around it did, for weeks. There seemed no end. The residents prayed for that new wind to blow the obstinate smell away, but no wind came and the air became stagnant and more foul as if the valley were next to an ancient cesspool that had suddenly ruptured after centuries of accumulations. The malodor permeated the wood of the houses, it tainted the fresh clothes hung to dry, and it entered the pores of everyone, making young and old smell bad even after a good scrubbing. The love lives of the residents became nonexistent.

"We gotta do somet'ing 'bout dis hauna," Joseph Correa complained. The retired sewers worker from the City and County sat on a chair under the eaves of an old abandoned store that fronted the main road.

"Yeah, but what?" said Bobby Ignacio. He turned his gaunt, expressionless face towards Correa, then returned to his meditation of birds eating the ripened fruits of a lichee tree across the road.

"You know, Bobby," Correa said in a voice shaded ominously, "I betchu dah gov'ment is behind all dis. Look how long dis hauna stay heah. Long time already. If was jus' one nat'ral t'ing, dah wind already blow 'em away."

Ignacio, a truck farmer up the road in the valley, spat disconsolately into the wild grass growing on the side of the store.

"But I tell you dis, Bobby. I betchu one day dah gov'ment goin' come down heah and dey goin' brag how dey can take dis hauna away. And den they *goin'* take 'em away. But I betchu little while aftah dat, dey goin' come back and try ask us for do dem one favor. You watch." Correa nodded his head. "No miss."

The farmer shrugged his narrow shoulders. "But you know what everybody saying?"

"Who everybody?"

"Everybody."

"So what everybody saying?"

"Dey saying old Jacob dah one doing all dis."

The old retiree nervously stretched out his tired legs, his head twitched a few times, then he looked out languidly towards the mango trees across the road.

"I nevah had no problems with old Jacob," Correa said weakly. "I was always good to him. I nevah talk stink 'bout him or anything li' dat."

The smell persisted, and somehow it infected the rich, famous soil of the valley. The earth began to emit a terrible odor of rotten fish. While plowing one corner of his sweet potato field, Tats Sugimura uncovered a hole full of fish scales and fish bones. He didn't think anything of it until his wife complained to him later how fishy everything smelled. The bad smell of the valley had numbed his nose so Tats couldn't really smell anything now. His wife, on the other hand, had a super-sensitive nose and she often would sniff the air in her kitchen and know exactly what the Rodriguez family was cooking a quarter of a mile down the road.

"Tats, you wen dump some rotten fish around here or what?" she said. Sugimura shook his head. He wasn't the talking type, even with his wife. "Den whas dat stink smell?"

He thought of telling her about the fish scales and bones, then he thought that perhaps a bunch of stray cats had had a feast in that corner of his field. The fish were probably tilapia or catfish the cats had caught in the nearby stream. But he was tired from working all day under the hot sun and in the stifling humid air and he didn't have the energy to describe to his wife what he had seen. The fish scales and fish bones were unimportant, and he shrugged his thin, wiry shoulders and said nothing.

But something bad was in the soil. When Tats and the other sweet potato farmers began harvesting their produce a few days later, they found abnormally small sweet potatoes, some having the peculiar shape of a penis.

"How dah hell we goin' sell dis kine produce?" complained Earl Fritzhugh, a part-Hawaiian sweet potato farmer. "Dey goin' laugh at us. So small. And look at dis one. Look like one prick!"

"Somet'ing strange goin' on in dis valley," said Darryl Mineda, another farmer. "Get dah story goin' around dat old Jacob doin' all dis to get back."

"Get back at who?" Fritzhugh asked irately.

"At us."

Fritzhugh looked at Mineda incredulously. "At us? Why dat old Hawaiian like get back at us fo'? He wen live by himself. Nobody wen bother him."

Mineda shook his head. "Somebody tol' me all dah land in dis valley used to be his family's land, long time ago. Den dah Cox family wen come in and take dah land away from his family. Somet'ing 'bout Jacob's family not paying dah land tax or water tax or somet'ing li' dat, and dah haole wen pay instead."

"But what got to do with us? I not responsible. Dah haole wen do it. Not me."

Mineda shrugged his shoulders.

"Eh, I was good to dah old man," Fritzhugh said. "I nevah bother him. When he used to go up and down dis road, he nevah said not'ing to me, so I never say not'ing to him." He paused. "But I wonder who goin' get his land now he ma-ke. He no mo' children, eh?"

Mineda shrugged his shoulders again. "Maybe das why," Mineda said.

"Maybe das why what?"

"Maybe das why he got all salty. Nobody pay attention to him. Nobody talk story with him. Nobody go bother him."

"So what you goin' do? Dah buggah dead already."

"What . . . you no believe in dah spirits?"

"Eh, no fut around."

"No. I asking you one simple question. You believe in dah kine Hawaiian spirits or what?"

"Yeah, I believe in dat kine," Fritzhugh said, looking warily across his sweet potato field, then back to Mineda's furrowed face. "But so what? Why . . . you think he wen curse dah valley or what?"

Mineda looked at his feet. He was silent for a while. "Crazy," he said finally. "All of dis. And how we going sell our produce to dah markets?"

A white car with the state emblem on the doors came by the store one day. Correa sat up and stared into the car curiously. Then he nodded his head. "You see, Bobby, you see," he said. "What I tol' you. Dah gov'ment goin' come down heah and try get somet'ing from us. I tol' you all along, dis hauna was from dah gov'ment. What I tol' you?"

Ignacio leaned forward, squinting his eyes to read the emblem. "Department of Agriculture," he muttered. He slouched back into his seat.

"What I tol' you, eh, Bobby? Look, dah Japanee going come out and he goin' try smooth talk us. You watch."

"Fritzhugh wen call dem fo' come down and try figure out whas wrong with dah dirt."

"Look dah buggah, nice clean cah, air conditionah and everyt'ing," Correa said sardonically, pretending he had not heard what his friend had said.

The man got out of the car and went up to the two men.

"Yes, sir," Correa said officiously. "What can I do fo' you today?"

The man crimped his nose at the fetid air. "You know where I can find Earl Fritzhugh?"

"Yeah—yeah. He live up dah valley. Whas dis fo'?" Correa asked.

"He called me about some problems you farmers having over here. Something about the soil."

"Not dah soil," Correa said. "Dah air. You cannot smell how hauna dah air is?"

The man nodded his head. "Yes . . . yes, the air kind of stink. Smell like rotten fish."

"Smell like somebody wen unload one big pile in dah middle of dah valley."

The man from the state grinned.

"So why you come," Correa asked pointedly, "and not one guy from dah Department of Air?"

The man from the state looked at Correa with dying interest. "You can tell me where Earl Fritzhugh lives?" he asked Ignacio.

"Yeah, brah," Ignacio said, pointing up the valley road. "You go up this road, maybe one mile into the valley. You goin' pass one big grove bamboo on the right side. The farm right after that going be the Fritzhugh farm. No can miss 'em."

The man thanked him, then got back into the car and left.

"You better call up Fritzhugh and tell him dah Japanee comin' up question him," Correa said.

Ignacio waved the flies away from his face, then spat into the grass.

There was nothing wrong with the soil, the state worker told them a few days after he had come up and taken samples to the downtown laboratory. Nothing was wrong. The farmers left that meeting with remorse. Then what was wrong with the crops?

A day later heavy rains came, and for three days the whole valley was inundated with torrents and flash floods. The residents welcomed the storm, for they believed that the rains would wash the soil of the inscrutable poison and cleanse the air of the bad smell. But came the fourth day and a bright sun and when the residents smelled the air again, the odor was still there, now more pronounced than ever and denser. It was as if the storm had nurtured the smell like water nourishes plants.

"You did anyt'ing to old Jacob?" people were now asking each other. And the answer was always, "No . . . but did you?" And when the informal polling was completed, it was determined that everybody in the valley had left old Jacob alone. But they all cast accusing looks at one another, as if everyone else but themselves were responsible for the curse that old Jacob seemed to have thrown over the once peaceful and productive valley.

One morning a haole salesman came to the doorsteps of one of the houses.

"Heard you folks here were having problems with fires," he said in a jovial voice, a Mid-Western accent.

"No," Tats Sugimura's wife said sourly. "Not fires. The smell. You cannot smell dah stink smell?"

The haole laughed. "Well, you know what they say," he said.

"No, what dey say?" Harriet said.

"They say that if you can't see it, then you can surely smell it." He laughed again. Harriet was about to ask who had said that when the salesman segued quickly into a sales pitch about a new fire prevention system his company was now offering in the area. And, for a limited time, he concluded, they would install the entire system without charge.

"We not interested," Harriet Sugimura said. "Go away. Go talk to somebody else."

"But you don't understand," the salesman said. "Along with this fire prevention system comes our new, revolutionary, home-odors maintenance system. And for a limited time, we will give it to you free if you purchase our fire prevention system. Here . . . smell this."

The salesman took out a small aerosol can and sprayed it inside the Sugimuras' house from the front door. Instantly, the spray cleared the air of the ugly smell that Harriet had almost gotten used to and the whole living room smelled fresh like roses.

"Your system can do this?" she gasped with delight.

"Yes, and more. Why, because our system is computer-controlled, you don't have to lift a finger. Everything will be done automatically."

Harriet's face beamed with promise. It had been so long since she smelled the scent of flowers. "So how much is it?"

"Retail, it sells for eight hundred and fifty dollars. But for this limited offer, we will sell it to you for two hundred and fifty dollars."

"Two hundred fifty!"

"Well, if you know of a friend or neighbor or family who would want this system too, I can give it to you for two-twenty-five."

"Hmm. Wait, let me call my neighbor."

Soon, the entire valley was buzzing on the telephone lines talking about that new machine that would wipe out the bad smell in the homes. If the valley was going to stay bad smelling, that didn't mean the homes had to have that smell, too. So almost every other household bought one of those systems, and the salesman, being a nice guy, even reduced the price by another twenty-five dollars, pre-payment, stating emphatically that the company was now making only a twenty-dollar profit from each unit sold. The residents waited impatiently for that big brown truck that the haole promised would bring the fire-prevention-home-odor-maintenance system, and they waited past the promised three days delivery period, but the truck never came.

The smell worsened to the point that every other person in the valley was getting a constant headache.

"Somet'ing has to be done about the smell," Ignacio said. "If we cannot do anyt'ing about it, den we gotta take dis to the state."

"Nah, how you can do dat?" Correa said. "Dah state already wen say dey cannot do not'ing about it."

"But something gotta be done," Ignacio said.

"Something gotta be done," Harriet Sugimura said to her husband, sheepishly, a few days after her husband, for the first time in seven years, had lost his temper when she told him how she had spent their tax refunds.

"If this smell continue on, I'm getting the hell out of this valley," Pat Fritzhugh said to her husband.

"Me, too," Fritzhugh replied.

"You know what the problem is?" Leimomi Vargas said to her neighbor, Elizabeth Kauhale. "The problem is nobody honest wit' everybody else. I betchu somebody wen get the old man real angry. Really angry. And das why he wen curse the valley wit' dis stink fut smell before he ma-ke."

"I think you right, Lei," Elizabeth said sadly. "We gotta be honest wit' each other. Das dah only way."

"Then maybe the old man going take back the curse," Lei said.

"Maybe we should go get one kahuna bless dah friggin', stinkin' place," Elizabeth said.

"You nevah know the old man was one kahuna?"

"I know, but he dead."

"Still yet."

"But I t'ink you right. We gotta get to the bottom of this. Find all the persons responsible for him cursing the valley. Then make them offer somet'ing to the old man's spirit. Or somet'ing like that. Whachu t'ink?"

So from that conversation, the two women went door to door, struggling with the others to be honest. For starts, Lei told about the time when she was a small girl and she went up to the old man's place and stole an egg from one of his hens. And Elizabeth said one time she saw her brother throw a rock at the old man as he was climbing the road to his hermitage, and because her brother was now living on the Big Island, she would take responsibility for his wrong action. Then, slowly, the others began to unfold their stories of wrongdoings against the old man, even Joseph Correa, who admitted that he wronged old Jacob when they were young men growing up in the valley and wooing the same girl and he had told her parents that Jacob didn't have a prick and that he was a mahu. About the only person who hadn't sinned against Jacob was Tats Sugimura, who lived the next lot down from Jacob's. In fact, he had been kind to Jacob, giving him sweet potatoes and letting him use his water at the far end of the field (where Tats had found the fish scales and bones, though Tats couldn't figure out that that was where Jacob used to clean his fish).

So they organized representatives from each household of the valley to go up the road and pay their homage to Jacob's vindictive soul. They went to his place one late Saturday afternoon when the sun was beginning to set behind the mountains, parking their cars and trucks at the end of the dirt road where the road turned into a trail that led into Jacob's forbidden plot of land. They brought taro, sweet potatoes, corn, watermelons, yams, several 'awa roots, a dozen cans of meat, a basket of freshly laid eggs, a tub of fish and another tub of crawling crabs, loads of ti leaves, bunches of green bananas, and a fifth of good bourbon so that Jacob could wash all of the offerings down. They silently climbed the narrow path that the valley road turned into, winding up through dense brush and trees towards old Jacob's place. Lei was the only one in the contingent who had been up to Jacob's place before, but that was years and years ago and all she had seen were the dilapidated chicken coops, and everyone's senses were suspended in fear, not knowing what they might expect or see at the end of the trail.

Finally, they reached a flat clearing where they saw a sweeping view of the precipitous mountain range. They searched anxiously for his house until finally Elizabeth Kauhale found it hanging a few feet above the ground, with vines attaching it to a giant kukui tree. It was made out of scrap wood and looked like a big crate with a small opening on the side where a tattered rope ladder hung down. The box house began to swing and there was heard hollow laughter coming from within. The entourage retreated a few steps, their faces blanched with the expectation that Jacob's ghost might leap out after them. The laughing stopped, and they quickly dropped their offerings in an untidy heap under Jacob's pendular house, not daring to glance up the rope ladder. Then, hurriedly, they filed down the trail.

When they reached the bottom, they stopped, looked back, and made sure everyone who had gone up was back down. After they finished counting heads, they ambled off to their cars, murmuring among themselves how they hoped things would come out all right and the smell would leave the valley. Then, suddenly, there came loud, crackling laughter from deep in the valley that made the plants and trees shake. Everyone crammed into whosoever's car was nearest. They raced down the road and did not stop until, breathless and terrified and worried for their very lives, they were down at the old abandoned store, and here they sat speechless until Leimomi Vargas shouted at the top of her lungs, "I think dis is all silly—us guys getting our pants scared off our 'okoles!"

Embarrassed smiles came upon everyone's face and there was heard some nervous laughter. Someone suggested that they celebrate in the memory of old Jacob, and, without further ado, they voted unanimously to go back to their homes and get what they had to eat and bring it all back down to the abandoned store where they would party for the rest of the night. So the people who were in the wrong cars got out and into the cars they had originally gone up the road with, and they all went back home and took boxes of chicken or beef or squid or whatever they had out of the freezers and thawed them under warm running water; the Ignacios brought down a pig Bobby had slaughtered that morning; the Fritzhughs brought a big barrel of fish their oldest son had caught that day; and Tats Sugimura trucked down a load of his miniature, mutant sweet potatoes; and the others went into backyards and lopped off hands of bananas and picked ears of corn and mangoes and carried off watermelons from the fields; and they brought all that food and all the beer and whiskey they had in their homes down to the store. Earl Fritzhugh and his two sons chopped up a large kiawe tree and made a roaring fire in the empty lot next to the store, and everyone pitched in and cooked the copious amounts of food in that sweet-smelling, charcoal inferno. Bobby Ignacio and friends—Earl Fritzhugh, Fritzhugh's youngest son, Sonny Pico's two boys and his daughter, Tats Sugimura's brother and Joseph Correa—brought down their ukes and guitars and a washtub bass and provided the entertainment that lasted exactly three nights and two days. And when the festivities finally ended—the smoke from the kiawe fire was still smoldering strongly—everyone at the old store began hugging each other and then meandered off to their homes.

But before they fell into deep sleep, Earl Fritzhugh and his wife made love for the first time since the smell began putrefying the air of the valley. And so did Tats and Harriet Sugimura. And there were at least a dozen or so illegitimate liaisons committed that festive time—for one, Elizabeth Kauhale saw her teenage son go in the bush with Bobby Ignacio's willowy daughter—which was probably the reason why weeks ahead there would be more festivities when three of those liaisons would be legitimized, and why months later, on the same day, there would be added three new members to the community.

And before he slept, old Joseph Correa dragged his feet to the old cemetery next to the clapboard Catholic church, and there he laid a bunch of wild orchids on the grave of his beloved wife, Martha, and he sat down on the soft, wet ground, though it was a struggle for his brittle old legs to do so, and he sang that song that was a favorite of his wife—"Pua Lilia"— because his wife's middle name was Lilia, and he had often sung that song to her when she was alive and he had sung that song to her when she was dying. And after that song, he gazed up the valley and apologized once again to his former friend, Jacob Hookano, for saying those damaging things about him in the past. "But she was worth fighting for," he said with a choke in his voice. "And you can see, my friend," he added with a touch of jealousy, "that you with her right now."

When the people of the valley finally woke up the next morning, or the next afternoon—or whenever—the first thing they noticed was the smell. The fresh clean smell of the ocean. It was the smell of salt, and the warm winds that carried it over the valley swept up to the highest ridges of the mountains, and there the warm air married with the cold dampness and thick clouds formed, and soon, with the shift in the trades, rain began to fall over the silent, peaceful valley.

PIGEONS OF AUTUMN
Karen Shishido

I was outside feeding my father's pigeons just before dinner when the air raid signal came. The siren was over across town, at Pā'ia fire station, but it always sounded like it was coming from somewhere over in the Taniokas' backyard. I waited for someone else to come outside. I could hear my father yelling in the parlor, then my older brother Masao came out, slamming the old screen door. His zoris scuffed the dirt as he crossed the yard. "Eh, Yosh. Never mind the birds. Come help me put the stuff up."

I knew it was just a drill, that no Japanese planes were about to come and bomb a tiny sugar plantation town where there were practically more chickens than people. Why would they, when they could go after O'ahu again? They had these drills three times a week at least. Every time we'd have to drag out the tarps and cover the windows and the car, and turn off all the lights in the house. At first it had been kind of fun, and I imagined myself like Buck Rogers, stealthily hiding away, waiting for the right moment to counterattack. Now it was just annoying. I put one last handful of corn and grit into the tin pan on the bottom of the coop. Buster, the spit-mean, one-eyed, balding king of the coop, started pecking away, hobbling on his bad foot and scolding the others who had come down from the roosts to eat.

Later that night, some of us were sitting in the parlor, lights back on since they had sounded the all-clear. My sister Betty was sewing a button back on a blouse. Probably she was about to go to the movies with her boyfriend, Jimmy Akana. I don't think my father knew that, though—probably he thought she was still going steady with Mits Takamoto. He would have been pretty mad if he knew, because he thought my sisters should date only straight-arrow Japanese guys like my brother Masao. I was waiting for Flash Gordon to come on the radio, popping a roll of Smarties in my mouth. My father was muttering something half to himself. "I can't believe that! . . ." He got up, the *Maui Daily Telegram* clenched in his clubbed fists, and started to walk around the table, like he did when something was getting to him.

"Shin, did you know they're still taking away the Japanese in California and Washington? Ten thousand already!" he said to my mother, who was in the kitchen getting some *sake* for him.

"What? *Araaaa*, so many?" she said gravely, setting the small cup and the bottle of my father's home brew down. My sister took the opportunity to make a quiet exit, closing the wooden shoe box almost noiselessly as she left.

"What kind is this? And not only the mainland, you know. They went take Endo-san and Fukada-san from Wailuku Town last week! They saying all them is spies for the Emperor."

"Michiko going have hard time now," my mother said, shaking her head. "She get seven kids, too. *Taihen, ne!*" She knew both families because she had grown up over by the mill in Wailuku and often went to visit my grandmother there.

At this point I entered the conversation, since Flash Gordon was running late and the Pepsodent commercial was singsonging on.

"Are you sure it's ten thousand, Pa?" It seemed too big a number to me. Maybe he had read it wrong. He only read the English language paper, unlike a lot of my friends' fathers, and even if his English was better than most people's, maybe he had misunderstood.

"Yeah, yeah, I telling you it's ten thousand. They no lie, you know. They taking anykine Japanese, even all the basans."

I shrugged, turning around to hear my program.

A minute later Masao came down from his room. He had put a shirt on, so I guessed he was going somewhere. He and his high school friends often went to the beach near Pā'ia School and drank beer. He had taken me once, but I had thrown up and he'd had to carry me home on his back.

"Eh, Ma, no forget the message, OK? The one I told you about Mrs. Endo." Masao was rooting around in the icebox for some eggs and Portuguese sausage to take along for the grill. His voice was loud but my mother couldn't understand him.

"What, what? Tell me again," she called to him. I heard him curse softly from the kitchen.

"I said," he sighed, coming out with his hands full, "she went send Mrs. Yamamoto to ask if you can walk Peggy and Clarence to the grammar school Wednesday and if Pa could drive her to town to the courthouse Thursday. She stay trying for get her old man out—"

"Wait, wait. What you talking? More slower," interrupted my mother. Even though she had been born on Maui, and my father had immigrated from Japan when he was nine, she had never learned English very well.

Masao was about to lose his temper, I could tell. Probably Chester Wakai and the others were already down at the beach. "Look, Ma . . . ." He stopped, sighing impatiently, deciding to try another tack. "*Endo-san, kodomo o gakko made Kayōbi ni tsurete itte kudasai . . . .*" Suddenly there was this huge bang. I wheeled around and saw that Father was standing, his fists on the table. His eyes were flashing. He jabbed a finger at my brother.

"Hey! I *said* you kids no talk Japanese! Only English! You *hear* me? You like they say you not one real American? Hah?"

Masao turned red, but then stiffened—he was a good six inches taller than my father, and just as strong in build. For a second, he just stared at my father, his lip curling. Then he spat in a low, tight voice, "Just because you talk Japanese no mean you one *Jap* Jap." He turned around and strode toward the door. "Goddamned old man."

The sound of the screen door slapping shut echoed in the silence. A few minutes later, I heard my father go outside, and the faint creaking of the door of the aviary being opened. I pretended to listen to the rest of the show, not turning around.

Going upstairs to sleep, I stopped at the small pane glass window near the landing of the stairs that overlooked our yard. In the bluish cast of moonlight, I saw my father. He was kneeling in front of the coop, the soft breeze flapping the tail of his work-shirt as his fingers stroked the tattered feathers of Buster, who lay still and silent on the pebbly dirt.

A CONSERVATIVE VIEW
Cathy Song

Money, my mother
never had much.
Perhaps that explains her life's
philosophy, the conservation of money,
the idea of money as a natural resource,
the sleepless nights worrying
whether there is enough of it.
According to her current calculations,
there isn't.

I used to think it was because she is Chinese,
proud of the fact that her practical
nature is due to her Chinese blood.
"We do not spoil our children"
she is fond of saying as an explanation
for never having given in to our demands.
"Take care of the needs but not the wants" is another.

Place a well-behaved child
in front of her and my mother will say,
"Chinese, eh?"
She believes Japanese and Korean
parents spoil their children.
"Doormats to their kids."
And the bok gwai?—well,
they ship their offspring to camp or boarding school, right?
For the Chinese, discipline begins at home.
And it begins with teaching the value of money.

There are two things in life
my mother vows never to pay for:
gift wrapping and parking.
It hurts her to cough up change for the meter.
Lucky is any day she can pull

into an empty space with time still running.
I was convinced my friends knew
that the birthday gifts I presented at parties
were wrapped in leftover sheets of our bathroom wallpaper.
—"Eh, how come dis paypa so tick?"

My mother's thrift frowns on the frivolous—
like singing in the shower
(it's a waste of water).
Her clear and practical sentences
are sprinkled with expressions
semantically rooted to the conservation of money.
They pepper her observations like expletives—
"Poho" if we bought something we couldn't use.
"Humbug" if we have to go out and buy
something we don't need.
"No need"—her favorite expression of all.

On shopping trips to the mall
she'll finger something soft and expensive,
letting her fingers linger on the exquisite
cut and fabric of a garment
when suddenly she'll exclaim,
like a kung fu battle cry,
"Pee-sa!"
(the one word she borrows liberally
from her Korean in-laws),
shuddering and releasing the price tag
as if she'd been bitten by a snake.

My sister and I agree
she takes the price of things too personally.
Every morning there is her wake-up call—
"Diapers on sale at Longs."
"Price of lettuce up at Star."—
as though she were reporting the Dow Jones Industrial Average.
If I answer in the negative
to her interrogative
"Did you use coupons to buy that?"
—that being chicken thighs or toilet paper,
I feel guilty.

My father doesn't help matters.
He has heard enough from Mother
about Koreans being big spenders, show-offs—
"champagne taste on a beer budget"—
to have his revenge.
He thinks Mao Tse-tung is the best
thing that ever happened to China.
"How else are you going to get those damn pa-kes to share?"

HOW THE ISLAND WORKS
Gary Tachiyama

Somebody wen' tell me no more fish,
then I wen' tell you no more fish,
then you wen' tell somebody,
and then they wen' tell.
Pretty soon, everybody know
no more nothing.

So when we go spearing
we poke everything
'cause we think no more nothing,
and we lucky see something.
Then, when we take 'em home,
our mothers tell us why bring home
this guppy-size kind, and our mothers
throw 'em outside for the cats.

And if we take 'em home,
and our mothers no stay,
if we put on the fire,
the frying pan, oil in that,
then cook the fish, eat 'em,
wipe the stove, so we no get lickens,
then clean the frying pan . . . you know,
too humbug to cook the manini-size kind,
so we throw 'em outside for the cats.

Pretty soon, everybody do that,
no more fish, only fat cats.
But you know this already,
'cause you know how the Island work, yeah.
Word of mouth, brah, word of mouth.

GOOD FO' BE ONE HAPA KID

Carrie Y. Takahata

Skin glows scarlet in the sun
without added yellow;
light ehu brown hair softens

noses built high with power
to hold glasses
without rubber nose pads.

People will say
eyes are big enough to see out of;
at least got height; lucky
get haole blood.

No matter too tall to see
people underneath, at least
never have to feel
too much of any kine:
she's so . . . oriental.

And pidgin can be Pidgin
without question.

I HAVE A STORY TO TELL
Carrie Y. Takahata

An educational video project for the State:
the mother-daughter interview lasts two hours and I go first.

Gordon asks questions about internment,
the Japanese American experience in Hawai'i,

and I don't know; I don't know
when grandpa came to Hawai'i and I don't know why;

I can't remember if I'm Sansei or if I'm Yonsei or
if it really matters. And did you tell me

you were interned in Arkansas the entire
three years? Where did you finally meet up with your father?

I can't say how long it was
your family remained apart; or how long

that ride on the *Lurline* took. I stare into the lights;
the interview begins when I move into the kitchen. You

explain how, at age four, internment began; how you were corralled
at Sand Island before you were *Lurlined* to the mainland;

how, at first, you actually looked forward to moving from Hawai'i
the name of the city seeming to call to you, *Heart Mountain*;

how, once there, you slept in a tin barrack with four other families and how
you had to move two times during two years to finally meet up with
grandpa in Arkansas.

You said you watched him carve a pair of one-inch zori
out of scrap wood from a nearby construction site;

and you loaned his yellowing camp pictures, self-laminated,
to exhibits touring nationally, pieces I'd never heard of.

I try to remember. The interview ends;
unconsciously, I thank the recorders for the opportunity.

We walk out the door and apologetically you explain
how "something's come up" and you

have to get back to the office; our dinner date postponed

again. I get into my car and watch you drive away.

MAKING YONSEI
Carrie Y. Takahata

Mom,
what are you saying?
What'd you mean,
How come I don't know? and *What kind*
Japanese are you? Don't act
like I'm supposed to know these words. You
never told them to me before. You always said,

> *three* not *chree*
> *I am* not *I stay*
> *like that* not *li-dat.*

How am I supposed to know
anything but   Buddha's
not just the sculpture in our living room,
the one my friends made fun of, he's a man
who sat under the bodhi tree and thought   thought   thought:

Call me at the office and if my secretary answers, give me a page; if I don't
        answer within five
minutes, call my cell; I'll keep it on just   for   you,

you told me that.

You only use these words now
because you know your friend

                                        likes them;

he thinks they're *neat*
and *interesting.*
I know what he wants.
He wants a little Local Japanese:
someone who will teach him
that this is

> *gohan* not *rice*
> *chazuke* not *rice and tea*
> *ko-ko* not *pickled cabbage*

the makings of the family meal;

someone who'll buy him
the 10,000 strand red-paper-fire-crackers before
they go on sale at Longs;
someone who will show him just how to eat
the konbu for happiness,
the mochi to make the family stick,
the soba for long life;
someone who will open up the butsudan
and give him "mantras"??

He looks at you
and that's what he sees;
he looks at me
and wonders
what went wrong.

JADE HEART from *A Little Too Much Is Enough*
Kathleen Tyau

I saw the light under your bedroom door. All these years, and that's the last thing I see before I go to sleep, the light under your door. Too bad you're not a baby. I could show you the moon and rock you back and forth. Now you are so big, I have to remind myself that you are my baby, I raised you from a pup.

Are you thinking about tomorrow? Still trying to decide what to take? You are worse than me. Don't worry. Just take it all. Uncle Wing can help us with the extra luggage. He knows somebody who can get your bags through.

Maybe you can take this wool coat too. You can wear it on the plane. I'm sure it gets cold in Oregon. I might need it sometime, but I can always borrow it back. In the meantime, you take it. I hate to see it go to waste in the closet.

Let me see you wear it. Oh, you look just like me. No wonder people call us sisters. My hair used to be long like yours, but I wore it pinned up on my head with flowers. I was so hau po back then. Do you know I bought this coat in San Francisco? It's older than you! So many years ago, but still in fashion. That's why I bought it simple, just a shawl collar, and navy blue is always good, never goes out of style. I wish it was red, but at the time I didn't want to stick out that much. I didn't like when people called me Jap. Makes me sick to my stomach just to think. I had a good time on my own, but sometimes I just wanted to fade away. I wanted to go home. When you wear this coat, I want you to think about how stupid that was. Wasting time being homesick, feeling sorry for myself when I could have been having fun.

Someday maybe, when I come up, we can go to San Francisco. We can dress up and go out to eat. We can ride the cable car to Fisherman's Wharf, just you and me, no uncles or aunties. Nobody telling us what to do. They can drop us off at the bus stop. We can go shopping. I'll show you Chinatown. Where I used to live, if they haven't torn it down.

I'm glad you're going to Oregon. I heard about Oregon when I lived in San Francisco. I hear they have plenty of trees up there. Not as many island people, but just as well. Better if you can get away from so many people telling you what to do. Then you can hear yourself talk. You can hear yourself think.

Sometimes I tell Kūhio, Let's just sell the house and go, but we're still here. I don't know where to go. I can't think of where I want to be. Something inside me just tells me Go, but not all the time. Just when I'm tired. Then I want to go where nobody knows me, where all I have to do is what Anna wants.

I hope you won't be too homesick. Don't worry about home. I'll write to you and you can write back. I'll send you anything you want. All the food you miss. Seed and mochi crunch. Portuguese sausage. Orchids too.

I'm so jealous. I wish I could be young again and go with you. We could have so much fun. But you can write and tell me. That will be good enough.

Tell me about school, what you are learning. Tell me about your friends, just don't tell me everything. What I don't know won't hurt me. I know you won't do anything bad. I know your father and I brought you up to think for yourself. You're a good girl. When the time comes, you'll know what to do.

Just don't shack up with a man. You might have to get married. Finish school first. Get your degree. These days, it's okay for a girl to be smart. Don't be afraid to speak up in school and let the teacher know you can think. I know you don't always get to say what you want to at home. This is your chance. You can say anything. You can do what you want.

And if it doesn't work out, you still have a home. Don't force yourself to stay away. Nobody's going to take your room. I'll keep your spread on the bed, all of your stuffed animals and books. Everything will still be here when you get back. You don't even have to go, but you know that already. You'll have a good time. I'm so proud of you.

I have only one more thing to give you. Don't worry, it's small. This jade heart. It's from your popo. I was saving it for your thirtieth birthday, Chinese style. But why wait? You might as well wear it now. Going away is just like thirty. You can wear it on the airplane. You can wear it all the time. Popo gave it to me because I was the oldest daughter. Now you are the first, so I give it to you.

Sometimes I think of how much you remind me of your popo. Maybe it is just the way you act. Think how brave she was, coming all the way from China. The only person she knew here was Goong Goong, and then she never went back. She never saw her family again. Lucky thing we have planes. We don't have to say goodbye forever. You can come home anytime.

Don't worry about losing this jade. Just wear it. That's what it's for. When I went to San Francisco, Popo gave me a jade pendant. It was a teardrop pendant, not a heart. I was only there for one month when I lost it. The clasp on the chain broke. I looked everywhere, at the bus stop, on the sidewalk, in front of my apartment. I was sure I dropped it going to class. I never found that jade. I cried for weeks. I didn't know how I was going to tell my mother. I felt like I had not only lost my jade but my whole family. But when I came home, Popo didn't scold. She just gave me another pendant, this heart, and a new gold chain with a better clasp. She said to me, You have not lost that jade. You will always remember it.

When I was in San Francisco, all I could think about was Hawai'i. Now that I am here, I cannot forget San Francisco. I have to remind myself that I have not lost it. It is still there, just like Hawai'i will still be here when you are in Oregon. Whatever is lost, you will remember. You will always hold it in your heart.

AFTERWORD

This Is a Fisherman by Barry Asato, Radford High School

I WUZ HEA

Eric Chock

I grew up on a lane named for the Hawaiians that lived on the other side of the lane. Herman, Tutu, Willy, Aunty Mary in her black holoku, Lydia, Alicia, and Vanessa will always remind me that what was Hawai'i was always right next door. Behind them, on a lane with their family name, behind a ten foot high log fence, was the home of a descendant of a local Hawaiian princess. A school nearby also bears that family name. On either side of our house were streams, little 'auwai, with taro still growing there in the soft mud that sucked you to your knees when you were foolish enough to step in. Our houselot was sold to my parents by the descendants of the royal family and is the only houselot on that side of the lane, surrounded by the acres of cemetery that used to be horse pasture and a neighborhood dump. Poi pounders and horseshoes were found when the foundations for our house were being dug. Most have somehow disappeared. To this day, raking under the mango tree can bring up small pieces of porcelain or colored glass.

When I was young, I played with the Japanese cemetery worker's children next door. They lived in cemetery worker housing, farmed extended vegetable gardens between their houses and the graves, and their grandfather went at night when it was legal for him to burn the bodies in the crematorium next door to us. The newest graves were being filled right behind my bedroom. What was our baseball field was being filled with Japanese names. Their stones were mostly gray or black granite. The older haole and Hawaiian stones were often white marble, as were many of the stones of the seamen and early 19th century adventurers. It was their cemetery at first, but later they let everybody else in. There was an oval section of what I found out were Jewish graves, all bearing the Star of David. Beyond that was a corner of Koreans. Between the Koreans and the famous local names, were a few fraternal plots whose stones all contained certain symbols. There were some military groups. There were a few Chinese names here and there, but most of them were in their own cemeteries.

When we were kids, we used to wander through the graveyard and count how many names of streets, boulevards, or famous people we could find on the marble and granite monuments. Or wonder who those Kalalau shootout victims were. Or marvel at the fact that a famous Hawaiian wrestler had the exact same name as one of the stones. I passed my grandparents on my weekly trips to the waterfall. Or I would notice that the college scholarship I was awarded was named after someone a few steps from my front door. I guess I have always felt that the whole world passes by our front door and that we are somehow connected. All were alive to me. After hours, I serenaded my benefactor with my local trumpeter's version of Herb Alpert's "The Lonely Bull" or an adolescent "As Tears Go By" on folk guitar. Sometimes I would spend afternoons searching for the oldest stone; a New England sailor I think from the early 1800s is the oldest I could find. Or I would marvel at the white-columned mansions hidden adjacent to the graveyard. These people not only had their street named for them, their missionary ancestor had his own mini mausoleum at the edge of their property, a white, plaster, one-room building with a black, wrought-iron fence and arch over the gate spelling out his name. Sometimes I would visit their Japanese servant's children.

In the rocks beyond the furthest graves, down toward another stream, were petroglyphs, now encased behind steel bars. In earlier days, it was sacred, too kapu to touch. The way we never stepped on or pointed at anyone's gravestone. Now the petroglyphs are vandalized too often by those who frequent the swimming hole beyond. Above the petroglyphs, every day we used to walk to school past the gold-tipped black spears of the wrought iron fence of the Royal Mausoleum, never thinking of any connection. All this within a five minute walk from my house. Yet I took it all for granted. It was just where I lived. In the center of local history. Only now looking back I put it all together.

When we ran out of room inside our house, I helped my father chisel out a space in the slope of solid lava rock underneath the house. We poured two flat beds of concrete just big enough to hold two small mattresses placed in a right angle. We screened in the space to minimize the mosquitoes. I would come home late at night, drive up the lane through the cemetery, walk down five steps, duck my head under the doorway, and crawl onto my rock nest. At least it was my own room. It was the first time I ever had my own space at home. Lying on my bed, with my back to the ground, I could reach up and touch the bottom of the floor above. How could I not feel connected to this locale?

When I was growing up, my bedroom window faced the smokestack of the crematorium and the spread of gravestones dotting the manicured lawn. We played cards in the breath of black diesel smoke as a latenight body was burned. Once, playing poker, my neighbor and I got locked inside the mausoleum when they closed up for the night. So what. As a teenager, the cemetery was a place to get away from the house, to feel at ease with myself, to think. Things pass away. Perhaps we memorialize them. I accepted that. Now, in my mind, I hold on more dearly to what I love. When I go back home and visit my folks and look into their faces or walk around the neighborhood, I know that what used to be called Local is just about gone—the people and places woven into meanings which even those people barely understood. Some will go back and try to keep the petroglyphs protected, the wrought iron shiny, the traditions and families perpetuated. But most things change. The rich man's mausoleum is gone, and the site is now owned by a Buddhist sect from Japan, and they have imported a beautiful full-size temple replica which is purportedly held together with no nails. The Japanese cemetery workers have been replaced by more recent immigrant Filipinos and Koreans. The vegetable gardens were contaminated with diesel fuel, and temporarily quarantined. The crematorium smokestack taints the air with its black smoke more than ever, but someday even it will be replaced by some more modern method which we cannot even imagine. When we do another edition of this book later in the 21st century, who knows what it will look like?

LISTENING WITH AN OUTSIDER'S EAR
Bill Teter

I didn't grow up local. Not here, not anywhere. My dad was a Marine, and our family moved more than a dozen times while I was growing up. At an early age I got to be really good with maps; I'd study them so that I could find my way around whatever our new home was going to be. And wherever we moved—Pittsburgh, Pennsylvania; Jacksonville, North Carolina; Vista, California—I tried to learn as much as I could about the place. It was a way of trying to blend in. And of course it never really worked.

One advantage, I guess you can call it that, of having no real home, no place I grew up, is that I always felt free to call anyplace home. Plus, I could dismiss any place I didn't want to be from. I say I grew up in California, even though I didn't move there for good until after my freshman year of high school. When I left for college in San Francisco, I knew after two days that I would call The City my home; I didn't have to check that feeling with anyone else.

But it was different when I came to Hawai'i twenty years ago. I learned very quickly that no one can call Hawai'i home until someone from here tells them they can. I also learned very quickly that that is okay. And it isn't enough just to like it here; you have to somehow "become" local. That is *nothing* like growing up local.

Every year I give the students in my class a writing assignment: I ask them to tell me what "local" means. In the past few years the answers have evolved in interesting ways. Regardless of the ethnicity or race of the writer, the answers have had little to do with ethnic or racial background. Instead, they have clustered around certain kinds of attitudes, experiences and values. These are the attributes of a local person, according to the students in my classes:

—*Love of the land.* The sea, the mountains, everything in between. There is a sense that *local* people actively cherish the land, enjoying what it has to offer and being concerned about its preservation.

—*Grinding.* Local people love to eat, love variety in what they eat, and love to talk about what they love to eat. (I remember sitting in a restaurant two summers ago in North Carolina with several Hawai'i high school speech coaches. We'd just finished a huge dinner; we could barely move, and a waiter's question about dessert brought a chorus of groans. While we drank coffee and tried to digest, we talked about our favorite plate lunch places back home. Local people talking serious grinding.)

—*Diversity*. You can't just tolerate differences. You have to celebrate them, revel in them, *know* what's going on. Take a look at a Bon Dance some summer evening, or an elementary school May Day celebration, or a neighborhood New Year's Eve, and you'll see what this means.

—*The Voice*. The debate over pidgin may rage in educational or academic circles, but there's no uncertainty among the students who answer my question every year: Pidgin is fo' real. Don't talk it if you can't talk it, they say—but don't dismiss it either. Even as pidgin evolves, it remains central to their understanding of what local is. Even kids who don't speak it enjoy it, understand it, recognize it as the sound of "home." If you wanna be local, gotta at least *appreciate* da kine.

I suppose I'm an outsider in the pidgin debate, but it's a debate I never have understood. The great pidgin writers of our islands stand in a rich and honorable tradition in literature. The American voice has *always* been a local voice—regional, heavily inflected, sometimes hard for others to understand. Hawthorne, Twain and Faulkner come immediately to mind. In our century, the voices of the south, Welty, O'Connor, and McCullers; the northwestern voice of Raymond Carver; the voices we have to our shame ignored for too long, only recently beginning to hear and appreciate them: Baldwin, Walker, Hong Kingston, Cisneros. The writers of these islands, in this book and elsewhere, are adding their voices to this impressive group. If I could wish this book could do one thing, it would be this: at long last to lay to rest the arguments over whether pidgin is "acceptable" or not in literature. To empower Hawai'i students (and other readers), to help them find their own voices, and to celebrate in writing the marvelous diversity of voices that make up Hawai'i. To help us all to see that more languages, more voices, more ways to speak and sing and be heard, is always better than fewer.

AUTHORS' NOTES

Clockwise:

untitled
by Jared Holman,
Radford High School

My Pet
by Kellie Ng,
Farrington High School

Albert Junior
by Alvah Maree Poscablo,
'Aiea High School

ALOHI AE'A
Kamehameha School

I know not what it meant to grow up local. I grew up —that is all I know. And now I stand here, trying to verbalize what it was that made me how I am, and I cannot.

This word "local"—it is the heaviest chain, yet my key to freedom. It is a blessing with a curse, an exclusively inclusive title. With this word I am bound to these islands, yet freed to live in them, granted a birthright yet held to its responsibilities, a member of an elite society that includes all who love this place.

It is the word that covers all of us—the surfer with golden morning light on his back; the jogger you see every evening; the mother driving her children to school; the man wearing khakis and an aloha shirt downtown; the old woman selling leis; the gardener trimming a tree; the farmer harvesting *kalo*; the construction worker pouring cement.

And me . . . a local girl, almost grown up, wanting to be faithful to my roots, yet not knowing how.

ANJANETTE BALINBIN
Lahainaluna HS 1992–1996

Born and raised on the west side of Maui, I am the 2nd of four, and the only girl. My mom is a school teacher and my dad is a cook. I have a pet lovebird named Hale-Bopp and my most immediate goal is to graduate college, teach English, and cultivate a love of reading and writing in my students.

To me, "growing up local" is all about growing up in the aloha spirit. More than anything about Hawai'i, it's the love and appreciation of all the differences we have that sets us apart, makes us unique, and makes the rest of the world want to live and vacation here.

As for how that relates to the story . . . well, much as I love it, even Paradise has its darker side. The story is half based on a guy I once dated, and mostly on a friend who was actually going through that situation. I think one of the reasons the story reads as well as it does, is because people can see the truth behind it. It's about them, or people they love. It's real, and people recognize it.

KATHY DEE KALEOKEALOHA KALOLOAHILANI BANGGO
Leilehua High School

K.D.K.K. Banggo enjoys surfing and writing. She was born and raised on the island of O'ahu, Hawai'i, and is of Hawaiian/Filipino ancestry. She has won various writing awards, including a 1995 Intro Award for Poetry from the Associated Writing Programs.

"I wrote 'No Mindless Digging' about seven years ago when construction of the H-3 freeway started again after all of those years of silence, no construction. Family members were involved in the excavations and actual building—they didn't like their jobs and what it meant to do what they were doing to survive, feed themselves, feed their families . . . . I think that here in Hawai'i we've learned to surrender what we love and believe in, at times, because of socio-economic reasons. In many ways, plantation days are still with us. We may feel angry, heartbroken, confused or betrayed, sorrowful, nostalgic—a host of emotions, but may not be so vocal or active in any way, and watch golf courses, condos, malls, etc., pop up everywhere. Change is inevitable. The struggle over land, political power, personal power, social class, identity and racism here in Hawai'i shaped me and my artwork for as long as I can remember."

ARLENE BIALA
Santa Clara High School (California)

Arlene Biala lives and works in the San Francisco Bay Area. Poetry book *Continental Drift* forthcoming from West End Press (New Mexico). "Kona Side" was inspired "by family on the Big Island, Junior's respect for the ocean, and luck!"

ERIC ALFRED BOTEILHO
Henry Perrine Baldwin High School

This piece, "Of Walls and Wheelbarrows," is one of a series of short stories and essays that I wrote for both the Hawai'i Education Association writing contests and the Language Arts Showcase writing contests throughout my years in high school. The intent was to show the lighter side of growing up in Hawai'i, the laughter and good times shared among family and friends. The piece is inspired by a true story—yes, it really happened, and to me, that makes it all the more humorous.

Growing up local has influenced me in ways which I still today am discovering (four years after writing this piece). A short time after this piece was written I left Hawai'i to attend college in Los Angeles. This is where the local influence becomes noticeable. No one understands you when you accidentally let slip an "all pau."

Artistically, however, Hawai'i has meant a great deal. I don't mean Hawai'i as a place, or Hawai'i as a people, but Hawai'i as an almost intangible entity which can only be felt when you need artistic influence. It is a combination of place and people and times which makes an artist of any genre or medium feel so welcome, so alive. If there are any doubts about this, try looking into Waimea Valley, or Haleakalā, or the faces of the people walking around the streets. It is there, and it influences people in different ways. That's the beauty of it all. So many different people living so many different lives, yet all living the same. The poet, musician, artisan, and sugar cane worker are all the same because of where they came from, where their roots are. This is Hawai'i to me and this is what makes it so special. "Of Walls and Wheelbarrows" is meant to show this in a very subtle way. Everyone, no matter who you are, knows about the hollow tile walls commonly seen in subdivisions in Hawai'i, and everyone knows about the Hawaiian rain—certainly not a force easily contended with. Above all, though, everyone laughs. And the bringing together of experiences in a funny way is what makes my work so much fun.

(Sorry if that was a bit long-winded—I'm chronically Portuguese.)

BRADAJO (JOZUF HADLEY)
University High School

Jozuf Hadley has facilitated creative experiences in the secondary art classroom since 1961, and is presently on the art faculty at Oxbow High School in Bradford, Vermont. Born in 1932 on Kaua'i, as was his mother before him, Hadley attended Kaua'i High School his 9th grade year, but continued at University High, finishing with the first graduating class of 23 in 1951. Following military service, Hadley received a bachelor's degree in art education at California College of Arts and Crafts, Oakland, in 1961. He earned a master's degree in sculpture at the University of Hawai'i—Mānoa in 1970 by molding people under a plaster-soaked sheet. Recent "figurecasting" works are on display at Polonaise Gallery in Woodstock, Vermont. Jozuf Hadley lives with his Russian wife Elena in West Newbury, Vermont.

"Having grown up on a Kaua'i sugar plantation, and sharing school life with perhaps the most diverse population known, Pidgin is part of my bones and marrow. And yes, I capitalize Pidgin because it deserves equal honor due any manifestation of a unique and distinctive culture. Pidgin is a culture, a dying culture fast fading into the mall-television culture enveloping the planet. Alas! Auwe!

"But it was my solitary life in the jungles between Līhu'e and Nāwiliwili that gifted me with appreciation for wilderness, an honoring of stillness; this and the great enthusiasm for the beauty, romance, and history of the Garden Island that I absorbed from Thelma Hopper Hadley, my mother.

"It's been thirty years since three friends and I climbed into Waimea Canyon and rock-hopped up the Koa'e tributary in an attempt to reach Alaka'i Swamp atop Mount Wai'ale'ale (dabeegeeneen). That powerful experience was literally the beginning of my written Pidgin. Suddenly, the poetic stuff I'd been jotting down in composition books began flowing out as this phonetic broken-English calligraphy that continues to this day. My first Pidgin piece, *chalookyu eensai* (Try Look Inside) was born of these early fragments.

"Thanks to Carl Lindquist, a book entitled *chalookyu eensai*, with an accompanying recording, was sold through Liberty House in 1972. We are re-issuing an expanded version of *chalookyu eensai* with photographs and a CD, hopefully by Christmas 1998."

The translation of bradajo's poems follows:

MY CAT STANLEY

My cat Stanley,
the Blue Cross (animal
hospital) went send 'um
one Christmas card, yuh?
He no stay now, but.
He stay free, that's why.
I went know
the mother before.
That's when I stay
Beretania Street, yuh?
She never like come close,
she stay wild,
that's why.

By and by,
she come pregnant.
Then come Stanley (from *On the
Waterfront*) and the brothers.
They stay wild too, yuh?

Morning time,
I watch 'um play
under the tree;
they like chase the leaves, yuh?

One time,
the mother,
she went get
squash
on top the road.
Then Stanley and the brother,
they come on top my step, yuh?
Stay hungry,
that's why.

Then, slow, slow,
he let me touch 'um.
But not the brother,
he scared.
And so,
me and Stanley,
we went make friend, yuh?
And by and by,
he come inside.

We went play
fight-fight, yuh?
Good fun, the kind.
I get scratch, but.
I went buy 'um
one small kind superball.
And when he whack 'um,
he bounce
anykind place.

One time,
I must move, yuh?
And Stanley:
What I going do with him?
Long time I think, yuh?
By and by I figure,
more better let him go
on top the mountain.
That's mean he's free, yuh?
No more the mans
going bother him.

So,
I put 'um inside the box,
and I tied 'um with the string,
and I drove to the mountain.

I seen 'um one time
after that.
He look like one ghost, yuh?
His hair
all stand up
from the cold.

He look me
long time, yuh?
Just like
he like tell me something.

Then,
he stay go.

PHYSICAL EDUCATION

Nine grade,
Kaua'i High School,
you gotta take
physical education . . .
you gotta wear the kind
jock strap!
And then they give you
the baggy red shorts.
Me, I like wear
my chopped pants, yuh?
But you no can!!

And then the Coach tell,
"Okay, boys,
today you are going learn
calisthenics."
So everybody—
Filipino, Portuguese,
Puerto Rican, Caucasian,
Japanese, Chinese, Hawaiian,
and a couple Blacks—
with the baggy red shorts,
jumping up and down
on top the grass.
Physical Education!

But the worst part coming up.
Because now,
you gotta go inside
take shower.
So everybody—
Filipino, Portuguese,
Puerto Rican, Caucasian,
Japanese, Chinese, Hawaiian,
and a couple Blacks—
running inside the locker room,
take off the baggy red shorts,
and the damn jock strap,
and go inside the shower.
That's when you find out:
everybody . . . same.

Next day,
you gotta go sit down
inside the quonset hut.
And then Coach tell,
"Okay boys, today
you going learn
sex education."
And then he unroll 'um
the big picture.
He tell,
"This is the testicle."
Nah!
And then you gotta look
the movie.

All
this
time,
the sun,
he shining,
the wave,
he breaking,
and you gotta sit down
inside there.

One girl,
she had go
Waianae High, yuh?
She tell me,
"When the big wave
he breaking,
the whole school
empty
Only the teacher
stay inside.
I no kid you!"

STACY CHANG
University Laboratory School

I feel incredibly lucky to have grown up in Hawai'i, with friends of different ethnicities, cultures, and customs. One disturbing trend I have seen regardless of these differences, however, has been girls' dissatisfaction with themselves and their looks. Feeling the emphasis society, media, and peers place on beauty, it has become hard for girls not to judge themselves by how pretty they look—and many let this become an obsession that takes over their lives and steals away their happiness.

STUART CHING
Kaiser High School

"Way Back to Pālolo" began with an image: four boys hiding behind wooden crates and realizing, at that moment, that each depended on the other for survival. Like much of my writing, "Way Back to Pālolo" is shaped by memory—not in an autobiographical sense, but in the way the imaginative work affirms a sense of self that I developed as a child and, despite numerous life-changes, that I still take with me wherever I go.

"Growing up local" in Hawai'i, I surfed at Waikīkī, Ala Moana, and Sandy Beach, and I spent many evenings playing 'ukulele and guitar with friends at island parks. I attended Kaiser High School (class of 1982). After earning a B.Ed. at the University of Hawai'i and an M.F.A. at Colorado State University, I taught in the Hawai'i public schools for six years. I now live in Nebraska, where I'm working on a Ph.D. in English at the University of Nebraska-Lincoln and teaching writing at Creighton University.

ERIC CHOCK
McKinley High School

Eric Chock graduated from McKinley High School in '68 after 12 years of classes with Darrell Lum. In his job as local literary activist he has taught poetry writing in grades K through graduate school, coordinated the Poets in the Schools program, co-edited Bamboo Ridge Press, masqueraded as president of the Hawai'i Literary Arts Council, been awarded the Hawai'i Award for Literature in 1996, and written occasional verse.

SHAYNA ANN A. COLEON
H. P. Baldwin High School

When I started writing this story, my mouth watered for my mom's tempura, my auntie's sushi, and Grandma's nishime. Growing up in Hawai'i, I value my mixed ethnicity with pride and uniqueness. With this in mind, I find it truest when I write about what I know and relate to. "The Tempura War" not only dealt with my own Japanese and Filipino culture, but local prejudices as well. One thing's for certain, I still can't get my boyfriend to eat tempura!

D. MĀHEALANI DUDOIT
Maryknoll High School

The writing of "My Father's Garden" began as the essay begins: me sitting at my computer, wracking my brains for a subject that would inspire me enough to meet the deadline for the next installment of my master's thesis. It was a day like today; in fact, although the coincidence may seem a fictionalized one, it was almost exactly three years ago that I wrote the piece.

It is the day before Easter Sunday and, again, the wind is blowing through my father's garden, scattering leaves and blossoms everywhere, telling me, like so many other things in this world, that my father is still alive. Hawai'i has changed so much since he was born in 1919; so much even since he passed way in 1983. Although the Hawaiian renaissance was past its infancy by the time my father died, it hadn't reached enough force to have saved him from the despair that he and so many Hawaiians felt, people whose native knowledge and experience were seen as primitive, without value, even criminal.

I wish my father had lived just a few years longer, so that he could have been part of the mighty upsurge of Hawaiian pride that has swept these islands in the last decade, and so that we, as a community, could have benefited more from those things that only our mākua and kūpuna (our parents and grandparents) can give us.

More than anyone else in my life, my father instilled in me the love for this land that is the root of our culture, a love that also engendered in both of us a terrible frustration and anger when seeing that land and culture desecrated and destroyed. To me, his life is emblematic of the struggle many of us have undergone in Hawai'i to recover our history, our dignity, and our self-worth, to stand up and say, "This is who I am, a child of these islands. These are the things I care about. This is what they mean to me." (author right front)

MARIE M. HARA
University of Hawai'i

Marie Virginia Murphy wrote a news story about
Elvis. She got a byline. He was gorgeous. Really.

MAVIS HARA

"What school you went?" I don't remember. But I used to hang out with
people from Kaimuki, Roosevelt, Farrington, McKinley, and Castle.

JAMES R. HARSTAD
South Kitsap High School
(Port Orchard, Washington)

Rub a dub dub, one kid in a tub on Hood
Canal in 1942. No, I'm not local, and as my students can tell you I'm not grown up
either. But I'm working on it. In 1966 I arrived in Hawai'i at age 26 and have been
growing up local-style ever since, first in Wai'anae, then in Mānoa, but most
recently—and mostly—in Pālolo.

I met Darrell Lum in Phil Damon's fiction-writing class at UH in 1970, and
we've been friends ever since. I've done a lot of literary growing up while admiring
the way Darrell and those who've followed him transform local speech into written
art. When he and Eric Chock established Bamboo Ridge Press in 1978, they made
it possible for the whole community to grow through its shared writing. Twenty
years later, the contribution of *Bamboo Ridge* to Hawaii's literature has grown
immeasurably vast. This book, for example, would not have been possible without
it.

Darrell and I have a longstanding joke that we'll spend our last days in the
Pālolo Chinese Home. Come visit us there in thirty years or so. I'll be almost
grown up and well over two-thirds local by then. By den try see if you can tell
which ol' buggah stay Daro an' which one stay *me!*

JOHN DOMINIS HOLT

John Dominis Holt is author of a three act play *Kaulana Na Pua - Famous
are the Flowers* (Topgallant, 1974), *Princess of the Night Rides and other tales*
(Topgallant, 1977), *Waimea Summer* (Topgallant, 1976) and *Recollections: Memoirs*

of John Dominis Holt (Ku Paa, 1993). He received the Hawai'i Award for Literature in 1985.

ASHLEY M. HOUK
Punahou School

I wrote this poem in my seventh grade English class at Punahou School. I am now a freshman attending Punahou. Our assignment was to write about a place that meant something to us. I had gone to Chinatown since I was little and being there had always seemed like a different world. Chinese is part of my background and my mom would take me there to teach me about my culture. Chinatown for me is part of growing up local because it was a place where my grandmother shopped for food and taught my mother to do the same. In Chinatown, our culture was passed down from the old generation to the new one.

CATHY KANOELANI IKEDA
Kamehameha, Class of '85

"Max" was written for my students at Hilo High. My 10th class reunion was coming up and I was talking about the things I did "back in the days." My students are often more concerned with today to look too much into the past, and they don't feel the future holds much hope. It made me think of my friends and the different journeys we've taken. Max is a wake up call for my students who think that what they are now is what they're going to be forever. Max is for the nerd in the library, the clown, the prom queen, the jock, the bully and all the Maxes that think that no one will care if they just disappear.

DARLENE M. JAVAR
Ka'u High & Pahala Elementary School

Growing up in little ol' Pahala Town was wonderful in many ways. Everybody was Aunty This or Uncle That. There was definitely a sense of safety and belonging. "No need lock." Attending Ka'u High & Pahala Elementary, kindergarten through twelfth grades was great also, especially for those of us who loved to "get involved." Embarrassing to recall, as a typical brown skinned local girl, not much "made me shame" back then. The world, as I knew it, seemed a friendly place.

My first plane ride took me to the University of Hawai'i at Mānoa. Even if I had never been away from home before, I felt I could take on the world. Then, I entered my first class. I remember stopping in the middle of the double doorway, looking up at all those chairs suddenly feeling very minuscule in the scheme of things. The fact sunk in at that moment. I was in a world outside of Ka'u.

"Shame and the First Day College" is not just about shame and the pidgin dialect. It's about feeling inferior, then taking that same energy and using it to build yourself into a stronger, vigorous goal achiever. And besides, who is to determine that you are inferior? Regardless of race, religion, gender, language, size of town, size of school, spot in the boonies—believe in yourself. Build a vision. Plan and prepare. Then see your goals to their ends. "I will. I can. I am."

Today I am a teacher at my alma mater. I turn the pidgin off and on as appropriate. For the most part I have my students write in standard English—the computer doesn't spell check pidgin, yet.

HINA KAHANU
"I one Makinley Hotcha."

We went to Eric's little apartment and in his living room we had a Poets-in-the-Schools boot camp. Priscilla Atkins shared this musical pattern based on the book *When I Was Young on a Mountain*. It was August. I needed a birthday poem gift for my brother.

Pearl Harbor influenced me because I am Japanese. Watching the new Lunalilo Freeway bury my Pirie mango tree friend, the death of Kāne'ohe Bay, the rebirth of the Hawaiian language.

After being invalidated for years by anti-local teachers, I studied and wrote with Phyllis Hoge and Nell Altizer and they helped unwash my brains and they gave free flying lessons.

I see Wini, Eric, Darryl, Gail, Dana, Pua, Tamara, Joe, Kamaka, Kaikilani, 'Imai, Māhe, Lika, Sher, and Ho'oipo.

LISA LINN KANAE
Kaimuki High School

I grad Kaimuki High '78. My alias was "Brandy," and I was the only "book-book"-looking one in a clique of Japanese girls. I bought all my mu'umu'us from Otaheite, and all my hip-hugger shorts from Jeans Machine. My high school counselor told me once that I would make a great stewardess. I walked out of her office determined to prove her wrong.

NORA OKJA KELLER
Punahou

While we were growing up, my mother spoke to her children in English, so we learned very little Korean. I think she was concerned about her own English, about becoming "American" and didn't want us to grow up feeling conflicted, split or "different."

We did anyway.

Not wanting anyone to link her "FOB" accent, her manners, her food, her beliefs, her "otherness" to me, I spent a chunk of my adolescence avoiding my mother and all things Korean. I was impatient and condescending, wanting only to be a "local" girl, not an immigrant's daughter.

In a way, my writing is an apology to my mother for that time in my life. I write to heal some of the pain we caused each other, and I write to rebuild bridges I once tried to burn.

Writing is also a way for me to understand and explore what being a Korean American woman in Hawai'i means to me. And what it might one day mean for my child.

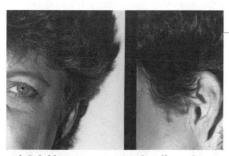

CHRISTINE KIRK-KUWAYE
Roosevelt High School, but . . .

Although this collection is called *Growing Up Local* and my story is included, I did not grow up local and I am not, even by the most imaginative folks among us, a local girl. I did begin growing up locally at the age of 13, when I arrived with my parents from Toledo, Ohio. I attended Stevenson Intermediate, then Highlands in Pearl City (which was a brand new school during my year there), then Waipahu High, then a year in Los Angeles. I came back to and graduated from Roosevelt High School. Being a haole from the mainland whose parents were working class put me in a separate category, not—kama'aina, not military. All that mattered to me in the 1960s when I was growing up in Hawai'i was that I stood a better than average chance of making local friends because I was not a military brat and not a Punahou haole.

I'm not sure what makes people want to write except liking to build things out of language and finding solace in the imagined world of poems, plays, and stories. For me, writing sometimes is preferable to being with real, living human beings, so that gives you some idea of how odd people who write might be. The piece included in this collection, "Sister from Another Planet," is called fiction although it is mostly true—many of the events did occur and names have been changed not so much to protect the innocent as to suggest connections to other pieces of literature, to make a joke, or to celebrate the sound of human language. But in spite of its facticity, this story is fiction because, for one thing, life goes on without narration and, for another, it is a whole lot messier than fiction.

I don't actually remember writing "Sister," but the characters, Pearl, her mother, Grace, and her step-father, are folks who have appeared in some of my other stories. What I do remember is that I was studying American history, slavery, and immigration when I wrote the story in 1993 or 1994. I was also attempting to learn as much as I could about Hawaiian sovereignty. What would someone from outer space make of the U.S. and Hawai'i at the end of the twentieth century and how would this alien communicate what was learned?—that is what I wondered. Fiction seemed a good way to explore that idea.

JULIET S. KONO
Hilo High School

Juliet S. Kono lives and works in Honolulu, Hawai'i. "The rain in Hilo; the humidity; growing up bare-footed; the mud oozing between the toes; Mr. Suga's hat flying off his head; Uncle Roy's dog, Cookie; swimming at N.A.S.; my grandparents, parents, my Aunts—Sue, Nancy, Elsie, Dot, Asayo; the cane fires; my friends and unfriends; traveling with my husband; Dee-dee and Sha-sha; children; a former marriage; the voices in my head—inform my writing."

LANNING LEE
University Laboratory School

The art of Shige Yamada can be found in collections throughout the world. You can see examples of his work at the State Convention Center, the University of Hawaii's Sakamaki Hall and Stan Sheriff Center, and at both the Honolulu International and Maui airports. Now retired from teaching, Mr. Yamada lives in Kihei, Maui, where he continues to paint and produce scupture and ceramics. It was a great honor to be taught by him; he remains one of three teachers who most influenced and shaped my life. Not only did I discover the beauty and pleasure of ceramic work, but I also learned how to concentrate, how to persevere, and how to imagine. This story, dear reader, does not in any way endorse breaking and entering, nor does it celebrate the suggestion of dishonoring school property in any way. But if I hadn't broken the law that fateful day long ago, I wouldn't be the person I am today. Thank you, Shig—uh, Mr. Yamada. Truly, your hide is far tougher than mine.

PETER C. T. LI
McKinley High School

Peter C. T. Li is a software engineer and web designer for ICE Systems, Inc. When not thinking about algorithms and data structures, he dreams about words and sentence structures.

VICTORIA LONO
Hana High School

I am currently a freshmen at Hana School and have been a student of this school for as long as I can remember. I have a pure Hawaiian as a father and a pure Haole for a mom. It is like I have lived two lives, one for each of them. I was always closer to my Hawaiian family rather then my mainland family when I was young. I was born proud of my Hawaiian race. I danced hula since I was 3-years-old. But one year my dad went to prison and since that year I have changed a lot. I have been living my haole half since then. I don't really seem to fit in though. I always feel different. Since my dad is not here to take me fishing and diving, I take myself out surfing. I love to surf. The ocean is the one place where I feel I belong. I feel free of my life on the shore, my life that was left so confused and angry. It is when I am angry that my more powerful writings come out. The kind that hit people's emotions where it hurts. One night after I had a bad day, I cried in bed at everything that was wrong with my life and wrote this story with the hate I felt towards all the world, "The Visit."

DARRELL H. Y. LUM
McKinley

Darrell Lum (on the left in the photo) has published two collections of short stories *Sun, short stories and drama* (Bamboo Ridge Press, 1980) and *Pass On, No Pass Back* (Bamboo Ridge Press, 1990). He received the Hawai'i Award for Literature in 1996.

LOCAL GIRLS

My two Chinese grandmothers were very different from each other, but when I was growing up, both were the personification of all things Chinese. They were as different from me as . . . as someone from China. I was a local boy, born and raised in Hawai'i. A true blue American, I thought. I felt superior to my parents (my father born in Canton, China, my mother in Waikāne Valley, O'ahu) and far more worldly than either grandmother who I scorned because they couldn't speak or read English: Ah Po Lum was barely able to mark a shaky "X" on the signature line of her insurance papers and Ah Po Lee never attended school. They were illiterate and old-fashioned and I barely paid attention to them because I could speak English (or so I thought) and could read (mostly comic books, Sergeant Rock battling Commie Chinks). I was American. No way was I Chinese. I refused to learn Chinese, could barely reply to my Chinese name or mutter "*tung-ah-jun*, one moment" when Ah Po called and asked to speak to my mother. My ears got hot when the girls in school chanted at jump rope, "Ching Chong Chinamen sitting on a fence, trying to make a dollar outa fifteen cents . . ." Or when I heard that rhyme:

> *Red, white and blue,*
> *Stars over you,*
> *Mama say, Papa say, "You Pa-ke."*

"You pa-ke." Chinese, all the slanty-eyed, tight-fisted, buck-toothed, Charlie Chan, suicidal-Commie-soldier cartoon images came to mind.

The truth is, the things Chinese that this local boy had managed to retain had been filtered through the years and perceptions of a couple of local girls, my grand-mothers. I realized that they were local girls in much the same way I thought myself a local boy. What did they know about China and high Chinese culture? Their direct knowledge of Chinese language and culture was stuck at the point when they arrived in the Hawaiian islands. For Ah Po Lee, coming to Hawai'i as a child from a life of poverty, knowledge of Chinese culture was likely formed by the community already here: the ladies at the temple, the butcher at the market, the lady she worked for. She spoke Cantonese, pidgin Hawaiian and pidgin English, evidence that she went far beyond the borders of Chinatown. Ah Po Lum came from more aristocratic begin-nings. Married to a scholar and government official, she came to the islands as the wife of the Chinese school teacher. But her bound feet hobbled her and she remained in the shadow of her husband, unable to get much beyond her own home.

The two women who I had thought were all things Chinese had picked their way through the rubble of Chinese language, culture, and tradition that remained in the midst of the languages, cultures, and traditions that surrounded them and created the practices of being "Chinese" against the backdrop of a dominant white, Western culture and a native Hawaiian host culture. They made for themselves, and ultimately for me, a local identity.

WING TEK LUM

Wing Tek Lum's first collection of poetry, *Expounding the Doubtful Points,* was published by Bamboo Ridge Press in 1987.

MAKIA MALO
Pauoa, Kawānanakoa, Kalaupapa, Hale Mohalu, UH Mānoa

I got into storytelling because I needed a job. I'd left Kalaupapa when I was 37 and started U. H. Because I'm blind and my hands don't feel, getting a job was hard. My boss at Parks and Recreation sent me to a storytelling workshop with Jeff Gere and I was hooked. Now I've got two audiotapes out, I'm a part-time Artist-In-Residence with Pacific Resources for Education and Learning (PREL), and I've performed from New Zealand to Spain and had a blast! In my mind, I am always on my porch talking to one friend and reliving my story. But it is the feedback I get from an audience that is the magic for me. Mahalo.

ELIZABETH MANLY
Niu Valley Intermediate, La Pietra

Although I now attend La Pietra, I wrote this story while I was a student at Niu Valley Intermediate School. I was born in Honolulu and have lived in Hawai'i all my life. I wove in elements of real-life experiences with fantasy. The year I was eight, I spent the summer in Poland, where I met a cousin whose leg had to be amputated due to osteogenic sarcoma. On several visits to the Big Island, I became acquainted with the real Pio, a pueo (the Hawaiian owl). Pio had been hit by a car. Though his injuries healed, they precluded him from flight. He lived out his life in the home of Ah Fat and Barbara Lee, who at that time were involved with the nene breeding program at Pōhakuloa. It was they who gave him the name Pio, which means "prisoner" in Hawaiian. The courtyard at the Hawai'i Academy of Arts is one of my favorite places. I imagined how it might look from the air after I went parasailing off the Kona coast.

BARRY MASUDA
Maui High School

Growing up "local" Japanese on Maui, I heard many, many fishing stories (not da Sakamoto kine) about how much tako, 'opihi, moi, or whatevah had in "da old days." Waste time ah, fishing "nowadays?" Brah, I could relate to some parts of the stories. Cuz me, I think that since Statehood, "progress" meant bombing Kaho'olawe so da military could practice for conquering people in Asia and da Pacific, evicting mostly local Hawaiians so rich people from da mainland, Europe, and Japan can cruise little while on da back of local and recent immigrant labor, state jobs for mostly local Japanese, and polluting good fishing grounds (with 'ōpala, tourists, whatevah). And displacing locals from those grounds too, like da goddam whale sanctuary and all da tourist boats from Ma'alaea everyday stay anchored in every single cove down Pali side. But I remember feeling that eh, you folks might be right about how tourism affects the amount of good kine fish can catch, but when you guys take time out from golf or home improvement for go fishing "nowadays," you still catch more than me and my friends. Maybe "nowadays" still get fish, but not as much, and only you guys know da spots, but you not going tell us, cuz 'ass "your" spot. And you complain about how much "crime" get "nowadays" so no can leave da car door unlocked when you go lay net down Waiehu or Makena, even Kaupo side. I guess you guys stay more worried about yo' cars dan local and non-local people who stay unemployed or who work 2-3 jobs just to get by. Anyways, 'ass why I when write dis poem. Some pretty, ah? (author on the left)

MICHAEL McPHERSON
Punahou, Kailua High School

      In high school, some friends and I went to Kaua'i to surf. We met an elderly gentleman named John Costa, who was sheriff of Makaweli. John told us that he never had been to O'ahu, or even off of Kaua'i, and besides that he had not been to Lihue in over twenty years. John was my idea of a very local person.

      Four-plus decades later, I still surf. I've abandoned any inclination to describe waves I ride by linear measurement. If someone asks me how big are the waves, I resort to the colors of waves when the sun is high. There are milk green waves, with white sand in them stirred up from the bottom. There are bigger, blue waves that reflect coral reef beneath them. On the Big Island where I live now, there are black water waves, from water so deep that the bottom might as well not even be there.

      I don't ride black water anymore. I'm too old and weak. The reflexes, stamina, strength, and courage required are history for me. Blue reef is my best-day limit. But in the imagined world of my writing, I still try to reach beyond my acknowledged limitations. I still dream of black water waves.

      I'm a Hawai'i writer. Born and raised, it's in my blood. I'm less local than folks like John Costa, surely, but Hawai'i is the only real home possible for me. I'd like to think I'm a black water writer, still pushing the edge. (Photo by Carole Chillingworth)

WENDY MIYAKE
Mililani High School

      Wendy Miyake is a poet and fiction writer. Her work is published in *Bamboo Ridge* and *Taxi*. Although she was raised in Mililani, she grew up in a family rich with stories of plantation life. Pu'unene and Waialua are as familiar to her as Mililani Town and, of course, Wonder Woman.

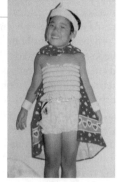

      "I think in growing up local, I am so conscious of place and how Hawai'i seems to manifest itself in everything, especially my writing. This place is so specific and detailed in its businesses, its natural resources, its people. You can never really describe your neighbor here in one sentence. We speak at length about people because their characters are so original and developed. All this detail gets transferred into the written stories. I grew up hearing stories told and retold and revised by various family members. My childhood was a lesson in embellishment and storytelling. I think till this day my mother's family is still not quite sure if my grandfather was the valedictorian of his ninth grade class. But who cares if it's true or not, the way he tells it, capturing the different voices, setting the scene, it's just a good story.

"Now growing up in Mililani is a whole other experience in growing up local. Not only are you in the land of red dirt and model homes but you live by rules—only earthtone paint for the house, no clotheslines seen from the street, no pigs as pets. I think existence in Mililani is strange—it's not quite a city nor is it the country. It's in between. Perhaps that is why I create characters who are sort of marginalized, who live on the edge, who don't quite fit in with the normal junior prom establishment.

"Yes, there is this thing embedded in your heart when you grow up local. If you don't believe me, move away. Distance always makes you remember."

BILL MIYASATO
Hilo High School, UH Mānoa

Growing up in the late '60s/early '70s in Hilo was an interesting dichotomy: the tail end of the counterculture era, the first results of the civil rights movement, the burgeoning Hawaiian Renaissance and the emergence of Ethnic Studies empowered and encouraged us to celebrate our differences, while coming of age in a small town in many ways reinforced conformity and created a longing need to belong. These colliding forces continue to infuse my work to this day. It was a great time to be a kid.

L. NISHIOKA
Kailua High School

Born in 1943 and raised in Kailua, Oʻahu during the '50s and '60s, I now live and teach in Mililani Town. I started writing after listening to local writer Juliet Kono talk about and share her poems on her mother. Eric Chock, Cathy Song, Lois-Ann Yamanaka, and Gary Pak have been my teachers.

"Growing Up Barefoot" was written as part of an ongoing exploration of local images and how they function in poetry. Coming from a traditional English teacher's background, I find myself having to make a conscious effort to recognize local images as "images" and as "poetic," being that they can, of course, be very different from those found in traditional literature.

Whenever I go shopping for shoes, my luau feet narrow choices down to extra wide styles. They cannot help but remind me of my childhood, running barefoot with my cousins through Grandpa Chinen's watermelon fields along the banks of Kawainui Canal.

I often begin the semester with my creative writing students by discussing objects from my memory box that can act as stimuli for writing. This begins the building of relationships that undergird our writing workshop. Students later share their memory boxes and write from them. One of the photos that I talk about is of my kindergarten graduation with me in my first, "real" pair of shoes. I also point out Peter V., whom students can readily see graduated barefoot. I then share with them the poem that resulted. Now, I'll be able to show them the same piece published!

SUSAN NUNES
Riverside Elementary, Hilo Intermediate, Hilo High
School, St. Ann's

This story was inspired by two articles printed
back-to-back in a newspaper recently. One was about
religious conflicts in interdenominational families, the
other about the religious war in Bosnia. It struck me
that a family is a kind of world and the world a kind of
family. And so I wanted to write a story that asked Willie's question: isn't love the
most transcending commandment and why can't everyone just get along?

Willie's story is not a religious story. It is not a putdown of Catholics,
Baptists, or Buddhists. It's about what a child does with the beliefs and stories of
her mixed heritage, how she accepts and eventually transcends them. I hope the
story is funny; it was meant to be. If Father Marius seems somewhat heavy-handed,
remember that he's stuck in the 1950s and much has changed since then, and that
what Father Marius says isn't as important as what Willie does. And if Mrs. Chaffee
seems well-meaning but insensitive about the beliefs of her neighbors, remember
that Hilo was a long way from Memphis, Tennessee in 1953.

I think I was lucky to grow up in a mixed family and a small but diverse com-
munity, both brim-full with the same contradictions and conflicts that Willie has to
face. Without contradiction and conflict, there are no stories. (author on the right)

JINA OSHIRO
This piece was written during my senior year of high School, for an English
Assignment—I believe the topic was "a humorous event from your past" or
something similar. While death may not exactly spring to mind when searching for
a lighthearted, fun topic to write about, this particular incident seemed
appropriate.

GARY PAK
Kāneʻohe Elementary, ʻIolani School

What school I went?
I was supposed to go Island Paradise. When I was
born, my parents were living on Matlock Avenue, right
down the street from the school, in this car garage
converted into a one-room bungalow. I was real small
when I started hearing my mom telling family and friends
that I was going to Island Paradise. I had my mind set at attending Island Paradise.
I used to think about carrying my books and running around in the playground.
When we walked by the school, my mom used to point at the children playing and
tell me that soon I'd be in there too. But we moved to Kāneʻohe when I was about

four, and now it was too far away to attend the school. So I guess Island Paradise is the school that I never got to go but was/is always in my heart as the school I was supposed to go. And it kind of broke my heart when I heard the recent story that Island Paradise, after so many years, is closing for good. Sad news, boy.

But now Kāneʻohe was my home. We lived near the bay and near the mountains, and these became my second homes. Which also became the setting for "The Gift." Growing up in my neighborhood was a real blessing. There were a lot of good friends. We had no television, so our entertainment was being and living in the outdoors: crabbing and swimming in the bay, hiking and camping up the mountains, all the stuff that I described in the story and more. It was a very happy time. Sodawater was ten cents. Didn't have to worry about speaking "correct" English or be ashamed about wearing out-of-style or worn-out clothes (wasn't even a consideration back then). Enjoyed the times when my cousin and/or friends could ride in the bed of my dad's '59 Chevy pickup truck. The only concern was staying away from the bullies. Life back then was very simple: there were simple joys, and there were simple hardships, and all of these were easy to understand. But then I also remember the time when the Cuban missile crisis happened, when all of a sudden— well, for me, as a child about to face a lot of changes hormonally and socially— things began to be a bit complex and confusing. I tried to capture that time of perplexity and rapture (don't know why, but now I didn't think it was too cool to toss toads at girls) in "The Gift." (A note: For those of you who know your history well, I did take "poetic license" when I had the missile crisis occur in the beginning of the summer of 1962; rather, that big showdown between Kennedy and Krushchev happened in October of 1962.)

What school I went?

Went to Kāneʻohe Elementary School, next to the cow pastures and near the Koʻolaus. Good friends and good teachers. I was considered naughty, at times. Throwing toads at the girls during recesses. Was the champion at Guess Hand, that game with marbles, 'cause I used "psycho-a-logy," a word/concept I picked up from my dad ("Whas dah stuff you use everytime you win?" James asks. "Psychoalogy," Gary answers. "Yeah, das dah one."). Was okay at "beefing" but took my share of lickings. Was an avid reader but disliked being called "Four-eyes" when started to wear glasses in the fifth grade. Got to be a decent kickball and football player in recess (third, maybe fourth to be picked).

Then it was off to ʻIolani School after the sixth grade. Where I read thick books that I could not understand. Where I learned that coming from a rich family meant something. Where I learned to be ashamed of my father's truck. Where I began to yearn for the opposite sex (it was an all-boys school when I went there). Where I learned that my English was not the "right" English. Where I learned good study skills. Where I developed a blind respect and affinity for haole culture. Where I started to listen to rock music.

Then it was off to Boston University and became very aware of America's contradictions in race relations and foreign policy. Found out that racial prejudice was not only a term from a textbook. Literature and Jazz became the artistic elements that I followed. Ah . . . the early seventies, the strong shadow of the mighty sixties.

Back home, for good, the local people became my new school. And I am still learning at this school. Don't want to ever leave this school. Will never leave it. My learning here prompted the story, "The Valley of the Dead Air." The community activism of the residents and supporters in the Waiāhole-Waikāne land eviction struggle, for example, was so moving for me. It was neat to see people of various persuasions, etc., throw down their differences and "come together, right now": humanity moving forward. Powerful. Powerful. Helped to develop my optimistic vision of humanity and the role of the masses in shaping the future.

BRONSON WAYNE KEALIIKOA RIVERA
Haleiwa Elementary

As a first grader, Bronson wrote the following when his poem was a winner in the 1996 HEA contest:

"I like fire trucks and sugar haulers. I wanted to be a sugar hauler driver like my dad, but the Waialua Sugar Company will close down in July 1996. So maybe I will be a fireman like my grandpa and drive the fire truck."

GRAHAM SALISBURY
Kailua Elementary, Hawai'i Preparatory Academy

Graham Salisbury's novels include *Blue Skin of the Sea* (1992), *Under the Blood-Red Sun* (1994), *Shark Bait* (1997), and *Jungle Dogs* (Fall 1998). Among other awards, *Under the Blood-Red Sun* won the 1995 Scott O'Dell Award for historical fiction, and the 1998 Nene Award, chosen by the young readers of Hawai'i. Today, he lives in Portland, Oregon, with his family.

"'You Would Cry to See Waiākea Town' grew out of a stunning memory: that of seeing Hilo's Waiākea Town days after it was flattened by a tidal wave. Parking meters bent to the ground. Vacant concrete pads where buildings once stood. Mud, debris, broken glass everywhere, and an eerie silence. I'd been in Waiākea Town several times before that awful day. I'd felt its life, breathed its humid air. Then, poof. Gone. Vanished from the face of the earth.

"My easy life on the sunny Kona coast had not known this kind of ocean power. I was a deckhand on my step-father's deep-sea charter fishing boat at the time, a tanned haole boy sweet-talking tourist girls. I was an innocent and an idiot. Facing the clean sweep of Waiākea Town took some of that innocence away. It also shook up the idiot. I have since come to believe that we are fortunate for such wrenching losses of innocence, for each loss strengthens our hearts. When you hear of a tornado in Florida decimating a trailer park you might think, hmmm, too bad. But if you'd ever seen something like Waiākea Town, you might not say anything. You'd just feel it somewhere deep in your gut.

"That's why I wrote this story, because of what I felt about it. Because of the way those flattened parking meters hit me dead on. Because of the silence, and the dryness on my tongue.

"Words can capture, assess, and make sense of the events in our often confusing lives. Isn't it miraculous that little black squiggles on white paper can make us laugh or move our hearts to tears? There is not one of us who does not have a story within. Not one. It's there. All you need to do is reach down and pull it out." (photo by Gary Nolton)

KAREN SHISHIDO
Pearl City High School

I just graduated from Occidental College in L.A. with a degree in English Literature and Asian Studies, which I hope will prove to be more "practical" than they all warned me. . . .

Of course I don't believe that a career as a writer is the only or best way to be an active participant in literature, reading or writing. I plan to enroll in an English graduate studies program in the future. For now I'll try to work and catch up on all the books and things that my liberal arts undergraduate education *didn't* expose me to!

CATHY SONG
Kalani High School

Kalani High, Class of '73. Cathy Song received the Hawai'i Award for Literature in 1993.

GARY TACHIYAMA
Kauluwela, Central, McKinley

The poem developed as a dialogue. The second voice was deleted. It was written as a counterpoint to the idea that "pidgin" was solely a language of comedy, of ignorance and of tactless put down and stereotype. Of course, the poem does not address this directly—that would be too straightforward and obvious, the misdirection of example is better. In the same light, the last several lines are excessive and overkill and maybe should be deleted. I think to say the poem is just a simple explanation of an observed fact, no fish/small fish, would be missing the darker underbelly of it. And, that's the counterpoint to the idea about pidgin as language.

CARRIE Y. TAKAHATA
Moanalua High School

I was born on the island of O'ahu. Although I spent my first four years living in Kāne'ohe, I actually grew up in Pearl City. I graduated from Moanalua High School in 1986 and then went on to the

University of Hawai'i, where I received a Bachelor of Social Work and a Master of Arts degree. The three pieces included in this anthology are examples of the many phases I've gone through while growing up in Hawai'i. "Growing up local" emphasizes the variety. The islands seem to represent a microcosm of the larger world and in it I am forced to evaluate who and what I am in relation to everyone and everything that surrounds me. As a direct result, my writing illuminates the various parts of me. "Making Yonsei" and "I Have a Story to Tell" were both written in 1995. During that time, I focused on what it meant to be who I am in relation to my ethnicity and in relation to my relations. "Good Fo' Be One Hapa Kid" was written in 1997 and began as a response to the feeling of inferiority to this sort of "local" ideal of beauty; however, as I study the piece now I realize that it is more of a comment on the reason why "the hapa" is seen as ideal . . . perhaps. And it is this kind of writing, the kind of writing that insists on commenting on the politics within, that because of its diversity Hawai'i insists on. (author on the left)

BILL TETER
Oceanside High School (Oceanside, California)

Eighth grade, St. Agnes School, West Mifflin, Pennsylvania, high up on a bluff overlooking McKeesport and the Monongahela Steelworks. Ours was a small class, I think there were about 20 of us. Not only was I the only kid in that class whose father was not a steelworker, I was the only one whose grandfathers (both sides of the family) hadn't been steelworkers. My father was a Marine, a recruiter, and the Corps moved our family around a lot. St. Agnes was my seventh school in nine years.

My classmates looked at me like I had dropped in from another planet. I remember how jealous I felt especially of those kids, but also of the classmates I had everywhere else I went to school. They had a history of their street, their neighborhood, their town, whether they knew it or not. I could tell you where I've been, but I couldn't tell you where I am from.

LEE A. TONOUCHI
'Aiea High School

Lee wen grad 'Aiea c/o '90. Dis story wuz one of da runners-up insai da 1997 *Honolulu Magazine* fiction contess. Lee considers himself deprived cuz he nevah get da opportunity fo' study da kine Local literature until he went college. Befo' dat he nevah even know had such ting.

Wen he wuz growing up his teachahs toll him dat he wrote like how he talked. And I guess dat wuz one problem to dem. Lee has finally found one creative outlet fo' himself and even if he no can make million dollahs wit dis whole writing deals he get one back-up plan in da works. He dunno nahting about computers, but Lee like create one program dat get da kine Pidgin grammar and spell check li' dat.

Da whole beauty of dis money-making scheme is dat da disc going be BLANK cuz in Pidgin no mo' right and wrong, ah?
K-bibadee.

JEAN YAMASAKI TOYAMA
Roosevelt High School

Roosevelt High School, that's where I graduated from. This may not mean anything today, but back then, Roosevelt was the Punahou of the public school system. To get in you either came from a "feeder school" or passed a test. We were proud to become Rough Riders. (It's Theodore Roosevelt and not Franklin D.) In fact, ours was the last so-called "English Standard class." Much effort was made drilling into us the finer points of this "foreign" language, and it was foreign to most of us because pidgin was likely the language spoken at home. For me this has been a mixed blessing. My English is a bookish kind. Grammatical and academic, it is suited for the kind of life that I have chosen for myself: Professor. But this language is not exactly me, because my intimate, my family language was a mixture of peasant Hiroshima Japanese, pidgin and an evolving English spoken by me and my sisters which we in turn were teaching to our parents. Since my separation from pidgin started in second grade—when my father decided to move us to a district with an English Standard feeder school—my pidgin today is limited.

Throughout my life I have been working on finding a language that is me. As a second grader I was told that the one I grew up with and spoke "naturally" was wrong, bad, needed to be changed. (I still remember my grades for English—3 minuses—ruined a perfect report card.) Later in college I chose to learn French, which ultimately became the language of my work. Then came Japanese. I'd also like to learn Hawaiian and Italian. I just like to play with language, which is why I write, sometimes.

"My Healer" has gone through several forms since I began it over thirteen years ago and received an honorable mention in the first *Honolulu Magazine* fiction contest and a Lorin Tarr Gill prize. It's directly inspired by my father's mother who practiced *reiki*, now becoming popular, and my mother-in-law, who had her own "practice" in Hawi, Hawai'i, using cups. It is not unlike the use of leeches.

Indirectly, though, the story is about mothers, and here, I am thinking especially about my own mother, who I have witnessed caring for my father, my uncles, my grandfather. These women by their very nature are all healers. (author on the left)

KATHLEEN TYAU

I attended public schools in Pearl City then went to St. Andrew's Priory for high school. I graduated from Lewis and Clark College with a B. A. in English.

You could say I spent my whole life getting ready to write my first novel, *A Little Too Much Is Enough*. I wanted to convey the local spirit—the exuberance, the craziness, and the often overwhelming generosity. So I wrote about food and eating—what else? I also shaped the book so that the chapters are like dishes at a potluck supper—some small, like pupus; some big, like main dishes. These chapters may be read independently, but together they tell the story of a girl growing up local in a big family with big appetites and big hearts.

KOBAI SCOTT WHITNEY
Mont LaSalle High School (Napa, California)

Kobai Scott Whitney is a freelance writer and contributing editor to *Honolulu Magazine* and to *Island Business*. His non-fiction book, called *Sitting Inside*, is out from Parallax Press in 1998.

"This story is built around a prom for the 1964 graudating class of Konawaena High on the Big Island. Although that was my graduating year, I was not there. I attended a Catholic boarding school in northern California, and I have never been to a prom in my life. But that is the beauty of fiction.

"Like my non-fiction work, this story was built up from the testimony of many sources. It contains the remembered details of local proms, told to me by friends at work, where we frequently reminisced in the lunch room about the thrills and traumas of growing up local—or just growing up at all. The plot, along with the narrator and her fellow characters, are all from my own alleged mind.

"Growing up is always a melodrama; it is always sad and inspiring and boring—often all at the same time. 'Truth,' fantasy writer Ursula LeGuin says, 'is a matter of the imagination,' and I am convinced that the only match for the dark and complicated truth of growing up is fiction."

ELIZABETH WIGHT
Punahou ("Nevah min' wha' ye-ah, no ask")

Eric Chock made me do it! Nah nah nah. He, Dennis Kawaharada, Richard Hamasaki, Gail Harada, and several other folks asked me to write down a presentation they heard. It felt too personal and intimate to put down on paper, but this popped out instead after Eric's pep talks. I hope it's the start of more writing about growing up hapa-Hawaiian in pre-freeway Honolulu in the '50s and '60s. How can I separate who I am from who my family is, from the stories I heard as a child, from my community, from the Mānoa rains that bring me peace, from poi dogs and "chop suey" people, "all mix up"? What sustains me flows from all of them, a spirit, a blessing, a connection, a beloved lei. Aloha.

LOIS-ANN YAMANAKA

I write with tears. One time, I told Eric Chock that I sobbed when I finished writing my poem called "Kid." He laughed a little too loud and a little too long. "That's your most clichéd poem," he said. Oh well, *I cried.* When I wrote "Boss of the Food," I laughed until tears flew out of my eyes. My sister Mona, the boss of the world of our childhood days, laughed tears of recognition.

But to write with tears involves risk and fearlessness. Growing up local on the Big Island, I always used to think to myself, "There must he a reason for all of this," whenever I couldn't understand hurt, violence, racial intolerance, shame, lies, inhumanity, cultural collisions, or betrayal. Growing up local, I felt I had no voice, but my mind never stopped pondering the big and the small. I could never understand why my grandpa's neighbor played hymns on his violin only when I was watching TV, why Aunty Vi's chicken crowed what I swore was "Hap-py Birth-day," why the naked hippies lived in tents, where my dog went after she died, what exactly Steely Dan meant by "Call me deacon blues," and what exactly was cremation?

I would grow up local in Kaunakakai, Hilo, Pahala, and Keauhou to write those stories. I promised myself that I would always write with tears. And little by little, I make sense of the reasons for all this. (author on the right)

PERMISSIONS

My Room by Jonathan Yi, Farrington High School

Some of the work in this anthology was previously published in slightly different versions in the publications listed below. They are reprinted by permission of the author or the copyright holder.

Balinbin, Anjanette, "Recollections," from *Write On, HEA!* (Hawai'i Education Association, 1996).

Banggo, Kathy Dee Kaleokealoha Kaloloahilani, "No Mindless Digging," from *Hawai'i Review #37* (Spring 1993).

Boteilho, Eric, "Of Walls and Wheelbarrows," from *Write On, HEA!* (Hawai'i Education Association, 1994).

Burgess, Puanani, "Hawai'i Pono'i," from *Bamboo Ridge #36* (Fall 1987).

Chang, Stacy, "Attack from Within," from *Write On, HEA!* (Hawai'i Education Association, 1997).

Chock, Eric, "Allowance," "Making Da Scene," and "My First Walk with Ashley," from *Last Days Here* (Bamboo Ridge, 1990),

Coleon, Shayna Ann A., "The Tempura War," from *Write On, HEA!* (Hawai'i Education Association, 1998).

Dudoit, D. Māhealani, "My Father's Garden," from *Southwest Review* (Winter 1997).

Hadley, Jozuf, "ma ket stenlei," from *chalookyu eensai* (Sandwich Islands, 1972).

Hara, Marie M., "Fourth Grade Ukus," from *Bananaheart & Other Stories* (Bamboo Ridge, 1994),

Hara, Mavis, "Carnival Queen," from *Sister Stew: Fiction and Poetry by Women*, edited by Juliet S. Kono and Cathy Song (Bamboo Ridge, 1991).

Holt, John Dominis, "Rainbows Under Water," from *Recollections: Memoirs of John Dominis Holt* (Ku Pa'a, 1993). Reprinted by permission of Allison Holt Gendreau.

Kahanu, Hina, "When I Was Young on an Island," from *Sister Stew: Fiction and Poetry by Women*, edited by Juliet S. Kono and Cathy Song (Bamboo Ridge, 1991).

Keller, Nora Okja, "Chapter 3" from *Comfort Woman* © 1997 by Nora Okja Keller. Published by Penguin Books USA, Inc. Reprinted by permission of Susan Bergholz Literary Services, New York. All rights reserved.

Keller, Nora Okja, "A Bite of Kimchee" was previously published as "My Mother's Food" © 1997 by Nora Okja Keller. First published in *Attachments/New Woman*, September 1997. Reprinted by permission of Susan Bergholz Literary Services, New York. All rights reserved.

Lono, Tori, "The Visit," from *Write On, HEA!* (Hawai'i Education Association, 1997).

Lum, Darrell, "Four Score & Seven Years Ago," from *Charlie Chan Is Dead: An Anthology of Contemporary Asian American Fiction*, edited by Jessica Hagedorn (Penguin, 1993). "Giving Tanks," from *Into the Fire: Asian-American Prose*, edited by Sylvia Watanabe & Carol Bruchac (Greenfield Review Press, 1996).

Lum, Wing Tek, "An Image of the Good Times," from *Bamboo Ridge* #44 (Fall 1989). "Childhood Memories," from *Bamboo Ridge* #60 (Fall 1993).

Malo, Makia, "The Rooster," adapted from *Tales of a Hawaiian Boyhood, Volume I: The Kalaupapa Years*, 1993.

Manly, Elizabeth, "The Dream Flyer," from *Write On, HEA!* (Hawai'i Education Association, 1995).

Masuda, Barry, "No Mo' Fish on Maui," from *Hawai'i Review* #37 (Spring 1993).

McPherson, Michael, "The Waking Stone" and "Up Mauka," from *Bamboo Ridge* #63-64 (Summer/Fall 1994).

Miyake, Wendy, "Woman Woman and My Junior Prom," from *Bamboo Ridge* #69 (Spring 1996).

Miyasato, Bill, "An Infinitely Subtle Shame," from *Bamboo Ridge* #44 (Fall 1989).

Oshiro, Jina, "The Monk and the Millipede," from *Write On, HEA!* (Hawai'i Education Association, 1994).

Pak, Gary, "The Gift" and "The Valley of the Dead Air," from *The Watcher of Waipuna and Other Stories* (Bamboo Ridge, 1992).

Rivera, Bronson W.K., "Broken Dream," from *Write On, HEA!* (Hawai'i Education Association, 1996).

Salisbury, Graham, "You Would Cry to See Waiākea Town," from *Bamboo Ridge* #44 (Fall 1989).

Song, Cathy. "Adagio," "A Conservative View, and "The Grammar of Silk," from *School Figures* (University of Pittsburgh Press, 1994).

Suzuki, M., "Childhood," from *Sister Stew: Fiction and Poetry by Women*, edited by Juliet S. Kono and Cathy Song (Bamboo Ridge, 1991).

Tachiyama, Gary, "How the Island Works," from *Bamboo Ridge* #36 (Fall 1987).

Tyau, Kathleen, "How to Cook Rice," "Mixing Poi," and "Jade Heart," from *A Little Too Much Is Enough* (Farrar Straus & Giroux, 1995). © Kathleen Tyau. Reprinted with permission of Sterling Lord Literistic.

Whitney, Kobai Scott, "Kona Glitter 1964: A Ghost Story," from *Bamboo Ridge* #69 (Spring 1996).

Yamanaka, Lois-Ann, "Boss of the Food," "Lickens," and "Tita: Boyfriends," from *Saturday Night at the Pahala Theatre*. ©1993 by Lois-Ann Yamanaka. Published by Bamboo Ridge Press. First published in *Bamboo Ridge, The Hawai'i Writers' Quarterly*. Reprinted by permission of Susan Bergholz Literary Services, New York. All rights reserved.